Small Differences That Matter

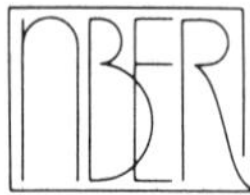

NBER Comparative Labor Markets Series
A National Bureau of Economic Research Series
Edited by Richard B. Freeman

Small Differences That Matter

Labor Markets and Income Maintenance in Canada and the United States

Edited by David Card and Richard B. Freeman

The University of Chicago Press

Chicago and London

DAVID CARD is professor of economics at Princeton University and a research associate of the National Bureau of Economic Research. RICHARD B. FREEMAN is professor of economics at Harvard University, program director of the National Bureau of Economic Research's Program in Labor Studies, and executive program director of the Comparative Labour Market Institutions Programme at the London School of Economics' Centre for Economic Performance.

The University of Chicago Press, Chicago 60637
The University of Chicago Press, Ltd., London

Printed in the United States of America

02 01 00 99 98 97 96 95 94 93   1 2 3 4 5
ISBN: 0-226-09283-6 (cloth)

Library of Congress Cataloging-in-Publication Data

Small differences that matter : labor markets and income maintenance in Canada and the United States / edited by David Card and Richard B. Freeman.
p. cm.—(NBER Comparative labor markets series)
Includes bibliographical references and index.
1. Labor market—Canada. 2. Labor market—United States. 3. Income maintenance programs—Canada. 4. Income maintenance programs—United States. I. Card, David E. II. Freeman, Richard B. III. Series.

362.5′82′0971—dc20   93–10513
HD5728.S54 1993   CIP

⊗ The paper used in this publication meets the minimum requirements of the American National Standard for Information Sciences—Permanence of Paper for Printed Library Materials, ANSI Z39.48-1984.

Relation of the Directors to the Work and Publications of the National Bureau of Economic Research

1. The object of the National Bureau of Economic Research is to ascertain and to present to the public important economic facts and their interpretation in a scientific and impartial manner. The Board of Directors is charged with the responsibility of ensuring that the work of the National Bureau is carried on in strict conformity with this object.

2. The President of the National Bureau shall submit to the Board of Directors, or to its Executive Committee, for their formal adoption all specific proposals for research to be instituted.

3. No research report shall be published by the National Bureau until the President has sent each member of the Board a notice that a manuscript is recommended for publication and that in the President's opinion it is suitable for publication in accordance with the principles of the National Bureau. Such notification will include an abstract or summary of the manuscript's content and a response form for use by those Directors who desire a copy of the manuscript for review. Each manuscript shall contain a summary drawing attention to the nature and treatment of the problem studied, the character of the data and their utilization in the report, and the main conclusions reached.

4. For each manuscript so submitted, a special committee of the Directors (including Directors Emeriti) shall be appointed by majority agreement of the President and Vice Presidents (or by the Executive Committee in case of inability to decide on the part of the President and Vice Presidents), consisting of three Directors selected as nearly as may be one from each general division of the Board. The names of the special manuscript committee shall be stated to each Director when notice of the proposed publication is submitted to him. It shall be the duty of each member of the special manuscript committee to read the manuscript. If each member of the manuscript committee signifies his approval within thirty days of the transmittal of the manuscript, the report may be published. If at the end of that period any member of the manuscript committee withholds his approval, the President shall then notify each member of the Board, requesting approval or disapproval of publication, and thirty days additional shall be granted for this purpose. The manuscript shall then not be published unless at least a majority of the entire Board who shall have voted on the proposal within the time fixed for the receipt of votes shall have approved.

5. No manuscript may be published, though approved by each member of the special manuscript committee, until forty-five days have elapsed from the transmittal of the report in manuscript form. The interval is allowed for the receipt of any memorandum of dissent or reservation, together with a brief statement of his reasons, that any member may wish to express; and such memorandum of dissent or reservation shall be published with the manuscript if he so desires. Publication does not, however, imply that each member of the Board has read the manuscript, or that either members of the Board in general or the special committee have passed on its validity in every detail.

6. Publications of the National Bureau issued for informational purposes concerning the work of the Bureau and its staff, or issued to inform the public of activities of Bureau staff, and volumes issued as a result of various conferences involving the National Bureau shall contain a specific disclaimer noting that such publication has not passed through the normal review procedures required in this resolution. The Executive Committee of the Board is charged with review of all such publications from time to time to ensure that they do not take on the character of formal research reports of the National Bureau, requiring formal Board approval.

7. Unless otherwise determined by the Board or exempted by the terms of paragraph 6, a copy of this resolution shall be printed in each National Bureau publication.

(Resolution adopted October 25, 1926, as revised through September 30, 1974)

Contents

Preface

This volume contains seven papers that explore and compare labor market and income maintenance policies and outcomes in the United States and Canada. The papers are the result of a comparative project on social policy and the labor market, executed as part of the program on United States-Canada comparative social policy of the William H. Donner Foundation, New York. We thank the William H. Donner Foundation for its support, and William T. Alpert, who served as program officer for this project, for his support and encouragement.

Six of the papers were presented at a conference held in Ottawa, Canada, 24–25 January 1991. We thank the many conference participants, and particularly the six discussants, for their valuable inputs to this project.

Introduction

David Card and Richard B. Freeman

Canada and the United States are as close economically and socially as any pair of countries in the world. The two nations share similar cultural traditions and enjoy comparable living standards. Both countries have highly educated and skilled work forces, with similar industrial and occupational structures. Many of the same firms and unions operate on both sides of the border. Large American firms such as DuPont are Canadian-owned, while American multinationals are active in virtually all areas of the Canadian economy.[1] The massive trade and capital flows that link the two economies promise to become even greater in the wake of the 1988 Canada-U.S. free trade agreement.

Throughout the past century Canada and the United States shared similar economic experiences. Both countries were major recipients of European immigration and capital flows; more recently, both have experienced large inflows of non-European immigrants. Both escaped the destruction of World Wars I and II. Both had "baby booms" in the 1950s that produced comparable demographic structures. And both developed broadly similar income security and labor market regulations over the course of the twentieth century.

But against this backdrop of similarity are "small differences" in policies, institutions, and economic outcomes. Although the United States initially led Canada in the adoption of a universal social insurance system, Canadian income maintenance programs are now more clearly redistributive than compa-

David Card is professor of economics at Princeton University and a research associate of the National Bureau of Economic Research. Richard B. Freeman is professor of economics at Harvard University, program director of the National Bureau of Economic Research's Program in Labor Studies, and executive program director of the Comparative Labour Market Institutions Programme at the London School of Economics' Centre for Economic Performance.

1. See U.S. Department of Commerce (1991, chap. 4) for an analysis of the importance of foreign ownership in the U.S. economy. The ownership status of DuPont is noted on p. 70 of the same document.

rable U.S. programs. Labor legislation and health policies in Canada reveal a greater reliance on collectivist solutions to economic problems. On the outcome side, unemployment rates and union membership rates in the two countries have diverged over the past two decades. Unemployment rates, which were nearly equal in the two countries in the 1950s and 1960s, were markedly higher in Canada in the 1980s. Unionization rates, comparable in the 1950s, were twice as high in Canada as in the United States by 1990. Family income inequality and poverty rates both increased in the United States over the 1980s, while they fell in Canada.

The mix of differences and similarities creates a valuable "natural experiment" for analyzing the effects of economic policy, institutions, and market shocks on labor market outcomes. If one wants to study the impact of differing unemployment insurance, income maintenance, or labor laws on economic behavior and outcomes, comparisons of Canadian and U.S. experiences hold out the promise of relatively straightforward inferences. A program that works in one country stands a good chance of working in a similar way in the other country because so much else is the same. Alternatively, if one wants to discover the sources of differences in wage structures, unemployment, unionization rates, or poverty, the basic similarities of the U.S. and Canadian economies make it easier to link the differences to specific causal factors.

Recognizing the potential for learning from each other, public policy debates within Canada and the United States frequently refer to the experiences of the other country to support or oppose particular initiatives. U.S. policy analysts routinely point to the Canadian example in arguing for more activist labor market or social policy. U.S. unionists look longingly at Canadian labor laws. Canadian analysts often cite the United States as an exemplar of reduced government intervention in the labor market and in economic affairs more generally. Liberals and social democrats worry about the viability of Canada's national health insurance and strong unions in a competitive international market.

In short, while Canada-U.S. comparisons are not ideal laboratory-style controlled experiments, they are highly credible sources from which to draw conclusions about economic behavior and the effect of institutions and policies on outcomes. Yet despite widespread interest in how things work across the border, detailed and systematic comparative studies of labor markets and income maintenance programs in the two countries have been surprisingly rare.

What are the principal differences in income inequality, poverty rates, unemployment, and other labor market outcomes between Canada and the United States in the 1980s? Can one plausibly relate these differences to differences in labor market and income maintenance policies? How did Canada's more redistributive policies affect economic outcomes in this difficult decade compared to the United States' greater reliance on unrestricted market forces?

What are the economic effects and costs of the "small differences" between Canadian and U.S. policy and institutions?

This volume seeks to answer these important questions. Some of the studies begin with differences in specific policies—immigration (George J. Borjas), unemployment compensation (David Card and W. Craig Riddell), income maintenance (Rebecca M. Blank and Maria J. Hanratty)—and examine how they have generated different economic outcomes. Other studies begin with differences in outcomes—educational wage differentials (Richard B. Freeman and Karen Needels), the extent of unionism (Riddell), the dispersion of earnings (Thomas Lemieux)—and seek to relate those differences to policies, economic shocks, and the operation of the labor market. The final chapter (McKinley L. Blackburn and David E. Bloom) brings together several of these themes in an overall comparison of income distributions in the two countries.

All the studies in this research project employ a similar methodology—one that has become feasible only with the recent computer data revolution in economics. Each study analyzes detailed microdata on thousands of individuals in Canada, the United States, or both countries, and bases its conclusions on comparisons of these data.

It is difficult to exaggerate the value of such data in a cross-country comparison. At one stage, researchers interested in why economic outcomes varied across countries were limited to aggregate statistics—twenty or thirty time-series observations, or published means from government surveys—that permitted only crude comparisons. Such limited data make it impossible to explore in depth how people in one country might respond to the incentives and institutions in another, or to assess how different market institutions might explain differences in outcomes. All too often, the addition of a few more years of data or another control variable would overturn the conclusions drawn from limited and highly collinear time series.

By contrast, the microdata sets available from Statistics Canada and the U.S. Bureau of the Census—drawn from similar monthly labor force surveys, annual supplementary surveys, and population censuses—permit an extraordinarily rich portrait of the labor markets in the two countries. With comparable information on tens of thousands of people differing only in country of residence, we can draw stronger inferences about differences between Canada and the United States than were previously possible. As a case in point, consider Card and Riddell's analysis of unemployment. They note that the divergence in unemployment rates between Canada and the United States reflects a change in labor supply behavior and argue that some Canadians with low work attachment tailor their work effort to Canada's more generous unemployment support program. In the absence of suitable microdata, it would be impossible to document the divergence in individual labor supply behavior, with the result that previous discussions of the unemployment gap have focused on differences in the extent of macroeconomic recession and recovery—differences that Card and Riddell reject as the prime cause of the differences in unemployment.

While any inference of individual behavior and market interactions from nonexperimental data across countries is fraught with problems, detailed microdata on individual decision units give economists and policy analysts at least a fighting chance of assessing whether "small differences" in policy and institutions matter between the United States and Canada.

Outcomes and Policies

The starting point for our project is the differences in outcomes between the Canadian and U.S. labor markets and in the institutions and policies that affected those outcomes in the 1980s. Some of the differences between the two countries arose only in the past decade, while others reflect longer-term trends.

Table 1 gives a capsule summary of the aggregate differences in labor market outcomes between the two countries. Line 1 illustrates the unemployment gap between Canada and the United States that developed in the 1980s, by comparing average decadal rates of unemployment. There are two possible explanations for this gap: failure of employment to expand in Canada as rapidly as in the United States, and increased labor force participation in Canada relative to the United States. The employment-population rates in line 2 show a small difference favoring the United States, but line 3 shows an opposite difference in labor force participation rates. After lagging the United States for many years, labor force participation rates in Canada surpassed U.S. rates in the 1980s. The gap in unemployment rates thus appears to be associated as

Table 1 Aggregate Labor Market Outcomes in Canada and the United States in the 1980s

	Canada	U.S.	Difference, Canada − U.S.
Average, 1981–90			
1. Unemployment rate	9.4	7.1	2.3
2. Employment-population rate	59.5	60.4	−0.9
3. Labor force participation rate	65.6	64.9	0.7
Average annual rate of change, 1979–90			
4. Employment	1.8	1.6	0.2
5. Real hourly earnings in manufacturing	0.6	−1.2	1.8
6. Real compensation per employee	0.8	−0.2	1.0

Sources: Lines 1–4—Card and Riddell, table 5.1 in this volume. Lines 5–6—*OECD Economic Outlook* (June 1992), table 54, 56, 59.

Note: Real earnings and compensation are deflated by GNP consumption deflator.

much with increased labor force participation as with the failure of the Canadian economy to generate jobs.

Lines 4–6 turn from decadal averages to growth rates over the 1980s. The employment growth rates in line 4 actually show slightly faster job creation in Canada, although we note that different beginning and ending dates would tip the balance the other way. We infer that both Canada and the United States had significant (and roughly comparable) employment growth in the 1980s in contrast, say, to Western Europe. The growth rates of real earnings in lines 5 and 6 also favor Canada—though in both countries earnings growth rates fell below the historical averages that gave North America one of the highest living standards in the world. We make little of the Canadian advantage here, because again other earnings series and other beginning and ending dates would give somewhat different relative standings. For instance, microdata on the earnings of family heads show earnings increasing more rapidly in the United States than in Canada from 1979 to 1987. The evidence does not support the conclusion that either country had markedly superior growth in real earnings or employment over the period, despite the emergence of an unemployment gap.

Inequality and Poverty

It is well known that the distribution of income in the United States widened substantially in the 1980s. Differentials between more- and less-educated workers and between white-collar and blue-collar workers grew sharply. Inequality also increased among those with similar nominal skills (Blackburn, Bloom, and Freeman 1990; Katz and Murphy 1992; Murphy and Welch 1992). Rising inequality combined with stagnant average real wages, declines in the real value of some economic transfers, and the continued growth of single-parent families to produce increases in poverty rates, particularly among children (Blank 1991). Did Canada have similar or different experiences?

Table 2 compares the changes in the distributions of earnings and income in Canada and the United States during the 1980s. The estimated earnings gap between male college graduates and male high school graduates in line 1 shows that Canada had a notably smaller increase in the college premium than did the United States. The pattern among female wage earners is similar (Freeman and Needels, chap. 2 in this volume). The measure of earnings inequality for male workers in line 2 (the variance of log earnings) shows that earnings inequality was greater in the United States at the beginning of the decade and that the intercountry difference grew over the 1980s. An even more striking pattern is revealed in line 3, which shows that family income inequality—measured by the Gini coefficient—actually fell in Canada at the same time it rose in the United States. Other measures of family income inequality tell a similar story (Blackburn and Bloom, chap. 7 in this volume).

Table 2 **Inequality and Poverty Outcomes in Canada and the United States in the 1980s**

	Country	1979	1986/87	Change
1. Education premium: difference in log weekly earnings between male college graduates and male high school graduates (adjusted)	Canada	0.29	0.33	0.04
	U.S.	0.23	0.39	0.16
2. Variance of log earnings of prime-age male workers	Canada	0.270	0.288	0.018
	U.S.	0.286	0.320	0.034
3. Gini coefficient of family income	Canada	0.373	0.371	−0.002
	U.S.	0.398	0.411	0.013
4. Poverty rate of nonelderly-headed families (%)	Canada	7.8	7.1	−0.7
	U.S.	9.0	11.6	2.6
5. Poverty rate of single-parent families with children (%)	Canada	31.5	25.9	−5.6
	U.S.	34.0	40.5	6.5

Sources: Line 1—Freeman and Needels, table 2.2, in this volume. Line 2—Blackburn and Bloom, table 7.10, in this volume. Line 3—Blackburn and Bloom, table 7.5, in this volume. Lines 4–5—Blank and Hanratty (1992), tables 5 and 6.

Given comparable employment-population ratios and rates of growth of average earnings in the two countries, and the differing trends in the distributions of income and earnings, one would expect to find relatively slower growth of poverty in Canada than in the United States. Lines 4 and 5 confirm this expectation and in fact show an even stronger relative trend: poverty rates fell in Canada over the 1980s while they rose in the United States. The relative divergence was particularly striking for single-headed families with children.

Institutions and Policies

What about economic policies and institutions? Do they differ between Canada and the United States in ways likely to explain the differing trends in labor market outcomes and family incomes?

At the outset it is important to recognize that both Canada and the United States are large and geographically diverse countries that operate under relatively decentralized federal systems. Provinces or states play a role in determining labor market regulations and income support policies. Some provinces of Canada are closer geographically and economically to nearby U.S. states than to other parts of Canada. Similarly, some U.S. border states look more like their nearest Canadian neighbor (in terms of resources, climate, and economic base) than like Mississippi or New Mexico. The province of Quebec differs in laws, culture, and predominant language from either English-speaking Canada or the United States.

Which particular policies are under federal as opposed to provincial or state control often differs between the countries. Even where Canadian provinces have considerable autonomy in determining laws or expenditures, however, they often show less regional variation than the individual states. Income support payments in Canada, for instance, vary less across provinces than Aid to Families with Dependent Children (AFDC) payments vary across states or regions in the United States. One important exception is labor law, which lies largely under provincial rule in Canada but is determined by the Congress in the United States (save for state and local employees).

Immigration policies in both countries are set nationally. Both Canada and the United States altered immigration laws in the 1960s to allow greater inflows of immigrants from non-European source countries. The United States adopted a policy that stressed family reunification, although admission of refugees and substantial inflows of illegal immigrants (Borjas, Freeman, and Lang 1991) meant that immigrants admitted under the quota system made up less than one-half of total immigrants in the 1980s. Canada adopted a point system for allocating visas, designed to produce a more skilled immigrant flow. These laws were later amended to allow a greater role for family reunification.

Following the example of the Wagner Act in the United States, Canadian labor laws were substantially modified during and after World War II. Despite this common heritage, Canadian laws have become more favorable to unions as institutions have evolved and economic circumstances have changed. Under Canadian law it is easier to unionize: in most cases, unions need only obtain the signatures of a majority of workers, and management has less scope to express opposition to unionism. Firms cannot permanently replace strikers, and legislation in some provinces makes even temporary strike replacements illegal. Quebec has Western European–style extension of union contracts to nonunion workers.

Whether because of differences in labor laws or other factors (Riddell, chap. 4 in this volume), the unionization rates in the two countries have diverged from rough equality in the 1950s to a substantial difference in the 1980s. The overall union density in Canada remained fairly stable in the 1980s (although it fell slightly in the private sector), while the unionization rate fell sharply in the United States.

Canadian and U.S. educational systems differ in ways that affect the supply of highly educated labor. The Canadian system varies across provinces, with high school graduation after 11 years of schooling in some provinces and after 12 or 13 in others. These differences feed into different paths to a university degree (a minimum of 3 years of university in Ontario; 2 years of CEGEP and 3 years of university in Quebec; 4 years of university elsewhere). In the United States all states have 4 years of high school and 4-year university programs.

Many more Canadian than U.S. students leave high school without completing the requirements to attend university, but many more attend vocational and community college programs. In the 1960s the United States expanded its higher education system more rapidly than Canada did, with the result that by

1987 18 percent of U.S. adults had 16 or more years of schooling compared to only 12 percent of Canadian adults. At the other end of the spectrum 8 percent of Americans had less than 8 years of schooling compared to 14 percent of Canadians.

Canada's unemployment compensation system is more generous than the United States' system, primarily because of its less restrictive eligibility requirements and the longer duration of benefits. Unemployment benefits are available for up to fifty weeks in Canada as opposed to only twenty-six weeks in the United States, although the U.S. government often extends benefit durations in major recessions. Less restrictive eligibility rules imply that a larger share of unemployed workers are eligible for benefits in Canada than in the United States. Benefits are also available for maternity leaves, sickness, and training in Canada. Finally, the take-up rate among those eligible for benefits is higher in Canada. For reasons that are poorly understood (Blank and Card 1991), many American workers fail to apply for the benefits available to them.

Like the unemployment insurance system, Canada's income support system for nonelderly persons is broader than the U.S. system. Canada's means-tested programs have wider eligibility and higher benefits than comparable U.S. programs. And Canada has universal non-means-tested programs that are not found in the United States. Canadian antipoverty transfer programs include family allowances (child bonuses of the form found in much of Western Europe), child tax credits, and, most important, social assistance to low-income families and individuals.[2] Comparable U.S. programs (AFDC, food stamps, and Earned Income Tax Credits) are more narrowly targeted and less generous. In addition, Canada allows greater discretion for caseworkers in determining benefits, making for a less bureaucratic and potentially more flexible and personalized system.

The Major Theme

The results of the studies in this volume relating economic outcomes to policies and institutions in the United States and Canada are striking. Although the chapters were written and can be read independently, they tell a surprisingly similar story that gives us the title for the book and shows the interrelations among the various policies, institutions, and outcomes, which make the book more than the sum of its parts. The most important theme in the volume is that small differences matter. Albeit in different ways, the studies show that differences in safety-net systems, labor market regulations, and labor market conditions have discernible effects on outcomes and explain a substantial share of the differing labor market and income experiences of the two countries in the 1980s.

2. The family allowance program was phased out as a universal program in Canada at the end of 1992.

One reason why small differences matter is that individuals and institutions respond in economically significant ways to incentives. Immigration patterns between Canada and the United States, for example, show evidence of self-selection consistent with the broader redistribution policies in Canada and with Canada's point-based immigration system. Canadians who migrate to the United States come from the upper part of the Canadian earnings and education distributions, whereas Americans who migrate to Canada come from relatively lower parts of the U.S. earnings and education distribution. The greater emphasis on skills in Canadian immigration rules has produced a more modest decline in the skills of immigrants compared to natives than in the United States. Annual labor supply patterns suggest that individuals adjust their work activity to the specific features of unemployment insurance systems. And changes in educational earnings differentials affect the pattern of enrollment in colleges and universities.

A second reason why small differences matter is that they interact in various ways. The convergence in educational attainments between Canada and the United States in the 1980s, due in part to differences in the timing of expansion of university education, contributed to the divergence in earnings differentials and income inequality. The convergence in female labor force participation rates likewise contributed to the relative rise in Canadian unemployment rates. Differing trends in union membership rates contributed to the divergence in earnings inequality. And differences in immigration policies brought a relatively more educated work force into Canada, with consequences for the distribution of earnings. Some of these relations—between stronger unions, unemployment, and income support—fit together in a systematic way that is consistent with a more collectivist and welfare-state orientation in Canada. A thorough understanding of labor market and income developments in the two countries thus requires an analysis of the full spectrum of small differences between the countries.

The chief empirical finding of the volume is that Canadian labor market and income support policies mitigated against the 1980s trend of rising inequality that swept the United States. By leaning against the wind, Canada managed to lower poverty rates during a decade when slow economic growth and structural economic and social change made it exceedingly difficult for less-skilled individuals to maintain their living standards. This finding emerges most clearly in the analyses of unemployment, poverty, and income distributions. Simulations by Blank and Hanratty suggest that if the United States had adopted Canada's welfare policies, it would have avoided the trend of rising child poverty that has cast such a pall over the future of U.S. society. Blackburn and Bloom's analyses show that Canada's income transfer system played a major role in keeping family income inequality from rising. And Card and Riddell's analysis of unemployment compensation suggests that the unemployment insurance system encouraged some persons with limited skills and labor force attachment to continue working just enough to maintain eligibility.

The finding that Canada's more activist labor market and income support policies successfully mitigated some of the adverse economic forces of the 1980s does not, of course, mean that these policies were ideal or indeed desirable. After all, there is no such thing as a free lunch: these programs cost real resources, which must be considered in evaluating their overall social merit.

Specific Findings

1. Canada's social safety net produced markedly lower poverty rates, especially for single-parent families, than did the United States' poverty programs, at a cost of two to three times the U.S. transfer expenditures.

As noted above, Canada's income support programs have higher benefit levels and greater eligibility than the United States' comparable programs. With poverty defined in the same manner, comparable U.S. and Canadian survey data show that, despite modestly lower average income in Canada, rates of poverty are lower than in the United States and the poverty gap—the amount of income necessary to bring families to the poverty line—is smaller. The difference in poverty rates is particularly large among single parents: 32 percent of single parents are poor in Canada, compared to 45 percent in the United States (Blank and Hanratty, chap. 7 in this volume).

To see whether the lower rates of poverty can be attributed to differences in policy, Blank and Hanratty compare U.S. and Canadian rates of poverty before and after government transfers, on the simplifying assumption that transfers do not affect other sources of income. They find that the Canadian transfer system is much more effective, reducing the poverty rate overall by 5.7 points compared to the 1.9 point reduction attributable to the U.S. transfer system. Among single-parent families, the transfer system lowers poverty by 14.3 points in Canada compared to 5.2 points in the United States.

Simulating the effect of applying Canada's transfer system to the United States—by giving Americans the transfers they would have received had they faced Canadian program rules and benefits—Blank and Hanratty find that the Canadian transfer program would essentially eliminate poverty among children in the United States. One possible problem with simulations like these is that a more generous transfer program might increase pretransfer poverty by reducing the work activity of those who receive the transfers. Blank and Hanratty show that this is unlikely to be important in the Canadian context, as one might suspect, given rising labor participation rates in Canada. The cost of the transfer program is not the indirect cost of lost labor supply, but rather the direct expenses: Canada spends two to three times as much per person on transfers as the United States does.

2. The divergence in Canadian-U.S. unemployment rates is due largely to changes in the fraction of nonworking time that is reported as unemployment. Canada's unemployment insurance system induced workers with low labor force attachment to offer low levels of labor supply, but differences between the U.S. and Canadian unemployment insurance systems contributed little to the rise in relative unemployment rates.

One way to obtain insight into the emergence of higher unemployment in Canada than in the United States is to analyze changes in relative unemployment rates among individuals with similar weeks of work. A decomposition of unemployment among individuals with differing amounts of weeks worked during the previous year reveals a relative increase in the likelihood that Canadian family heads, especially women, report nonworking time as time spent unemployed rather than out of the labor force. For instance, Canadian women with 4 weeks of work in 1979 reported 8.2 weeks of unemployment, compared to 4.5 weeks of unemployment reported by comparable U.S. women. In 1986 women with the same work activity reported 16.6 weeks of unemployment in Canada and 6.3 weeks of unemployment in the United States—a relative increase of 6.6 weeks of unemployment in Canada (Card and Riddell, chap. 5 in this volume).

The effect of Canada's more generous unemployment insurance system is revealed by the emergence of spikes in distributions of weeks worked at 10 and 12 weeks. Under the Canadian system, individuals in many regions are eligible for unemployment insurance with a minimum of 10 or 12 weeks of work a year. The relative increase in the fraction of Canadian workers with this low level of annual labor supply, coupled with increases in reported unemployment by these workers, accounts for part of the relative increase in Canadian unemployment. Nevertheless, more generous unemployment benefits are not the only cause of the increase in Canadian unemployment. Much of the relative increase in male unemployment occurred among men with 0 weeks of work—a group with declining unemployment insurance recipiency rates in Canada. In addition, the reductions in maximum unemployment insurance eligibility weeks in the late 1980s failed to reduce the high levels of unemployment.

3. Educational earnings differentials increased less in Canada than in the United States, in large part because of the greater relative increase in the supply of college-educated workers in Canada.

One striking change in the American earnings distribution in the 1980s was the huge increase in the differential between more- and less-educated workers. This increase was particularly large among younger workers, who are more likely to be on the active job market than older workers ensconced in their careers. In Canada, educational differentials between university-educated and high school–educated workers increased very modestly for both men and women. Between 1979 and 1986/87 differentials rose by .16 log points for 25–64-year-old American men compared to .04 points for Canadian men and by .10 points for American women compared to .04 points for Canadian women. Among 25–34-year-olds the increase for Canadians was .04 for men and for women versus an increase for Americans of .21 (men) and .10 (women) (Freeman and Needels, chap. 2 in this volume).

Associated with differing trends in educational wage premiums were differing rates of growth in the relative supply of more-educated workers in Canada and the United States. In the U.S. labor force as a whole the trend rate of growth in the ratio of college to high school graduates decelerated over the 1980s. Among young male workers the ratio of college graduates to high school graduates actually fell during the 1980s. By contrast, in Canada the ratio of college to high school graduates increased rapidly. Using time-series estimates of the effect of relative supplies on relative earnings, Freeman and Needels estimate that the greater growth of the relative supply of educated workers in Canada explains over one-half of the divergence in Canada-U.S. educational differentials. Although other factors—differing shifts in labor demand, greater unionization and income support in Canada—may also have played a role, the effect of supply is consistent with evidence from other countries that relative supplies are a key determinant of relative earnings by education (Freeman 1976; Katz and Murphy 1992; Schmidt 1992; Edin and Holmlund 1992).

4. Income inequality among families increased in the United States but not in Canada, in part because of increased transfer income in Canada and in part because of smaller increases in earnings inequality.

The distribution of income among families depends on the age and size composition of families, the number of earners, the distribution of earnings among the employed, the distribution of property income, the effect of income transfer programs (including unemployment compensation), and the correlations among these factors. Using several summary measures of the distribution of family incomes, Blackburn and Bloom show that inequality in family incomes increased in the United States but not in Canada in the 1980s, and decompose the differential pattern into its immediate causes.

The faster growth of single-parent families in the United States than in Canada contributed little to the relative change in family income inequality. In fact, microdata show that inequality rose in almost all family types in the United States but in almost no family type in Canada. Inequality of total family earnings and earnings of full-time year-round male workers rose in both the United States and Canada, ruling out a pure labor market explanation for the differing trends in family income inequality. Nevertheless, the smaller increase in earnings inequality for male workers in Canada (due to the slower rise in education differentials, among other factors) ameliorated the rise in income inequality among Canadian families.

The primary explanation for the differential trend in inequality was the differential growth of transfer income. Transfer income had a sizable equalizing impact on the distribution of income in Canada but did little to offset the forces producing income inequality in the United States. That income inequality fell among Canadian families headed by females, whose incomes are most directly affected by transfer policy, while rising among U.S. families headed by females provides strong support for this conclusion.

5. The higher rate of unionization in Canada than in the United States accounts for a sizable part of the difference in earnings inequality between the countries, and the divergence in unionization rates contributed to the more rapid growth of earnings inequality in the United States.

It is well established that unions reduce income inequality, in large part through standardization of wages within the organized sector (Freeman 1980). Both Card (1991) and Freeman (1991) attribute about one-fifth of the recent rise in male earnings inequality in the United States to the decline in unionization. Not only can the higher unionization rate in Canada potentially explain part of the Canadian-U.S. difference in earnings inequality, but the diverging trend in unionization between the countries ought to account for some of the divergence in earnings inequality in the 1980s.

Using cross-section and longitudinal data on Canadian earnings and union membership, and comparing these data with Card's (1991) analysis for the United States, Lemieux shows that these expectations are correct. The effect of unions on the distribution of earnings depends on the size of the union wage premium, the position of organized workers in the nonunion earnings distribution, and the effects of unions on inequality within the organized sector. Lemieux finds that unions in Canada have similar relative wage effects to those in the United States, and similar effects on the extent of wage inequality among union workers. In both Canada and the United States, private sector unionization rates are highest for workers in the middle of the skill distribution. In Canada, however, the high level of unionization among public sector workers implies that unionization rates in the economy as a whole rise with skill levels. Taking all these factors into account, Lemieux shows that in Canada as in the United States the presence of trade unions reduces the variance of earnings among men. About 40 percent of the Canadian-U.S. difference in earnings inequality is due to difference in unionization. In contrast, unionization raises inequality among Canadian women relative to their U.S. counterparts.

Studies that infer union wage effects from cross-section data are subject to the problem of selectivity of union members along unobservable dimensions. Lemieux's analysis of longitudinal changes in the wages of workers who involuntarily lose their jobs and switch union status shows that correcting for selectivity in this manner has little effect on the estimated pattern of union wage differentials but does substantially reduce the estimated effect of unions on the dispersion of earnings in the union sector. However, he attributes this to the peculiarities of the small sample of changers and concludes the cross-sectional differences give better estimates of the union effect on within-group variance.

Given the approximate seven-point drop in union density in the United States relative to Canada in the 1980s, as much as 45 percent of the relative increase in the variance of earnings among U.S. men can be attributed to the differential trend in unionization.

6. Union coverage is approximately twice as high in Canada as in the United States, an outcome that is largely attributable to the higher probability that Canadian workers who desire union representation are unionized.

The differential rate of unionization in Canada and the United States has aroused considerable debate among labor specialists, in large part because of the implications for policy. Four hypotheses have been offered to explain the differential patterns and trends. First is the claim that differences in union rates result from differences in economic structure: U.S. unionization is falling, as employment shifts to traditionally nonunion private sector industries, whereas Canada's greater governmental employment buttresses the unionization rate. By calculating unionization rates for workers classified by gender, age, industry, occupation, public or private sector employment, and education, Riddell shows that this explanation of the differing rate of union density is false. Comparable differences in union rates are found in all groups. A second hypothesis is that the U.S.-Canada gap in union coverage is due to differences in social attitudes toward unions: Canadians like unions and Americans do not. Survey data on whether people think unions are good or bad or whether they approve or disapprove of trade unions show no difference in attitudes or in trends in attitudes, indicating that this explanation is also false.

Two serious contenders for explaining the different level and trend remain: U.S. workers have less desire for unions than do Canadian workers, and U.S. employers and/or institutions afford workers less possibility for organizing unions when they want to organize, compared to Canadian employers/institutions.

Riddell puts these explanations in the context of a demand-supply framework (developed by Farber [1983]), in which workers demand union representation, and firms and labor market institutions supply union jobs. Comparing Canadian and U.S. surveys on the desire for unionization, he finds that desire for union representation is about 28 percent higher in Canada than in the United States, but that the bigger difference between the two countries is in the higher Canadian unionization rate conditional on the desire for unions. Of Canadians who want to be unionized, 76 percent are in unions, compared to 44 percent of Americans, a difference that remains after controlling for differences in the characteristics of workers. Although Riddell does not explore the reasons for this difference, an obvious candidate is the difference in labor laws and institutions that permit U.S. management greater opportunity to deter unionization through hostile actions (Freeman 1988; Weiler 1990).

7. Canada's point-based immigration system produces a more skilled flow of immigrants than the United States' family unification–based system, largely because it draws more immigrants from industrialized European countries.

Changes in immigration laws in Canada and the United States in the 1960s were associated with changes in skill composition of immigrants. In the early 1960s immigrants to Canada had fewer years of schooling than those to the United States (though more schooling than native-born Canadians). By the 1970s this situation had reversed: immigrants to Canada averaged nearly a year more of schooling than immigrants to the United States. In addition, largely because of the relative difference in schooling, the immigrant-native earnings gap was greater in the United States than in Canada in the 1970s.

Immigrants from the same source country tend to have about the same education and relative earnings in the United States and in Canada. Consequently, the main explanation for the differing education and earnings of immigrants in the two countries is the national origin of immigrants. Although the fraction of immigrants from Asia and Latin America increased in both countries, Canada maintained a larger share of European immigrants, presumably because they better fit the skills requirement for Canadian visas.

Costs of Transfer Policies

As noted, the conclusion that Canada's labor market institutions and income support programs have reduced income inequality and lowered poverty rates does not mean that they are better or more successful than comparable U.S. institutions and programs. Canadian transfer programs expanded through the 1980s in a period of sluggish economic growth. This expansion came at the cost of higher taxation rates and sharp relative increases in government indebtedness in Canada.

The expansion of transfer spending in Canada in the 1980s and the dramatic comparison with U.S. trends over the decade are illustrated in table 3. Here we give a thirty-year perspective on social spending for three main sets of transfer programs: needs-based cash and in-kind transfers for the nonelderly (including payments to blind and disabled individuals but excluding medical payments); unemployment insurance; and cash-based child support programs (Family Allowance and Child Tax Credit programs in Canada, Earned Income Tax Credits in the United States). These programs account for virtually all of

Table 3 Transfer Program Expenditures in the United States and Canada, 1960–90 (percentage of GNP)

	Country	1960	1965	1970	1975	1980	1985	1990[a]
1. Need-based transfers including disabled[b]	Canada	0.66	0.98	1.37	1.69	1.76	2.15	2.20
	U.S.	0.80	0.89	1.10	1.72	1.70	1.40	1.30
2. Unemployment insurance	Canada	1.22	0.54	0.78	1.81	1.28	2.13	1.77
	U.S.	0.59	0.44	0.38	0.87	0.68	0.46	0.32
3. Child programs: tax credits and family allowance[c]	Canada	1.36	1.05	0.63	1.06	0.86	0.82	0.77
	U.S.	—	—	—	0.06	0.05	0.04	0.09
4. Sum of three programs	Canada	3.24	2.57	2.78	4.56	3.90	5.10	4.74
	U.S.	1.39	1.33	1.48	2.65	2.43	1.90	1.71

Sources: For Canada, *Canada Year Book* (1980–81, 1991). For the United States, *Social Security Bulletin Annual Statistical Supplement* (1991); *1992 Green Book.*

[a]1990 data for Canada; 1989 data for the United States.

[b]Canadian data include expenditures under the Canada Assistance Program and earlier programs for disabled people, as well as provincial and municipal welfare. U.S. data include AFDC, SSI, food stamps, general assistance, and other categorical payments under the Social Security Act *excluding* Medicaid expenditures.

[c]Canadian data include FA and CTC. U.S. data include the refunded portion of EITC.

the measured transfer income of individuals and families in the two countries (see Blank and Hanratty, chap. 6 in this volume), although they ignore government spending on health care, housing, and education.

Spending on need-based transfers (line 1) shows a rising trend in both the United States and Canada during the 1960s and 1970s. Although spending was lower in Canada in 1960, by 1975 the percentages of national income devoted to needs-based transfer programs was about equal in the two countries. During the 1980s spending rose sharply in Canada (a 25 percent increase to 2.2 percent of GNP), while it fell sharply in the United States (a 25 percent cut to 1.3 percent of GNP).

Line 2 of table 3 shows that spending on unemployment insurance programs was higher in Canada than in the United States throughout the 1960s and 1970s. Nevertheless, the relative ratio of spending was roughly constant—at about 2 : 1—from 1960 to 1980. During the 1980s Canada again had a large increase in spending, while the U.S. unemployment insurance program contracted. By the close of the decade Canadian spending on unemployment compensation was five times greater as a fraction of national income.

The entries in line 3 show that expenditures on Child Tax Credit and Family Allowance have declined in Canada over the past three decades. Spending on tax credits in the United States, by comparison, actually rose over the 1980s (albeit from a very modest base). As in the previous lines, however, the main contrast is in the substantially higher level of spending in Canada. When the three sets of programs are added together (in line 4 of the table), the higher overall level of Canadian spending and the divergence in spending trends after 1980 stand out very clearly.

How has Canada financed its more generous transfer spending? The answer is revealed in figures 1 and 2, which show average "taxation" rates (total government tax revenues divided by total income) and government borrowing rates (total government budget deficits divided by total income) in the two countries.[3] During the past two decades total government revenues followed roughly parallel trends in the two countries. Throughout the period Canadian governments collected about 5 percentage points more of national income. The two countries also had similar (and relatively small) net government borrowing rates in the early 1970s. In the late 1970s and especially after 1980, however, government borrowing increased sharply in Canada relative to the United States. Although the borrowing gap narrowed in the late 1980s, it is clear that Canada paid for its relative expansion in government spending through larger deficits, transferring the burden of this spending to future tax liabilities.

3. We define government spending to include all levels of government: federal, provincial, and local in Canada: federal, state, and local in the United States. Comparisons of the level of government spending in the two countries are affected by the composition of health care spending, which is mostly government spending in Canada.

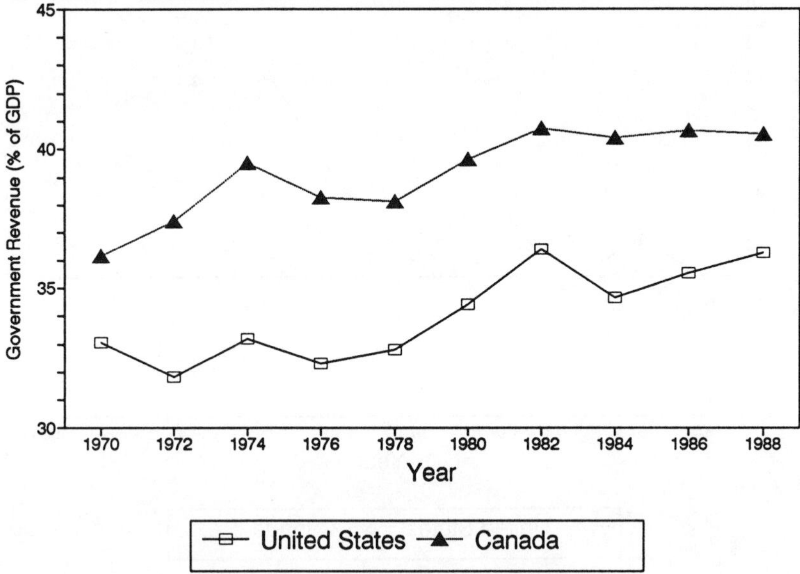

Fig. 1. Government revenue as percentage of GDP, United States and Canada, 1970–88

Sources: For the United States, GDP data are from the *Economic Report of the President* (1992), table B-1; government expenditures data (for all levels of government) are from *Statistical Abstract of the United States* (1982–83 to 1991). For Canada, GDP data are from Statistics Canada, *National Income and Expenditure Accounts Annual Estimates, 1926–86* (1988) and *Bank of Canada Review* (July 1992), Table H-2; government expenditures data (for all levels of government) are from *Canada Year Book* (1975–1988) and International Monetary Fund, *Government Finance Statistics Yearbook* (1991).

Neither source of funding is costless: both taxes and deficits introduce a variety of distortions, which add to the inefficiency of the economy (Romer 1988). Whether the cost of transfer spending in the United States or Canada is greater or less than the benefits created by this spending is beyond the scope of this volume. We note that in the late 1970s the two countries were much closer in the fraction of incomes raised as taxes, borrowed, and spent on income transfer programs. Over the 1980s they diverged, with some of the consequences we have documented here.

Conclusion

The 1980s provided a challenging period in which to judge the effects of more and less activist policy on diverse economic outcomes. It was a decade that featured both the highest unemployment rates and the longest peacetime recovery since the Great Depression. Even with the lengthy recovery, productivity growth was sluggish and unemployment rates never fully recovered to the levels of the previous decade. Diverse forces—new technology, shifts in

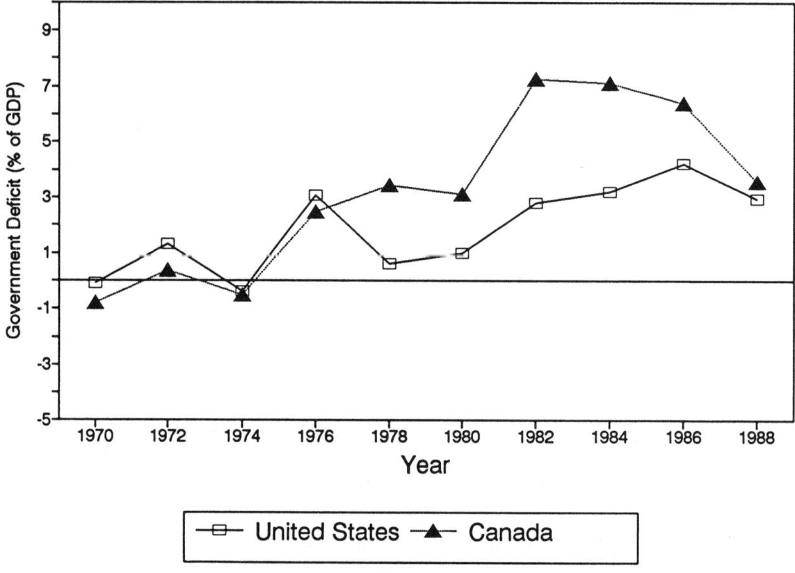

Fig. 2. Government Deficit as percentage of GDP, United States and Canada, 1970–88
Sources: See figure 1.

relative labor supplies, opening of trade—made it difficult for less-skilled workers throughout North America to compete and survive. The United States chose to give relatively free play to market forces during this decade. Canada chose a more activist strategy of providing broader social safety nets and labor regulations and institutions more favorable to trade unionism. U.S. policies generated substantial employment growth but did little to mitigate market forces that redistributed income toward higher-income workers and families. Canadian policies generated comparable employment growth but also mitigated the forces that tended to increase inequality and poverty. The experiences of the decade suggest that policy differences—even small differences—can matter in economic outcomes, albeit with associated costs. With a modestly different set of policies, the United States could have had labor market and income outcomes comparable to those in Canada. With a modestly different set of policies, Canada could have looked more like the United States. The reasons why the two countries chose different strategies for coping with the problems of the 1980s, and the longer-run consequences of these choices, lie beyond the scope of our project, though they are certainly interesting to explore.

References

Blackburn, McKinley L., David E. Bloom and Richard B. Freeman. 1990. The Declining Economic Position of Less Skilled American Men. In Gary Burtless, ed., *A Future of Lousy Jobs? The Changing Structure of U.S. Wages*. Washington, DC: Brookings Institution.

Blank, Rebecca. 1991. Why Were Poverty Rates So High in the 1980s? NBER Working Paper no. 3878. Cambridge, MA: National Bureau of Economic Research, October.

Blank, Rebecca, and David Card. 1991. Recent Trends in Insured and Uninsured Unemployment: Is There an Explanation? *Quarterly Journal of Economics* 106 (November): 1157–89.

Blank, Rebecca, and Maria Hanratty. 1992. Down and Out in North America: Recent Trends in Poverty Rates in the United States and Canada. *Quarterly Journal of Economics* 107 (February): 233–54.

Borjas, George J., Richard B. Freeman, and Kevin Lang. 1991. Undocumented Mexican-Born Workers in the United States: How Many, How Permanent? In John M. Abowd and Richard B. Freeman, eds., *Immigration, Trade, and the Labor Market*. Chicago: University of Chicago Press.

Card, David. 1992. The Effect of Unions on the Distribution of Wages: Redistribution or Relabelling? NBER Working Paper no. 4195. Cambridge, MA: National Bureau of Economic Research, October.

Edin, Per-Anders, and Bertil Holmlund. 1992. The Swedish Wage Structure: The Rise and Fall of Solidaristic Policy. Paper presented at the NBER Summer Labor Studies Program, Cambridge, MA, August.

Farber, Henry. 1983. The Determination of the Union Status of Workers. *Econometrica* 51 (September): 1417–37.

Freeman, Richard B. 1976. *The Overeducated American*. New York: Academic Press.

———. 1980.q Unionism and the Dispersion of Wages. *Industrial and Labor Relations Review* 34 (October): 3–23.

———. 1988. On the Divergence of Unionism among Developed Countries. NBER Working Paper no. 2817. Cambridge, MA: National Bureau of Economic Research, January.

———. 1991. How Much Has De-unionization Contributed to the Rise in Male Earnings Inequality? NBER Working Paper no. 3826. Cambridge, MA: National Bureau of Economic Research, August.

Katz, Lawrence F., and Kevin M. Murphy. 1992. Changes in Relative Wages, 1963–1987: Supply and Demand Factors. *Quarterly Journal of Economics* 107 (February): 35–78.

Murphy, Kevin M., and Finis Welch. 1992. The Structure of Wages. *Quarterly Journal of Economics* 107 (February): 285–326.

Romer, David. 1988. What Are the Costs of Excessive Deficits? In Stanley Fischer, ed., *NBER Macroeconomics Annual 1988*. Cambridge, MA: MIT Press.

Schmidt, John. 1992. The Changing Structure of Earnings in Britain. Paper presented at the NBER Summer Labor Studies Program, Cambridge, MA, August.

U.S. Department of Commerce. Economics and Statistics Administration Office of the Chief Economist. 1991. *Foreign Direct Investment in the United States: A Review of Analysis and Current Developments*. Washington, DC: Office of Macroeconomic Analysis, U.S. Department of Commerce, August.

Weiler, Paul. 1990. *Governing the Workplace: The Future of Labor and Employment Law*. Cambridge, MA: Harvard University Press.

1 Immigration Policy, National Origin, and Immigrant Skills: A Comparison of Canada and the United States

George J. Borjas

1.1 Introduction

Both Canada and the United States are important participants in the immigration market. These two countries admitted over 12 million immigrants between 1959 and 1981. In recent years, their immigration policies have diverged considerably. Prior to the early 1960s, both Canada and the United States used national origin to allocate the scarce number of visas among the many applicants, preferring persons originating in northwestern European countries.[1] During the 1960s, the two countries enacted major immigration policy changes. As a result, the United States began to award entry permits on the basis of the applicant's family ties with U.S. residents or citizens, whereas Canada began to allocate visas on the basis of the applicant's observable socioeconomic characteristics.

The historical comparison of immigrant skills and labor market performance between Canada and the United States, therefore, can provide useful lessons in the benefits and costs of skill-based immigration policies. Earlier work has documented important differences between the Canadian and U.S. experiences.[2] This paper continues this line of research and documents that many of the differences in the economic impact of foreign-born workers on Canada and the United States can be understood in terms of a simple hypoth-

George J. Borjas is professor of economics at the University of California, San Diego, and a research associate of the National Bureau of Economic Research.

The author is grateful to Michael Abbott for useful comments and to the National Science Foundation (grant no. SES-8809281) for financial support.

1. There was also a sizable transnational migration between Canada and the United States. The size and skill composition of this flow is discussed in detail below.

2. See Abbott and Beach 1987; Bloom and Gunderson 1991; Borjas 1990; Chiswick 1987; and Tandon 1978.

esis: the national-origin composition of immigrants in the two host countries is different.

The source-country distribution of immigrant flows plays a crucial role because of substantial dispersion in skills and labor market performance among national-origin groups (Borjas 1987; Jasso and Rosenzweig 1986). In general, immigrants originating in industrialized economies are more skilled and are more successful in the host country's labor market than are immigrants originating in the less-developed countries. The empirical analysis below shows that the observed differences between Canada and the United States in the average skill level of foreign-born workers can mostly be "explained" by differences in the national-origin mix of the immigrant flows admitted into the two countries.

This finding raises important questions about the efficacy of Canada's point system. My empirical analysis indicates that the point system works not because it attracts more skilled workers from a particular source country, but because it alters the national-origin mix of the immigrant flow.[3] This implication of the empirical evidence provides a very different understanding of how a point system increases the average skills of foreign-born workers.

1.2 Immigration Policies between 1960 and 1980

Prior to the 1965 amendments to the Immigration and Nationality Act, U.S. immigration policy was guided by the national-origins quota system.[4] Entry visas allocated to countries in the Eastern Hemisphere depended proportionately on their representation in the national-origin composition of the U.S. population in 1920. Because the ancestors of the great majority of U.S. residents originated in northwestern Europe, the United Kingdom was allocated 65,721 visas (almost half of the 150,000 available visas) and Germany was allocated 25,957 visas, whereas Italy was allocated 5,802 and Russia was allocated 2,784 visas. To prohibit the entry of Asian immigrants, Asian countries were generally allocated 100 visas per year.

The national-origins quota system applied only to visa applicants originating in countries in the Eastern Hemisphere. Applicants from North and South America were exempt from the quotas and faced no numerical restrictions on the number of visas, presumably because of the close economic and political ties between the United States and its geographic neighbors. These visas were awarded on a first-come, first-served basis as long as the applicants satisfied a long list of requirements regarding their health and their political and moral backgrounds.

3. See Duleep and Regets (1990) for additional evidence that the skills of immigrants from specific source countries vary little between Canada and the United States.

4. Borjas (1990) presents a comparative review of Canadian and U.S. immigration policies. See also Boyd (1976) and Keely and Elwell (1981).

The 1965 amendments (and subsequent revisions) regulated the process of legal immigration throughout the 1970s and 1980s. Under the 1965 amendments, the United States permitted the entry of 270,000 persons per year, with no more than 20,000 immigrants originating in any particular country of origin. Instead of emphasizing national origin, the 1965 amendments made family reunification the central objective of immigration policy. This was accomplished through several provisions. First, 80 percent of the 270,000 numerically limited visas were awarded to "close" relatives of U.S. citizens or residents. These close relatives included unmarried adult children of U.S. citizens, siblings of adult U.S. citizens, and spouses of resident aliens. The remaining 20 percent of the visas were allocated to persons on the basis of their skills. A large number of these 54,000 visas, however, went to the families of the skilled workers who qualified for the visa.

Furthermore, parents, spouses, and minor children of adult U.S. citizens could bypass the numerical restrictions specified in the legislation. These "immediate" relatives automatically qualified for entry and did not have to apply for one of the 270,000 numerically limited visas. By the late 1980s, more immigrants were entering under this single provision of the law than under all the family reunification preferences combined.

Until 1961, Canadian immigration policy, like that of the United States, permitted the entry of persons originating in only a few selected countries, such as the United Kingdom, Ireland, and the United States, or of persons who were dependents of Canadian residents. Major policy changes in 1962 and 1967 removed the national-origin restrictions and shifted the emphasis in the visa allocation system toward skills requirements. Under the new regulations, applicants for entry into Canada were classified into three categories: sponsored immigrants (which included close relatives of Canadian residents), nominated relatives (which included more distant relatives of Canadian residents), and independent immigrants.

Beginning in 1967, visa applicants in the last two of these categories were screened by means of a point system. Potential immigrants were graded and given up to 100 points. Points were awarded according to the applicant's education (a point per year of schooling, up to 20 points), occupational demand (up to 15 points if the applicant's occupation was in strong demand in Canada), age (up to 10 points for applicants under the age of 35, minus 1 point for each year over the age 35), arranged employment (10 points if the applicant had a job offer from a Canadian employer), a "personal assessment" by the immigration officer based on the applicant's motivation and initiative (up to 15 points), and other factors. Generally, an applicant needed to obtain 50 out of the 100 total points in order to pass the test and be awarded an entry visa.

In 1976, Canada amended its Immigration Act and made it easier for the families of Canadian residents to migrate there. This was accomplished through a revised point system that, in essence, awarded extra points to nominated relatives. To some extent, Canada enacted a weak version of the 1965 amendments eleven years after the United States.

Certainly the most noticeable consequence of the major policy shifts in Canada and the United States is the change that occurred in the national-origin mix of the immigrant flow. Table 1.1 summarizes the national-origin distribution of the immigrant flows admitted between 1959 and 1981. During the 1960s, about 40 percent of immigrants entering the United States originated in Europe. This had declined to 17 percent by the 1970s. In contrast, only 12.8 percent of immigrants in the 1960s originated in Asian countries, and this tripled to 37.2 percent by the 1970s.

Similar changes were also observed in Canada. For instance, 70 percent of immigrants entering Canada in the 1960s originated in the United Kingdom or in other European countries. During the 1970s, the fraction of the immigrant flow originating in Europe was cut by half, to 37 percent. On the other hand, the fraction of immigrants originating in Asia almost quadrupled, from 8 percent in the 1960s to 29 percent in the 1970s.

Although the trend away from European immigration and toward Asian immigration characterizes the experience of both Canada and the United States, it is important to note that there were significant differences in the national-origin mix of the immigrant flow between the two host countries in the 1970s. The fraction of immigrants originating in Europe was more than twice as large

Table 1.1 Migration Flows into Canada and the United States, 1959–81

	1959–70		1971–81	
Origin	Number (in 1000s)	% of Total	Number (in 1000s)	% of Total
	Canada			
Africa	34.1	2.1	71.5	4.6
Americas	283.5	17.5	427.9	27.3
Asia	136.3	8.4	457.3	29.1
United Kingdom	381.2	23.5	237.8	15.2
Europe (excluding United Kingdom)	745.4	46.0	340.1	21.7
Oceania and other	40.2	2.5	34.3	2.2
Total	1,620.7		1,568.9	
	United States			
Africa	43.2	1.1	106.5	2.0
Americas	1,792.0	46.6	2,175.7	42.7
Asia	492.2	12.8	1,898.1	37.3
United Kingdom	268.8	7.0	138.5	2.7
Europe (excluding United Kingdom)	1,228.2	31.9	729.5	14.3
Oceania and other	23.4	0.6	41.5	0.8
Total	3,847.8		5,089.8	

Sources: Leahy (1983); U.S. Immigration and Naturalization Service (various years).

in Canada, while the fraction of immigrants originating in the Americas (primarily Latin America) was almost three times as large in the United States. I will show that these national-origin differentials explain a major portion of the gap in average skills between immigrants in Canada and the United States.

1.3 Education and the "Choice" of a Host Country

As a result of changes in immigration policy (as well as changes in economic conditions in the host and source countries), the relative size and skill composition of immigrant flows into Canada and the United States changed drastically in recent years. This section and the next describe the extent of these changes.

Consider the population of persons who immigrate at any given time period into either Canada or the United States. These data can be used to calculate the fraction of immigrants who "choose" one country over the other. Table 1.2 reports the fraction of immigrants, by cohort and educational attainment, who migrated to the United States.

I estimate the fraction of immigrants who chose the United States using the public use samples of the 1971 and 1981 Canadian censuses and the 1970 and 1980 U.S. censuses. The 1971 data are drawn from a 1/100 random sample of the Canadian population, while the 1981 data are drawn from a 2/100 sample. The 1970 U.S. census data for immigrants are a 2/100 random sample of the immigrant population, while the 1980 data are a 5/100 sample. The 1970/71 censuses are used to estimate the choice probabilities for the cohorts that migrated during the 1960s, and the 1980/81 censuses are used for estimating the choice probabilities of the cohorts that migrated in the 1970s.[5] Finally, the probabilities are calculated in the sample of immigrants (both men and women) aged 18–64.

Between 1960 and 1980, 81.5 percent of the immigrants "chose" to reside in the United States. Note, however, that this statistic increased rapidly during the period. In the early 1960s, 77.2 percent of the sample migrated to the United States, while in the late 1970s 86.1 percent chose the United States. This reallocation of immigrants in the North American continent is due to policy changes in the United States that increased the annual number of immigrants, while the size of the annual immigrant flow in Canada remained relatively constant (see table 1.1).

A more interesting result revealed by table 1.2 concerns the differential trends in the choice probability across schooling groups. Although the fraction of immigrants ending up in the United States increased in most schooling

5. The intervals reporting the immigrant's year of entry into the host country differ between the Canadian and U.S. censuses. For the post-1960 cohorts, however, these variations are relatively unimportant. The probabilities reported in table 1.2 weigh the observations in each of the censuses so as to ensure that the underlying time period defining each cohort has the same duration in the two host countries.

Table 1.2 **Immigration to Canada and the United States, by Cohort and Education (fraction of immigrants "choosing" the United States)**

	Education				
Cohort	Less than High School	High School	Some College	College Graduate	All
1960–64	.721	.864	.750	.824	.772
1965–70	.719	.780	.578	.770	.719
1970–74	.821	.798	.740	.828	.804
1975–80	.869	.851	.831	.890	.861
All	.815	.825	.765	.849	.815

Sources: The data for the 1960–64 and 1965–70 cohorts are drawn from the 1971 Canadian census and the 1970 U.S. census. The data for the 1970–74 and 1975–80 cohorts are drawn from the 1981 Canadian census and the 1980 U.S. census. The statistics are calculated in the sample of immigrants aged 18–64.

groups, the increase was largest among the least educated. In the early 1960s, 72.1 percent of immigrants who did not have a high school diploma migrated to the United States. By the late 1970s, this statistic was 86.9 percent, an increase of almost 15 percentage points. In contrast, in the early 1960s, 82.4 percent of immigrants with a college diploma chose the United States, but by the early 1970s, the fraction increased to only 89.0 percent, less than 7 percentage points.

Immigration policy reforms in Canada and the United States are probably responsible for these trends. Prior to the enactment of the point system in Canada, relatively more college graduates "chose" the United States as a destination point. By the late 1970s, after Canada began to restrict the entry of high school dropouts, the fraction of persons choosing the United States was the same for high school dropouts as for college graduates.

1.4 Immigrant Earnings in Canada and the United States

Suppose two census cross-sections are available in a particular host country (the 1971 and 1981 censuses in Canada, or the 1970 and 1980 censuses in the United States), and the following regression model is estimated within a host country:

$$\log w_{ij} = X_j\beta_i + \alpha_1 y_j + \alpha_2 y_j^2 + \sum_j \beta_t C_t + \gamma_i \pi_j + \varepsilon_{ij}, \quad (1)$$

and

$$\log w_{n\ell} = X_\ell \beta_n + \gamma_n \pi_\ell + \varepsilon_{n\ell}, \quad (2)$$

where w_{ij} is the wage rate of immigrant j;$w_{n\ell}$ is the wage rate of native person ℓ; X is a vector of socioeconomic characteristics (e.g., education, age); y is a variable measuring the number of years that the immigrant has resided in the host country; C is a vector of dummy variables indicating the calendar year in which the migration occurred; and π is a dummy variable set to unity if the observation is drawn from the 1980/81 census, and to zero otherwise. The vector of parameters (α_1,α_2), along with the age coefficients in the vector X, measures the assimilation effect (i.e., the rate at which the age-earnings profile of immigrants is converging to the age-earnings profiles of natives), while the vector of parameters β estimates the cohort effects. The period effects are given by γ_i for immigrants and by γ_n for natives.

It is well known that the parameters of the system in (1) and (2) are not identified unless some normalization is made about either the aging, cohort, or period effects (Borjas 1991). In other words, two cross-sections cannot identify three separate sets of coefficients, and something must be assumed about one of the effects in order to identify the other two. I chose the normalization that the period effect experienced by immigrants (γ_i) is identical to the period effect experienced by natives (γ_n). This normalization, of course, implies that the relative wage differential between immigrants and natives is invariant to the business cycle.

The data used to estimate (1) and (2) are drawn from the Canadian and U.S. censuses described in section 1.3. The regression analysis is restricted to prime-age men (aged 25–64) who are not self-employed, whose records report the relevant information needed to calculate a wage rate in the year prior to the census, and who are not residing in group quarters. Although all immigrant observations are used in the analysis, I use random samples of the native population in the United States because of the large number of natives surveyed.[6]

The mean characteristics in these samples are reported in table 1.3 for the post-1960 cohorts. The descriptive data yield a number of important results. The U.S. census clearly documents the importance of cohort effects in immigrant labor market performance. The most recent arrivals in the 1970 census (i.e., the 1965–69 cohort) have −0.3 fewer years of education than natives and earn about 16 percent less than natives. By 1980, the most recent arrivals (i.e., the 1975–79 cohort) have −0.8 fewer years of schooling and earn almost 30 percent less than natives.

Remarkably, despite the enactment of the point system, the Canadian data show a somewhat similar pattern. The educational attainment of the most recent immigrants in 1971 is 12.0 years, while that of the most recent immigrants in 1981 is 12.6 years, an increase of over half a year in schooling. At the same time, however, the educational attainment of recent immigrants relative to Canadian natives declined from a 2.1-year advantage in 1971 to a 1.3-year advantage in 1981, and the relative wage of recent immigrants decreased from −2.1 percent in 1971 to −17.2 percent in 1981. Although the educa-

6. The 1970 U.S. native sample is a 1/1,000 extract, while the 1980 U.S. native sample is a 1/2,500 extract.

Table 1.3 **Education and Wages of Immigrants in Canada and the United States, by Cohort**

	1971			1981		
Cohort	Education	Relative Education	Relative Wage	Education	Relative Education	Relative Wage
			Canada			
1960–64	10.506	0.599	−.008	11.217	−0.086	.048
		(4.51)	(−0.44)		(−0.94)	(3.37)
1965–70	12.043	2.136	−.021	12.351	1.048	.065
		(21.34)	(−1.51)		(15.69)	(6.24)
1970–74	—	—	—	12.370	1.067	−.084
					(13.55)	(−6.83)
1975–80	—	—	—	12.603	1.300	−.172
					(16.32)	(−13.86)
			United States			
1960–64	10.959	−0.556	−.051	11.913	−0.793	.009
		(−9.21)	(−5.79)		(−14.91)	(1.18)
1965–70	11.179	−0.336	−.160	11.418	−1.288	−.069
		(−6.01)	(−19.75)		(−25.75)	(−9.90)
1970–74	—	—	—	11.091	−1.614	−.200
					(−33.31)	(−29.43)
1975–80	—	—	—	11.859	−0.846	−.299
					(−17.54)	(−44.28)

Notes: The *t*-ratios are reported in parentheses. The sample sizes are 1971 Canadian census, 8,018 immigrants and 28,049 natives; 1981 Canadian census, 17,417 immigrants and 61,205 natives; 1970 U.S. census, 32,491 immigrants and 20,978 natives; 1980 U.S. census, 134,254 immigrants and 15,071 natives.

tional attainment of successive immigrant waves rose over time, the educational attainment of the native Canadian population was rising even faster.

This result, however, should not obscure the fact that the point system "attracted" a more educated immigrant flow into Canada. In the early 1960s, prior to the immigration reform in Canada, the typical immigrant entering Canada had 0.4 fewer years of schooling than did the typical immigrant entering the United States (where the educational attainment is measured as of 1970/71). The Canadian disadvantage in immigrant schooling disappeared by the late 1960s, when the typical new immigrant in Canada had almost 1 year more schooling than did the typical new immigrant in the United States, and this gap remained roughly constant throughout the 1970s.

The dependent variable in equations (1) and (2) is the logarithm of the wage rate. I use two different specifications for the vector X. The first includes an intercept, age, and age squared, while the second adds education, marital status, whether the individual lives in a metropolitan area, and whether the individual's health limits work (available only for the United States). The estimated regressions are presented in appendix Table 1A.1 for Canada and 1A.2

Table 1.4 **Predicted Entry Wages and Growth Rates for Immigrants in Canada and the United States**

	Canada		U.S.	
	(1)	(2)	(1)	(2)
Cohort				
1960–64	−.0325	−.0242	−.0975	−.0932
	(−1.16)	(−0.90)	(−5.18)	(−5.22)
1965–69	.0045	−.0255	−.1547	−.1200
	(0.20)	(−1.13)	(−9.23)	(−7.53)
1970–74	−.1043	−.1320	−.2353	−.1632
	(−4.33)	(−5.69)	(−15.08)	(−10.97)
1975–80	−.1531	−.1839	−.2941	−.2290
	(−7.32)	(−9.11)	(−20.18)	(−17.21)
Growth rate at $y = 10$ years	.0032	.0006	.0051	.0054
	(2.09)	(2.81)	(5.01)	(9.23)
Growth rate at $y = 20$ years	.0033	.0008	.0020	.0027
	(2.08)	(2.75)	(5.09)	(9.21)
Holds constant demographic characteristics	No	Yes	No	Yes

Notes: The *t*-ratios are reported in parentheses. The vector X in the regressions underlying the estimates in column 1 includes age and age squared. The regressions in column 2 add education, marital status, metropolitan residence, and an indicator of whether health limits work (available only in the United States).

for the United States. Table 1.4 summarizes the implications of the regressions by reporting the wage differential between immigrants and natives at the time of entry into the host country (assuming immigration takes place at age 20), and the rate of growth of immigrant earnings relative to natives at $y = 10$ and $y = 20$.[7]

The results indicate that immigrants in Canada have substantially higher entry wages (relative to natives) than immigrants in the United States if the regressions do not control for differences in educational attainment and other socioeconomic characteristics. For instance, the typical person who migrated to Canada in the late 1970s earned about 15 percent less than natives at the time of arrival, while the typical person who migrated to the United States at the same time earned about 29 percent less than natives. The superior economic performance of immigrants in Canada, however, largely disappears after controlling for differences in observed demographic characteristics (particularly education) between immigrants and natives in each host country. The predicted difference between the (log) wage of immigrants who arrived in the

7. The growth rates are evaluated by calculating the slope of the age earnings profile at the relevant age and years-since-migration values. The statistics reported in table 1.4 differ slightly from those that can be calculated from tables 1A.1 and 1A.2 because of rounding errors in the reporting of the regression coefficients.

late 1970s and demographically comparable natives is −0.18 in Canada and −0.23 in the United States. The skill-filtering explicit in Canadian immigration policy, therefore, leads to higher-wage immigrants not because of unobserved factors such as ability and training, but because of more education.

The data in table 1.4 indicate that the enactment of a point system in Canada could not prevent a decline in the relative skill level of immigrants across successive waves. In both countries, the entry wage of immigrants is higher for the earlier cohorts than for the later cohorts. The decline in immigrant skills (as measured by the unadjusted wage), however, is much steeper in the United States, where the (relative) entry wage fell from −0.10 in the early 1960s to −0.29 in the late 1970s. By contrast, in Canada, the entry wage fell from −0.03 to −0.15 during the same period.

1.5 National Origin and the Canada-U.S. Skill Differential

This section shows that one single factor, the different national-origin mix of immigrants in Canada and the United States, explains most of the differences in skills and relative wages of the foreign-born between these two countries. In section 1.2 I documented that the national-origin mix of the immigrant flow differs between Canada and the United States. Substantial dispersion in skills and wages also exists across national-origin groups in each of the host countries.

I focus on three measures of skills: years of educational attainment, the log wage rate (relative to natives), and the log wage differential between immigrants and natives adjusted for differences in socioeconomic characteristics (such as education and age) between the two groups. To calculate the adjusted wage, I first estimated log wage regressions separately for each national origin group and for natives in each of the four censuses available (two censuses per host country). Using the estimated coefficients, I calculated the wage differential between each immigrant cohort and natives using the mean of the socioeconomic characteristics observed in the immigrant population. The statistics for the cohorts that migrated during the 1960s are obtained from the 1970/71 censuses, while the statistics for the cohorts that migrated in the 1970s are obtained from the 1980/81 censuses. To illustrate the large dispersion that exists across national-origin groups, table 1.5 reports the educational attainment, relative wage, and adjusted wage for the cohort that migrated in the late 1970s for fifteen national-origin groups (which are the fifteen groups that can be matched exactly among the four censuses).[8]

The average educational attainment level of immigrants from Greece who arrived in Canada in the late 1970s was 8.3 years, while the average education

8. The U.S. census reports many more source countries than the Canadian census does. The main drawback of the Canadian census is that the specific source country of Asian or Latin American immigrants is not identified.

Table 1.5 **Schooling and Wages by National Origin, 1975–80 Cohort**

	Canada			U.S.		
Country of Origin	Education	Relative Wage	Adjusted Wage	Education	Relative Wage	Adjusted Wage
Europe						
Belgium	16.600	.661	.411	16.239	.456	.293
France	13.359[a]	−.004[a]	−.037[a]	15.626	.252	.161
Germany	13.705[a]	.084	−.008	15.237	.293	.171
Greece	8.271[a]	−.482	−.310	11.058	−.311	−.183
Ireland	13.333	−.443	−.514	13.803	−.114	−.121
Italy	9.833	−.212	−.153	10.567	−.133	−.065
Netherlands	13.333[a]	−.194[a]	−.235[a]	15.939	.311	.172
Poland	14.500[a]	.096[a]	−.049[a]	12.742	−.342	−.339
United Kingdom	13.068[a]	.062[a]	−.021[a]	15.047	.221	.118
USSR	14.455	−.099	−.311	14.328	−.257	−.386
Other Europe	9.648[a]	−.101	−.026	11.118	−.141	−.061
Africa	13.772[a]	−.159	−.264	15.362	−.210	−.268
Asia	12.860[a]	−.290	−.348[a]	13.966	−.250	−.294
Latin America	11.706[a]	−.354[a]	−.369	8.551	−.532	−.365
Other	12.698	−.062	−.103	12.017	−.230	−.126

[a]The difference between Canada and the United States is significantly different from zero at the 5 percent level.

level of immigrants from Belgium was 16.6 years. Similarly, in the United States, the average education level of immigrants who arrived in the same period ranged from 8.6 years for immigrants from Latin America to 16.2 years for immigrants from Belgium. The relative wage of immigrants exhibits similar dispersion across national origin groups. The relative (log) wage ranges from −0.48 (Greek immigrants) to 0.66 (Belgian immigrants) in Canada, and from −0.53 (Latin American immigrants) to 0.46 (Belgian immigrants) in the United States.

As suggested by these descriptive data, there is a very strong correlation between the skills of national-origin groups in Canada and the skills of the corresponding group in the United States. Table 1.6 presents regressions that describe the relationship between the skills of national-origin groups across host countries. These regressions are of the form

$$(3) \qquad y_{iu}(t) = \rho_0 + \rho_1 y_{ic}(t) + \nu_i,$$

where y_{iu} is the value of the skill variable for immigrants belonging to national-origin group i who migrated to the United States at time t; $y_{ic}(t)$ is the value of the skill variable for the same immigrant cohort in Canada.[9] The

9. Because the dependent variables are themselves estimates of the true means, the regressions are estimated using generalized least squares. It is worth noting, however, that the unweighted regressions lead to the same qualitative conclusions as the GLS regressions.

regressions reported in table 1.6 provide one very interesting insight. For the post-1965 cohorts, with only one exception, the slope coefficient ρ_1 is insignificantly different from unity, and the intercept is insignificantly different from zero. Moreover, the explanatory power of these regressions is quite high: the R^2 is on the order of .5 to .8. These results imply that the expected skills or wages of a specific national-origin group in Canada and the United States (in the 1965–80 period) are identical. There is no evidence, therefore, to suggest that the point system generated a more skilled flow into Canada from *within* a source country.

The finding that, on average, immigrants in Canada are more skilled than immigrants in the United States is attributable to another factor. I now show that the different national-origin composition of immigrant flows in the two countries accounts for much of the Canadian advantage. Let $Y_r(t)$ be the average value for a particular characteristic (i.e., education or wage) observed in the immigrant flow in year t in host country r. By definition, $Y_r(t)$ can be written as

$$Y_r(t) = \sum_j p_{jr}(t)\, y_{jr}(t), \tag{4}$$

Table 1.6 Relationship between Skills and Wages of National-Origin Groups in the United States and Canada, by Cohort

Variable	1960–64	1965–70	1970–74	1975–80
Dependent variable = mean education of national-origin group in United States				
Intercept	3.864[a]	0.471	−0.502	−1.832
	(1.298)	(1.646)	(2.963)	(4.556)
Canada mean	0.670[b]	0.954	1.072	1.196
	(0.120)	(0.139)	(0.241)	(0.366)
R^2	.708	.785	.602	.451
Dependent variable = mean wage of national origin group in United States				
Intercept	.040	−.016	.070[a]	.063
	(.030)	(.043)	(.033)	(.057)
Canada mean	0.349[b]	0.910	1.469[b]	1.275
	(.197)	(.283)	(.215)	(.228)
R^2	.195	.443	.782	.707
Dependent variable = adjusted wage of national origin group in United States				
Intercept	.043	.032	.031	.065
	(.027)	(.042)	(.027)	(.042)
Canada mean	0.426	1.017	0.799	1.068
	(.259)	(.259)	(.128)	(.150)
R^2	.173	.543	.751	.797

Note: The standard errors are in parentheses.

[a]Significantly different from zero at the 5 percent level.

[b]Significantly different from one at the 5 percent level.

where $y_{jr}(t)$ is the average value for the labor market characteristic observed among persons who migrated from source country j into host country r in year t; and $p_{jr}(t)$ is the fraction of the host country's immigrant flow in year t originating in source country j.

It is useful to define the average labor market performance that would have been observed if a different national-origin mix had migrated to host country r, such as the national-origin mix observed in host country s, $p_{js}(t)$. This is given by

$$Y(t,s) = \sum_{j} p_{js}(t)\, y_{jr}(t). \tag{5}$$

The impact of a changing national-origin mix is then given by the difference between equations (4) and (5):

$$Y_r(t) - Y(t,s) = \sum_{j} y_{jr}(t)\, [p_{jr}(t) - p_{js}(t)]. \tag{6}$$

The decomposition implicit in equation (6) is similar to that commonly used to measure wage discrimination (Oaxaca 1973) and has its roots in the statistical literature (Kitigawa 1955). Using this methodological framework, table 1.7 decomposes the differences observed in educational attainment and relative wages between Canada and the United States for each of the immigrant waves arriving between 1960 and 1980.

To understand the nature of the results, it is instructive to consider first the cohort that migrated to Canada or the United States in the late 1970s. The average education level of those who migrated to Canada was 12.6 years, while the average education level of those who migrated to the United States was 11.9 years, a difference of 0.7 years. Column 3 of table 1.7 reports the prediction of what the education level of immigrants in Canada would have been had Canada admitted immigrants on the basis of the U.S. national-origin mix. In other words, it presents the prediction from equation (5) using the 1975–80 means of educational attainment in Canada and the 1975–80 national-origin mix observed in the United States. This prediction is 12.3 years, so that the average educational attainment of this immigrant wave would have been 0.3 years lower. National-origin differences, therefore, explain almost half of the observed gap between the educational attainment of the 1975–80 immigrant wave in Canada and the United States.

It is also possible to estimate what the average educational attainment of immigrants in the United States would have been had the United States accepted immigrants on the basis of Canada's national-origin mix. In other words, equation (5) is estimated using the 1975–80 means of educational attainment in the United States and the national-origin mix observed in Canada in 1975–80. This prediction, reported in column 4 of table 1.7, is 13.1 years. In other words, the educational attainment of U.S. immigrants would have increased from 11.9 to 13.1 years due solely to changes in the national-origin

Table 1.7 **Decomposition of Differences between Canada and the United States**

Cohort	Canada Average (1)	U.S. Average (2)	(1) − (2)	Predicted Averages: If Canada Had U.S. Mix (3)	Predicted Averages: If U.S. Had Canada Mix (4)	(4) − (2)	(1) − (3)
Education							
1960–64	10.506	10.959	−0.453	11.202	10.768	−0.191	−0.696
1965–70	12.043	11.179	0.864	11.818	11.694	0.515	0.225
1970–74	12.370	11.092	1.278	12.042	12.602	1.510	0.328
1975–80	12.603	11.860	0.743	12.302	13.102	1.242	0.301
Wage							
1960–64	−.008	−.051	.043	.053	.038	.089	−.061
1965–70	−.021	−.160	.139	−.087	−.044	.116	.066
1970–74	−.084	−.200	.116	−.174	−.070	.130	.090
1975–80	−.172	−.299	.127	−.254	−.161	.138	.082
Adjusted wage							
1960–64	−.049	−.063	.014	−.063	.029	.092	.014
1965–70	−.097	−.159	.062	−.155	−.070	.089	.058
1970–74	−.161	−.159	−.002	−.233	−.094	.065	.072
1975–80	−.224	−.258	.034	−.293	−.170	.088	.069

mix. This increase is greater than the observed difference between Canada and the United States, so that national origin overexplains the observed difference.

Table 1.7 reports a similar decomposition for both wages and adjusted wages for the 1975–80 cohort, as well as for all other post-1960 cohorts. It is evident that differences between the two host countries in the national-origin mix are largely responsible for the post-1965 differences in educational attainment, wages, and adjusted wages. For instance, the difference in relative wages between the immigrant wave that arrived in Canada and the United States in 1965–70 is 0.139, of which at least one-half is attributable to differences in national origin. The observed difference for the waves that arrived during the 1970s is around 0.12, and over two-thirds of this gap is attributable to national origin.[10]

In contrast to the post-1965 cohorts, the results in table 1.7 show that national origin played a different role among persons who migrated in the early 1960s. These data do not indicate that immigrants in Canada were unambiguously more skilled than immigrants in the United States. Moreover, the differences in the national-origin mix of this immigrant flow sometimes worked to the advantage of the United States. The mean educational attainment of immigrants in Canada would have increased from 10.5 to 11.2 years if Canada had had the national-origin mix of the United States. The decomposition of the wage differential between the two host countries, however, does not yield an unambiguous indication that either country had a more "desirable" national-origin mix.

The central implication of these results is clear. Differences in the national-origin mix of immigrants arriving in Canada and the United States since 1965 are mainly responsible for the higher average skills and relative wages of immigrants in Canada. In view of this finding, it is worth reassessing the role that immigration policy, and in particular a point system, can play in generating a more skilled immigrant flow. To the extent that the point system is intended as a way of increasing the skill level of immigrants from a given source country, the results in tables 1.6 and 1.7 are discouraging. A point system seems to have little effect on the education level or relative wages of specific national-origin groups.

This does not imply, however, that the point system is ineffective. An alternative, though little discussed, effect of the point system is to reallocate visas *across* source countries. Consider, for instance, the impact of the educational requirements in the point system. A visa applicant is given one point per year of education, and only fifty points are needed to "pass the test." Persons originating in countries with high mean educational attainment are more likely to qualify for entry into Canada than persons originating in countries with low educational attainment. The population of the source countries differs sub-

10. These education data are reported in Borjas (1991, table 2) and give the average educational attainment of the population of the source countries in the late 1970s.

stantially in mean education levels. For instance, the average educational attainment is 3.2 years in Haiti, 6.1 years in Mexico, 10.7 years in the United Kingdom, and 11.1 years in France.[11] It is likely, therefore, that the point system plays an important role in determining the national-origin mix of the immigrant flow.

The extent to which the point system actually redistributes visas among source countries has not been analyzed. As a preliminary way of establishing this link, I calculated the fraction of immigrants that migrated to Canada (out of the total number of immigrants into Canada and the United States) for forty source countries in the late 1970s.[12] The relationship between this "choice" variable and mean educational attainment in the source country is summarized by

$$(7) \qquad \log[P/(1-P)] = \underset{(-3.58)}{-2.3035} + \underset{(2.67)}{.1971\,\bar{S}}, \qquad R^2 = .178,$$

where P is the fraction of the immigrant flow that "chose" Canada, $\bar{S}$ is the mean educational attainment in the source country, and the t-statistics are reported in parentheses. Equation (7) was estimated using a minimum χ^2 grouped-logit estimator. Evaluated at the mean probability, an increase of one year in the average schooling level of the source country increases the likelihood that immigrants "choose" Canada by about 3.6 percentage points.

This preliminary analysis thus suggests that the point system plays a subtle, but crucial, role: it biases the admission of immigrants toward national-origin groups that originate in high-income, high-skill countries. My findings imply that it is this feature of the point system that is mostly responsible for the different performance of immigrants in Canada and in the United States during the post-1965 period.[13]

11. It is of interest to determine the extent to which these findings are driven by the presence of large numbers of relatively unskilled Latin American immigrants in the United States. I reestimated the statistics reported in table 1.7 after omitting the sample of Latin Americans from the analysis. Suppose, for instance, that there were no Latin American immigrants in the 1975–80 cohort in either Canada or the United States. The average wage of immigrants would be −0.144 in Canada and −0.173 in the United States. If Canada had the same national-origin mix as the United States, the predicted wage would be −0.198, while if the United States had the same national-origin mix as Canada the predicted wage would be −0.099. Therefore, the results indicate that, although Latin American immigrants in the United States substantially reduce the average skill level of U.S. immigrants, differences in the national-origin composition of the immigrant flow *still* favor Canada.

12. The forty countries included in this analysis are listed in Borjas (1987).

13. The empirical analysis presented in section 1.4 also indicated a sizable decline in skills among successive immigrant waves in both host countries, with the decline being much steeper in the United States. I have shown elsewhere (Borjas 1992) that much of the U.S. trend can be attributed to the changing national-origin mix of immigrant flows. Preliminary calculations (not reported) indicate that national origin plays a weaker (though still important) role in explaining the declining skills of immigrants in Canada.

1.6 Migration Flows between Canada and the United States

The large migration flows between Canada and the United States provide further evidence on the limitations and effectiveness of Canada's point system.[14] In 1980–81, nearly 850,000 persons born in Canada resided in the United States, and over 300,000 persons born in the United States resided in Canada. The emigration of Americans accounted for 8 percent of the foreign-born population in Canada, while the emigration of Canadians accounted for 6 percent of the foreign-born population in the United States.

Table 1.8 reports the mean educational attainment and relative wages for several waves of transnational migrants. These data yield several interesting facts. In general, Canadian immigrants in the United States do quite well in the labor market. The most recent arrivals enumerated in the 1980 census earn about 20 percent higher wages than American natives and have about 2 years more schooling. In contrast, American immigrants in Canada are less successful. The most recent arrivals enumerated in the 1981 census earn 4.5 percent less than Canadian natives yet have 4.5 years *more* schooling.

In addition, the data indicate little growth in immigrant earnings over time (relative to natives). For instance, the U.S. census shows that the most recent arrivals enumerated in the 1970 census had 14.9 percent higher wages than natives. By 1980, this differential had increased to only 17.2 percent. In Canada, the typical immigrant who arrived in the late 1960s earned 30 percent more than natives in 1970, but earned only 10.6 percent more than natives in 1980. There is little evidence of assimilation in these data. In fact, the Canadian census suggests the possibility of "disassimilation."

Finally, there was a sizable decline in skills among successive waves of American immigrants in Canada, but an increase among successive waves of Canadians in the United States. In 1970, the newly arrived Americans had 6.5 more years of schooling and earned 29 percent more than natives, but by 1980 the most recent American immigrants had 4.5 more years of schooling and earned 4.5 percent less than natives. In contrast, the newly arrived Canadians enumerated by the 1970 U.S. census had 1.4 more years of schooling and 14.9 percent higher wages than natives, but the most recent Canadian immigrants in 1980 had 1.9 more years of schooling and earned 20.2 percent more than natives.

Some of the statistics in table 1.8 may be contaminated by the migration of draft avoiders to Canada in the late 1960s and early 1970s. A presidential pardon allowing their reentry into the United States was declared in 1978. Because the empirical analysis below uses the 1971–81 Canadian censuses to track the wages of cohorts of American migrants, it is possible that the influx

14. These flows have long been of interest to Canadian demographers. See Boyd (1981), Lavoie (1972), and the many references in U.S. Bureau of the Census (1990).

Table 1.8 Education and Wages of Transnational Immigrants, by Cohort

	Americans in Canada				Canadians in U.S.			
	1971		1981		1971		1981	
Cohort	Education	Relative Wage	Education	Relative Wage	Education	Relative Wage	Education	Relative Wage
1960–64	15.698	.3924	15.262	.0248	11.366	.1248	12.756	.1427
		(5.01)		(0.34)		(4.21)		(7.13)
1965–70	16.444	.2897	16.205	.1059	12.599	.1488	12.599	.1722
		(6.14)		(2.59)		(4.72)		(7.00)
1970–74	—	—	15.985	.0819	—	—	13.748	.1124
				(1.81)				(3.35)
1975–80	—	—	15.809	−.0454	—	—	14.604	.2021
				(−0.89)				(7.90)

Notes: The *t*-ratios are reported in parentheses. The mean educational attainment of natives in Canada was 9.907 in 1971 and 11.303 in 1981. The mean educational attainment of natives in the United States was 11.515 in 1971 and 12.706 in 1981. The sample sizes are 1971 Canadian census, 511 American immigrants and 28,049 natives; 1981 Canadian census, 924 American immigrants and 61,205 natives; 1970 U.S. census, 3,430 Canadian immigrants and 20,978 natives; 1980 U.S. census, 7,083 Canadian immigrants and 15,071 natives.

of the draft avoiders enumerated in the 1971 Canadian census, and their possible return migration to the U.S. prior to the 1981 census, biases the analysis.

There are no reliable estimates of the number of draft avoiders nor of their return migration rates. The 1971 Canadian census enumerated only 4,800 American-born young men (aged 18–25) who had migrated between 1966 and 1971. The 1981 Canadian census enumerated 4,250 American-born men aged 28–35 (who had migrated in 1966–71). Both the size of this migration flow and the return migration rate are relatively small. It is unlikely, therefore, that the migration of Vietnam draft avoiders is driving the results of the analysis (and this flow could certainly not explain the increasing skills of Canadian immigrants in the United States).

Within each host country, the samples of natives and of transnational migrants were used to estimate the earnings functions (1) and (2). I then predicted the (relative) entry wage of the transnational migrants in each of the host countries, as well as the growth rate after ten and twenty years in the host country. These summary statistics are reported in table 1.9.

The most recent Canadian immigrants in the United States (i.e., the 1975–80 wave) entered the labor market with essentially the same wage as natives, while the most recent Americans in Canada entered the Canadian labor market with much lower wages than natives. This situation is quite different from what was observed in the early 1960s. At that time, the most recent Canadians in the United States had slightly lower wages than natives (though the differ-

Table 1.9 Predicted Entry Wages and Growth Rates for Transnational Immigrants in Canada and the United States

	Americans in Canada		Canadians in U.S.	
	(1)	(2)	(1)	(2)
Cohort				
1960–64	.2055	.0607	−.0509	−.0952
	(1.90)	(0.59)	(−1.10)	(−2.21)
1965–69	.1098	−.0426	−.0150	−.0509
	(1.29)	(−0.52)	(−0.37)	(−1.36)
1970–74	.0120	−.1174	−.0674	−.1182
	(0.14)	(−1.34)	(−1.47)	(−2.78)
1975–80	−.2368	−.3275	.0521	−.0231
	(−2.79)	(−4.06)	(1.45)	(−0.81)
Growth rate at y = 10 years	−.0053	−.0084	.0097	−.0119
	(−6.79)	(−5.98)	(0.37)	(1.55)
Growth rate at y = 20 years	−.0018	−.0018	.0046	.0059
	(−6.68)	(−5.91)	(0.22)	(1.69)
Holds constant demographic characteristics	No	Yes	No	Yes

Notes: The t-ratios are reported in parentheses. The vector X in the regressions underlying the estimates in column 1 include age and age squared. The regressions in column 2 add education, marital status, metropolitan residence, and an indicator of whether health limits work (available only in the United States).

ence was not statistically significant), while Americans in Canada entered the labor market with much higher wages than natives.

The relatively better performance of recent Canadian immigrants in the U.S. labor market may be a result of a different selection process guiding the migration of persons across the U.S.-Canada border. In earlier work (Borjas 1987), I argued that international differences in the rate of return to skills are the main determinants of the skill composition of immigrant flows. The results presented in tables 1.8 and 1.9 are consistent with this hypothesis if Canada has a lower rate of return to skills than does the United States. In fact, the available evidence suggests that the Canadian income distribution is more compressed than that of the United States, so that skilled Canadians are likely to have greater incentives to migrate to the United States than unskilled Canadians do (McWatters and Beach 1989).

Regardless of the validity of this hypothesis, the results presented in this section suggest that the point system plays a much weaker role than would have been presumed. Because of the skill filters explicitly built into Canadian immigration policy and the absence of such filters in U.S. immigration policy, it is not unreasonable to expect that American immigrants in Canada would do well in the Canadian labor market and that Canadian immigrants in the

United States would be less successful. The facts, however, are exactly the opposite. The self-selection generated by the differential economic opportunities available to skilled and unskilled workers in the two countries greatly dilutes the expected impact of Canada's point system.

1.7 Summary

Because immigration policies in Canada and the United States differ in their objectives, the comparison of the economic impact of immigrants in the two countries provides a benchmark for assessing the role played by policy in determining the skill composition of the immigrant flow. This paper presented a description of the trends in immigrant skills and labor market performance in both Canada and the United States, and interpreted these trends in terms of the underlying policy changes that occurred between 1960 and 1980 in both host countries.

The data provide a clear and unambiguous picture of the skills and labor market performance of immigrants in the two countries. Immigrants in Canada are, on average, more skilled than immigrants in the United States. This result is evident from comparisons of educational attainment, where immigrants in Canada have about a year more schooling at the time of arrival than immigrants in the United States, as well as in terms of immigrant wages, where the wage disadvantage of immigrants (relative to natives) is substantially greater in the United States.

The empirical analysis suggests a simple explanation for the skill differential. The average skill level of specific national-origin groups is about the same in Canada and the United States, so that Canada's point system does not attract more skilled workers from a given source country. The national-origin mix of the Canadian immigrant flow, however, is more heavily weighted toward national-origin groups that tend to perform well in both the Canadian and U.S. labor markets. It is this compositional effect that explains most of the observed differences in the educational attainment and wages of immigrants in Canada and the United States.

In effect, the point system works because it alters the national-origin mix of immigrant flows. This finding has important, if unpalatable, implications for the ongoing debate over the role that the skills of visa applicants should play in determining entry into Canada or the United States. To a large extent, skill filters are effective because they alter the allocation of visas across source countries. The data analyzed in this paper, therefore, suggest an important tradeoff between the average skill level of immigrant flows and their ethnic diversity. The existence and implications of this tradeoff are likely to play an important role in future discussions of immigration policy.

Appendix

Table 1A.1 Log Wage Regressions on Pooled 1971 and 1981 Canadian Censuses

	(1)		(2)	
Variable	Natives	Immigrants	Natives	Immigrants
Intercept	1.0613	.9275	.3231	.4655
	(36.37)	(15.52)	(11.17)	(7.96)
Education	—	—	.0438	.0344
			(84.79)	(43.25)
Age	0.0563	.0556	.0564	.0498
	(36.89)	(19.16)	(40.49)	(17.80)
Age squared	−0.0006	−.0006	−.0006	−.0005
	(−36.55)	(−19.08)	(−36.12)	(−17.07)
Years since migration	—	.0043	—	.0054
		(2.06)		(2.72)
Years since migration, squared	—	.00002	—	−.00003
		(.39)		(−0.76)
1970–74 cohort	—	.0488	—	.0519
		(2.73)		(3.05)
1965–69 cohort	—	.1576	—	.1584
		(9.66)		(10.17)
1960–64 cohort	—	.1206	—	.1597
		(5.84)		(8.06)
1950–59 cohort	—	.1139	—	.1597
		(5.04)		(7.32)
Pre-1950 cohort	—	.1046	—	.1773
		(3.28)		(5.71)
Observation from 1971 census	−0.9651	−.9651	−.9427	−.9427
	(−248.35)	(−248.35)	(−238.28)	(−238.28)
R^2	.399		.456	
holds constant demographic characteristics	No		Yes	

Notes: The *t*-ratios are reported in parentheses. The regressions in column 2 also control for marital status, metropolitan residence, and an indicator of whether health limits work (available only in the United States). The index indicating if the person migrated after 1975 is the omitted dummy variable. The sample size is 114,689.

Table 1A.2 Log Wage Regressions on Pooled 1971 and 1981 U.S. Censuses

Variable	(1) Natives	(1) Immigrants	(2) Natives	(2) Immigrants
Intercept	.8298	.4387	−.1012	−.0483
	(17.43)	(17.41)	(−2.18)	(−1.99)
Education	—	—	.0558	.0442
			(63.12)	(143.54)
Age	.0560	.0628	.0490	.0494
	(24.05)	(50.88)	(22.31)	(42.24)
Age squared	−.0006	−.0007	−.0005	−.0005
	(22.27)	(48.82)	(−18.91)	(−38.05)
Years since migration	—	.0053	—	.0090
		(5.07)		(9.16)
Years since migration, squared	—	−.0001	—	−.0001
		(−4.00)		(−7.34)
1970–74 cohort	—	.0588	—	.0659
		(7.95)		(9.43)
1965–69 cohort	—	.1395	—	.1090
		(14.86)		(12.31)
1960–64 cohort	—	.1967	—	.1358
		(15.64)		(11.44)
1950–59 cohort	—	.2414	—	.1554
		(15.08)		(10.26)
Pre-1950 cohort	—	.2798	—	.1523
		(12.92)		(7.44)
Observations from 1971 census	−.6837	−.6837	−.6105	−.6105
	(−133.23)	(−133.23)	(−125.07)	(−125.07)
R^2	.192		.289	
holds constant demographic characteristics	No		Yes	

Notes: The *t*-ratios are reported in parentheses. The regressions in column 2 also control for marital status, metropolitan residence, and an indicator of whether health limits work (available only in the United States). The index indicating if the person migrated after 1975 is the omitted dummy variable. The sample size is 210,732.

References

Abbott, Michael G., and Charles M. Beach. 1987. Immigrant Earnings Differentials and Cohort Effects in Canada. Queen's University, Kingston, Ontario. Mimeo.

Bloom, David E., and Morley K. Gunderson. 1991. An Analysis of the Earnings of Canadian Immigration. In *Immigration, Trade, and the Labor Market,* ed. John M. Abowd and Richard B. Freeman. Chicago: University of Chicago Press.

Borjas, George J. 1987. Self-Selection and the Earnings of Immigrants. *American Economic Review* 77:531–53.

———. 1990. *Friends or Strangers: The Impact of Immigrants on the U.S. Economy.* New York: Basic Books.

———. 1991. Immigration and Self-Selection. In *Immigration, Trade, and the Labor Market,* ed. John M. Abowd and Richard B. Freeman. Chicago: University of Chicago Press.

———. 1992. National Origin and the Skills of Immigrants in the Postwar Period. In *Immigration in the Work Place: Economic Consequences for the United States and Source Areas,* ed. George J. Borjas and Richard B. Freeman. Chicago: University of Chicago Press.

Boyd, Monica. 1976. Immigration Policies and Trends: A Comparison of Canada and the United States. *Demography* 13:83–104.

———. 1981. The American Emigrant in Canada: Trends and Consequences. *International Migration Review* 15:650–70.

Chiswick, Barry R. 1987. Immigration Policies, Source Countries, and Immigrant Skills. Mimeo.

Duleep, Harriet Orcutt, and Mark C. Regets. 1990. Some Evidence on the Effect of Admission Criteria on Immigrant Assimilation: The Earnings Profiles of Asian Immigrants in Canada and the United States. Mimeo.

Jasso, Guillermina, and Mark R. Rosenzweig. 1986. What's in a Name? Country-of-Origin Influences on the Earnings of Immigrants in the United States. *Research in Human Capital and Development* 4:75–106.

Keely, Charles B., and P. Elwell. 1981. International Migration: The United States and Canada. In *Global Trends in Migration,* ed. Mary Kritz and Silvano Tomasi. New York: Center for Migration Studies.

Kitigawa, Evelyn M. 1955. Components of a Difference between Two Rates. *Journal of the American Statistical Association* 50:1168–94.

Lavoie, Yolande. 1972. *L'Emigration des Canadiens aux Etats-Unis avant 1930.* Montreal: Canada Presses de l'Université de Montréal.

Leahy, F. H., ed. 1983. *Historical Statistics of Canada.* 2d edition. Ottawa: Statistics Canada.

McWatters, Catherine G., and Charles M. Beach. 1989. The Changes behind Canada's Income Distribution: Cause for Concern? Mimeo.

Oaxaca, Ronald. 1973. Male-Female Wage Differentials in Urban Labor Markets. *International Economic Review* 14:693–709.

Tandon, B. B. 1978. Earnings Differentials among Native Born and Foreign Born Residents of Canada. *International Migration Review* 12:406–10.

U.S. Bureau of the Census. 1990. *Migration between Canada and the United States.* Washington, D.C.: U.S. Government Printing Office.

U.S. Immigration and Naturalization Service. Various years. *Statistical Yearbook.* Washington, D.C.: U.S. Government Printing Office.

2 Skill Differentials in Canada in an Era of Rising Labor Market Inequality

Richard B. Freeman and Karen Needels

2.1 Introduction

In the 1980s differentials in earnings and employment between more and less educated or skilled workers widened greatly in the United States (Murphy and Welch 1988; Katz and Revenga 1989; Blackburn, Bloom, and Freeman 1990). The pay of college graduates, of professionals and managers, and of other white-collar workers increased relative to the pay of less-educated and blue-collar workers; joblessness increased among the less-educated but not among college graduates. Dispersion of earnings within educational groups increased. The rise in earnings and employment differentials was greatest among younger men: from the early 1970s through the 1980s the real earnings of 25–34-year-old men with high school or less education fell by some 20 percent. Their employment-population rate dropped by over 10 percentage points, while college graduates suffered no such losses.

What happened to earnings and employment differentials between more- and less-educated workers in Canada in this era of rising economic inequality in the United States? Did supply and demand for labor shift in the same way in Canada as in the United States? Did Canadian wage-setting institutions respond "more gently" to the market twist against the less skilled than those of the United States? What does the Canadian experience tell us about the causes of the 1980s rise in skill differentials in the United States?

To answer these questions we analyze data from the Canadian Survey of

Richard B. Freeman is professor of economics at Harvard University, program director of the National Bureau of Economic Research's Program in Labor Studies, and executive programme director of the Comparative Labour Market Institutions Programme at the London School of Economics' Centre for Economic Performance. Karen Needels is a graduate student in economics at Princeton University.

Research for this paper was supported by the Donner Foundation, Princeton University, and the National Science Foundation.

Consumer Finances (SCF) for 1976, 1980, 1987, and 1988 and the Canadian Census of Population (Census) for 1971, 1981, and 1986. The SCF surveys some 36,000–40,000 Canadian households as a supplement to the annual labor force survey and obtains individual and family incomes for the previous year.[1] The Census surveys also provide income information for the previous year, but for much larger samples than does the SCF. For U.S. comparisons we use the public use tapes of the March Current Population Survey (CPS), which asks 50,000–60,000 households their previous years' earnings and weeks worked.

Our major finding is that the college–high school differential increased much less in Canada than in the United States. We also find that within educational groups the distribution of earnings widened, gender pay gaps narrowed, and age pay gaps increased in Canada as in the United States. The greater growth of the college graduate proportion of the work force in Canada than in the United States is one important reason why differentials rose more modestly in Canada than in the United States. The greater strength of Canadian unions in wage setting, and the faster growth of real national output and better trade balance in Canada may also have contributed to the lesser rise in differentials. Because Canada and the United States have so many characteristics in common, we interpret our results as indicating that the massive rise of skill differentials in the United States was not the result of some inexorable shift in the economic structure of advanced capitalist countries, but rather reflected specific developments in the U.S. labor market and the way in which the country's decentralized wage-setting system adjusted to these developments. We cannot, however, rule out the possibility that Canada may be lagging the United States in the rise in inequality.

2.2 Canadian Micro Earnings Data

To see how educational earnings differentials changed in the 1980s in Canada, we calculated mean earnings by education and estimated regression coefficients on education dummy variables in log earnings equations using public use data tapes from the SCF and the Census. Paralleling work on differentials in the United States (Blackburn, Bloom, and Freeman 1990), we examined only workers aged 25–64 and refer to 25–34 years old as the younger subset. U.S. studies have found that the 1980s rise in educational differentials was concentrated among the young (as was the fall in differentials in the 1970s), presumably because young workers are more likely to be on the "active job market" and are thus more sensitive to changing market conditions than are older workers who are protected by seniority and specific training. We measured earnings by wages and salaries, limited our samples to civilian nonagricultural workers, and (where possible) excluded persons still in school. In

1. See Statistics Canada 1976, catalogue 71-526 and 1979, catalogue 71–528.

addition, we examined several measures of employment status: weeks worked, employment-population ratios, and unemployment rates.

There are problems with both of the Canadian data sets that we used. The 1986 Census did not distinguish persons by school-enrollment status, leading us to estimate differentials from the 1986 Census and earlier Censuses for samples that include those in school. This creates a possible bias in comparisons with estimated differentials from samples that exclude persons in school. To assess the potential magnitude of the bias, we estimated skill differentials in the SCF and in the earlier Censuses for samples that include those in school and for samples that exclude those in school. These estimates revealed only minor differences between the results for the two groups (presumably because there are relatively few in-school earners among persons aged 25 or more). Failure to determine enrollment status in the 1986 Census thus does not appear to mar our Census-based estimates of the change in differentials.

The SCF public use files that we use are limited to heads of households and spouses. We were able, however, to assess the potential magnitude of the problem of excluding other individuals by estimating earnings equations from the 1987 SCF individual file and the 1987 SCF household-head file. We obtained similar results, indicating that for the 25-and-older age group on which we focus analysis of the household-head files does not seriously bias estimated differentials in earnings by education. For comparability over time, we limit analysis of SCF data to family heads and spouses for all years.

Finally, both the Census and SCF files exclude individuals with "extremely unusual characteristics." The U.S. CPS files also go through a cleaning up process, and in addition contain extrapolated figures based on the "hot deck" procedure (U.S. Bureau of the Census 1976). Differences in the way statistical offices handle aberrant observations may affect the extremes of the earnings distributions but are unlikely to affect central tendencies or changes over time.

In addition to data problems, differences between the Canadian and American education systems complicate comparisons of educational earnings and employment differentials. Although Canadians and Americans attain roughly the same years of schooling, Canadians do not follow the same pattern of attainment as Americans. In some provinces Canadians graduate high school after 11 years of schooling, while in others they graduate after 12 or 13 years, compared to the uniform 12 years in the United States. Canadians are more likely than Americans to leave school before completing high school but are also more likely to obtain post–high school nonuniversity training. The education questions in the SCF and Census reflect these differences, producing different categorizations than in the U.S. CPS.[2] We deal with this problem by

2. The SCF does not provide information to tell if a person graduated school. The 1981 and 1986 Censuses do provide such information, and we make use of it in determining education status. The education groups for which data are provided are 0–8 years; 9–10 years; 11–13 years; some postsecondary with no certificate, degree, or diploma; some postsecondary with a certificate, degree, or diploma; university degree received.

focusing on the difference between Canadian university graduates (comparable to Americans with 16 or more years of education) and persons with 11–13 years of school and no further training (comparable to Americans with 12 years of schooling).[3]

2.3 Weekly Earnings Differentials among Men

Table 2.1 records the mean real (1975 Canadian dollars) weekly earnings[4] of 25–64- and 25–34-year-old Canadian men with 11–13 years of schooling and with university degrees and the log differentials between those means from the 1970s through the 1980s. We summarize the changes in terms of average annual changes measured in log units (= differences in the log of earnings between years divided by the number of years). Multiplied by 100, the annual changes can be interpreted as approximate percentage growth rates of earnings: the −.001 for university graduates in the 1979–87 column represents a 0.1 percent average decrease in the real earnings of those workers per year—which cumulates to an approximate 0.8 percent decrease over the eight-year period.

The annual change in real earnings in the 1980s for each group is negative, implying that the decade was one of falling real earnings for male Canadians. This finding is consistent with the results in other data sets that show declining real pay for substantial groups of Canadians in the 1980s. Statistics Canada reports that real compensation per hour fell from 1981 to 1987 and that most union wage settlements in the 1980s were below the rate of inflation (Kumar, Coates, and Arrowsmith 1988, 668, 679). OECD data indicate that over the same period real average weekly earnings in manufacturing fell by 0.5 percent per year in Canada, making Canada second to the United States in loss of real earnings among OECD countries (OECD 1989, 90). Finally, note that the decline in real earnings in table 2.1 is greater for 25–34-year-old men than for 25–64-year-olds in all educational groups. This implies that the age-earnings profile shifted dramatically against younger workers in the 1980s in Canada. This is consistent with results reported by Myles, Picot, and Wannell (1988) using the 1981 Work History Survey and the 1986 Labour Market Activity Survey.

The rows labeled "log earnings differentials" in table 2.1 give log differences between the earnings of college and high school graduates and the annual change in those differentials over time. Despite differences in sampling design and years covered, the SCF and Census show a similar pattern

3. In the SCF we used the categories in the survey. For the Census, we followed a more complex procedure, using questions on degrees completed as well as years of schooling. We also examined workers with 0–8 years of schooling, but pay little attention to their earnings in this paper.

4. Because most variation in annual hours worked is due to variation in weeks worked rather to variation in hours per week, weekly earnings are a good measure of rates of pay.

Table 2.1 Weekly Earnings of Canadian Men Aged 25–64 and 25–34, by Education, 1970–87 (1975 dollars)

	Survey of Consumer Finances				
	Levels			Annual Change in Log Points	
	1975	1979	1987	1975–79	1979–87
Men 25–64					
Real earnings					
College degree	382	370	367	–.008	–.001
11–13 years school	271	275	252	.003	–.011
Log earnings differentials, college degree/11–13	.34	.30	.38	–.010	.010
Men 25–34					
Real Earnings					
College degree	302	306	286	.000	–.008
11–13 years school	243	258	223	.015	–.018
Log earnings differentials, college degree/11–13	.22	.17	.25	–.013	.010
	Census of Population				
	Levels			Annual Change in Log Points	
	1970	1980	1985	1970–80	1980–85
Men 25–64					
Real earnings					
College degree	418	395	388	–.006	–.004
11–13 years school	262	283	263	.008	–.014
Log earnings differentials, college degree/11–13	.47	.33	.39	–.014	.012
Men 25–34					
Real earnings					
College degree	291	308	292	.006	–.010
11–13 years school	236	257	234	.009	–.018
Log earnings differentials, college degree/11–13	.21	.18	.22	–.003	.008

Sources: Tabulated from the relevant SCFs and Censuses. Note for consistency of trends over time the Census data include persons in school, while the SCF data exclude them.

of change: a decline in the college premium in the 1970s consistent with Dooley's (1986) finding of falling educational earnings differentials for full-year full-time workers in that decade, followed by an increase in differentials in the 1980s. The magnitude of the 1980s increase differs modestly between the Census and the SCF. For 25–64-year-olds the SCF shows a rise in the college–high school premium of roughly 1 percent (.010 ln points) per year, while the Census gives an annual increase of 1.2 percent per year. For 25–34-year-olds the increase in the premium in the SCF is 1 percent per year, while the increase in the Census is 0.8 percent per year.

To obtain measures of college–high school pay differentials net of other wage-determining factors, we estimated log weekly earnings equations that control for age, region, and marital status. The earnings differentials in the regressions differ from the differences in table 2.1 for two reasons: addition of covariates (primarily for age) and differences between the log of the geometric mean (the regression concept) and the log of the arithmetic mean (the table 2.1 measure). Table 2.2 summarizes the results of our regressions for Canadian men aged 25–64 and 25–34 in terms of the estimated college–high school earnings differentials in each year and the annual log point changes over time. In addition, it gives comparative differentials and changes in differentials for the United States based on essentially identical regressions. All of the estimated differentials have sufficiently small standard errors to justify omitting standard errors from the table for ease of presentation.

The data for Canada and the United States in the column "annual change" in table 2.2 show that Canada experienced much smaller increases in educational earnings differentials in the 1980s than did the United States. For 25–64-year-old men, the Census-based 0.4 percent annual increase in the college premium in Canada and the SCF-based 0.5 percent annual increase are far below the 2.0 percent increase in the United States. As college–high school differentials declined in Canada by about as much as in the United States in the 1970s (from 1975 to 1979 the drop in the SCF was .05 compared to a .05 drop in the CPS), this conclusion holds up even if we extend the period covered several years back. For 25–34-year-olds, the Canadian Census-based increase in the differential is one-sixth as large as the CPS-based increase in the United States, while the SCF-based increase is one-fifth as large as the U.S. increase. From 1979 to 1987 the college–high school differential among 25–34-year-olds rose by 0.21 log points in the United States but by just 0.04 log points in Canada! Extending the comparison back to 1975 makes the differences even more striking. Canadian differentials fell from 1975 to 1979, though here we caution that U.S. differentials fell sharply from 1969 to 1975 (Freeman 1976), so that 1975–87 comparisons may overstate the change. Still, it is evident from table 2.2 that something very different was going on in the labor markets in the two countries, particularly for young men, during this period.

Table 2.2 Regression Estimates of College–High School Ln Weekly Earnings Differentials, Canadian and U.S. Men Aged 25–64 and 25–34, 1970–87

	1970 (1)	1975 (2)	1979/80 (3)	1985 (4)	1987 (5)	Annual Change 1979/80 to 1985/87 (6)
Men 25–64						
Canada						
SCF	—	.34	.29	—	.33	.005
Census	.40	—	.32	.34	—	.004
United States						
CPS	—	.28	.23	—	.39	.020
Men 25–34						
Canada						
SCF	—	.22	.16	—	.20	.005
Census	.21	—	.19	.21	—	.004
United States						
CPS	—	.14	.12	—	.33	.026

Sources: Canadian figures were estimated by regression analyses from the relevant data sources, with the following control variables: nine dummies for province; two dummies for married and for marital status other than single; eight age dummies, covering five-year groups. The regressions also included persons with other years of schooling. The number of observations was limited by the number of people who reported both weeks worked and earnings. Depending on the year they ranged from 8,729 to 13,370 for 25–64-year-olds in the SCF, from 38,071 to 76,483 for 25–64-year-olds in the Census, from 2,933 to 4,537 for 25–34-year-olds in the SCF, and from 12,037 to 24,820 for 25–34-year-olds in the Census.

U.S. figures were estimated by regression analyses from the March CPS tapes, with the following control variables: three dummies for region; two dummies for married and for marital status other than single; eight age dummies, covering five-year groups. The regressions also included persons with other years of schooling. The number of observations was limited by the number of people who reported both weeks worked and earnings. Depending on the year they ranged from 21,172 to 26,144 for 25–64-year-olds and from 7,317 to 9,379 for 25–34-year-olds.

Notes: Data for 1979/80 are 1979 for SCF and CPS and 1980 for Census. Data for 1985/87 are 1985 for Census, 1986 for SCF, and 1987 for CPS. SCF and Census figures include persons in school; CPS figures do not.

2.4 Differentials in Labor Utilization

Shifts in labor market conditions can alter labor utilization as well as rates of pay. In the United States the increased pay differential among education groups was accompanied by increased differences in unemployment rates, employment-population ratios, and weeks worked—a pattern that implies that changes in weekly earnings differentials understate the market shift against the less-educated. Is the same true in Canada? Were the smaller increases in earnings differentials in Canada offset by larger increases in labor utilization differentials, so that educational differentials overall increased as much in Canada as in the United States?

To answer these questions we estimated 1980s changes in differentials in weeks worked, unemployment, and employment-population ratios in Canada and in the United States. Our evidence, summarized in table 2.3 and in figures 2.1 and 2.2, shows that the employment prospects of male high school graduates worsened relative to that of male college graduates, particularly among the young, in the 1980s in Canada as well as in the United States. Most but not all of the statistics show greater declines in the relative utilization of the less-educated in Canada. Consider first the estimated log differentials in weeks worked in Canada in table 2.3. These differentials are based on regressions of log weeks worked on education and age dummies and the same additional control variables as in the table 2.2 weekly earnings regressions. Both the Census and the SCF data show an increase in the differential in weeks worked between high school and college graduates in Canada. The Census places most of the rise in weeks worked differentials in the 1970s, while the SCF places most of the rise in the 1980s.[5] For 25–64-year-olds the increase in the differential in weeks worked is larger in Canada than in the United States. However, Blackburn, Bloom, and Freeman (1990) report that employment-population and unemployment rate differentials among educational groups widened more in the 1970s than in the 1980s in the United States, raising the possibility that the greater increase in differentials in weeks worked in Canada in the 1980s may largely be a matter of timing. Among 25–34-year-olds, the SCF shows a larger increase in the differential in weeks worked between college and high school graduates in Canada than in the United States. But the Census shows no increase in the differential in Canada at all in the 1980s, giving an ambiguous picture overall.

Figure 2.1, which records unemployment rates for college and high school men in Canada and the United States, gives greater support to the proposition that the job prospects of the less-educated deteriorated more in Canada than in the United States. Between 1976 and 1987, when the unemployment rate of 25–64-year-old college graduates was virtually unchanged in Canada and the United States, the rate of unemployment of 25–64-year-old high school men increased by 4.3 points in Canada compared to a 1974–88 increase of 2.7 points in the United States. Over the same period the rate of unemployment of 25–34-year-old high school men in Canada increased by 5.4 points compared to a 3.1 point increase in the United States. Greater growth in the unemployment of less-educated men in Canada than in the United States is consistent, we note, with the greater increase in the aggregate unemployment rates in Canada than in the United States after the 1973 oil shock (Ashenfelter and Card 1986).

The employment-population ratios in figure 2.2 present a more mixed pic-

5. The difference between the two data sets does not appear to be due to differences in the groups covered (inclusion of persons in school in the Census figures), to definitions of the education groups, to the precise earnings variables used, or to the slight differences in years covered.

Table 2.3 **Differentials in Weeks Worked and Annual Earnings between Male College and High School Graduates Aged 25–64 and 25–34: Canada versus United States, 1970–87**

	Men 25–64			Men 25–34		
	SCF	Census	U.S.	SCF	Census	U.S.
	Estimated differential in ln weeks worked					
1970	—	−.02	—	—	−.07	—
1975	.02	—	.06	−.02	—	—
1979/80	.03	.02	.04	.01	.01	.00
1985	—	.03	—	—	.01	—
1987	.07	—	.05	.08	—	.03
Annual changes						
1979/80 to 1985/87	.005	.002	.001	.009	.000	.003
	Estimated differential in ln annual earnings					
1970	—	.37	—	—	.13	—
1975	.36	—	.34	.26	—	.20
1979/80	.30	.34	.27	.17	.20	.16
1985	—	.37	—	—	.22	—
1987	.40	—	.44	.28	—	.39
Annual changes						
1979/80 to 1985/87	.013	.006	.021	.014	.004	.029

Sources: Estimated by regression analysis, as described in the sources for table 2.2, with dependent variables ln weeks worked and ln annual earnings. Sample sizes are larger than in table 2.2 because some persons reported weeks worked and not annual earnings, while others reported annual earnings but not weeks worked.

ture of the changes in relative labor utilization in the two countries due to differences in the timing of the deterioration of the position of the less-educated. In the United States, the employment-population ratio for high school men fell in the late 1970s, then roughly stabilized, while in Canada the employment-population ratio of high school graduates fell largely in the 1980s. The larger drop in the employment-population ratio in Canada in the 1980s is consistent with the notion that Canada responded to the deteriorating job market for the less-educated with a relatively greater quantity adjustment than with price adjustment. But the decline in employment-population ratios for high school graduates in the United States in the late 1970s suggests that the timing of the drop in employment-population ratios may be the key differentiating feature between the two labor markets: male U.S. high school graduates took their hit in employment in the 1970s while their Canadian peers took their hit in the 1980s.

2.5 Annual Earnings

To what extent do differences in the pattern of change in labor utilization between the United States and Canada alter our principal claim, that educa-

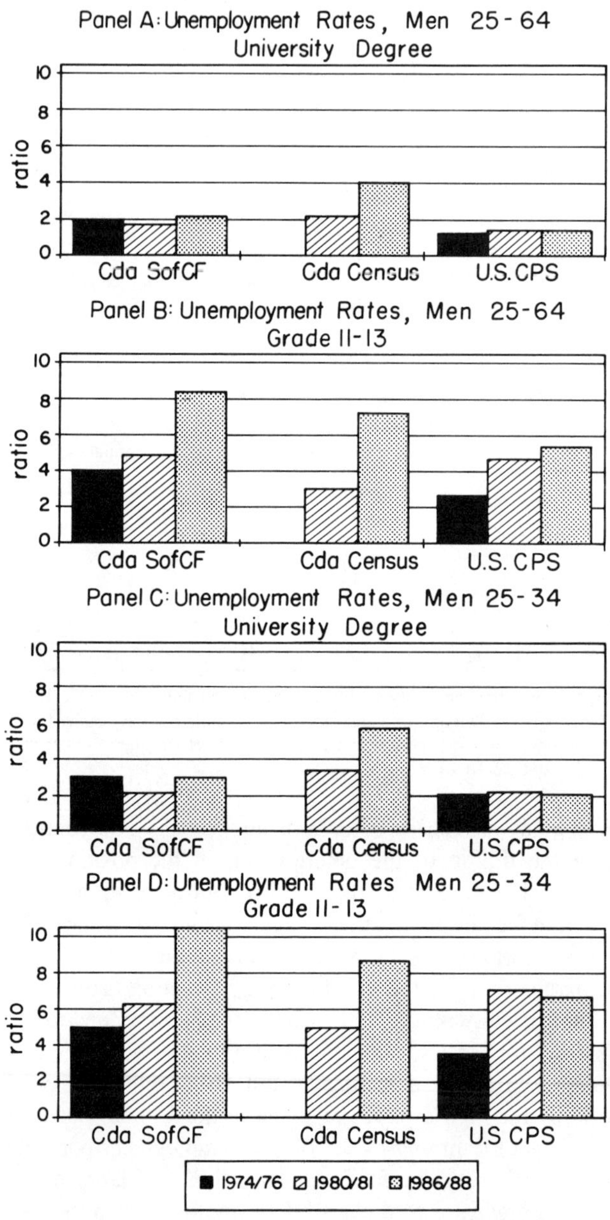

Fig. 2.1 Unemployment rates for men, by education, Canada versus the United States, 1974–88

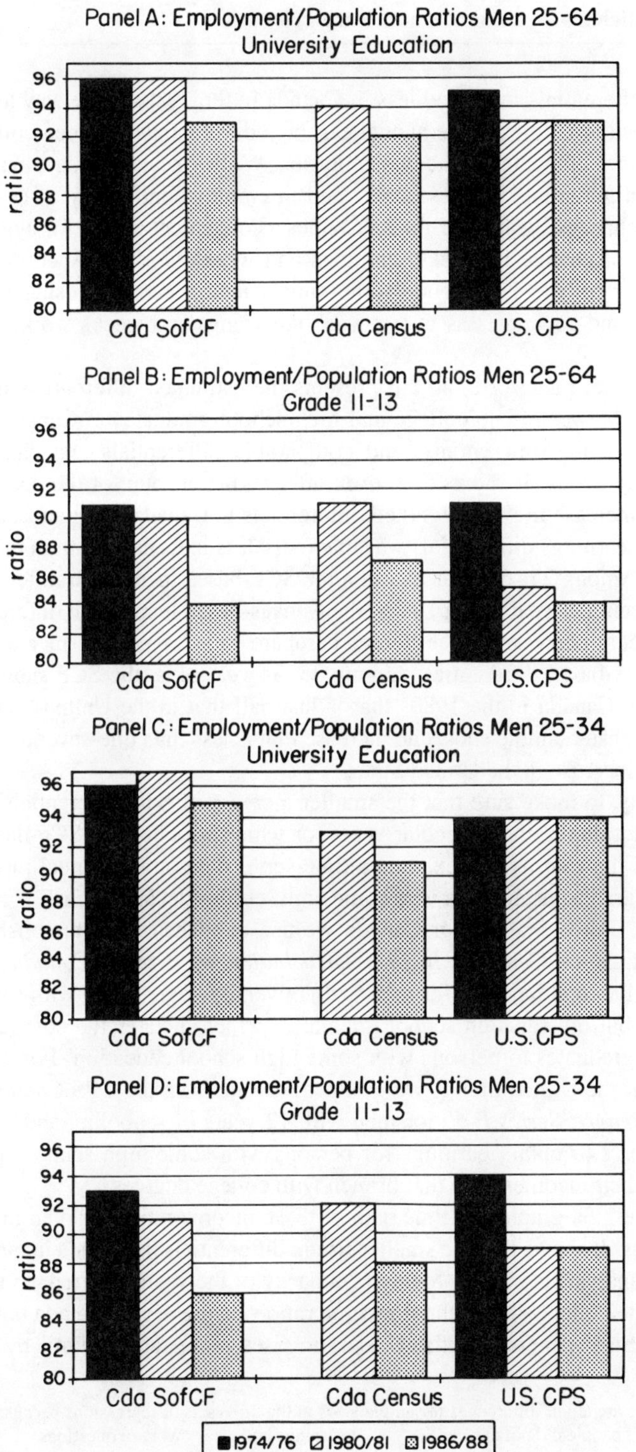

Fig. 2.2 Employment-population rates for men, by education, Canada versus the United States, 1974–88

tional differentials increased less in Canada in the 1980s? One way to answer this question is to estimate annual earnings differentials between college and high school graduates in the two countries. While one can argue about how to weight differentials in rates of pay and in employment in any assessment of overall changes, yearly earnings provides a convenient metric for aggregating patterns of change in weekly earnings and weeks worked. Accordingly, we estimated college–high school differentials in log earnings using the same samples and covariates as in our weekly earnings and weeks worked regressions.[6]

The lower panel of table 2.3 presents the estimated differentials in yearly earnings between male college and high school graduates in Canada, annual changes in the differentials, and comparable differentials and changes for American males. It shows that, even after taking account of the occasionally greater increase in weeks worked differentials in Canada, the increase in educational earnings differentials was markedly less in Canada than in the United States. Among 25–64-year-old men the SCF-based increase in differentials is 1.3 percent per year in the 1980s; the Census-based increase in differentials is 0.6 percent per year. These figures compare to a 2.1 percent increase in the U.S. CPS-based differential. Among 25–34-year-olds, the SCF shows an increase in Canada in the 1980s that is just half that in the United States. The larger Census sample shows an increase that is less than one-seventh the comparable increase in the United States.

Finally, to make sure that the smaller increase in skill differentials in Canada is not due to the particular years for which we obtained SCF data or the years of the Census, we examined time-series data on the annual incomes of college graduates and men with some high school education yearly for Canada and the United States. For Canada we use published and unpublished data from Statistics Canada's *Income Distribution by Size in Canada* reports, which give total incomes for men with university degrees and with some high school, but not for high school graduates, which dictates the comparison of college graduates to persons with some high school education. For comparability for the United States, we grouped income from the CPS *Current Population Report, Series P-60* for men with 12 years of schooling and men with 9–11 years to obtain earnings for persons with some high school, and contrasted their incomes with that of men with college degrees.

Figure 2.3a graphs the time path of these income ratios for men in the two countries. It shows that the smaller rise in differentials in Canada in our microsurvey analysis is not due to any peculiarity of the years covered. In the mid-1970s the college–high school income ratio was greater in Canada than in the United States; thereafter the U.S. ratio rises more rapidly until by 1987 it

6. There are slight differences in sample sizes in the three sets of regressions because different numbers of people did not answer the annual earnings and weeks worked questions.

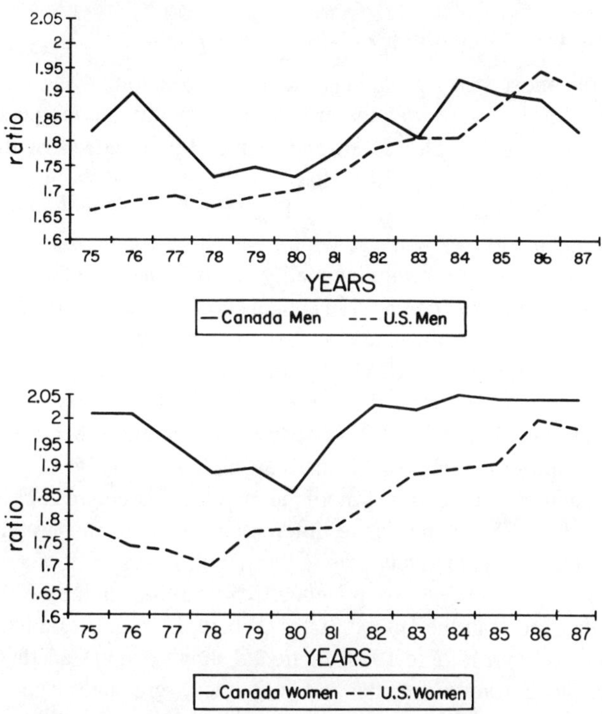

Fig. 2.3 Mean income ratios, college–some high school, Canada versus the United States, 1975–87

Sources: For Canada: calculated from Statistics Canada, *Income Distribution by Size in Canada,* table "Percentage Distribution of Individuals by Income Groups, Education and Sex," various years. For the United States: calculated from *Current Population Reports, Series P-60,* table "Education and age—Persons 25 yrs. old and over by total money income, by race and sex," various years.

exceeds the Canadian ratio. If we carried the U.S. figures back further, we would find a marked decline in the differential from the late 1960s through the mid-1970s (Freeman 1976), similar to the decline in Canada from 1976 through 1980. This finding again suggests that part of the difference in the pattern of changes in earnings differentials may be due to differences in the timing of changes between the two countries but does not gainsay the more modest 1980s rise in educational differentials in Canada.[7]

7. The year-to-year variation in the Canadian college–high school differential shown in figure 2.3 does little to explain the difference between the 1980–85 Census contrasts and the 1979–86 SCF contrasts. The relevant income ratios fall from 1979 to 1980 but also from 1985 to 1986, roughly balancing out any difference due to the SCF's covering 1979–86 and the Census's covering 1980–85.

2.6 Within Education and Overall Inequality

One of the most striking changes in the distribution of earnings in the United States in the 1980s was the growth of inequality among persons with the same education (Murphy, Juhn, and Pierce 1993). Indeed, within-group dispersion rose even in the 1970s, offsetting the effects of the falling college premium on overall earnings inequality. Has there been an analogous increase in earnings inequality for workers within educational categories in Canada? How do changes in within-group inequality compare between the countries?

Figure 2.4 records ln differences in annual earnings between the highest and lowest deciles for male college and high school graduates in Canada in 1975, 1979, and 1986 from the SCF. The figures show that earnings inequality increased among workers with the same educational attainment in Canada. Among college graduates aged 25–64, the log differential between those in the top and bottom deciles rose from 1.39 in 1979 to 1.55 in 1986, while among men with 11–13 years of school the increase is even greater.[8] Similarly, among men aged 25–34 the decile differential increased moderately among college graduates and massively among those with 11–13 years of school. The pattern of increasing within-group inequality in earnings in the 1980s is comparable to that found in the United States. Where the countries differ is in the 1970s changes. From 1975 to 1979, figure 2.4 shows that in Canada the decile differentials were roughly unchanged for college graduates and rose only modestly for high school men—in contrast to the increase in earnings inequality within education groups found in the United States in the 1970s.

The absence of increased within-group inequality in Canada in the 1970s and the more modest increase in educational differentials in Canada than in the United States in the 1980s have an important implication for the overall pattern of earnings inequality among men in the two countries. They imply that from the 1970s through the 1980s inequality among male workers increased less in Canada than in the United States.

2.7 Female Workers

In the United States the college–high school earnings differential increased in the 1980s among female as well as among male workers. In the same period male-female earnings gaps fell within education groups. What happened to the college–high school differential among women and to female-male differentials in Canada?

To answer this we estimated log weekly and annual earnings equations for working women in the SCF and Census data sets, using the same regression

8. This is partly due to the worsened weeks worked of high school men in the period, and is likely to be much less pronounced with weekly earnings.

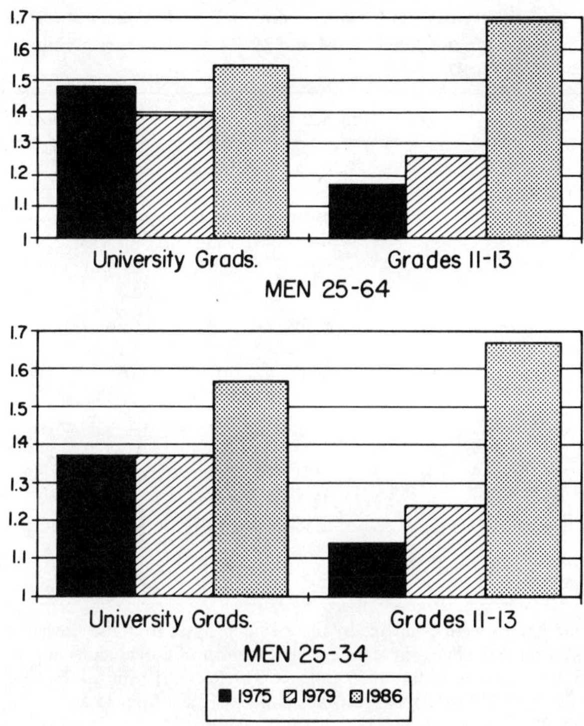

Fig. 2.4 Ln high/low decile annual earnings differential, Canada (SCF)

model that we used to analyze male earnings. For comparative purposes we estimated the same equations for women in the United States, using the relevant March CPS files. The results of this analysis, given in table 2.4 for weekly and annual earnings, tell a clear story about changes in the 1980s. The top panel reveals that there was at most a modest increase in college–high school weekly earnings differentials among women in Canada. The Census data show effectively no change in the college–high school premium (paralleling the small increase in the premium found among men in the Census), while the SCF data shows 0.5 percent increases per annum in the premium for both 25–64-year-olds and 25–34-year-olds compared to much larger rises in the college premium of 1.3 percent for 25–64-year-old U.S. women and 1.4 percent for 25–34-year-old U.S. women. The annual earnings differentials tell a similar story. Among 25–64-year-olds, the Census shows a decline in the college–high school differential in Canada from 1980 to 1985, while the SCF shows smaller increases than are found in the United States from 1979 to 1987. Among 25–34-year-olds, the Census also shows a drop in differentials, but the SCF shows a rise in differentials only modestly less than that in the

Table 2.4 Differentials in Earnings between Female College and High School Graduates Aged 25–64 and 25–34: Canada versus United States, 1975–87

	Women 25–64			Women 25–34		
	SCF	Census	U.S.	SCF	Census	U.S.
	Estimated differential in ln weekly earnings					
1975	.43	—	.35	.40	—	.37
1979/80	.49	.50	.38	.46	.45	.41
1985	—	.50	—	—	.45	—
1987	.53	—	.48	.50	—	.52
Annual changes						
1979/80 to 1985/87	.005	.000	.013	.005	.000	.014
	Estimated differential in ln annual earnings					
1975	.53	—	.40	.51	—	.48
1979/80	.61	.56	.42	.58	.52	.51
1985	—	.52	—	—	.47	—
1987	.66	—	.55	.67	—	.62
Annual changes						
1979/80 to 1985/87	.006	−.008	.016	.011	−.004	.014

Sources: Canadian figures were estimated by regression analyses from the relevant data sources, using the same control variables as in table 2.2. The number of observations ranged from 4,453 to 7,774 for 25–64-year-olds in the SCF, from 16,917 to 54,019 for 25–64-year-olds in the Census, from 1,793 to 3,112 for 25–34-year-olds in the SCF, and from 35,809 to 70,277 for 25–34-year-olds in the Census.

U.S. figures were estimated by regression analyses from the March CPS files, using the same control variables as in table 2.2. The number of observations ranged from 15,184 to 23,168 for 25–64-year-olds and from 5,246 to 8,616 for 25–34-year-olds.

United States. The sharper rise in differentials in annual earnings than in weekly earnings for young women in Canada implies a large increase in the weeks worked advantage of female college graduates over high school graduates, relative to the change in the United States.

As a final check on the pattern of change in educational differentials in Canada, we used published and unpublished figures on the annual incomes of college graduate women and of women with some high school to estimate educational differentials over the entire 1975–87 period. The income ratios in figure 2.3b show that the years covered in our regression estimates do not distort the pattern in differentials and suggest that even over the longer period differentials increased less in Canada. In the mid- and late 1970s educational income differentials among women were considerably greater in Canada than in the United States. The gap between the differentials narrowed, however, in the 1980s, so that by 1987 the Canadian ratio was only slightly higher than the U.S. ratio. We conclude that educational earnings differentials increased less among Canadian women than among U.S. women in the period under study, just as they increased less among Canadian men than among U.S. men.

Table 2.5 records statistics on another aspect of the changing job market for women in Canada: the level and pattern of change in earnings differentials between men and women within educational groups. The first two columns give the ratios of the mean earnings of women to men from the SCF for 1975, 1979, and 1986. The second two columns give comparable differentials for the United States based on mean earnings tabulated from the March CPS tapes. In the college column for Canada, the 0.55 for 1975 indicates that Canadian female graduates earned 55 percent of the earnings of male graduates in 1975, while the 0.61 figure for 1986 shows that women's earnings were 61 percent of men's, and thus women gained 6 percentage points, or 10 percent, relative to men. The table shows roughly comparable gains of female college and high school graduates relative to their male peers in Canada, and more rapid gains in annual earnings differentials than in weekly earnings differentials due to a huge increase in weeks worked by Canadian women within edu-

Table 2.5 Female-Male Earnings Ratios, by Education and Age Group, Canada and the United States

	Canada		United States	
	College	11–13	College	High School
		A. Women 25–64		
Annual earnings				
1975	.45	.37	.49	.44
1979	.52	.39	.51	.44
1986	.54	.46	.57	.53
Δ	.09	.09	.08	.09
Weekly earnings				
1975	.55	.48	.55	.48
1979	.59	.47	.56	.48
1986	.61	.52	.60	.55
Δ	.06	.04	.05	.07
		B. Women 25–34		
Annual earnings				
1975	.53	.37	.59	.46
1979	.58	.38	.61	.47
1986	.66	.48	.67	.57
Δ	.13	.11	.08	.11
Weekly earnings				
1975	.65	.53	.65	.51
1979	.66	.47	.68	.52
1986	.70	.56	.70	.61
Δ	.05	.03	.05	.10

Sources: For Canada, tabulated from SCF tapes. For the United States, tabulated from March CPS tapes.

Note: Year used for Canada was 1986; for the United States, 1987.

cational groups. The comparative U.S. figures show a somewhat different pattern of increases in female pay relative to male pay by educational group. Here, females made larger gains in weekly earnings ratios among high school graduates than among college graduates. This reflects the particularly poor labor market for male high school graduates in the United States. In both countries 24–34-year-old women have earnings closer to that of their male peers than women aged 25–64. The gains of the younger women are not markedly different than those of all women, measured in percentage points of the earnings ratios.[9]

2.8 Why Did Differentials Increase Less in Canada?

The question that naturally arises from our major finding is, Why did educational differentials increase less in Canada than in the United States in the 1980s? What factors moderated the growth in wage differentials between these two broadly similar economies?

There are, in our view, two potential sorts of explanatory candidates: differences in "exogenous shocks" impacting the Canadian and American labor markets and differences in the response of wage setting and other market institutions to the shocks. We consider the effect of these forces in a simple model of changes in relative wages:

$$RW' = u_d D' - u_s S' + vI', \tag{1}$$

where RW measures the relevant wage differential; D is the relative demand for skills; S is the relative supply of skills; I refers to institutional or other factors that affect differentials independently of supply and demand; and $'$ denotes log differentials (i.e., $D' = \ln D$).

If institutional factors have no influence on wages ($v = 0$) and the market clears, and if we properly measure shifts in supply and demand, the coefficients in (1) have a ready structural interpretation: $u_d = u_s =$ the inverse of the sum of the relative demand and supply elasticities for the groups (see Blackburn, Bloom, and Freeman 1990). Otherwise, (1) should be viewed simply as a reduced-form equation assessing the response of wages to measured supply shifts, demand shifts, and institutional factors.[10] To the extent that those measured factors differ between Canada and the United States, the intercountry differences in the pattern of educational earnings differentials

9. The question of whether the gains are greater for 25–34-year-olds hinges on the metric used to measure the gains. If we use a metric of percentage declines in the difference between the female/male ratio and equality in earnings, the gains are greater for 25–34-year-olds. If we use a metric of percentage changes in the ratios, the gains are greater for all women in most of the data in the table.

10. The specification is not completely innocuous. It makes institutional factors orthogonal to market forces—a crude simplifying assumption but one consistent with traditional studies of union and other wage differentials.

over time may be at least partly explained. Given available data, we focus on the following factors: the ratio of college to high school populations, the level of real national product, the trade balance as a percentage of national output, and the percentage unionized.

The ratio of college to high school workers should reduce the college–high school differential as increases in relative supply move market wages down the relative demand curve (Freeman 1976; Katz and Revenga 1989; Blackburn, Bloom, and Freeman 1990; Katz and Murphy 1992). In the United States the growth of the ratio of college graduates to high school graduates decelerated among 25–64-year-old men in the 1980s. Among the 25–34-year-old men for whom the college–high school differential rose the most, the deceleration was so great that the ratio of college to high school graduates actually fell—the lagged response to the decline in enrollments induced by the falling return to college of the 1970s. Data from Statistics Canada's *The Labour Force* show a very different pattern of change in Canada: from 1979 to 1987 the ratio of 25–64-year-old male college graduates to men with high school training rose by 0.18 ln points compared to a CPS-based increase in the college–high school ratio in the United States of 0.05 ln points. Unpublished SCF data show that among 25–34-year-old men, the number with university education relative to those with just high school training increased by 0.04 ln points from 1981 to 1987, compared to a 0.16 ln point drop in the ratio in the United States.[11] Thus, we expect differences in the growth of relative supplies to help account for the smaller growth of the college–high school differential in Canada.

On the demand side, the overall state of the economy, as reflected in the national output, is likely to reduce the educational differential because the less-skilled benefit most from a rapidly expanding economy (Blackburn, Bloom, and Freeman 1990, table 7). Since GDP grew by 2.9 percent per year in Canada from 1979 to 1987, compared to 2.6 percent for the United States, this may also help explain the smaller increase in the differential. The trade balance has been hypothesized to have contributed to the increased educational differentials in the United States because less-skilled workers are adversely affected by imports (Murphy and Welch 1988; Blackburn, Bloom, and Freeman 1990). The large trade surpluses in Canada in the 1980s compared to the large deficits in the United States[12] suggest that the difference in the relative trade balance between the countries may help explain the slower increase in skill differentials in Canada.

Finally, on the institutional side, because trade unions generally organize

11. We record 1981–87 changes because these are the best data we have on the numbers of workers by age and education from unpublished Statistics Canada sources.

12. In 1979–87 Canada had an average trade surplus of 2.2 percent of GNP, while the United States had an average deficit of 2.0 percent of GNP (OECD 1989).

less-educated blue-collar workers to a greater extent than more-educated white-collar workers, and often have a bigger effect on the wages of the former, the decline in union density has also been proposed as a cause of the increased educational earnings differentials in the United States (Freeman 1992). U.S. union density fell in the 1970s and 1980s, while Canadian density held roughly constant. Even in manufacturing, where Canadian density dropped in the 1980s (Kumar, Coates, and Arrowsmith 1988), U.S. density fell more. The different changes in union representation might also have contributed to the differing change in educational differentials between the two countries (see Lemieux, chap. 3 in this volume, for evidence on the effect of unionism on earnings inequality in the United States and Canada).

We examine the effects of these factors on college–high school earnings differentials for men using U.S. and Canadian time-series data. For the United States the CPS provides sufficiently lengthy time-series data for estimating the effect of the four factors on earnings differentials (see Freeman 1976; Blackburn, Bloom, and Freeman 1990; Katz and Revenga 1989). For Canada changes in educational classifications in 1975 give us a very limited time series, but one that in conjunction with the U.S. data provides some evidence on potential determinants of change.

Table 2.6 presents our estimates of equation (1). In addition to relative supply, real GDP, the trade balance, and union density, each equation includes a linear time trend. Columns 1 and 2 give the coefficients and standard errors from our analysis of the Canadian data, with unionization excluded from the first equation and included in the second equation. Columns 3 and 4 give the results from analysis of differentials for all men in the United States; column 5 presents the results of a pooled sample of data from the two countries; columns 6 and 7 give results for men aged 25–34 in the United States. Exclusive of the time trend, only one variable has a significant coefficient in all specifications: relative supplies. The log of real GDP has a substantial negative effect on the earnings differential in the U.S. equations and in column 1 for Canada but not in column 2. The trade balance has a strong effect in the U.S. data but not in the Canadian data. Unionization substantially reduces earnings differentials in the United States but has a positive effect on differentials in Canada, which makes us uneasy about using the time series to assess the effect of unionism. In the pooled sample we excluded unionization and obtained strong statistical results on relative supplies and the log of real GDP.

The one solid inference from these calculations is that relative labor supplies have an important effect on relative earnings. Indeed, given the estimated coefficients in the table, the faster growth of the relative supply of college graduates in Canada accounts for two-thirds or so of the slower growth of educational earnings differentials in Canada. Specifically, from 1979 to 1987 the college–high school differential rose among 25–64-year-old men by 0.04 points in Canada compared to 0.16 points in the U.S. (table 2.2), producing a 0.12 smaller increase in Canada. The difference in the growth of the

Table 2.6 **Estimates of Supply and Demand Effects on College–High School Earnings Differentials of Men, Canada 1975–87 and the United States 1967–87**

	All Men					Men 25–34	
	Canada		United States		Pooled	United States	
	(1)	(2)	(3)	(4)	(5)	(6)	(7)
Intercept	3.55	−3.36	−1.84	.33	−.31	−1.02	.05
Log relative	−.53	−.99	−.59	−.35	−.68	−.33	−.25
supply	(.38)	(.34)	(.12)	(.08)	(.14)	(.04)	(.08)
Log real GDP	−.97	−.10	−.67	−.52	−.53	−.62	−.63
	(.46)	(.49)	(.26)	(.14)	(.24)	(.25)	(.25)
Trend	.051	.030	.036	.012	.037	.024	.025
	(.021)	(.018)	(.009)	(.006)	(.009)	(.007)	(.010)
Trade balance/	−.006	−.001	−.008	−.008	−.001	−.006	−.008
GDP times	(.011)	(.009)	(.004)	(.002)	(.004)	(.004)	(.004)
100 (%)							
Union (%)		.030		−.016			−.021
		(.011)		(.003)			(.008)
Canada dummy					3.96		
					(1.89)		
N	13	13	21	21	34	21	21
R^2	.50	.74	.79	.94	.90	.86	.88

Sources: Estimated from time-series data. For United States, data are reported in Blackburn, Bloom, and Freeman (1990). For Canada, relative incomes are from published and unpublished SCF data; relative supply is from Statistics Canada, *The Labour Force;* real GDP is from OECD, *National Accounts;* trade balance is from *International Financial Statistics Yearbook 1990;* union is from Kumar, Coates, and Arrowsmith 1988.

ratio of college to high school male workers between the countries was 0.11 ln points. Multiplying 0.11 by the −.68 coefficient in our pooled regression in table 2.6 yields a predicted difference of 0.07 points. Similarly, the difference in the increase in the college–high school premium between the United States and Canada among 25–34-year-old men was .17 points (table 2.2). The difference in the growth of the ratio of college to high school men aged 25–34 between the countries was 0.20. Multiplying .20 by −.68 yields a 0.14 predicted difference; multiplying .20 by the smaller −0.33 estimated coefficient in column 6 of table 2.6 yields a 0.07 contribution of relative supplies to the slower growth of the college premium in Canada among 25–34-year-olds.

As another way to demonstrate the effect of relative supplies, we used our pooled Canadian-U.S. data to calculate differences between the countries in the college to high school earnings differentials. We regressed the difference in the differentials on a linear trend and obtained a coefficient (standard error) of −.005 (.002). When we added the difference in relative supplies to the equation, the coefficient on the trend term fell by 60 percent, to −.002 (.001).

The evidence that differential shifts in relative supplies of labor dominate the time-series data does not, of course, mean that greater growth in the relative supply of college graduates is the only reason for the slower growth of the educational differential in Canada, but does reaffirm the fact that the time-series evidence supports a strong role for relative supplies. Other factors—growth of GDP, unionization, trade balance—may very well have contributed to the slower growth of relative earnings in Canada, but here the time-series evidence is more mixed: the U.S. data show substantial effects while the limited Canadian data do not. In addition, it is possible that shifts in demand for educated labor that we have failed to measure, say, due to technological factors that alter the demand for educated workers within sectors (Mincer 1991; Allen 1991; Osberg, Wolff, and Baumol 1989), may have been more extensive in the United States than in Canada. Our evidence is silent on this point.

2.9 Summary

This study has shown that during the 1980s decade of rising educational earnings differentials in the United States, weekly and annual earnings differentials between male and female college and high school graduates widened less sharply in Canada than in the United States. We also found growing gaps in weeks worked, employment-population ratios, and unemployment rates between more- and less-educated men in Canada. As far as we can tell, the major cause of the more modest rise in educational earnings differentials in Canada, at least among men, was the greater expansion in the relative number of college-educated workers, though other factors—unionization, trade, growth of real output, technological change—may also have played a part in accounting for the differences between the countries.

References

Allen, Steve. 1991. Technology and the Wage Structure. North Carolina State, Raleigh. Mimeo.

Ashenfelter, Orley, and David Card. 1986. Why Have Unemployment Rates in Canada and the United States Diverged? *Economica* 53 (supplement): S171–96.

Blackburn, McKinley L., David E. Bloom, and Richard B. Freeman. 1990. The Declining Economic Position of Less Skilled American Men. In Gary Burtless, ed., *A Future of Lousy Jobs? The Changing Structure of U.S. Wages*. Washington, D.C.: Brookings Institution.

Dooley, Martin. 1986. The Overeducated Canadian? Changes in the Relationship among Earnings, Education, and Age for Canadian Men: 1971–81. *Canadian Journal of Economics* 19:142–59.

Freeman, Richard B. 1976. *The Overeducated American*. New York: Academic Press.

———. 1992. How Much Has De-unionization Contributed to the Rise in Male Earnings Inequality? In Sheldon Danziger and Peter Gottschalk, eds., *Uneven Tides*, pp. 133–63. New York: Sage Press.

Katz, Lawrence F., and Kevin Murphy. 1992. Changes in Relative Wages, 1963–87:

Supply and Demand Factors. *Quarterly Journal of Economics* 107 (February): 35–78.

Katz, Lawrence F., and Ana L. Revenga. 1989. Changes in the Structure of Wages: The United States versus Japan. *Journal of the Japanese and International Economies* 3 (December): 522–53.

Kumar, Pradeep, Mary Lou Coates, and David Arrowsmith. 1988. *The Current Industrial Relations Scene in Canada 1988*. Queen's University Press, Kingston, Ontario.

Mincer, Jacob. 1991. Human Capital, Technology, and the Wage Structure: What Do Time Series Show? NBER Working Paper 3581. Cambridge, Mass.: National Bureau of Economics Research, January.

Murphy, Kevin, C. Juhn, and B. Pierce. 1993. Wage Inequality and the Rise in Returns to Skill. *Journal of Political Economy,* forthcoming.

Murphy, Kevin, and Finis Welch. 1988. Wage Differentials in the 1980s: The Role of International Trade. Mont Pelerin Society Meeting, September, Stockholm.

Myles, J., G. Picot, and T. Wannell. 1988. Wages and Jobs in the 1980s: Changing Youth Wages and the Declining Middle. Social and Economic Studies Division Working Paper no. 17. Ottawa: Statistics Canada.

OECD. 1989. *Historical Statistics 1960–1987*. Paris: OECD.

———. Various years. *National Accounts*. Paris: OECD.

Osberg, Lars, E. Wolff, and W. Baumol. 1989. *The Information Economy: Implications of Unbalanced Growth*. Halifax: Institute for Research on Public Policy.

Statistics Canada. Various years. *Income Distribution by Size in Canada*. Ottawa.

———. Various years. *The Labour Force*. Ottawa.

———. 1976. *Methodology of the Canadian Labour Force Survey.* Ottawa.

———. 1979. *Guide to Labour Force Survey Data*. Ottawa.

U.S. Bureau of the Census. Various years. *Current Population Reports, Series P-60*. Washington, D.C.: GPO.

3 Unions and Wage Inequality in Canada and the United States

Thomas Lemieux

3.1 Introduction

Throughout the past decade, Canadian workers were twice as likely to be covered by a collective bargaining agreement as their U.S. counterparts (Riddell, chap. 4 in this volume). Over the same period of time, wages were more equally distributed in Canada than in the United States (Blackburn and Bloom, chap. 7 in this volume). These two observations raise the obvious question of whether the different unionization rates in Canada and the United States can explain the difference in wage inequality between the two countries. Several U.S. studies suggest this might be the case. These studies find that unionization narrows the overall distribution of wages among men.[1] It is thus reasonable to expect that the higher rate of unionization in Canada may narrow even more the distribution of wages.

The purpose of this paper is to compare the effects of unionization on wage inequality in Canada and in the United States. After a short discussion of the role of union wage policies in the distribution of wages in section 3.2, the paper begins by describing the patterns of unionism and wages using compa-

Thomas Lemieux is assistant professor of economics at the University of Montreal, an associate fellow at the Centre de Recherche et Développement en économique, and a faculty research fellow of the National Bureau of Economic Research.

The author thanks Orley Ashenfelter, David Card, Richard Freeman, Nicole Fortin, and seminar participants at the Princeton Labor Lunch for helpful discussions, and the Industrial Relations Section at Princeton University for financial support. This analysis is based on Statistics Canada microdata tapes 7426NT and 7079NT, which contain anonymized data collected in the 1986 and 1987 Labour Market Activity Survey. All computations on these microdata were prepared by the author, and the responsibility for the use and interpretation of these data is entirely that of the author.

1. U.S. studies that try to assess the impact of unions on the overall distribution of wages of men include Freeman (1980, 1984) and Card (1992). See also Lewis (1986, chap. 10) for a critical survey of additional studies. Swidinsky and Kupferschmidt (1991) present evidence on the impact of unions on residual wage inequality in Canada.

rable cross-sectional data for Canada (the 1986 Labour Market Activity Survey[LMAS]) and for the United States (the 1986 outgoing rotation group file of the Current Population Survey [CPS]) in section 3.3. Cross-sectional estimates of the effects of unions on wages may be afflicted by selectivity biases since union workers are a nonrandom sample of the population. Panel data methods are thus used to estimate selection-adjusted effects of unions on the level and on the variance of wages in Canada in section 3.4. These estimates are used to measure the overall effects of unions on wage inequality in Canada in section 3.5. The estimated effects of unions on wage inequality in Canada are compared to the effects estimated by Card (1992) for the United States in section 3.6. The main finding of the paper is that, for men, differences in unionization rates account for 40 percent of differences in the variance of wages between Canada and the United States.

3.2 Union Wage Policies and Overall Wage Inequality

3.2.1 Efficiency and Equity Issues

There is a long tradition in public policy analysis of evaluating government interventions in terms of efficiency and equity (see, for example, Okun 1975). Union wage policies can also be studied in such terms. In the traditional analysis of union behavior, it is postulated that unions use their monopoly power to set the wages of their members above their competitive level. By creating a wedge between wages and the opportunity cost of labor, unions thus create a deadweight loss measured by the surface of the usual Harberger triangle (see Harberger 1971).

It has long been recognized, however, that union wage policies also have an important impact on the distribution of wages and thus on welfare inequality. On the one hand, unions tend to reduce wage inequalities by standardizing wages within the workplace. On the other hand, union wage policies may exacerbate existing inequalities, as they benefit union workers at the expense of nonunion workers. Existing studies for the United States suggest that, overall, unions reduce wage inequality among male workers (Freeman 1980, 1984). There may thus be a tradeoff between the efficiency costs of unions and the redistributive aspects of union wage policies.[2]

Most empirical studies for Canada and the United States have implicitly focused on the efficiency aspect of union wage policies by estimating the av-

2. Unions may have other roles aside from their effects on the level and distribution of wages. For instance, unions may also increase productivity by giving a "voice" to workers (Freeman and Medoff 1984). In addition, unions are positively associated with nonpecuniary benefits such as pensions and health insurance. Unfortunately, nonpecuniary workers' benefits and productivity effects are harder to quantify than wage effects in standard household surveys like the CPS. By contrast, several data sets for both Canada and the United States contain good information on wages. For these reasons, the paper focuses on the wage effects of unions.

erage effect of unions on the level of wages. The recent widening of the distribution of wages in the United States, however, has revived interest in the redistributive aspects of union wage policies. For example, Card (1992) concluded that 20 percent of the increase in the variance of wages of men in the United States from 1973 to 1987 was attributable to deunionization. Freeman (1991) reported similar findings for the 1978 to 1987 period.

Measuring the deadweight loss of union wage policies is now a standard textbook case that will not be discussed here.[3] The remainder of the section will explain in some detail how union wage policies affect the overall distribution of wages in the economy.

3.2.2 The Effects of Unions on the Distribution of Wages

The effect of unions on the distribution of wages does not simply depend on the size of the average union wage differential. It depends on the joint distribution of unionization and of wages (union and nonunion) in the work force. To see this, consider the nonunion wage of a worker i with observed characteristics x_i:

$$w_i^N = w^N(x_i) + \varepsilon_i^N,$$

where ε_i^N is an error term with zero conditional mean and a conditional variance $\sigma_N^2(x_i)$. The wage for this same worker in the union sector is given by

$$w_i^U = w^U(x_i) + \varepsilon_i^U,$$

where ε_i^U has zero conditional mean and a conditional variance $\sigma_U^2(x_i)$. Consider $\bar{U}(x_i)$, the probability that worker i is unionized. Consider also the union wage gap $\Delta_w(x_i)$ for that worker,[4]

$$\Delta_w(x_i) = w^U(x_i) - w^N(x_i),$$

and the union variance gap $\Delta_v(x_i)$,

$$\Delta_v(x_i) = \sigma_U^2(x_i) - \sigma_N^2(x_i).$$

3. The standard formula for the deadweight loss is simply $DW \approx (.5\bar{\eta}\bar{\Delta}_w^2)wL$, where $\bar{\eta}$ is the (average) labor demand elasticity, $\bar{\Delta}_w$ is the (average) union wage gap, and wL is the wage bill in the union sector (see Harberger 1971 and Rees 1963 for an application to this particular problem). Note, however, that the simple formula is only valid when Δ_w, η, and the unionization rate are either constant or independently distributed across skill groups. In general, the deadweight loss with heterogeneous skill groups j is $DW = \Sigma_j(.5\eta_j\Delta_{wj}^2)w_jL_j$.

4. Note that it is implicitly assumed in this section that negotiated wages in the union sector have no effect on wages in the nonunion sector. This assumption is unlikely to hold, since general equilibrium considerations (Johnson and Mieszkowski 1970) suggest unions have a negative impact on wages in the nonunion sector, while union threat effects (Rosen 1969) suggest the opposite. The wages that prevail in the nonunion sector might thus be different from the wages that would prevail in the absence of unions. Lewis (1986) has convincingly argued that it was not possible to estimate the wages that would prevail in the absence of unions using standard household-based surveys. The more limited goal of this paper is therefore to compare the actual distribution of wages to the distribution of wages that would prevail if all workers were paid according to the wage schedule observed in the nonunion sector.

For convenience, call the group of workers with a given set of characteristics x a "skill group." The average wage $\bar{w}(x)$ of workers in skill group x is given by

$$(1) \qquad \bar{w}(x) = w^N(x) + \bar{U}(x)\Delta_w(x),$$

while the variance of wages among these workers, $\sigma^2(x)$, is given by[5]

$$(2) \qquad \sigma^2(x) = \left[\sigma_N^2(x) + \bar{U}(x)\Delta_v(x)\right] + \left[\bar{U}(x)(1 - \bar{U}(x))\Delta_w(x)^2\right].$$

The first component in square brackets is the average within-sector (union and nonunion) variance of wages, while the second component in square brackets is the between-sector variance of wages.

Now consider the overall variance of wages, which is a standard measure of wage dispersion. There are two components to the overall variance of wages among workers: the variance of wages among workers with a given set of characteristics x and the variance of wages between workers with different characteristics x. It follows from a standard variance decomposition that the overall variance of wages among nonunion workers is

$$(3) \qquad \mathrm{Var}(w_i^N) = \mathrm{Var}(w^N(x)) + E(\sigma_N^2(x)),$$

while the overall variance of wages among all workers is

$$(4) \qquad \mathrm{Var}(w_i) = \mathrm{Var}(\bar{w}(x)) + E(\sigma^2(x)).$$

Substituting equations (1) and (2) into equation (4) yields

$$(5) \qquad \begin{aligned} \mathrm{Var}(w_i) = {} & \mathrm{Var}[w^N(x)] + \mathrm{Var}[\bar{U}(x)\Delta_w(x)] + 2\mathrm{Cov}[w^N(x), \bar{U}(x)\Delta_w(x)] \\ & + E[\sigma_N^2(x)] + E[\bar{U}(x)\Delta_v(x)] + E[\bar{U}(x)(1 - \bar{U}(x))\Delta_w(x)^2]. \end{aligned}$$

The overall effect of unions on the variance of wages is then obtained by subtracting equation (3) from equation (5):

$$\begin{aligned} \mathrm{Var}(w_i) - \mathrm{Var}(w_i^N) = {} & \mathrm{Var}[\bar{U}(x)\Delta_w(x)] + 2\mathrm{Cov}[w^N(x), \bar{U}(x)\Delta_w(x)] \\ & + E[\bar{U}(x)\Delta_v(x)] + E[\bar{U}(x)(1 - \bar{U}(x))\Delta_w(x)^2]. \end{aligned}$$

The effect of unions on the variance of wages is thus attributable to three separate factors:

1. how unions change the relative position of each skill group in the wage distribution,

$$(6) \qquad \mathrm{Var}[\bar{U}(x)\Delta_w(x)] + 2\mathrm{Cov}[w^N(x), \bar{U}(x)\Delta_w(x)];$$

5. This formula is derived as follows:

$$\begin{aligned} \sigma^2(x) & = \mathrm{Var}\,(w_i|x) = E_U[\mathrm{Var}(w_i|x,U)] + \mathrm{Var}_U[E(w_i|x,U)] \\ & = (1 - \bar{U}(x))\mathrm{Var}(w_i^N|x) + \bar{U}(x)\mathrm{Var}(w_i^U|x) + \mathrm{Var}_U[w^N(x) + \bar{U}\Delta_w(x)] \\ & = (1 - \bar{U}(x))\sigma_N^2(x) + \bar{U}(x)\sigma_U^2(x) + \bar{U}(x)(1 - \bar{U}(x))\Delta_w(x)^2. \end{aligned}$$

2. how unions increase the variance of wages *between* union and nonunion workers in a skill group, averaged over skill groups,

$$E[\bar{U}(x)(1 - \bar{U}(x))\Delta_w(x)^2]; \tag{7}$$

3. how unions affect the residual variance of wages within union workers in a skill group, averaged over skill groups,

$$E[\bar{U}(x)\Delta_v(x)]. \tag{8}$$

A brief examination of effects 1 and 2 indicates that they depend on the *joint* distribution of $w^N(x)$, $\bar{U}(x)$, and $\Delta_w(x)$. It is therefore necessary to estimate this joint distribution to evaluate the overall impact of unions on wage inequality. The sign of effect 1 may be either positive or negative, depending on whether the covariance term is negative enough to offset the variance term. This covariance term is negative whenever the net union wage effect $\bar{U}\Delta_w$ is larger for workers at the low end of the skill distribution (workers with a low w^N) than for workers at the high end of the skill distribution.

Effect 2 is always positive, since union wage policies pull union workers apart from nonunion workers. On the other hand, effect 3 is usually believed to be negative, as unions tend to standardize wages among union workers ($\Delta_v < 0$).

If all the productive characteristics of workers were observed in the data, it would be straightforward to estimate $\Delta_w(x)$, $\Delta_v(x)$, $w^N(x)$, and thus $\text{Var}(w_i) - \text{Var}(w_i^N)$. Most estimation problems arise when some of these characteristics are unobserved in the data. Consistent estimation of $\Delta_w(x)$, $\Delta_v(x)$, and $w^N(x)$ in that context will be addressed in section 3.4. Note also that the effect of unions on the variance of wages between union and nonunion workers (effect 2) is no longer given by formula (7) when x only represents a subset of the relevant productive characteristics. The point is that union and nonunion workers with the same x's could have systematically different wages even in the absence of unions because of differences in unobserved characteristics. That underlying difference in wages would simply be $\bar{\Delta}_w(x) - \Delta_w(x)$, where $\bar{\Delta}_w(x)$ is the observed difference in wages between union and nonunion workers, while $\Delta_w(x)$ is the properly estimated effect of unions on wages. The effect of unions on the variance of wages between union and nonunion workers would thus become

$$\bar{U}(x)(1 - \bar{U}(x))\left[\bar{\Delta}_w(x)^2 - [\bar{\Delta}_w(x) - \Delta_w(x)]^2\right]. \tag{7'}$$

The formulas for the effects 1 and 3 would remain unchanged.

3.3 Data and Basic Empirical Regularities

The effect of unions on the variance of wages can be obtained by estimating the various components of equations (6), (7′), and (8). Before doing so, it is useful to describe the data used in this paper along with the basic empirical regularities in these data. The various components of equations (6), (7′), and (8) will be estimated in section 3.4.

3.3.1 Data

The Canadian data used for this study were obtained by merging the 1986–87 longitudinal file of the Canadian LMAS to the 1986 cross-sectional file of the LMAS. The 1986 LMAS was administered in January, February, and March 1987 to five rotation groups of the Canadian Labour Force Survey (LFS).[6] The public use sample consists of 66,934 people aged 16–69. It contains detailed information on up to five jobs held in 1986, including the usual hourly wage rate on all paid (except self-employed) jobs and the union status on the job.[7] In this paper, workers are classified as union when they are members of the union that collectively bargained with the employer, or are covered by a collective agreement. Otherwise, they are classified as nonunion. The LMAS also contains detailed information on the work history of each individual, including the reason a worker changed jobs. It is thus possible to reconstruct the precise timing of job changes and to know why people did change jobs.

Most of the people who were initially surveyed in 1987 (1986 LMAS) were reinterviewed in 1988 (1987 LMAS).[8] Like the 1986 LMAS, the 1987 LMAS contains information on up to five jobs held during the year. The 1986–87 longitudinal file was created by Statistics Canada by matching the information from the 1986 and 1987 cross-sections. The longitudinal file thus contains information on up to ten jobs held over the 1986–87 period. Since the LMAS is a work history survey, availability of the 1987 LMAS is not crucial for fixed effect estimation. It simply doubles the length of the work history. In addition, the 1987 LMAS contains useful information on ethnic origin, race, immigrant status, and mother tongue. These questions were not asked in the 1986 LMAS.

For the sake of comparability with other studies, this paper uses a sample of men and women aged 20–64 who hold jobs in nonagricultural industries. This subsample is also restricted to people who have worked for at least four weeks on a paid, but not self-employed, job in 1986. Jobs with a usual wage rate of less than $1.00 or more than $75.00 an hour are also excluded from the sample. A total of 34,765 workers satisfied the various sample selection criteria.[9]

6. The LFS sample design is based on six rotation groups including approximately 130,000 people. People remain in the sample for six consecutive months, at which time they are replaced.

7. The definition of a job in the LMAS is "usual duties performed at a usual wage or salary" (Statistics Canada 1988, sec. 4.1).

8. Statistics Canada managed to reinterview more than 90 percent of the people surveyed in the 1986 LMAS, including several thousands who had moved between the two interviews.

9. Of these workers, 32,696 were reinterviewed for the 1987 LMAS. The variables on ethnic origin, immigrant status, race, and mother tongue are only available for these 32,696 workers.

The U.S. data used to describe the basic empirical regularities on unions and wages come from the 1986 merged outgoing rotation group file of the CPS. Both the Canadian and the U.S. data are thus based on earnings supplements to very similar surveys (the LFS and the CPS). The sample selection criteria used to construct the final U.S. data set are also similar to the ones used for the Canadian data.[10] A sample of 161,195 workers satisfied these sample selection criteria. More details on the U.S. data and its comparability with the LMAS data are provided in appendix A.

3.3.2 Empirical Regularities

As mentioned earlier, the effect of unions on the distribution of wages depends on the joint distribution of unionization rates, union wages, and nonunion wages. This joint distribution is analyzed empirically by first tabulating unionization rates and wages over a set of workers and jobs characteristics. Table 3.1 presents the distribution of these characteristics in the sample, along with the unionization rate for workers with these characteristics.

Columns 5 and 6 indicate that the fraction of workers covered by collective bargaining agreements was 45.8 percent among men and 36.4 percent among women in Canada in 1986. In the LMAS sample, women account for 45.5 percent of the work force and for 39.9 percent of all workers covered by collective bargaining agreements. Furthermore, most women holding union jobs work in the public sector, where the union density is 67.3 percent, as opposed to 18.9 percent in the private sector.[11] The union density is also higher in the public sector than in the private sector for men. Overall, 45.1 percent of Canadian workers covered by collective bargaining agreements work in the public sector.

The composition of the Canadian and U.S. samples reported in table 3.1 are similar with a few exceptions. One difference is the race composition of the two samples. There are also some differences in educational achievement in the two countries, in part because of differences in the questions used in the two surveys.[12] Finally, the public sector employs relatively more people (es-

10. The only sample selection criterion that was not used is the condition that the job must last at least four weeks (job duration is not available in the CPS data used). See appendix A for more details.

11. The definition of the public sector used for Canada includes the health and welfare industry in addition to education services and public administration. This definition is used because the LMAS does not contain direct information on whether a job is in the public or in the private sector. Such information is available, however, in the 1984 Survey of Union Membership. Using these data, Riddell (chap. 4 in this volume) estimates the private sector density at 29 percent (men and women together). The definition of the private sector used in this paper would imply a union density of 28 percent (my calculation using table 2 in Kumar 1988), which is a satisfactory approximation to the true union density in the private sector.

12. In the LMAS, educational achievement is classified in five categories: none or elementary, high school (some or completed), some postsecondary, postsecondary certificate or diploma, and university. These five categories were mapped into the five following ranges of years of schooling completed in the CPS: 0–7, 8–12, 13, 14–15, 16 and more.

Table 3.1 Sample Characteristics and Unionization Rates in Canada and the United States

	Sample Composition (%)				Unionization Rate (%)			
	Canada		U.S.		Canada		U.S.	
	Men (1)	Women (2)	Men (3)	Women (4)	Men (5)	Women (6)	Men (7)	Women (8)
Total	54.53	45.47	53.49	46.51	45.78	36.39	25.63	16.60
Age								
20–24	15.12	18.03	14.27	15.63	26.25	20.25	12.90	7.71
25–34	32.19	33.60	33.80	32.30	43.04	37.71	21.74	14.82
35–44	25.50	25.25	24.96	25.60	51.92	43.30	30.60	19.78
45–54	16.44	15.18	16.15	16.19	54.04	40.72	33.18	21.16
55–64	10.75	7.94	10.82	10.28	54.25	37.24	31.88	20.62
Education								
Primary	11.20	7.37	3.30	1.94	57.21	32.17	23.42	15.12
High school	47.38	47.64	50.73	53.54	47.18	30.76	30.94	15.11
More than high school	10.51	11.35	7.06	8.26	38.38	29.31	27.35	12.15
Some post-secondary	14.56	18.80	13.87	14.64	42.27	44.12	22.18	11.91
University degree	16.35	14.84	25.03	21.62	41.79	52.22	16.59	25.31
Marital status								
Single	28.81	33.20	33.18	42.05	35.93	33.30	20.09	16.00
Married	71.19	66.80	66.82	58.95	49.77	37.93	28.39	17.04
Race								
White	93.72	93.69	87.10	85.01	46.78	37.02	24.96	15.37
Nonwhite	6.28	6.31	12.90	14.99	38.74	32.80	30.15	23.57
Part-time status								
Full-time	94.46	75.36	93.48	76.41	46.83	38.57	26.58	18.73
Part-time	5.54	24.64	6.52	23.59	27.95	29.73	12.00	9.70
Private sector	80.93	63.87	83.90	79.97	39.21	18.89	21.55	10.19
Public sector	19.07	36.13	16.10	20.03	73.67	67.33	46.93	42.19
Occupation								
White-collar	53.20	89.89	54.28	87.66	38.15	36.18	18.40	15.23
Blue-collar	46.80	10.11	45.72	12.34	54.45	38.34	34.22	26.35
Mother tongue								
English	59.02	61.50	—	—	42.51	34.15	—	—
French	26.30	24.70	—	—	54.30	45.26	—	—
Others	14.68	13.80	—	—	47.00	33.10	—	—

Sources: Canadian data are from the 1986 cross-sectional file and the 1986–87 longitudinal file of the LMAS. Sample size is 34,765, except for the tabulations for mother tongue and race, which are based on a matched sample of 32,696 observations. U.S. data are from the 1986 merged outgoing rotation group files of the CPS. Sample size is 161,195.

Note: The estimated frequency distributions are all weighted.

pecially women) in Canada, as it is defined to include the health and education sectors.

Table 3.2 presents ordinary least squares (OLS) estimates of standard log hourly wage equations in which the following regressors are included: an indicator variable for union coverage, the set of worker and job characteristics listed in table 3.1, and controls for industry, occupation, and region. The estimated union wage gap is comparable for men in Canada (0.198) and in the United States (0.180). It is much larger, however, for women in Canada (0.287) than for women in the United States (0.156). With the exception of women in Canada, the estimated union wage gaps reported here are consistent with previous findings in the literature.[13] The other estimated wage effects are similar in the two countries except for the effect of part-time employment, which is much larger in absolute value in the United States. Although the estimated returns to education are hard to compare for reasons discussed above, the estimated university–high school wage differentials are similar in Canada (0.257 for men, 0.271 for women) and in the United States (0.247 for men, 0.223 for women).[14]

The average union wage gaps reported in table 3.2 are estimated under the implicit assumption that the wage gap is the same for all workers. As mentioned in section 3.2, differences in the wage gap $\Delta_w(x)$ and in the union density $\bar{U}(x)$ by skill groups may play an important role in the overall impact of unions on the distribution of wages. The relationships among $\Delta_w(x)$, $\bar{U}(x)$, and the nonunion wage $w^N(x)$ are examined graphically by fitting simple index models for these three variables. More specifically, a log wage equation for the sample of nonunion worker is fit to the set of region dummies, indicator variables for marriage and race, and fully interacted age and education dummies. The nonunion wage index for a worker with characteristics x_i is then defined as the predicted wage from that regression (excluding the effect of province, on the assumption that regional wage differences reflect cost of living rather than skill differences). This nonunion wage index can be interpreted as a general skill index. A similar union wage index is constructed by running a wage regression on the sample of union workers. The union wage gap for a

13. Results from American studies are surveyed by Lewis (1986). See also Freeman and Medoff (1984). For Canadian studies that focus on the estimation of the average union wage gap, see Evans and Clark (1986); Grant, Swidinsky, and Vanderkamp (1987); Kumar and Stengos (1985, 1986); Maki and Ng (1990); Robinson (1989); Robinson and Tomes (1984); and Simpson (1985). The finding that the union wage gap is larger for women than for men in Canada is at odds with the results of Maki and Ng (1990) (similar wage gaps for men and women), who used data for 1981. The finding is consistent, however, with the fact that the unadjusted union wage gap was substantially larger for women than for men in Canada in 1984, 1986, and 1987 (Labour Canada 1991).

14. The estimated returns for education are different from those reported by Freeman and Needels (chap. 2 in this volume) because of the inclusion of industry and occupation dummies in the wage regression.

Table 3.2 **OLS Estimates of the (Log) Wage Equation**

	Canada		U.S.	
	Men (1)	Women (2)	Men (3)	Women (4)
Covered by collective bargaining	0.198 (0.007)	0.287 (0.007)	0.180 (0.004)	0.156 (0.004)
Age 25–34	0.211 (0.010)	0.180 (0.009)	0.209 (0.005)	0.180 (0.005)
Age 35–44	0.340 (0.011)	0.221 (0.010)	0.335 (0.005)	0.231 (0.005)
Age 45–54	0.372 (0.012)	0.234 (0.011)	0.376 (0.006)	0.231 (0.005)
Age 55–64	0.332 (0.013)	0.207 (0.013)	0.355 (0.006)	0.226 (0.006)
High school	0.138 (0.010)	0.090 (0.012)	0.273 (0.009)	0.252 (0.011)
More than high school	0.197 (0.013)	0.148 (0.015)	0.362 (0.010)	0.315 (0.012)
Some postsecondary	0.267 (0.012)	0.228 (0.014)	0.386 (0.009)	0.366 (0.012)
University degree	0.395 (0.014)	0.361 (0.016)	0.520 (0.009)	0.475 (0.012)
Married	0.111 (0.007)	0.012 (0.007)	0.109 (0.003)	0.012 (0.003)
Nonwhite	−0.075 (0.016)	−0.006 (0.017)	−0.093 (0.004)	−0.030 (0.004)
Part-time	−0.124 (0.013)	−0.016 (0.007)	−0.299 (0.006)	−0.169 (0.004)
Mother tongue				
French	−0.014 (0.011)	−0.004 (0.011)	—	—
Not English or French	−0.027 (0.011)	−0.017 (0.011)	—	—
Gender dummy[a] (women = 1)	−0.262 (0.008)		−0.241 (0.002)	
Observations	18,679	16,086	84,275	76,920
R^2	0.368	0.430	0.415	0.402
Root mean squared error	0.388	0.372	0.407	0.395
Mean of dependent variable	2.422	2.088	2.250	1.906

Sources: Canadian data are from the 1986 cross-sectional file and the 1986–87 longitudinal file of the LMAS. U.S. data are from the 1986 outgoing rotation group file of the CPS. The dependent variable is the log of the hourly wage rate. All specifications also include region dummies (ten provinces in Canada, nine regions in the United States), seven industry dummies, and eight occupation dummies. The base group is age 20–24, primary education, single, white, mother tongue English (Canada only).

[a]Estimated from a separate pooled regression for men and women.

given value of the nonunion wage index is simply the difference between the union and the nonunion wage index. Finally, a union density index is constructed by fitting a linear probability model and using the procedure discussed above to predict the probability of union coverage.[15]

The predicted union wage gap and the predicted unionization rate are plotted against the nonunion wage index for the sample of Canadian men in figure 3.1a. The fitted lines in the figure are obtained by regressing the predicted wage gap and the predicted unionization rate on a third-degree polynomial of the nonunion wage index.[16] The graph indicates that the union wage gap declines with skill. It is even negative for workers at the high end of the skill distribution. The graph also indicates that the unionization rate increases with skill among workers at the low end of the skill distribution. The unionization rate then remains more or less constant for workers at the middle and high ends of the skill distribution.

Figure 3.1a thus suggests that, for men in Canada, unions have a mixed impact on the distribution of wages across skill groups. The wage gap for low-skill men is large, but few of these men are unionized, while the opposite is true for high-skill men. This patterns hides important differences, however, between the impact of unions in the private and in the public sector. On the one hand, Figures 3.1b and 3.1c show that the wage gap declines with skill in both sectors. On the other hand, the figures show different patterns of unionization in the two sectors. While the unionization rate rises steadily to reach 80 percent at the high end of the skill distribution in the public sector, it peaks around 40 percent and then declines with skill in the private sector. Union workers are thus concentrated in the middle of the skill distribution in the private sector, but at the high end of the skill distribution in the public sector. The unionization rate is thus high for highly skilled men in Canada because of the pattern of the unionization in the public rather than in the private sector.

Figure 3.1d shows the same plots for men in the United States. Like Canadian union workers in the private sector, union workers in the United States are concentrated in the middle of the skill distribution. The union wage gap also declines with skill, though not monotonically, and is negative for workers at the high end of the skill distribution. Unions thus have similar relative wage effects in Canada and in the United States. Union workers are more skilled in Canada than in the United States, however, because of the high level of unionization among public sector workers.

Figure 3.2 shows analogous plots for women. These figures suggest two

15. Since age and education dummies are fully interacted, the predicted probabilities from a linear probability model are almost identical to the predicted probabilities from a probit or logit model (they would be numerically equivalent if all the regressors were fully interacted).

16. Only the fitted values (from a cubic regression) of the union wage gap and of the unionization rates, as opposed to the predicted values of these variables for each age-education-race–marital status cell, are plotted to simplify the graphs.

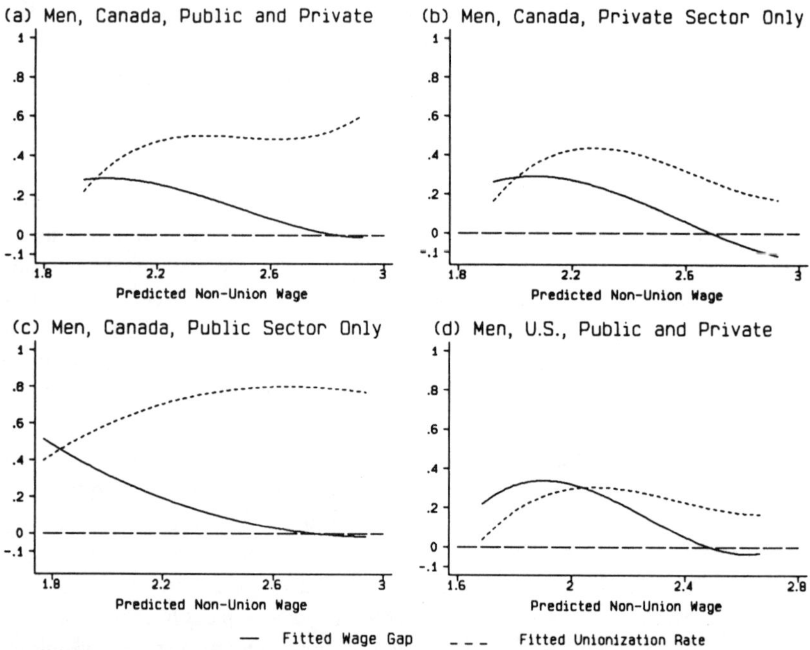

Fig. 3.1 Predicted union wage gap and predicted unionization rate by skill level: men

Note: Fitted values from a cubic regression of the predicted union wage gap (or unionization rate) on the predicted nonunion wage by age-education-race–marital status cell (see text for details).

major differences in the patterns of unionization and wages between men and women. First, the predicted union wage gap declines much less with skill for women than for men. The predicted union wage gap is always at least half as large for women at the high end of the skill distribution as for women at the low end of the skill distribution. It is almost a flat function of skills for women in Canada when private and public sector workers are pooled (figure 3.2a). A second major difference between men and women is that, for women, unionization is concentrated at the high end of the skill distribution in both Canada and the United States. The breakdown between the private and the public sector in Canada (figures 3.2b and 3.2c) suggests this overall pattern is due to concentration of union jobs in the public sector.

The division of union jobs between the public and the private sectors thus goes a long way toward explaining the patterns of unionization along skill lines for men and women in Canada and the United States. The fraction of union workers who hold a public sector job is 29 percent for U.S. men, 31 percent for Canadian men, 51 percent for U.S. women, and 67 percent for Canadian women. Figures 3.1 and 3.2 show that, as this fraction increases,

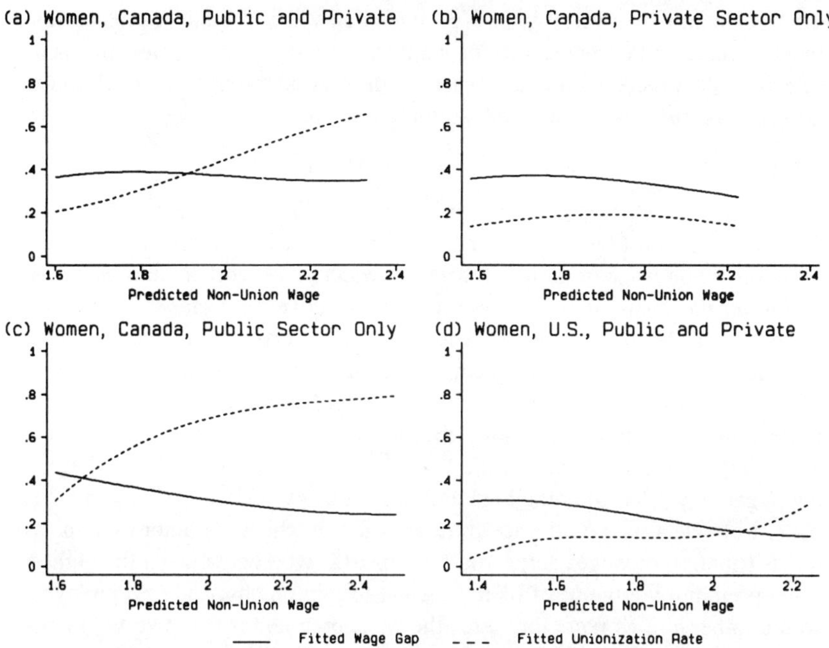

Fig. 3.2 Predicted union wage gap and predicted unionization rate by skill level: women

Note: Fitted values from a cubic regression of the predicted union wage gap (or unionization rate) on the predicted nonunion wage by age-education-race–marital status cell (see text for details).

the distribution of unionization gets more and more skewed to the right of the skill distribution.

The other main conclusion to be drawn from figures 3.1 and 3.2 is that the union wage gap declines in the skill level. This negative relationship is stronger for men than for women. The same basic conclusions are reached using a more standard regression-based approach for Canada (see appendix table 3B.1). Appendix table 3B.2 summarizes the results of that regression-based approach by showing the effects of unions on a selected number of wage differentials such as the university–high school wage differential and the white-collar/blue-collar wage differential.

3.4 Fixed Effect Estimation

The descriptive analysis of section 3.3 indicates substantial diversity in the role of unions for various subgroups of the work force. This section presents detailed estimates of the effects of unions on both the level and the variance of wages for some of these subgroups. These estimates will be used in section

3.5 to calculate the overall impact of unions on wage inequality. This section first discusses the importance of adjusting these estimates for the self-selection of workers into the union sector for each subgroup of the work force. The actual estimates are reported later in the section.

3.4.1 Self-selection and the Fixed Effects Method

The pattern of the union wage gap along skill lines documented in section 3.3 raises the question of whether the estimated gaps represent "true" effects of unionism on wage or merely reflect the selection of workers into the union sector on the basis of their unobserved productive characteristics. For instance, it may be that, among workers with low observed skills, only the most qualified are hired by unionized employers. It may also be that most workers with high observed skills do not get many benefits for joining unions, so only those with low unobserved skills join unions. As a result, union workers might be positively selected at the low end of the observed skill distribution but negatively selected at the high end of the observed skill distribution. This pattern of selection would arise from a model in which (1) unions compress the distribution of wages across skill groups, (2) workers who get the highest wage premium are the most likely to want to join unions, and (3) employers would rather hire workers for which the wage premium is the lowest.[17] In this model, union employers do not want to hire low-skill workers as they command a high wage premium, while high-skill workers do not want union jobs because their wage gain from unionization is low or negative. Unionization is thus concentrated among workers in the middle of the skill distribution. Since total skills are the sum of observed and unobserved skills, union workers with low observed skills tend to have high unobserved skills (positive selection) and vice versa. This model thus generates a pattern of selection that could explain why the estimated wage gap declines with skill.

The fixed effect approach is a standard technique used to consistently estimate the effects of union on wages when workers are selected in the union sector on the basis of unobservable characteristics.[18] The approach has the advantage of being robust to the complicated pattern of selection mentioned above. The goal of this section is thus to consistently estimate the union wage gap $\Delta_w(x)$ and the union variance gap $\Delta_v(x)$ by exploiting the panel data aspect of the LMAS and of the (matched) CPS data. Several recent U.S. studies, including Card (1992), have used fixed effect methods with the CPS data to estimate the effects of unions on wages. Since Card also addresses measure-

17. These are the building blocks of the queuing model of unionization of Abowd and Farber (1982).

18. See, for example, Chamberlain (1982) and Freeman (1984), who use various versions of the fixed effect approach to estimate the average union wage gap in the United States. There is a large debate on whether or not the fixed effect approach appropriately adjusts the wage gap estimates for the selection of union workers. Lemieux (1992) discusses these issues in detail. The results reported there suggest that fixed effect estimates adjust for most of the selection bias.

ment issues specific to the matched CPS data that are beyond the scope of this paper (see appendix A), his results will be directly used here and compared to the results obtained using the LMAS data.

One shortcoming of the fixed effect approach is that, in the LMAS data, it is only applicable to the limited sample of workers who changed jobs at least once during the 1986–87 period. This reduces the precision of the estimates and limits the ability to measure the effect of unions for small subgroups of the work force. It is thus important to use a parsimonious approach to get precise enough estimates while still letting the effect of unions vary along the lines suggested in section 3.3. In light of the results in section 3.3, it was decided to analyze men and women separately and to further break down the data into workers in the public and private sectors. It is also important to allow for some heterogeneity in the effect of unions by skill level. For the sake of comparability with the study of Card (1992) for the United States, the sample will thus be divided into three skill group (tiers) on the basis of workers' predicted wage in the nonunion sector.[19]

3.4.2 Dividing the Sample in Three Tiers

The sample of men and the sample of women are divided into three tiers by first fitting log wages to a regression of province, language, race, and marital status dummies, and age and education dummies fully interacted. A predicted nonunion wage is then constructed from all these variables except the province dummies (see section 3.3.2). This predicted wage is used to separate workers into three skill groups (lower tier, middle tier, and upper tier) of approximately equal sizes.[20]

Table 3.3 reports average nonunion wages, union wages, and unionization rates for the three tiers of the sample of Canadian men (columns 1–3). It also presents OLS estimates of the average union wage gap for each tier. The OLS estimates reported in column 4 are obtained by regressing log hourly wages on a dummy variable for union coverage, province and marital status dummies, age and education dummies fully interacted, and an extensive set of job characteristics available in the LMAS data.[21] Table 3.4 reports analogous estimates for the sample of Canadian women.

19. Card (1992) uses the large samples of the 1987–88 matched files of the CPS and divides his sample of men aged 24–66 in five quintiles. The Canadian sample is divided in three tiers only to improve the precision of the estimates (the Canadian sample is much smaller than the U.S. sample).

20. Dividing the sample in three tiers is simply one method among others to let the effects of unions vary over workers with different skill levels. A different but related method is used by Simpson (1985), who divides workers on the basis of the skill requirements of the occupation they hold. In addition, since workers are divided into tiers on the basis of a *predicted* wage, estimates by tier are not biased, while they would be if workers were divided into tiers on the basis of their *actual* wage (the dependent variable).

21. These job characteristics include a part-time dummy, seven occupation dummies, three tenure dummies, and four firm-size dummies.

Table 3.3 OLS and First-Differenced Wage Gap Estimates by Tier for Men in Canada

	Nonunion Wage (1)	Union Wage (2)	Unionization Rate (3)	Wage Gap Estimates[a] OLS (4)	First-Differenced (5)	Selection Bias (6)
			Public and private pooled			
Tier 1	2.010	2.407	38.2	0.232	0.207	0.025
				(0.011)	(0.035)	
Tier 2	2.312	2.534	50.3	0.129	0.220	−0.091
				(0.011)	(0.038)	
Tier 3	2.597	2.713	50.5	0.044	0.006	0.038
				(0.013)	(0.059)	
All	2.305	2.550	46.3	0.133	0.163	−0.030
				(0.007)	(0.024)	
			Private sector only			
Tier 1	2.016	2.417	34.9	0.223	0.190	0.033
				(0.012)	(0.038)	
Tier 2	2.309	2.547	45.8	0.131	0.229	−0.098
				(0.012)	(0.040)	
Tier 3	2.577	2.678	35.9	0.049	0.076	−0.027
				(0.017)	(0.088)	
All	2.300	2.547	39.1	0.139	0.162	−0.023
				(0.008)	(0.026)	
			Public sector only			
Tier 1	1.950	2.366	59.2	0.308	0.302	0.006
				(0.033)	(0.084)	
Tier 2	2.346	2.488	76.6	0.106	0.161	−0.055
				(0.029)	(0.101)	
Tier 3	2.703	2.743	77.6	0.028	0.074	−0.046
				(0.022)	(0.092)	
All	2.332	2.532	73.6	0.111	0.166	−0.055
				(0.015)	(0.050)	

Notes: Based on 18,679 observations (14,773 in the private sector, 3,906 in the public sector) divided into tiers on the basis of the predicted nonunion wage (see text). The public sector accounts for 13.5 percent of employment in tier 1, 14.6 percent in tier 2, and 20.9 percent in tier 3.

[a]Both OLS and first-differenced estimates are obtained by fitting log hourly wage regressions that also include controls for age, education, marital status, part-time status, tenure, firm size, industry, and occupation. The first-differenced estimates are based on a sample of 1,559 involuntary job changers (744 in tier 1, 480 in tier 2, and 335 in tier 3).

The results show the same patterns that were observed in figures 3.1 and 3.2. In the case of men, the union wage gap declines in the skill level while the unionization rate first increases and then remains constant in the middle and upper tiers. The results for women indicate that the union wage gap slowly declines in the skill level. For both men and women, public sector unionization increases in the skills of workers, while private sector unioniza-

Table 3.4 OLS and First-Differenced Wage Gap Estimates by Tier for Women in Canada

	Nonunion Wage (1)	Union Wage (2)	Unionization Rate (3)	Wage Gap Estimates[a]: OLS (4)	Wage Gap Estimates[a]: First-Differenced (5)	Selection Bias (6)
			Public and private pooled			
Tier 1	1.748	2.150	27.0	0.229	0.190	0.039
				(0.012)	(0.037)	
Tier 2	1.904	2.273	33.6	0.230	0.077	0.153
				(0.013)	(0.051)	
Tier 3	2.165	2.538	53.4	0.178	0.191	−0.013
				(0.015)	(0.054)	
All	1.934	2.319	37.9	0.212	0.167	0.045
				(0.008)	(0.026)	
			Private sector only			
Tier 1	1.736	2.078	17.3	0.200	0.146	0.054
				(0.015)	(0.045)	
Tier 2	1.889	2.241	19.8	0.231	0.152	0.079
				(0.017)	(0.066)	
Tier 3	2.103	2.391	17.0	0.170	0.320	−0.150
				(0.027)	(0.107)	
All	1.908	2.236	18.2	0.206	0.186	0.020
				(0.011)	(0.037)	
			Public sector only			
Tier 1	1.814	2.217	56.4	0.299	0.267	0.032
				(0.024)	(0.058)	
Tier 2	1.987	2.296	65.1	0.246	−0.022	0.268
				(0.020)	(0.074)	
Tier 3	2.288	2.558	75.0	0.187	0.153	0.034
				(0.017)	(0.108)	
All	2.028	2.355	68.4	0.231	0.150	0.081
				(0.011)	(0.035)	

Notes: Based on 16,086 observations (9,788 in the private sector, 6,298 in the public sector) divided into tiers on the basis of the predicted nonunion wage (see text). The public sector accounts for 24.8 percent of employment in tier 1, 30.4 percent in tier 2, and 62.8 percent in tier 3.

[a]Both OLS and first-differenced estimates are obtained by fitting log hourly wage regressions that also include controls for age, education, marital status, part-time status, tenure, firm size, industry, and occupation. The first-differenced estimates are based on a sample of 1,268 involuntary job changers (552 in tier 1, 362 in tier 2, and 354 in tier 3).

tion is concentrated in the middle of the skill distribution. The average union wage gaps are similar in the public and in the private sector.

3.4.3 Longitudinal Data for Fixed Effect Estimation

A data set like the LMAS, containing detailed information on work histories of individuals, has several advantages over standard panel data sets, such as matched CPS's, for estimating the union wage gap by fixed effect methods. A first advantage is that it is known from the work history whether a worker changed jobs. This information reduces the odds of misclassification errors in recorded changes in the union status, since union status changes *only* for job changers. Intuitively, observing a change in union status is not surprising when it is known that the worker has changed jobs. By contrast, observing a change in union status is surprising for a worker who has not changed jobs.[22] The probability that a recorded union status change for a non–job changer is due to misclassification errors is thus high. Since true job changes are infrequent events, a large number of the recorded changes in union status are likely to be spurious when job movers and job stayers are pooled. This problem is avoided by limiting the longitudinal analysis to workers who are known to have changed jobs.[23]

A second advantage of the LMAS is that it records the reason a worker changed jobs. It is thus possible to separate workers who quit their jobs voluntarily from workers who did not. In the presence of endogenous job search, fixed effect estimates based on a sample of voluntary quitters are likely to be biased. It is thus useful to estimate the model separately for involuntary job changers to see whether the results are robust to the choice of sample.

To be classified as a job changer, a worker has to hold consecutive jobs for two different employers over the 1986–87 period. The job changer also has to work at least four weeks on each of these jobs. On the one hand, workers holding two jobs simultaneously for more than a week are not classified as job changers. On the other hand, workers who are recorded to hold two jobs simultaneously during the transition week are also classified as job changers, to account for the possibility of job changes during the transition week as opposed to over the weekend. Finally, job changers are divided into a sample of voluntary quitters and involuntary changers on the basis of their response to the question, "What was the main reason . . . left that job or business?"[24] A sample of 5,200 job changers, including 2,826 involuntary changers and 2,374 voluntary quitters, were selected on the basis of their answer to that question. A panel of two jobs is available for both type of job changers.

3.4.4 Fixed Effect Estimates by Tier

The fixed effect estimates of the union wage gap are reported in column 5 of tables 3.3 and 3.4. The estimates are obtained by fitting to the sample of involuntary job changers a first-differenced version of the regressions used to

22. True transitions would only occur when the job became organized or decertified, which is a very unlikely event.

23. See Krueger and Summers (1988) for some evidence on this point in the context of estimating interindustry wage differentials.

24. Voluntary quitters left their job for one of the following reasons: low pay, no opportunity of advancement, no opportunity to use training or skills, working conditions, other reasons for which they were dissatisfied, or a decision to quit for no particular reason.

compute the OLS wage gaps (column 4). The first-differenced regressions also include a dummy variable indicating whether the second job was recorded in the 1987 LMAS, as opposed to the 1986 LMAS, to account for growth in log wages between 1986 and 1987. To improve the precision of the results, the first-differenced wage gap estimates in the private and public sectors are obtained by fitting a regression for the pooled sample in which the union coverage variable is interacted with a public sector dummy (a public sector dummy is also included separately). Note that, since there are only two observations per worker, first-differenced estimates are equivalent to standard within estimates.

The first-differenced wage gap estimates for men reported in table 3.3 are always *larger* than the OLS estimates when the three tiers are pooled. On average, men holding union jobs are thus negatively selected in both the private and the public sectors. The selection bias (the difference between the OLS and the first-differenced wage gap estimates) is reported in column 6. There is also some evidence that men in the lower tier are positively selected, while men in the middle and upper tiers are negatively selected in both private and public sector union jobs. It is nevertheless clear that the selection-adjusted wage gaps decline with skill. The selection mechanism only accentuates this pattern.

The results reported in table 3.4 indicate that, unlike men, women holding union jobs are positively selected in both the public and the private sector. As in the case of men, the selection is negative for lower-tier women and for upper-tier women working in the public sector. Unlike men, however, middle-tier women and upper-tier women in the private sector are positively selected into the union sector. Overall, the selection-adjusted estimates reinforce the conclusion that there is little systematic relationship between the union wage gap and the skill level of women in Canada.

The differences in the pattern of wage differentials for men and women can be restated in terms of selection-adjusted returns to skills in the union and the nonunion sectors. These returns to skills are calculated as the difference between the predicted wage of an average worker in the upper tier and the predicted wage of an average worker in the lower tier. These predicted wages $\hat{w}^N(G)$ and $\hat{w}^U(G)$ for tier G are defined as $\hat{w}^N(G) = \bar{w}(G) - \bar{U}(G)\Delta_w(G)$ and $\hat{w}^U(G) = \hat{w}^N(G) + \Delta_w(G)$, where $\bar{w}(G)$ is the average wage in tier G, $\bar{U}(G)$ is the unionization rate, and $\Delta_w(G)$ is the first-differenced wage gap estimate. Applying these formulas to the estimates reported in tables 3.3 and 3.4 yields an estimated return to skill for men of .37 in the union sector, and of .57 in the nonunion sector. The estimated return to skill is equal to .46 for women in both the union and the nonunion sector.

The union wage gap is thus the same for lower-tier and upper-tier women because the returns to skills for women are lower in the nonunion sector *and* higher in the union sector. Relative to men, the skills of women are thus more rewarded in the union than in the nonunion sector. This explains why high-skill women are relatively more likely than high-skill men to select the union sector. This pattern of self-selection is even stronger in the public sector, suggesting that public sector unions play a very different role for men than they do for women. Controlling for observables, unionized jobs in the public sector seem to attract relatively skilled women and relatively unskilled men. A potentially fruitful area of research would be to explore how differences in both wages and benefits packages, such as maternity leaves, make unionized public sector jobs particularly attractive to high-skill women.

The validity of these findings relies heavily, however, on the assumption that first-differenced wage gap estimates for the sample of involuntary job changers are consistent estimates of the true wage gap. Since first-differenced wage gap estimates are overidentified, it is possible to perform specification tests of these estimates. One straightforward test is to compare the wage gap estimates for union joiners and union leavers. These two wage gaps are estimated by interacting the union coverage variable with a dummy variable indicating whether the worker is a union joiner or a union leaver, and then fitting a first-differenced version of that enlarged wage equation.

The wage gap estimates for union joiners and union leavers are reported in columns 2 and 3 of appendix table 3C.1. The wage gap estimates for joiners and leavers are very similar, especially for men, which suggests the first-differenced model for the sample of involuntary leavers is well specified. The table also shows additional evidence of robustness of the main findings by presenting estimates for the sample of all job changers and for a sample of dual-job holders.

Most of the results presented in table 3C.1 are more directly comparable to the results of Card (1992), as they include demographic and location characteristics but not job characteristics in the wage equations being fitted.[25] Figure 3.3 compares the pattern of the union wage gap and of the unionization rate for men in Canada and the United States. The Canadian wage gap estimates are taken from column 1 of table 3C.1. The U.S. wage gap estimates are Card's (1992) wage gap estimates by quintile averaged in three tiers. The figure indicates similar patterns of selection-adjusted wage differentials in the two countries. The figure also indicates the unionization rates in the two countries diverge at the high end of the skill distribution, as was discussed in section 3.3. Note also that Card finds no evidence of selection bias, on average. He finds some evidence of positive selection at the lower end and negative selection at the upper end of the skill distribution, but the two effects cancel out in the aggregate.

3.4.5 Estimates of the Union Variance Gap in Canada

Of the main components of equations (6), (7′), and (8), only the variance gap $\Delta_v(x)$ remains to be estimated. One estimator of the variance gap is the

25. The covariates used are thus the regressors used in the predicted nonunion wage equation on the basis of which workers are divided in tiers (or quintiles).

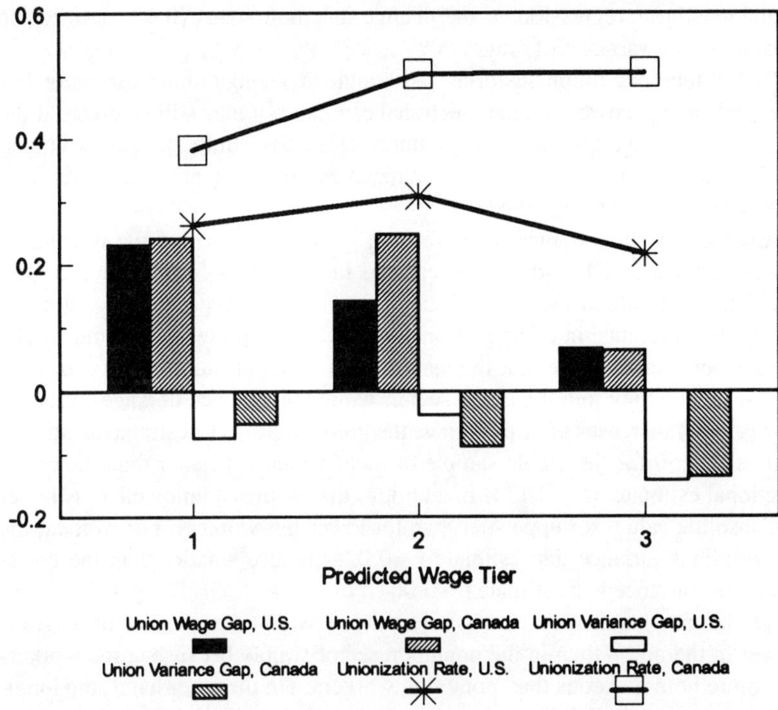

Fig. 3.3 Union wage effects and unionization rates by predicted wage tier for men in Canada and the United States

Sources: Rows 1, 4, and 5 of tables 3.6 and 3.8.

difference between the cross-sectional variance of wages in the union and in the nonunion sector. One problem with that approach is that it fails to distinguish whether unions reduce the variance of wages from whether union workers are more homogeneous than nonunion workers (Freeman 1984). This cross-sectional estimator is thus potentially afflicted by selectivity biases. One alternative panel data estimator of the variance gap that is not afflicted by selectivity biases is obtained by contrasting the change in the variance of wages of union joiners to the change in the variance of wages of nonunion stayers:

$$(V_2^{01} - V_1^{01}) - (V_2^{00} - V_1^{00}),$$

where V_t^{jk} is the variance of wages on job t ($t = 1,2$) among workers with union history $U_{i1} = j$ and $U_{i2} = k$. Another estimator is obtained by comparing union leavers to union stayers:

$$-[(V_2^{10} - V_1^{10}) - (V_2^{11} - V_1^{11})].$$

Both of these estimators of the variance gap are consistent but inefficient. The efficient longitudinal estimator of the variance gap is obtained by fitting a weighted linear regression of the change in union status (0,1, −1,0) to the change in the variance of wages ($V_2^{00} - V_1^{00}, V_2^{01} - V_1^{01}, V_2^{10} - V_1^{10}, V_2^{11} - V_1^{11}$) for the four union histories. Although this longitudinal estimator has clear advantages over the cross-sectional estimator, it may still be biased if the sample of job changers is small and unrepresentative. Both the cross-sectional and the longitudinal variance gap estimates are thus potentially biased. Both estimates will be presented below.

Changes in the variance of wages, $V_2^{jk} - V_1^{jk}$, for each of the four union histories 00, 01, 10, and 11 are reported in columns 1–4 of table 3.5. The efficient longitudinal estimate of the variance gap is reported in column 5, while the difference in cross-sectional variances is reported in column 6. The results for men indicate that the variance of wages of union joiners (01) decreases when they join the union sector, while the variance of wages of union leavers (10) increases after they leave the union sector. The estimated variance gap is −0.50 for the whole sample of men, which is smaller than the cross-sectional estimate of −0.134. In addition, the estimated union effect is larger (in absolute value) for upper-tier than for lower-tier workers. For women, the longitudinal variance gap estimate (−0.029) is also smaller than the cross-sectional variance gap estimate (−0.064).

On the one hand, these results reject the view that the variance of wages is lower in the union than in the nonunion sector simply because union workers are more homogeneous than nonunion workers. On the other hand, the longitudinal estimates of the variance gap are less than half of the cross-sectional variance gaps.[26] Correcting for selection biases thus has a bigger impact on the variance gap estimates than on the wage gap estimates reported in tables 3.3 and 3.4. There is some evidence, however, that part of the discrepancy between the cross-sectional and the longitudinal estimates of the variance gap is due to the composition of the sample of involuntary job changers. While the cross-sectional estimates of the variance gap are equal to −.134 for men and −.064 for women in the full sample, they are equal to only −.077 and .033 in the sample of involuntary changers. Furthermore, the preferred estimate of the variance gap in Lemieux (1992) is closer to the cross-sectional variance gap for the full sample than to the longitudinal variance gap for the sample of involuntary changers.[27] The cross-sectional estimates of the variance gap (table 3.5, column 6) will thus be used to calculate the overall impact of unions on the variance of wages.

The estimated variance gaps for men in Canada and the United States are

26. This was also noted by Swidinsky and Kupferschmidt (1991).

27. Lemieux (1992) also finds that the composition of the sample of involuntary job changers does not significantly affect the longitudinal estimates of the union wage gap (effect on level of wages). The composition problem occurs because unions flatten the returns to the permanent component of unobservable characteristics and the dispersion of these unobservable characteristics is small among job changers. The flattening effect thus reduces the variance of wages of job changers by less than it reduces the variance of wages of all union workers.

Table 3.5 Change in Variance of Wages for Job Changers in Canada

	Change in Variance by Union History				Estimates of the Union Variance Gap	
	00 (1)	01 (2)	10 (3)	11 (4)	Longitudinal[a] (5)	Cross-sectional (6)
			A. Men			
Public and private sectors						
Tier 1	−0.020	0.009	0.039	0.007	−0.018	−0.052
Tier 2	−0.009	−0.033	0.034	0.029	−0.033	−0.088
Tier 3	0.003	−0.027	0.078	−0.025	−0.057	−0.136
All tiers	−0.011	−0.019	0.074	0.007	−0.050	−0.134
Private sector only						
All tiers	−0.001	−0.004	0.040	−0.004	−0.024	−0.134
Public sector only						
All tiers	−0.107	−0.123	0.210	0.059	−0.181	−0.208
			B. Women			
Public and private sectors						
Tier 1	−0.018	−0.047	0.036	−0.068	−0.042	−0.037
Tier 2	0.031	−0.040	0.049	0.042	−0.044	−0.094
Tier 3	−0.001	−0.122	−0.063	−0.092	−0.024	−0.097
All tiers	−0.002	−0.051	0.008	−0.064	−0.029	−0.064
Private sector only						
All tiers	−0.005	0.038	0.006	−0.063	0.019	−0.054
Public sector only						
All tiers	0.010	−0.180	0.005	−0.075	−0.071	−0.133

[a]Estimated by fitting a weighted linear regression of the change in union status to the change in variance of wages for the four union histories. See text for more details.

compared in figure 3.3 (the estimates for the United States are in row 5 of table 3.8). As in the case of the wage gap, the estimated variance gaps follow similar patterns in Canada and in the United States. In both countries, the estimated variance gaps tend to be larger for high-skill men than for low-skill men.

3.5 The Overall Impact of Unions on Wage Inequality

This section uses the fixed effect, or selection-adjusted, estimates to calculate the impact of unions on the overall variance of wages. Following the discussion in section 3.2, the effect of unions on the overall variance of wages can be divided in three parts: (1) the effect of unions on the relative position of each skill group in the wage distribution; (2) the effect of unions on the between-sector variance of wages in a skill group, averaged over skill groups; and (3) the effect of unions on the within-sector variance of wages in a skill group, averaged over skill groups. The formulas (6), (7′), and (8) can be thus be used directly to compute these effects by replacing the general skill categories x by an index G for the three tiers defined above (G = lower tier, middle tier, and upper tier). These formulas depend on the nonunion wage $w^N(G)$, the unionization rate $\bar{U}(G)$, the union wage gap $\Delta_w(G)$, the union variance gap $\Delta_v(G)$, and the unadjusted wage gap $\bar{\Delta}_w(G)$. For Canada, estimates of $\bar{U}(x)$, $\Delta_w(x)$, $\Delta_v(x)$, and $\bar{\Delta}_w(x)$ are available from tables 3.3–3.5 and 3C.1, while $w^N(G)$ is obtained from the formula $w^N(G) = \bar{w}(G) - \bar{U}(G)\Delta_w(G)$ ($\bar{w}(G)$ is the average wage in the tier).

The calculations of the overall impact of unions on the variance of wages in Canada are reported in table 3.6 for men and in table 3.7 for women. For both men and women, the effect of unions on the within-sector variance of wages (row 6) is smaller than the effect of unions on the between-sector variance (row 7) in the lower tier. The reverse holds in the middle tier and the upper tier. Unions thus reduce the within-tier variance of wages by 0.029 for men and by 0.003 for women (row 8). In the case of men, unions also reduce the between-tier (across skill groups) variance of wages by 0.011 (row 9). The total impact of unions on the variance of wages is thus equal to −0.040, which represents a 14.5 percent reduction in the overall variance of wages.

As mentioned before, the impact of unions on the relative position of the

Table 3.6 Effects of Unions on Wage Inequality: Men in Canada

	Tier 1	Tier 2	Tier 3	All
1. Unionization rate ($\bar{U}_G$)	38.2	40.3	50.5	46.3
2. Mean log wage				
Nonunion	2.010	2.312	2.597	2.305
Union	2.407	2.534	2.713	2.550
Unadjusted wage gap ($\bar{\Delta}_{wG}$)	0.397	0.222	0.116	0.245
3. Standard deviation of log wages				
Nonunion	0.436	0.448	0.532	0.530
Union	0.371	0.335	0.383	0.383
4. Estimated union wage gap (Δ_{wG}, table 3C.1, col. 1)	0.242	0.248	0.064	—
5. Estimated union variance gap (Δ_{vG}, table 3.5, col. 6)	−0.052	−0.088	−0.136	—
Effect of unions on within-tier variance				
6. Effect on within-sector variance (row 1) * (row 5)	−0.020	−0.044	−0.069	−0.044
7. Effect on between-sector variance ($\bar{U}_G(1 - \bar{U}_G)[\bar{\Delta}^2_{wG} - (\bar{\Delta}_{wG} - \Delta_{wG})^2]$)	0.032	0.012	0.003	0.015
8. Total effect (row 6 + row 7)	0.012	−0.032	−0.066	−0.029
Effect of unions on between-tier variance				
9. ($\mathrm{Var}_G(\bar{U}_G\Delta_{wG}) + 2\mathrm{Cov}_G(w^N_G, \bar{U}_G\Delta_{wG})$)	—	—	—	−0.011
Total effect on variance of wages				
10. (row 8 + row 9)	—	—	—	−0.040

Table 3.7 **Effects of Unions on Wage Inequality: Women in Canada**

	Tier 1	Tier 2	Tier 3	All
1. Unionization rate (U_G)	27.0	33.6	53.4	26.4
2. Mean log wage				
Nonunion	1.748	1.904	2.165	1.934
Union	2.150	2.273	2.548	2.319
Unadjusted wage gap ($\bar{\Delta}_{wG}$)	0.402	0.369	0.373	0.375
3. Standard deviation of log wages				
Nonunion	0.395	0.437	0.496	0.466
Union	0.345	0.312	0.386	0.392
4. Estimated union wage gap (Δ_{wG}, table 3C.1, col. 1)	0.245	0.205	0.264	—
5. Estimated union variance gap (Δ_{wG}, table 3.5, col. 6)	−0.037	−0.094	−0.097	—
Effect of unions on within-tier variance				
6. Effect on within-sector variance (row 1) * (row 5)	−0.010	−0.032	−0.052	−0.031
7. Effect on between-sector variance ($\bar{U}_G(1 - \bar{U}_G)[\bar{\Delta}^2_{wG} - (\bar{\Delta}_{wG} - \Delta_{wG})^2]$)	0.027	0.024	0.031	0.028
8. Total effect (row 6 + row 7)	0.017	−0.008	−0.021	−0.003
Effect of unions on between-tier variance				
9. ($\mathrm{Var}_G(\bar{U}_G\Delta_{wG}) + 2\mathrm{Cov}_G(w^N_G, \bar{U}_G\Delta_{wG})$)	—	—	—	0.013
Total effect on variance of wages				
10. (row 8 + row 9)	—	—	—	0.009

tiers in the overall wage distribution is very different for men and women. For women, the union wage gap is more or less stable across tiers, and upper-tier women are disproportionately represented in the union sector. As a result, unions worsen the relative position of lower-tier women and increase the between-tier variance of wages by 0.013 (table 3.7, row 9). Overall, unions thus increase the variance of wages among women by 0.009, which represent 4.1 percent of the overall variance of wages. The finding that unions reduce the variance of wages of men but increase the variance of wages of women is robust to the choice of estimator of the variance gap. If longitudinal estimates of the variance gap were used instead of cross-sectional estimates, the estimated effect of unions on the variance of wages would become −0.013 (instead of −0.040) for men and 0.022 (instead of 0.009) for women.

The estimates can also be used to compute the overall effect of unions on the variance of wages of Canadian men and women pooled together. This effect depends on (1) the effect of unions on the variance of wages within men and within women, and (2) the effect of unions on the wage differential between men and women. The first component of the overall effect is simply the weighted sum of the effects reported in row 10 of tables 3.6 and 3.7. It is equal to −0.017, which represents a 6.1 percent reduction in the variance of wages. The second, or "between," component is given by

$$[s_m(\bar{w}_m - \bar{w})^2 + s_w(\bar{w}_w - \bar{w})^2] - [s_m(w_m^N - w^N)^2 + s_w(w_w^N - w^N)^2],$$

where s_m and s_w are the proportion of men and women in the work force, and $\bar{w}$ is the average wage for men and women. This component is equal to −0.002, which indicates that unions slightly improve the position of women relative to men in the wage distribution. Overall, unions thus reduce the variance of wages for Canadian men and women by 0.019 (0.017 plus 0.002).

Finally, the results for men in the United States are reported in table 3.8. These results are obtained by transforming the estimates reported in table 8 of Card (1992) by quintiles into estimates by tier. The relationship between the estimates by tier ($T1$ to $T3$) and the estimates by quintile ($Q1$ to $Q5$) is given by the weighted averages $T1 = .6Q1 + .4Q2$, $T2 = .2Q2 + .6Q3 + .2Q4$, and $T3 = .4Q4 + .6Q5$. As in the case of men in Canada, the effect of unions on the within-sector variance (−0.020) is larger than the effect on the between-sector variance (0.009). Unions thus reduce the average within-

Table 3.8 **Effects of Unions on Wage Inequality: Men in the United States**

	Tier 1	Tier 2	Tier 3	All
1. Unionization rate ($\bar{U}_G$)	26.2	30.9	21.7	26.4
2. Mean log wage				
Nonunion	1.973	2.276	2.636	2.274
Union	2.325	2.480	2.602	2.460
Unadjusted wage gap ($\bar{\Delta}_{wG}$)	0.352	0.204	−0.034	0.186
3. Standard deviation of log wages				
Nonunion	0.446	0.483	0.523	0.568
Union	0.362	0.342	0.362	0.380
4. Estimated union wage gap	0.232	0.142	0.067	—
5. Estimated union variance gap	−0.075	−0.038	−0.142	—
Effect of unions on within-tier variance				
6. Effect on within-sector variance (row 1) * (row 5)	−0.019	−0.010	−0.031	−0.020
7. Effect on between-sector variance ($\bar{U}_G(1 - \bar{U}_G)[\Delta^2_{wG} - (\bar{\Delta}_{wG} - \Delta_{wG})^2]$)	0.021	0.009	−0.003	0.009
8. Total effect (row 6 + row 7)	0.002	−0.000	−0.034	−0.009
Effect of unions on between-tier variance				
9. ($\mathrm{Var}_G(\bar{U}_G\Delta_{wG}) + 2\mathrm{Cov}_G(w^N_G, \bar{U}_G\Delta_{wG})$)	—	—	—	−0.010
Total effect on variance of wages				
10. (row 8 + row 9)	—	—	—	−0.019

Notes: The estimates were obtained by transforming the estimates reported in Card (1992) by quintiles into three tiers. The relationship between the estimates by tier ($T1$ to $T3$) and the estimates by quintile ($Q1$ to $Q5$) is given by the following weighted averages: $T1 = .6Q1 + .4Q2$, $T2 = .2Q2 + .6Q3 + .2Q4$, and $T3 = .4Q4 + .6Q5$.

tier variance of wages by 0.011. Unions also reduce the between-tier variance of wages by 0.008, for a total effect of −0.019, or 6.3 percent of the overall variance of wages.

3.6 Unions and Relative Wage Inequality in Canada and the United States

The results reported in table 3.8 indicate that unions reduce the variance of men's wages in the United States by 0.019, which is half of the estimated effect for Canada (0.040, table 3.6). The difference is mostly attributable to the larger effect of unions on the within-tier variance in Canada than in the United States. Authors such as Freeman (1991) and Card (1992) have argued that a significant fraction of the increase in wage inequality in the United States over the last two decades is attributable to the decline of unionism in the United States. Does the Canadian evidence support the view that wage inequality among men would be lower in the United States if American unions were "as strong" as Canadian unions? To answer this question, consider what would happen to wage inequality in the United States if the Canadian, as opposed to the U.S., distribution of unionism was to prevail, holding constant the U.S. wage structure. Alternatively, consider what would happen to wage inequality in Canada if the U.S., as opposed to the Canadian, distribution of unionism was to prevail, holding constant the Canadian wage structure. The results of these experiments are reported in table 3.9.

The first row of table 3.9 indicates that there is a gap of 0.050 between the actual variance of wages of men in Canada and in the United States. Row 4 indicates that if the extent of unionization in the United States were the same as in Canada, this gap would be reduced to 0.030. The gap would also be reduced to 0.030 if the extent of unionization in Canada was the same as in the United States (row 3). It would be reduced to 0.029 if there were no unions in either Canada or the United States (row 2). Taken together, these results suggest that differences in the pattern and extent of unionism in Canada and in the United States explain 40 percent of the difference in wage inequality of men between the two countries.

The results reported in column 1 also indicate that the variance of wages of Canadian women, unlike men, would be essentially unchanged if the unionization rate was the same as in the United States. This result is consistent with the overall finding that unions have a small, though positive, effect on the variance of wages of women.

The evidence from the Canada-U.S. comparison for men thus yields similar conclusions to the longitudinal comparison between the United States in the 1970s and in the late 1980s (Card 1992, and Freeman 1991). These studies find that deunionization in the United States between 1973 (or 1978) and 1987 accounts for 20 percent of the increase in wage inequality over that period. The unionization rate was relatively constant in Canada over the same period.

Table 3.9 **Relative Impact of Unions on Wage Inequality in Canada and in the United States**

	Women	Men		
	Canada (1)	Canada (2)	U.S. (3)	Difference between U.S. and Canada (4)
1. Actual variance of wages	0.228	0.234	0.284	0.050
2. Variance of wages that would prevail in the absence of unions[a]	0.219	0.274	0.303	0.029
3. Variance of wages that would prevail with U.S. unionism[b]	0.226	0.254	0.284	0.030
4. Variance of wages that would prevail with Canadian unionism[c]	0.228	0.234	0.264	0.030

[a]Actual variance of wages minus the estimated effect of unions on the variance of wages (tables 3.6–3.8, row 10).

[b]Actual variance of wages minus the effect of unions on the variance of wages calculated by replacing the actual unionization rates by the U.S. unionization rates in row 1 of table 3.5. The U.S. unionization rates for women are calculated from the 1986 CPS data used in tables 3.1 and 3.2 (11.7 percent in the lower tier, 15.4 percent in the middle tier, and 20.1 percent in the upper tier).

[c]Actual variance of wages minus the effect of unions on the variance of wages calculated by replacing the actual unionization rates by the Canadian unionization rates in row 1 of table 3.6.

Can changes in unionization rates between Canada and the United States explain the finding by Blackburn and Bloom (chap. 7 in this volume) that inequality in earnings increased by 0.034 in the United States but only by 0.018 in Canada over the 1979 to 1986 period? Although this paper does not provide direct evidence on that question, some back-of-the-envelope calculations can be made by combining some results from Riddell (chap. 4 in this volume) with the main findings of this paper. Table 4.1 in Riddell shows that the U.S. union density fell by 6 points relative to the Canadian density from 1980 to 1986. These 6 points represent a third of the gap in unionization rates between the two countries in 1986. Since the gap in unionization rates explains 0.020 of the gap in the variance of wages, a third of the unionization rate gap must explain a third of 0.020 (0.006 to 0.007). This represents 40 to 45 percent of the relative increase in earnings inequality of 0.016 (0.034 − 0.018) reported by Blackburn and Bloom. The strength of the union movement in Canada thus seems to be a major factor in explaining why wage inequality did not increase as quickly in Canada as it did in the United States.

From a social welfare perspective, these benefits of unionization do not necessarily come at no cost. As mentioned in section 3.2, unions may also cause efficiency losses by raising wages above their competitive level. Standard calculations indicate these losses are of the order of 0.2 percent of GNP in the United States and 0.5 percent of GNP in Canada.[28] These costs are small and would be even smaller if labor contracts were negotiated efficiently.[29] They nevertheless illustrate the tradeoff Canada would face if it were to move to more "U.S.-like" labor market institutions. GNP per capita would increase by 0.3 percent, but the variance of wages of men would increase by 8.5 percent (40 percent of 0.050/0.234).

3.7 Conclusion

The recent divergence in the extent of unionism in Canada and in the United States yields a unique opportunity to measure the impact of unionism on the distribution of wages using a comparative perspective. The major findings of the paper are the following:

1. Union relative wage effects are similar in Canada and in the United States. In the case of men, the union wage differential is negatively related to skills. This negative relationship is much less accentuated for women.
2. Private sector unionization is concentrated in the middle of the skill distribution, while public sector unionization is concentrated in the upper end of the skill distribution. This explains why unionization in Canada and among women is more skewed toward the upper end of the skill distribution.
3. The selection process into unionized jobs is different for men and women in Canada. For women, the permanent unobservable component of wages is positively correlated with the union status, while it is negatively correlated with the union status for men. This is particularly true in the public sector. There is no evidence of selection bias (on average) for men in the United States.
4. Unions reduce the within-sector variance of wages for both men and women.
5. Unions reduce the overall variance of wages by 14.5 percent for men in Canada and by 6.3 percent for men in the United States, but they increase the variance of wages of Canadian women by 4.1 percent. Differences in the pattern and extent of unionism in Canada and in the United States explain 40 percent of the difference in wage inequality of men between the two countries.

28. The efficiency losses computed over the three tiers are equal to $\Sigma\theta_G(.5\eta_G\Delta^2_{wG})$, where θ_j is a weight that represents the fraction of the total wage bill that goes to union workers in tier G ($\theta_G \approx [\bar{w}(G)/\bar{w}]\bar{U}(G)/3$). The labor demand elasticities η_G chosen for the calculations are .5 in the upper tier, .75 in the middle tier, and 1 in the lower tier.

29. The efficiency loss in the monopoly model of union occurs because the negotiated outcome is not Pareto efficient. This result is very sensitive, however, to the assumption that unions cannot bargain over employment. Labor contracts are said to be efficient when the firm and the union bargain over wage and employment simultaneously. Under the strong version of efficient contracts (Brown and Ashenfelter 1986), the negotiated wage is purely an instrument to redistribute rents between the parties. Unions cause neither efficiency losses nor employment distortions.

These findings shed new light on the role of unions in the relative distribution of wages of men and women in Canada and in the United States. More remains to be learned, however, on why unions have such a different impact on the wage distribution of men and women. A more thorough analysis of the role of unions in the provision of nonwage benefits such as maternity leaves and the role of unions in promoting wage equity in the workplace could shed considerable light on these issues. It would also be interesting to measure more directly the impact of unions on changes in wage inequality in Canada during the eighties.

Appendix A
Data

A Comparison of the LMAS and CPS Samples

The wage data used for Canada and the United States are based on supplements to very similar labor force surveys (the LFS in Canada and the CPS in the United States). The structures of the supplements are quite different, however. The Canadian LMAS is based on a work history that asks workers about all the jobs they held during the previous year. By contrast, the outgoing rotation group supplement of the CPS asks people about the job they held during the week of the survey. In both surveys, the earnings questions refer to usual, as opposed to actual, earnings and hours. The earnings in the LMAS may nevertheless be more noisy than in the CPS because of the recall bias problem.

On the one hand, the sampling frame for *jobs* (but not individuals) is different in the two samples, since the CPS is only a snap shot while the LMAS captures all the jobs held during the year. Short-duration jobs are thus more likely to be captured in the LMAS. On the other hand, the LMAS sample used in the cross-sectional analysis is limited to one job per person, and to jobs lasting at least four weeks. These sample selection criteria reduce the probability of sampling a short-duration job and thus make the LMAS sample more comparable to the CPS sample.

Another difference between the two samples is that earnings are top coded at 999$ a week in the CPS, while there is essentially no top coding in the LMAS.[30] In addition, only unallocated wages are used in the CPS, while all wages are used in the LMAS because there are no allocation flags in the LMAS.

The nature of the longitudinal data used is also quite different in the two

30. The LMAS user's guide indicates that "two records with total earnings from all jobs in 1986 in excess of $150,000 have had their hourly wage rates reduced to values which yield totals close to 150,000$."

surveys. The longitudinal CPS sample is obtained by matching people interviewed twice in one year (rotation groups 4 and 8). The matching is imperfect, and the measurement error in changes in the union status variable is substantial for the reasons mentioned in section 3.4. Card (1992) handles the measurement error problem by using additional information from the CPS validation study. The longitudinal LMAS sample is discussed in the main text.

Description of the Variables Used

The public use sample of the LMAS contains only bracketed information on age and education. This explains why the continuous version of these variables is not used in the analysis. The CPS age and education variables were grouped in these five categories to make them comparable with the LMAS data. The seven industry categories used in table 3.2 are primary industries, manufacturing, construction, transportation and communication, trade, services, and government (including health and education). The eight occupation categories are managers, professionals, nurses, clerical workers, sales workers, service workers, manual workers, and craft workers. The first six categories are considered white-collar workers, while the last two categories are considered blue-collar workers.

Appendix B

A Regression-based Approach to Analyze the Patterns of Unionization and Wages

Figures 3.1 and 3.2 indicate how $\bar{U}(x)$ and $\Delta_w(x)$ depend on a particular function of worker's characteristics, namely the estimated nonunion wage index. Similar findings are obtained using a regression-based approach that describes how $w^N(x)$, $\bar{U}(x)$, and $\Delta_w(x)$ jointly depend on worker, job, and location characteristics. Most of this analysis is limited to the case of Canada.

Table 3B.1 reports the differences in nonunion wages, unionization rates, and the union wage gap associated with changes in various individual characteristics of workers, when all other characteristics are held constant at their sample mean. The first row of the table gives average values of the three outcome variables by gender. Subsequent rows show the deviations from the overall means associated with a particular characteristic (e.g., age 20–24) *holding constant* all other characteristics. For simplicity, these deviations are called excess predicted nonunion wages, union rates, or union wage gaps.

The entries in table 3B.1 are calculated on the basis of separate wage regressions fit to the union and nonunion sectors. These regressions include the explanatory variables listed in table 3B.1 plus a full set of interactions between age and education dummies. The pattern of results for age and educa-

Table 3B.1 **Excess Nonunion Wage, Excess Union Density, and Excess Wage Gap by Demographic Characteristics and Job Characteristics in Canada**

	Men			Women		
	Excess Nonunion Wage (1)	Excess Density (2)	Excess Wage Gap (3)	Excess Nonunion Wage (4)	Excess Density (5)	Excess Wage Gap (6)
Average	2.361	0.463	0.136	2.006	0.379	0.211
	(0.005)	(0.003)	(0.007)	(0.005)	(0.003)	(0.008)
Age						
20–24	−0.233	−0.063	0.066	−0.127	−0.034	0.014
	(0.012)	(0.010)	(0.019)	(0.009)	(0.008)	(0.016)
25–34	−0.039	−0.002	0.017	0.029	0.008	−0.010
	(0.007)	(0.005)	(0.010)	(0.006)	(0.005)	(0.009)
35–44	0.102	0.011	−0.038	0.051	0.018	−0.012
	(0.008)	(0.006)	(0.010)	(0.007)	(0.005)	(0.010)
45–54	0.101	0.023	−0.039	0.022	0.004	0.006
	(0.011)	(0.008)	(0.015)	(0.010)	(0.008)	(0.016)
55–64	0.014	0.027	0.015	−0.054	−0.028	0.041
	(0.017)	(0.012)	(0.024)	(0.016)	(0.013)	(0.028)
Education						
Primary	−0.159	−0.014	0.041	−0.140	−0.031	0.012
	(0.014)	(0.010)	(0.020)	(0.016)	(0.014)	(0.031)
High school	−0.053	0.007	0.018	−0.057	−0.001	−0.011
	(0.005)	(0.003)	(0.006)	(0.004)	(0.003)	(0.006)
More than high school	0.007	0.007	−0.019	−0.025	−0.006	0.010
	(0.013)	(0.010)	(0.020)	(0.013)	(0.011)	(0.024)
Some postsecondary	0.070	0.002	0.006	0.069	0.006	0.020
	(0.011)	(0.008)	(0.014)	(0.009)	(0.007)	(0.013)
University	0.254	−0.018	−0.094	0.216	0.019	0.001
	(0.013)	(0.010)	(0.018)	(0.013)	(0.010)	(0.019)
Mother tongue						
English	0.007	−0.011	−0.001	0.006	−0.005	−0.005
	(0.005)	(0.004)	(0.007)	(0.005)	(0.004)	(0.007)
French	−0.011	0.011	0.011	−0.003	0.014	0.020
	(0.012)	(0.009)	(0.016)	(0.011)	(0.009)	(0.017)
Others	−0.010	0.023	−0.014	−0.017	−0.005	−0.015
	(0.014)	(0.010)	(0.018)	(0.012)	(0.010)	(0.006)
Race						
White	0.004	0.002	0.000	−0.002	0.002	0.006
	(0.001)	(0.001)	(0.002)	(0.001)	(0.001)	(0.002)
Nonwhite	−0.060	−0.032	−0.007	0.024	−0.031	−0.093
	(0.014)	(0.016)	(0.030)	(0.020)	(0.016)	(0.031)
Marital status						
Single	−0.080	−0.011	0.043	−0.008	−0.006	0.000
	(0.008)	(0.006)	(0.010)	(0.006)	(0.005)	(0.009)
Married	0.028	0.004	−0.015	0.004	0.003	−0.000
	(0.003)	(0.002)	(0.004)	(0.003)	(0.002)	(0.004)

Table 3B.1 (continued)

	Men			Women		
	Excess Nonunion Wage (1)	Excess Density (2)	Excess Wage Gap (3)	Excess Nonunion Wage (4)	Excess Density (5)	Excess Wage Gap (6)
Province						
Newfoundland	−0.109	0.008	−0.067	−0.112	0.053	0.003
	(0.017)	(0.012)	(0.022)	(0.017)	(0.013)	(0.024)
Prince Edward Island	−0.131	−0.032	−0.019	−0.097	−0.022	0.030
	(0.023)	(0.018)	(0.033)	(0.021)	(0.017)	(0.032)
Nova Scotia	−0.093	−0.046	−0.013	−0.075	−0.043	−0.041
	(0.014)	(0.011)	(0.020)	(0.013)	(0.011)	(0.021)
New Brunswick	−0.090	−0.037	0.026	−0.104	−0.039	0.051
	(0.014)	(0.010)	(0.019)	(0.013)	(0.010)	(0.020)
Quebec	−0.019	0.095	0.020	0.014	0.079	−0.018
	(0.010)	(0.007)	(0.013)	(0.010)	(0.007)	(0.013)
Ontario	0.046	−0.014	−0.008	0.032	−0.060	−0.001
	(0.008)	(0.006)	(0.010)	(0.007)	(0.006)	(0.011)
Manitoba	−0.068	−0.034	0.059	−0.019	−0.001	0.009
	(0.015)	(0.011)	(0.021)	(0.014)	(0.010)	(0.020)
Saskatchewan	0.019	−0.001	−0.014	−0.006	0.043	0.024
	(0.014)	(0.010)	(0.018)	(0.012)	(0.009)	(0.018)
Alberta	0.073	−0.083	−0.020	0.068	−0.028	−0.018
	(0.010)	(0.007)	(0.014)	(0.009)	(0.007)	(0.014)
British Columbia	0.095	0.082	0.022	0.054	0.053	0.008
	(0.014)	(0.009)	(0.017)	(0.012)	(0.009)	(0.017)
Part-time status						
Full-time	0.007	0.004	−0.007	−0.002	0.010	−0.004
	(0.001)	(0.001)	(0.001)	(0.002)	(0.002)	(0.004)
Part-time	−0.118	−0.072	0.125	0.006	−0.027	0.011
	(0.016)	(0.013)	(0.025)	(0.007)	(0.005)	(0.010)
Firm size						
Less than 20	−0.116	−0.213	0.051	−0.090	−0.172	−0.001
	(0.007)	(0.006)	(0.013)	(0.006)	(0.005)	(0.013)
20–99	−0.054	−0.086	0.021	−0.008	−0.024	0.002
	(0.009)	(0.007)	(0.013)	(0.009)	(0.007)	(0.014)
100–499	0.020	0.047	−0.011	0.044	0.087	−0.018
	(0.012)	(0.008)	(0.015)	(0.012)	(0.008)	(0.015)
500 and more	0.099	0.124	−0.049	0.084	0.121	−0.022
	(0.007)	(0.004)	(0.009)	(0.007)	(0.005)	(0.010)
Don't know	−0.020	0.073	0.026	−0.032	0.027	0.061
	(0.011)	(0.007)	(0.014)	(0.010)	(0.007)	(0.014)
Tenure (years)						
Less than 1	−0.134	−0.084	0.024	−0.131	−0.076	0.039
	(0.009)	(0.007)	(0.014)	(0.008)	(0.006)	(0.013)
1–5	−0.030	−0.045	−0.002	−0.034	−0.032	0.009
	(0.006)	(0.005)	(0.009)	(0.005)	(0.004)	(0.008)
5 and more	0.062	0.054	−0.006	0.098	0.068	−0.028
	(0.005)	(0.003)	(0.006)	(0.005)	(0.004)	(0.008)

(continued)

Table 3B.1 (continued)

	Men			Women		
	Excess Nonunion Wage (1)	Excess Density (2)	Excess Wage Gap (3)	Excess Nonunion Wage (4)	Excess Density (5)	Excess Wage Gap (6)
Occupation						
Managers	0.136	−0.253	−0.048	0.169	−0.168	−0.073
	(0.011)	(0.009)	(0.018)	(0.015)	(0.012)	(0.026)
Professional	0.029	−0.072	−0.006	0.065	0.037	0.050
	(0.015)	(0.011)	(0.021)	(0.019)	(0.012)	(0.026)
Nurses	−0.060	0.024	−0.067	0.165	0.055	−0.088
	(0.059)	(0.029)	(0.066)	(0.020)	(0.012)	(0.026)
Clerical	−0.064	0.010	−0.048	0.027	−0.055	−0.046
	(0.018)	(0.012)	(0.023)	(0.012)	(0.009)	(0.019)
Sales	−0.003	−0.150	−0.033	−0.057	−0.090	0.001
	(0.015)	(0.013)	(0.030)	(0.016)	(0.014)	(0.037)
Service	−0.161	−0.047	0.055	−0.198	−0.026	0.079
	(0.014)	(0.010)	(0.019)	(0.013)	(0.010)	(0.022)
Manual workers	−0.030	0.096	0.029	−0.073	0.353	0.101
	(0.008)	(0.006)	(0.012)	(0.092)	(0.068)	(0.151)
Craft workers	0.061	0.132	−0.014	−0.038	0.387	0.165
	(0.011)	(0.008)	(0.015)	(0.119)	(0.090)	(0.190)
Industry						
Primary	0.165	−0.139	−0.061	0.194	−0.288	0.069
	(0.017)	(0.014)	(0.028)	(0.034)	(0.031)	(0.097)
Manufacturing	0.029	−0.033	−0.036	0.017	−0.251	−0.078
	(0.013)	(0.009)	(0.018)	(0.055)	(0.041)	(0.090)
Construction	0.052	−0.108	0.138	0.126	−0.225	−0.176
	(0.020)	(0.016)	(0.031)	(0.030)	(0.028)	(0.126)
Transportation and	−0.008	0.042	0.052	0.078	0.122	0.094
communication	(0.015)	(0.010)	(0.019)	(0.022)	(0.014)	(0.029)
Trade	−0.096	−0.159	0.015	−0.100	−0.172	0.055
	(0.010)	(0.009)	(0.018)	(0.010)	(0.008)	(0.022)
Services	−0.071	−0.129	−0.061	−0.027	−0.164	−0.031
	(0.016)	(0.013)	(0.029)	(0.011)	(0.008)	(0.020)
Public sector	0.015	0.301	−0.001	0.040	0.256	0.012
	(0.016)	(0.011)	(0.023)	(0.011)	(0.008)	(0.017)

Sources: Data from the 1986 cross-sectional file and the 1986–87 longitudinal file of the LMAS.

Note: The excess nonunion wage for a given value of a characteristic is the difference between the predicted wage of a worker with that value of the characteristic, holding all other characteristics at their observed frequency distributions, and the mean wage in the sample.

tion is similar to the pattern uncovered in figures 3.1 and 3.2. The excess wage gap is inversely proportional to the excess nonunion wage (skills) for men, but remains more or less constant for women. Table 3B.1 also shows the relationship among the excess predicted values of $w^N(x)$, $U(x)$, and $\Delta_w(x)$ for a variety of other worker, job, and location characteristics.

The estimates in table 3B.1 are summarized in table 3B.2 by looking at the impact of unions on a selected number of wage differentials. Similar regressions are estimated using the CPS sample for the United States except that mother tongue is not included in those regressions. These union wage gaps are calculated by adding the average wage gap to excess wage gaps like the ones reported in table 3B.1 (the wage gaps used are similar but not identical to those in table 3B.1, since the underlying regressions are more parsimonious).

The results indicate that unions reduce the university–high school differential for men in Canada and the United States, but increase it for women in Canada. This is simply a restatement in regression terms of the findings illustrated in figures 3.1 and 3.2 (unions help more high-skill women than low-skill women, especially in Canada). Unions also tend to help public sector workers and blue-collar workers relative to private sector and white-collar workers. Unions also revert the small wage disadvantage of French speakers relative to English speakers in Canada, mostly because of the high unionization rates in Quebec. Finally, unions increase the wage differential between

Table 3B.2 Effect of Unions on Selected Wage Differentials

	Canada		U.S.	
	Men (1)	Women (2)	Men (3)	Women (4)
Mature workers (35–44) versus young workers (20–24)				
Wage differential	0.399	0.265	0.378	0.280
Effect of unions	−0.035	−0.005	0.027	0.025
University graduates versus high school graduates				
Wage differential	0.393	0.353	0.399	0.412
Effect of unions	−0.054	0.076	−0.065	0.003
White versus nonwhite				
Wage differential	0.098	−0.023	0.147	0.071
Effect of unions	0.022	0.046	−0.019	−0.021
White-collar versus blue-collar				
Wage differential	−0.042	0.008	0.056	0.096
Effect of unions	−0.040	0.003	−0.060	−0.044
Public sector versus private sector				
Wage differential	0.032	0.117	−0.003	0.073
Effect of unions	0.044	0.132	0.032	0.051
English-speaking versus French-speaking				
Wage differential	0.023	0.027	—	—
Effect of unions	−0.037	−0.057	—	—

Notes: These effects are found by estimating separate wage regressions for union and nonunion workers: the covariates used are the age dummies, the education dummies, the region dummies, and dummy variables for marital status, part-time status, race, blue-collar, public sector, and mother tongue (only for Canada). The regressions are used to calculate a union wage gap Δ_w for each category of worker listed in the table. The effect of unions on the wage differential between two groups A and B is simply $\bar{U}_A\Delta_{wA} - \bar{U}_B\Delta_{wB}$.

whites and nonwhites in Canada. This goes in opposite direction to what is typically found in the United States (here and in Ashenfelter 1972).

Appendix C
Robustness of the First-Differenced Estimates

Detailed first-differenced estimates for union joiners and union leavers are reported in columns 2 and 3 of table 3C.1 for men and women in Canada. The results reported in columns 1–5 are obtained by fitting first-differenced regressions that do not include controls for job characteristics. More precisely, consider the following wage equation in which control variables are omitted for the sake of clarity:

$$w_{it} = \gamma_t + U_{it}\Delta_w + \theta_i + \varepsilon_{it},$$

where γ_t is a time effect, θ_i is a time-invariant person-specific effect (fixed effect), and Δ_w is the union wage gap. The first-differenced version of this equation is

$$\Delta w_{it} = \Delta\gamma_t + \Delta U_{it}\Delta_w + \Delta\varepsilon_{it}.$$

OLS estimates of the first-differenced version of the wage equation yield consistent estimates of Δ_w even when θ_i is correlated with the union coverage variable U_{it}. Separate wage gap estimates Δ_w^{01} for union joiners ($U_{i1} = 0$ and $U_{i2} = 1$) and Δ_w^{10} for union leavers ($U_{i1} = 1$ and $U_{i2} = 0$) are obtained by fitting the following regression:

$$\Delta w_{it} = \Delta\gamma_t + U_i^{01}\Delta_w^{01} - U_i^{10}\Delta_w^{10} + \Delta\varepsilon_{it},$$

where U_i^{01} is an indicator variable equal to one for union joiners, while U_i^{10} is an indicator variable equal to one for union leavers.

Column 6 reproduces the estimates that were reported in tables 3.3 and 3.4, with job characteristics included as regressors. Job characteristics are not used in columns 1–5 for the sake of comparison with the results of Card (1992), and because there are few degrees of freedom available in the small samples of union joiners, union leavers, and dual-job holders. On the one hand, it is preferable to include job characteristics in the regression when we try to measure the union wage gap for the same kind of workers holding the same kind of jobs. This may be particularly important when involuntary job leavers are concentrated in few particular industries, for example, because of industrial restructuring. On the other hand, jobs are choice variables, and it is not clear they should be included in the definition of *skills* used for the analysis by tier. In any case, whether or not job characteristics are included in the regressions does not affect the substance of the results.

Table 3C.1 Robustness of First-Differenced Estimated for Canada

	Demographic Controls Only					Demographic and Job Controls
	Involuntary Job Changers					
	All (1)	Union Joiners[a] (2)	Union Leavers[a] (3)	All Changers (4)	Dual-Job Holders (5)	All Involuntary Job Changers (6)
			A. Men			
Public and private pooled						
Tier 1	0.242	0.209	0.270	0.243	0.219	0.207
	(0.034)	(0.054)	(0.048)	(0.025)	(0.079)	(0.035)
Tier 2	0.248	0.288	0.217	0.221	0.580	0.220
	(0.036)	(0.058)	(0.051)	(0.029)	(0.082)	(0.038)
Tier 3	0.064	0.060	0.068	0.064	0.636	0.006
	(0.055)	(0.090)	(0.079)	(0.040)	(0.106)	(0.059)
All tiers	0.204	0.202	0.207	0.196	0.376	0.163
	(0.034)	(0.037)	(0.033)	(0.017)	(0.052)	(0.024)
Private sector only						
All tiers	0.207	0.201	0.206	0.210	0.380	0.162
	(0.026)	(0.042)	(0.036)	(0.019)	(0.067)	(0.026)
Public sector only						
All tiers	0.191	0.195	0.205	0.126	0.347	0.166
	(0.050)	(0.074)	(0.072)	(0.039)	(0.090)	(0.050)
Observations	1,559	1,559		2,789	425	1,559
			B. Women			
Public and private pooled						
Tier 1	0.245	0.254	0.236	0.238	0.319	0.190
	(0.035)	(0.053)	(0.052)	(0.026)	(0.057)	(0.037)
Tier 2	0.205	0.198	0.212	0.197	0.371	0.077
	(0.046)	(0.070)	(0.070)	(0.032)	(0.097)	(0.051)
Tier 3	0.264	0.380	0.157	0.254	0.255	0.191
	(0.049)	(0.077)	(0.073)	(0.036)	(0.054)	(0.054)
All tiers	0.240	0.281	0.200	0.233	0.308	0.167
	(0.025)	(0.038)	(0.037)	(0.018)	(0.038)	(0.026)
Private sector only						
All tiers	0.256	0.244	0.223	0.224	0.416	0.186
	(0.035)	(0.052)	(0.055)	(0.024)	(0.063)	(0.037)
Public sector only						
All tiers	0.197	0.289	0.147	0.204	0.182	0.150
	(0.035)	(0.052)	(0.048)	(0.026)	(0.049)	(0.035)
Observations	1,268	1,268		2,789	425	1,268

[a]These estimates are obtained by estimating a first-differenced version of a wage equation in which the union coverage variable is interacted with dummy variables for whether the worker is a union leaver or a union joiner. There are 141 union joiners and 188 union leavers among the sample of men, while there are 137 union joiners and 145 union leavers among the sample of women.

In the case of men, the wage gap estimates for union joiners (0.202) and union leavers (0.207) are nearly identical when all skill groups are pooled. The estimated wage gaps differ more substantially for women (0.281 and 0.200). First-differenced estimates for the sample of all job changers, as opposed to involuntary changers only, are reported in column 4. The wage gap estimates for that sample are very similar to the estimates for the sample of involuntary changers only. Finally, the first-differenced procedure is applied to an alternative sample of dual-job holders. This sample consists of workers who hold two jobs simultaneously over a period of at least four weeks at any time in 1986–87. The job on which the worker usually spends the most hours per week is classified as the main job; the other job is classified as the secondary job. An alternative wage gap estimate is thus obtained by fitting the difference in wages on the two jobs to the differences in the characteristics of the two jobs, including the union coverage status. The results are reported in column 5.

Consider the results for all tiers together. The wage gap estimates based on the sample of dual-job holders are larger (0.376 for men, 0.308 for women) than any of the wage gap estimates based on samples of job changers. They also imply that men are negatively selected into the union sector, while women are positively selected into the union sector, as was found in tables 3.3 and 3.4. More research is nevertheless needed to explain why these wage gap estimates are as large as they are.

References

Abowd, John, and Henry S. Farber. 1982. Job Queues and the Union Status of Workers. *Industrial and Labor Relations Review* 35 (April): 354–67.

Ashenfelter, Orley. 1972. Racial Discrimination in Trade Unions. *Journal of Political Economy* 80 (May/June): 435–64.

Brown, James, and Orley Ashenfelter. 1986. Testing the Efficiency of Employment Contracts. *Journal of Political Economy* 94 (June): S40–S87.

Card, David. 1992. The Effect of Unions on the Distribution of Wages: Redistribution or Relabelling? NBER Working Paper no. 4195. Cambridge, Mass.: National Bureau of Economics Research, October.

Chamberlain, Gary. 1982. Multivariate Regression Models for Panel Data. *Journal of Econometrics* 18 (January): 5–46.

Evans, M. G., and R. L. Clark. 1986. The Effect of Unionization on Wages: Some Canadian Evidence. *Relations Industrielles* 41 (Fall): 572–77.

Freeman, Richard. 1980. Unionism and the Dispersion of Wages. *Industrial and Labor Relations Review* 34 (October): 3–23.

———. 1984. Longitudinal Analyses of the Effects of Trade Unions. *Journal of Labor Economics* 2 (January): 1–26.

———. 1991. How Much Has De-unionization Contributed to the Rise in Male Earnings Inequality? NBER Working Paper no. 3826. Cambridge, MA: National Bureau of Economic Research, August.

Freeman, Richard B., and James L. Medoff. 1984. *What Do Unions Do?* New York: Basic Books.

Grant, E. Kenneth, Robert Swidinsky, and John Vanderkamp. 1987. Canadian Union-Nonunion Wage Differentials. *Industrial and Labor Relations Review* 41 (October): 93–107.

Harberger, Arnold C. 1971. Three Basic Postulates for Applied Welfare Analysis: An Interpretive Essay. *Journal of Economic Literature* 9 (September): 785–97.

Johnson, Harry G., and Peter Mieszkowski. 1970. The Effects of Unionization on the Distribution of Income: A General Equilibrium Approach. *Quarterly Journal of Economics* 84 (November): 539–61.

Krueger, Alan B., and Lawrence H. Summers. 1988. Efficiency Wages and the Inter-industry Wage Structure. *Econometrica* 56 (March): 259–94.

Kumar, Pradeep. 1988. Estimates of Unionism and Collective Bargaining Coverage in Canada. *Relations Industrielles* 43 (Winter): 757–79.

Kumar, Pradeep, and Thanasis Stengos. 1985. Measuring the Union Relative Wage Impact: A Methodological Note. *Canadian Journal of Economics* 18 (February): 182–89.

———. 1986. Interpreting the Wage Gap Estimate from Selectivity Correction Techniques Using Micro Data. *Economic Letters* 20:191–95.

Labour Canada. 1991. *Women in the Labour Force, 1990–91 Edition.* Ottawa: Ministry of Supply and Services.

Lemieux, Thomas. 1992. Estimating the Effects of Unions on Wage Inequality in a Two-Sector Model with Comparative Advantage and Non-random Selection. Princeton University, mimeo, May.

Lewis, H. Gregg. 1986. *Union Relative Wage Effects: A Survey.* Chicago: University of Chicago Press.

Maki, Dennis, and Ignace Ng. 1990. Effects of Trade Unions on the Earnings Differential between Males and Females. *Canadian Journal of Economics* 23 (May): 305–11.

Okun, Arthur M. 1975. *Equality and Efficiency: The Big Tradeoff.* Washington, DC: Brookings Institution.

Rees, Albert. 1963. The Effects of Unions on Resources Allocation. *Journal of Law and Economics* 6 (October): 69–78.

Robinson, Chris. 1989. The Joint Determination of Union Status and Union Wage Effects: Some Tests of Alternative Models. *Journal of Political Economy* 97 (June): 639–67.

Robinson, Chris, and Nigel Tomes. 1984. Union Wage Differentials in Public and Private Sectors: A Simultaneous Equations Specification. *Journal of Labor Economics* 2 (January): 106–27.

Rosen, Sherwin. 1969. Trade Union Power, Threat Effects, and the Extent of Organization. *Review of Economic Studies* 36 (April): 185–96.

Simpson, Wayne. 1985. The Impact of Unions on the Structure of Canadian Wages: An Empirical Analysis with Micro Data. *Canadian Journal of Economics* 18 (February): 106–27.

Statistics Canada. 1986. *Labour Market Activity.* Micro Data Set. Ottawa.

———. 1988. *Labour Market Activity Survey: Microdata Data User's Guide.* Ottawa: Statistics Canada.

Swidinsky, Robert, and M. Kupferschmidt. 1991. Longitudinal Estimates of the Union Effect on Wages, Wage Dispersion, and Pension Fringe Benefits. *Relations Industrielles* 46 (Winter): 819–33.

4 Unionization in Canada and the United States: A Tale of Two Countries

W. Craig Riddell

It was the best of times, it was the worst of times.
Charles Dickens, *A Tale of Two Cities*

"Similar but different" provides a succinct yet reasonably accurate summary of many dimensions of life in Canada and the United States. This description certainly applies to the role played by unions and collective bargaining in the two societies. Countries vary greatly in their industrial relations systems—the legal and institutional arrangements affecting labor-management relations—and in the context of the differences among such countries as Australia, Germany, France, Japan, Sweden, and the United Kingdom, the Canadian and U.S. industrial relations systems are very similar. Yet there are important differences. Perhaps the most significant of these is the substantial differential that has emerged in the past two to three decades in the extent of union organization in the two countries. The purpose of this paper is to examine this differential. I begin by describing the salient features of the extent of unionization in Canada and the United States. I proceed to examine possible explanations for the differences in unionization that have recently emerged, including the role that public policies pursued in the two countries may have played in this phenomenon.

4.1 The Broad Picture

Between 1920 and 1960 union growth in Canada exhibited a pattern broadly similar to that in the United States (see table 4.1 and figure 4.1). The

W. Craig Riddell is professor of economics at the University of British Columbia.

This paper was prepared for the U.S. and Canadian Labour Markets project sponsored by the Donner Foundation (U.S.) and the National Bureau of Economic Research. The author thanks Denise Doiron, Richard Freeman, Alan Krueger, Ian Macredie, Noah Meltz, Pradeep Kumar, and Anil Verma for helpful comments and Garry Barrett, Woo-Yung Kim, Tim Sargent, and Shaun Vahey for valuable research assistance. One of the data sets used in the paper is based on a survey carried out by Decima Research for the Canadian Federation of Labour (CFL). The author is grateful to the CFL for providing access to this survey and to Stephen Kiar (CFL) and Steven O'Malley (Decima) for their assistance in this regard. The analysis and conclusions are those of the author and do not necessarily reflect the views of the CFL or Decima Research.

Table 4.1 **Union Membership as a Percentage of Nonagricultural Paid Workers in Canada and the United States, 1920–90**

Year	Canada (1)	U.S. (2)	Canada (3)	U.S. (4)	Canada (5)
1920	16.0	17.6			
1925	14.4	12.8			
1930	13.9	12.7			
1935	14.5	13.5			
1940	16.3	22.5			
1945	24.2	30.4			
1950	28.4	31.7			
1955	33.7	31.8			
1960	32.3	28.6			
1965	29.7	30.1			30.0
1970	33.6	29.6			33.1
1975	35.6	28.9			32.2
1980	37.1	23.2			32.2
1981	36.7	22.6	34.2		32.9
1982	37.0	21.9	—		33.3
1983	37.9	20.7	—	20.4	35.7
1984	37.9	19.4	37.5	19.1	35.1
1985	38.1	—	—	18.3	34.4
1986	37.7	—	35.7	17.8	34.1
1987	37.0	—	—	17.0	33.3
1988	36.5	—	35.5	17.0	33.7
1989	36.2	—	—	16.4	34.1
1990	36.2		33.1	16.1	

Sources: Column 1: Labour Canada, *Directory of Labour Organizations in Canada 1990/91* (Ottawa: Ministry of Supply and Services). The 1950 observation is for 1951. 2. L. Troy and N. Sheflin, *Union Source Book: Membership, Finances, Structure, Directory* (West Orange, N.J.: Industrial Relations Data and Information Services, 1985). 3. Data from the following special supplements to Statistics Canada's Labour Force Survey: Survey of Work History (1981); Survey of Union Membership (1984); Labour Market Activity Survey (1986–90). These observations include union membership in agriculture and are expressed as a percentage of all paid workers. 4. U.S. Bureau of Labor Statistics, *Employment and Earnings,* various years. 5. Statistics Canada, *Corporations and Labor Unions Returns Act,* various years. Due to amendments to the act that became effective in 1983, the pre-1983 observations are not comparable to subsequent observations. See Statistics Canada (1992a, 43) for the impact of these amendments. These data include union membership in agriculture and are expressed as a percentage of all paid workers.

extent of union organization—as measured by the proportion of nonagricultural paid workers who are union members[1]—fell during the 1920s in both countries, bottoming out at 12 to 14 percent at the beginning of the Great Depression. Union density grew modestly during the early 1930s and then dramatically—from about 14 percent to over 30 percent—between 1935 and

1. Other measures of the extent of union organization—such as union membership as a percentage of paid workers or collective agreement coverage as a percentage of nonagricultural paid employment—display similar qualitative trends in both countries.

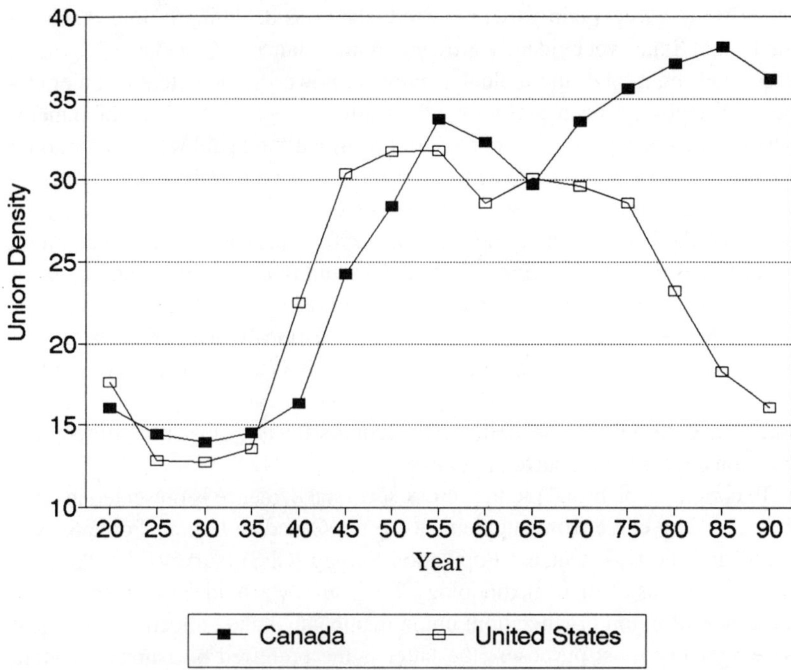

Fig. 4.1 Union density in the United States and Canada, 1920–90
Sources: See table 4.1.

the early 1950s. During this period union growth in Canada lagged behind that in the United States, possibly reflecting the later passage in Canada of the key legislation providing workers with the right to form and join unions.[2] Nonetheless, by 1952 the extent of union organization in Canada had caught up with that in the United States. Subsequently, union density declined in a parallel fashion in both countries. This period of slower growth in union membership than in the labor force was sharply reversed in Canada in the early 1960s but continued—indeed accelerated—in the United States. Thus for most of the past three decades, a growing gap has developed in the quantitative significance of unions and collective bargaining in the two societies (fig. 4.1).

Until recently, Dickens's characterization that "it was the best of times, it was the worst of times" seemed as apt a description of the state of unions and collective bargaining in the two countries of North America as of the cities of London and Paris during the French Revolution. The challenge for social

2. The key legislation in Canada, the National War Labour Order, Order-in-Council P.C. 1003, enacted in 1944, was to a considerable degree modeled on the U.S. National Labor Relations Act (Wagner Act) of 1935.

scientists was to explain why organized labor was declining in importance in the United States yet evidently growing in importance in Canada.

As both figure 4.1 and table 4.1 indicate, however, the extent of unionization in Canada has been declining, albeit slowly, since 1985 when union membership reached a peak of 38 percent of nonagricultural paid workers, or about 30 percent of the civilian labor force. Union density also declined during the 1980s in a number of other countries—including Japan, the Netherlands, Italy, and the United Kingdom (Freeman 1990). This suggests that a common set of forces may be affecting collective bargaining in several countries, albeit having an earlier and more dramatic impact in the United States.

Whether or not this is the case, two key questions remain. First, after following a broadly similar pattern over much of this century, why have the fortunes of the Canadian and American labor movements diverged dramatically since the early 1960s? Second, what accounts for the substantial differential in union coverage that currently exists?

To complete the broad picture, cross-sectional evidence is presented in table 4.2. The data come from supplements to the Canadian Labour Force Survey (LFS) and the U.S. Current Population Survey (CPS), surveys that are very similar in terms of their methodology. Each survey provides two measures of the extent of union organization: union membership and collective agreement coverage. For most purposes, the latter is the preferred measure. A feature common to Canadian and American labor legislation is the principle of exclusive jurisdiction, which states that, once certified, the union represents all workers in the bargaining unit, whether or not they are union members. Thus if the purpose of the extent of union organization variable is to measure the proportion of workers whose wages and working conditions are determined by collective bargaining, the preferred statistic is collective agreement coverage.

Table 4.2 shows this preferred measure of unionization disaggregated by age, sex, full-time and part-time employment, occupation, and industry. The remarkable feature revealed by these statistics is that union density in Canada is approximately double that in the United States across a wide range of industries, occupations, and types of workers. These tabulations suggest that a good rule of thumb is that in the United States the probability of any particular type of worker being represented by a union is about half that of the same type of worker in Canada. This observation suggests that the current differential in union coverage is a pervasive phenomenon that is not confined to specific segments of the labour force.

Inspection of table 4.2 also reveals that the Canada-U.S. unionization differential widened during the 1984–90 period. Union density declined in both countries, but more rapidly in the United States, and thus the ratio of Canadian to U.S. union coverage increased from 1.9 to 2.1. In addition, these data indicate that the extent to which Canadian union coverage exceeds that in the United States is often greatest (and is increasing most rapidly) in those seg-

Table 4.2 **Percentage of Employed Paid Workers Covered by a Collective Agreement by Age, Sex, Employment Status, Occupation, and Industry in Canada and the United States, 1984, 1986, and 1990**

	1984			1986			1990		
	Canada	U.S.	Ratio	Canada	U.S.	Ratio	Canada	U.S.	Ratio
Both sexes	41.8	21.6	1.9	39.9	19.9	2.0	37.6	18.3	2.1
16–24[a]	23.0	9.5	2.4	20.9	8.4	2.5	19.7	7.7	2.6
25–34	44.4	21.3	2.1	40.8	18.4	2.2	36.8	16.1	2.3
35–44	50.6	27.4	1.8	48.1	25.3	1.9	44.4	22.8	1.9
45–54	49.2	28.8	1.7	48.4	27.4	1.8	48.3	25.0	1.9
55–64	49.4	27.8	1.8	47.0	26.5	1.8	45.4	24.3	1.9
Males	46.0	25.7	1.8	43.7	23.7	1.8	40.5	21.4	1.9
16–24[a]	25.6	11.6	2.2	22.8	10.3	2.2	20.8	9.5	2.2
25–34	46.8	24.5	1.9	42.8	21.4	2.0	38.6	18.5	2.1
35–44	55.3	32.5	1.7	51.8	30.2	1.7	47.4	26.1	1.8
45–54	55.4	34.3	1.6	54.2	32.8	1.7	54.1	29.8	1.8
55–64	54.7	32.7	1.7	53.3	31.4	1.7	52.1	28.7	1.8
Females	36.6	16.8	2.2	35.2	15.5	2.3	34.3	14.9	2.3
16–24[a]	20.3	7.3	2.8	18.9	6.4	3.0	18.4	5.8	3.2
25–34	41.5	17.2	2.4	38.5	14.7	2.6	34.9	13.2	2.6
35–44	44.8	21.3	2.1	43.5	19.7	2.2	41.5	19.2	2.2
45–54	40.8	22.0	1.9	40.6	21.1	1.9	41.8	19.8	2.1
55–64	40.9	21.7	1.9	36.4	20.5	1.8	35.8	19.2	1.9
Full-time	45.5	24.5	1.9	43.2	22.5	1.9	40.0	20.5	2.0
Part-time	23.4	9.0	2.6	24.6	8.4	2.9	27.6	8.4	3.3
Occupation									
Managerial, professional, technical	47.0	19.6	2.4	43.0	18.1	2.4	42.7	17.4	2.5
Clerical	35.3	17.4	2.0	36.0	16.3	2.2	31.5	16.1	2.0
Sales	12.1	7.4	1.6	12.1	7.1	1.7	11.2	5.9	1.9
Service	32.1	17.2	1.9	33.2	15.9	2.1	32.3	15.6	2.1
Primary, except mining	24.6	6.4	3.8	18.4	6.9	2.7	19.6	5.5	3.6
Processing, machining, laborers	54.2	34.6	1.6	51.6	32.2	1.6	49.6	28.1	1.8
Transportation, moving	49.4	37.0	1.3	50.4	32.8	1.5	42.4	30.7	1.4
Materials handling	52.0	29.4	1.8	50.0	26.5	1.9	47.9	24.5	2.0
Industry									
Agriculture	2.8	3.3	0.8	5.4	2.9	1.9	6.7	2.1	3.2
Mining	36.5	19.8	1.8	38.2	19.1	2.0	40.9	20.2	2.0
Construction	42.3	24.8	1.7	37.1	23.4	1.6	35.2	22.2	1.6
Manufacturing	49.0	28.4	1.7	46.8	25.8	1.8	43.5	22.2	2.0
Durable	52.2	30.0	1.7	50.4	27.3	1.8	44.4	23.7	1.9
Nondurable	45.9	25.8	1.8	42.8	23.5	1.8	42.8	20.0	2.1
Transportation	58.4	39.4	1.5	55.9	36.4	1.5	51.5	34.1	1.5
Communication, utilities	71.5	45.4	1.6	72.3	40.7	1.8	66.2	38.3	1.7
Wholesale trade	16.2	9.5	1.7	16.5	8.2	2.0	14.2	7.3	1.9
Retail trade	15.9	8.7	1.8	15.8	7.7	2.1	15.6	6.9	2.3

(continued)

Table 4.2 (continued)

	1984			1986			1990		
	Canada	U.S.	Ratio	Canada	U.S.	Ratio	Canada	U.S.	Ratio
Finance, insurance, real estate	12.9	4.0	3.2	11.7	3.6	3.3	13.1	3.4	3.9
Services	43.4	8.8	4.9	41.1	7.8	5.3	38.8	7.1	5.5
Public administration	74.7	43.9	1.7	75.1	43.2	1.7	72.3	43.3	1.7

Sources: Statistics Canada, unpublished data from the 1984 Survey of Union Membership and the 1986 and 1990 Labour Market Activity Surveys, supplements to the Labour Force Survey; U.S. Bureau of Labor Statistics, *Employment and Earnings,* January 1985, January 1987, and January 1992.

[a]In Canada, 15–24 years.

ments of the labor force that are growing quickly and that have typically had low degrees of unionization: females (2.3 in 1990); part-time employment (3.3 in 1990, up from 2.6 in 1984); managerial, professional, and technical occupations (2.5 in 1990); service industries such as retail trade (2.3), finance, insurance, and real estate (3.9), and services (5.5). These observations suggest that Canadian unions have been more successful in organizing those segments of the labor force experiencing the greatest net growth in employment.

4.2 Alternative Explanations

The decline in U.S. union density in the past three decades has attracted considerable attention. This keen interest is certainly appropriate. Whether one believes it to be a good thing, a bad thing, or a bit of both, the substantial fall in union strength in the United States is one of the most significant social phenomena of the postwar period. Not all of the discussion has been about the causes of the decline in union strength—social scientists and others have also debated both the consequences of the decline and the role of public policies (e.g., labor law reform) to deal with consequences believed to be socially harmful (see, for example, Edwards 1986; Strauss, Gallagher, and Fiorito 1991; Weiler 1983, 1984). Nonetheless, a key aspect of any social phenomenon is understanding its origin(s); accordingly, there has been a good deal of research on the causes of the decline in unions in the United States (e.g., Dickens and Leonard 1985; Farber 1985, 1990; Freeman 1985, 1989; Neumann and Rissman 1984).

Much of the research initially focused exclusively on the United States. Beginning with Weiler (1983), however, the value of adopting a comparative Canada-U.S. perspective has increasingly been recognized. In particular, the many similarities between the two countries' economies and industrial relations systems may result in a situation with elements similar to a controlled experiment, thus perhaps enabling some explanations of the decline in unions in the United States to be rejected because these explanations cannot account for the observed behavior in Canada. As stated by Richard Freeman (1988, 69): "A persuasive explanation of the decline in union density in the United States should also explain why density did not decline in Canada in the same time period [1970–85]." For this reason, the various explanations examined in this paper are phrased in terms of their potential ability to account for both the decline in union density in the United States and the divergence in the extent of union organization between the United States and Canada.

Perhaps the most common explanation has to do with the changing structure of the economy and the labor force. Specifically, most of the employment changes that have occurred in the past three decades—away from manufacturing and toward services; away from blue-collar and toward white-collar; away from male and full-time and toward female and part-time—represent declines in the relative importance of sectors that traditionally have been highly unionized and increases in the relative importance of sectors that traditionally have had low union density. Thus if union density remained constant in each sector or for each type of worker, the economy-wide extent of union organization would decline due to these structural shifts.

Another explanation involves changes in the U.S. legal regime (the laws, their interpretation, and their administration and enforcement) relating to unions and collective bargaining during the post–World War II period. Differences between Canada and the United States in such areas as certification and decertification procedures, bankruptcy and succession rights, first contract negotiation, and union security arrangements are argued to be factors contributing to the differential in union coverage.

A related view is that the decline in unionization in the United States can largely be attributed to the rise in management opposition, both legal and illegal, to unions (Freeman 1985, 1988). The dramatic rise in unfair labor practices is evidence of a broader attempt by U.S. management to operate in a "union-free environment." The rise in unfair labor practices is not surprising, given the incentives facing employers (Flanagan 1987). Increased management opposition to unions can be attributed in part to a more competitive economic environment and to the substantial union-nonunion wage differential.

A fourth hypothesis is that there has been a reduction in the desire for collective representation because of the growth of substitute services. There are two variants of this view. One is that governments have gradually provided more of the employment protection and nonwage benefits that were originally important factors underlying workers' desire for organizing collectively (Neumann and Rissman 1984). The other is that employers have become increasingly sophisticated in their human resource practices and now provide many of the services (e.g., grievance procedures) that workers previously received only in unionized firms (Kochan, Katz, and McKersie 1986).

A final explanation, which is in many ways the simplest and most profound, is that there has been in the United States a reduction in public sympathy toward unions and collective bargaining (Lipset 1986). This shift in attitudes has resulted in a decline in workers' desire for collective forms of representation and a decline in the public support for achieving the goals of the labor movement via the political process. A corollary of this thesis is that the Canada-U.S. differential in union coverage can be attributed to fundamental value differences between the two societies—with Canada being a society that relies more on government, state intervention in the economy, and collective forms of organization and the United States being a society that emphasizes free enterprise and individual rather than collective rights and freedoms (Lipset 1986).

The remainder of the paper assesses these explanations, using the "natural experiment" provided by the differential experience of Canada and the United States. To as great an extent as possible, I attempt to use data and other information that are comparable between the two countries. The analysis begins by examining the extent to which the differential in union coverage can be attributed to differences between Canada and the United States in the demand for unionization versus differences in the supply of unionization.

4.3 The Demand for and Supply of Collective Representation: A Canada-U.S. Comparison

The growth and incidence of union organization can be analyzed using a demand and supply framework (Ashenfelter and Pencavel 1969; Pencavel 1971). The demand for union representation emanates from employees and depends on the expected benefits and costs of collective representation. The supply of unionization emanates from the organizing and contract administration activities of union leaders and their staff. Employers can affect the demand for union representation by altering the costs and/or benefits as perceived by unorganized employees. Employers can also alter the supply side by changing the costs and/or benefits to union leaders of representing existing members and organizing new members.

This framework may be useful in the present context because several of the hypotheses discussed above differ in their implications for the demand for and supply of unionization. For example, the "growth of union substitutes" view predicts that the observed behavior is due to a pure decline in demand, while the changes in the legal regime are expected to reduce both demand and supply. On the other hand, the structural shift hypothesis implies that there have been no changes in either demand or supply for a given type of worker (and union leader); rather, the aggregate behavior is due to the changing composition of the labor force.

For these reasons, this section provides an empirical analysis that attempts to determine the extent to which the Canada-U.S. differential in union coverage can be attributed to differences in the demand for union representation versus differences on the supply side.[3]

Unfortunately, it is generally difficult with the available data to determine the extent to which observed behavior is due to demand-side factors, supply-side factors, or both. For example, there is a strong relationship between union incidence and establishment size. This relationship could be due to a stronger desire for union representation among workers in large establishments—for example, because they have more need for a collective voice than do workers in small establishments. However, the relationship could also exist because union leaders target large establishments in their organizing drives in an attempt to maximize the number of potential new members per dollar of organizing expenditure. Similarly, the finding that, holding wages constant, workers with more education are more likely to be unionized could be due to these workers being more likely to choose jobs in the union sector or due to unionized employers choosing from the pool of applicants (for a job at a given wage) those with the most qualifications.

The problem here is one of identification. It is difficult to determine from observations on the union status of individual workers and such employee and employer characteristics as age, education, and establishment size the separate influences of the choices made by workers, employers, and union organizers. The additional information used here—as in Farber (1983, 1990)—is a measure of the desire for union representation by currently unorganized workers.

An individual worker will desire union representation if the expected net benefit of a union job is positive. Let z_i be the difference between the expected utility of a union and nonunion job for individual i. This (unobserved) utility gain or loss depends on certain observable and unobservable variables, including the wage differential between union and otherwise similar nonunion jobs.

$$z_i = X_i b + u_i \tag{1}$$

Let DES_i be a discrete variable that takes on a value of unity for individuals who prefer union status and zero for individuals who prefer nonunion status. Then

$$\text{Prob}(DES_i = 1) = \text{Prob}(z_i > 0) = \text{Prob}(u_i > -X_i b). \tag{2}$$

If it is known which individuals prefer to be unionized, the parameters in equation (2) can be estimated.

In most microdata sets only the union status of individual workers is observed. Let $US_i = 1$ for individuals in the union sector and $US_i = 0$ for non-

3. The methodology is due to Farber (1983) and was used by Farber (1990) to examine changes over time in the demand for and supply of unionization in the United States.

union workers. If individuals have sorted themselves into the sectors of their choice, then it would be the case that

$$\text{(3)} \qquad \text{Prob}(US_i = 1) = \text{Prob}(z_i > 0) = \text{Prob}(u_i > -X_i b).$$

In this case the parameters determining the demand for unionization could be estimated with information on union status alone.

However, there are several reasons to expect that not all individuals who prefer a union job will in fact be represented by a union. It may be costly for an individual worker to initiate or help organize a union organizing drive, especially if the employer attempts to dissuade employees from attempting to organize. Thus even if the expected net benefits from union representation are positive, these may become negative when the costs of organizing the workplace are taken into account. In addition, not all the benefits of collective representation accrue to those employees who make the investment in organizing a union; some accrue to existing employees who "free ride" (i.e., do not participate in the organizing drive), while others accrue to future employees. Thus there may be workplaces that remain nonunion even though a majority of current and future employees would prefer collective representation in the absence of organizing costs.

There may also be workplaces in which a minority of the current employees prefer union status. In this case the workplace would remain nonunion even in the absence of organizing costs. If it were costless to change jobs, those employees who prefer union jobs would leave. Changing jobs is often not costless, however, especially when workers have considerable specific human capital. Thus an unsatisfied demand for union representation may remain in nonunion firms.

If union organizing is costly to individual employees, which is particularly likely when employers adopt strong anti-union strategies, a queue for high-paying union jobs will emerge—even in a situation of full employment.[4] Evidence that such queues exist in the United States is provided in studies by Abowd and Farber (1982) and Farber (1983). In these circumstances, union status is determined not only by the preferences of the individual worker (i.e., whether $z_i > 0$) but also by which individuals are chosen from the pool of applicants by the unionized employer.[5] Thus there will be individuals in the nonunion sector ($US_i = 0$) who would prefer a union job ($DES_i = 1$).

Comparative evidence on the significance of this "unsatisfied demand" for union representation can be obtained from two surveys sponsored by union federations in the United States and Canada. The first, referred to here as the

4. Of course, there may be periods in which there are queues for most jobs, but that is another issue.

5. This discussion assumes that hiring decisions are made by the employer—by far the most common arrangement in North America. The analysis would need to be modified for situations in which employment decisions are made using union hiring halls.

AFL survey, was conducted in 1984 by Louis Harris and Associates, Inc., for the American Federation of Labor–Congress of Industrial Organizations.[6] The second, referred to here as the CFL survey, was carried out in 1990 by Decima Research for the Canadian Federation of Labour/Fédération Canadienne du Travail.

Both surveys ask respondents about their union status. Unorganized workers are also asked about their desire for union representation. However, individuals who are currently members of a union or covered by a collective agreement are not asked whether they would prefer their job to be nonunion. Thus US_i is observed for all respondents, and DES_i is observed for workers in the nonunion sector.

Although the AFL and CFL surveys are similar in a number of respects, three differences limit our ability to draw strong conclusions from a comparative analysis. First is the time lag between the two surveys. In effect the analysis represents a comparison between the United States in 1984 and Canada in 1990. Because union coverage was declining in both countries during the 1984–90 period, this comparison will overstate the Canadian-U.S. differential in 1990.

The two surveys were also conducted during very different phases of the business cycle in the two countries. The 1984 AFL survey was conducted at a time when the U.S. economy was just past the trough of a major recession, while the February 1990 CFL survey was carried out just prior to the peak of the 1983–90 business cycle in Canada.

The third factor involves differences between the two surveys in the critical (for this analysis) question of the desire for union representation among unorganized workers. The U.S. question is, for the purpose of this analysis, very precise: "If an election were held tomorrow to decide whether your workplace would be unionized or not, do you think you would definitely vote for a union, probably vote for a union, probably vote against a union, or definitely vote against a union?" Individuals who responded that they would definitely or probably vote for a union are assigned $DES_i = 1$, and those who responded that they would definitely or probably vote against a union are assigned $DES_i = 0$.

The Canadian question was, "Thinking about your own needs, and your current employment situation and expectations, would you say that it is very likely, somewhat likely, not very likely, or not likely at all that you would consider joining or associating yourself with a union or a professional association in the future?" Individuals who responded "somewhat likely" or "very likely" are assigned $DES_i = 1$, and those who responded "not very likely" or "not likely at all" are assigned $DES_i = 0$.

The measurement of the desire for collective representation among unorga-

6. See Farber (1990) for a more detailed discussion and analysis of this survey.

nized workers differs between the two surveys in two ways. One is the actual phrasing of the key question.[7] The CFL question is somewhat broader and vaguer and could be interpreted to involve a job other than the job currently held, whereas the AFL question is both precise and clearly focused on the existing job. For those not currently employed, the CFL question could be interpreted as asking about whether their job search will be focused on the union or nonunion sector. This difference in focus is not a problem in this paper because the analysis is restricted to those currently employed. Nonetheless, even among those currently employed, the CFL question may measure a somewhat broader concept of the desire for collective representation than does the AFL survey, which is more narrowly focused on the current job. The fact that the Canadian question is less precise may also bias the responses, although the direction of bias is unclear.

The second difference is that the AFL question was asked of all those not currently union members, whereas the CFL survey was structured such that this question was asked only of those not members of a union or professional association. Thus the concept of collective representation in the CFL survey is broader (those members of a union or professional association), and accordingly the question is only asked of a narrower group (those not members of a union or professional association).[8]

These two differences between the surveys may offset each other. The CFL question on the desire for collective representation is somewhat broader, which may result in a larger measured desire for union representation. The CFL question is asked of a narrower group, which will tend to reduce the measured desire for collective representation among the currently unorganized.

The two surveys differ in another respect. The CFL survey was designed to yield a representative sample of the Canadian labor force, whereas the AFL "quota sampled" union members because its primary purpose was to assess the attitudes of nonunion workers. Thus nonunion workers were oversampled (by about 10 percent) in the AFL survey. I deal with this in the same fashion as Farber (1990), by randomly omitting 10 percent of the observations on nonunion workers.

A feature common to the two surveys is that union members (and members of professional associations in the case of the CFL survey) were not asked if they would prefer a nonunion job. Because union representation is a majority decision, there may be some individuals covered by a collective agreement who would prefer nonunion status. The number of such individuals is un-

7. It is important to point out that, because union certification decisions in most Canadian jurisdictions are not based on voting, the U.S. question would probably not be appropriate in Canada even if both surveys were intending to measure the same phenomenon.

8. Unfortunately it is not possible to separate union members from members of professional associations because some workers report belonging to both. Furthermore, the critical question on the desire for union representation is only asked of those not members of either.

known, but their treatment in the same fashion by the two surveys should not significantly affect the comparative analysis.

As in Farber (1983, 1990), I assume $DES_i = 1$ for all those with $US_i = 1$. Excluded from the analysis are those not currently employed, the self-employed, managers, and those who did not respond to the questions on union status, desire for union representation, public or private sector employment, and demographic variables common to the two surveys (age, education, sex). After these exclusions and the adjustment to the AFL survey for quota sampling, there are 517 observations from the CFL survey (out of 1,000 interviews) and 890 observations from the AFL survey (out of 1,452 interviews). Some of the key statistics are summarized in table 4.3. The top part of the table shows these statistics for each of the full samples while the bottom part splits the samples into the public and private sectors.

These surveys confirm that the probability that a randomly selected Canadian worker is unionized is more than double that of a U.S. worker (0.48 versus 0.22). To some extent this differential is overstated by the inclusion of members of professional associations in the Canadian data but not in the U.S. data.[9] The remainder of this large differential can be accounted for by three factors. First, the desire for union representation in Canada is about 28 percent higher than that in the United States (Prob($DES_i = 1$) of 0.64 versus 0.50). There is also less unsatisfied demand for union status in Canada; Prob($DES_i = 1/US_i = 0$) is 0.30 in Canada versus 0.36 in the United States. However, the most remarkable difference between the two countries is clearly the greater supply of unionization conditional on desire for union status; Prob($US_i = 1/DES_i = 1$) is 0.76 in Canada versus 0.44 in the United States, that is, 73 percent higher in Canada. These summary statistics indicate that Canada's higher union density is due to both greater demand for and greater supply of union coverage in Canada, but that intercountry differences in the supply of union representation appear to be relatively more significant.

In order to assess the relative importance of demand and supply factors, the relationship $\text{Prob}(US_i = 1) = \text{Prob}(US_i = 1|DES_i = 1) * \text{Prob}(DES_i = 1)$ can be decomposed into two components corresponding to differences in the demand for and supply of unionization:

$$
\begin{aligned}
(4)\qquad \Delta\text{Prob}(US_i = 1) &= \Delta\text{Prob}(DES_i = 1) * \text{Prob}(US_i = 1|DES_i = 1) \\
&\quad + \text{Prob}(DES_i = 1) * \Delta\text{Prob}(US_i = 1|DES_i = 1) \\
&= 0.14 * 0.6 + 0.565 * 0.32 \\
&= .084 + .181 = 0.265,
\end{aligned}
$$

9. Union membership as a percentage of paid workers was 37 percent in Canada in 1984 and 16 percent in the United States in 1990, a differential of 21 percentage points. Collective agreement coverage as a percentage of paid workers was 42 percent in Canada in 1984 and 18 percent in the United States in 1990, a differential of 24 percentage points. The sources for these statistics are the surveys reported in table 4.2.

Table 4.3 AFL and CFL Surveys of Desire for Union Representation

	CFL Survey	AFL Survey
Number of Observations		
Union	250	196
Nonunion	267	694
Total	517	890
Prob ($US_i = 1$)	0.48	0.22
Prob ($DES_i = 1$)	0.64	0.50
Prob ($DES_i = 1 \mid US_i = 0$)	0.30	0.36
Prob ($US_i = 1 \mid DES_i = 1$)	0.76	0.44

	CFL Survey		AFL Survey	
	Public	Private	Public	Private
Number of observations				
Union	125	125	63	133
Nonunion	54	213	153	541
Total	179	338	216	674
Prob ($US_i = 1$)	0.70	0.37	0.29	0.20
Prob ($DES_i = 1$)	0.84	0.54	0.62	0.45
Prob ($DES_i = 1 \mid US_i = 0$)	0.46	0.26	0.46	0.31
Prob ($US_i = 1 \mid DES_i = 1$)	0.83	0.69	0.47	0.44

where Δ Prob($US_i = 1$) = 0.26 is the difference between the unionization rate in Canada and that in the United States, Δ Prob($DES_i = 1$) = 0.14 and Δ Prob($US_i = 1 \mid DES_i = 1$) = 0.32 are Canadian minus U.S. differences, and Prob($US_i = 1 \mid DES_i = 1$) = 0.60 and Prob($DES_i = 1$) = 0.565 are averages of the U.S. and Canadian levels.[10]

This decomposition implies that about two-thirds of the Canada-U.S. differential in union coverage is due to the difference in the supply of union representation (the second term in the above decomposition) and one-third to differences between Canada and the United States in the demand for union representation (the first term).[11]

Both the CFL and AFL surveys permit identification of public versus private sector respondents, and the bottom part of table 4.3 contains the same analysis for the private and public sectors separately. This analysis is worthwhile for two reasons. Explanations of Canadian-U.S. differences in the extent of union organization have often stressed the relative importance of Can-

10. Evaluating the approximation at the averages of the U.S. and Canadian levels gave a smaller approximation error than did using either country as the base.

11. In a recent contribution, Farber and Krueger (1992) employ an alternative decomposition: Prob($US_i = 1$) = Prob($DES_i = 1$) − Prob($DES_i = 1$ and $US_i = 0$). The first term constitutes intercountry differences in demand and the second intercountry differences in "inverse supply," or the amount of unsatisfied demand for union representation as a fraction of the entire labor force. This decomposition attributes 0.14 (or 54 percent) of the intercountry unionization differential of 0.26 to differences in demand and 0.12 (or 46 percent) to differences in inverse supply.

ada's public sector (Meltz 1985; Troy 1990). In addition, some explanations of the decline in unionization in the United States imply different outcomes in the U.S. private and public sectors (Freeman 1986, 1988).

The two surveys differ in their questions about public sector status. The AFL survey asked, "Do you work for federal, state or local government?" Those who answered yes are regarded in what follows as being in the public sector; the remainder are treated as being in the private sector. The CFL survey asked, "Do you work in a large business, small business, or the public sector?" Thus the meaning of "public sector" in the Canadian survey is both self-reported and potentially broader than that of federal, provincial, or local government employment. As discussed in more detail later, the broader notion of public sector in Canada is to an important extent an appropriate reflection of the greater government involvement in the Canadian economy. However, the differences between the two surveys in this respect also imply that caution is appropriate in interpreting the results.

According to these surveys, the Canada-U.S. unionization gap is larger in the public than in the private sector; a Canadian public sector worker is more than twice as likely to be unionized than the U.S. counterpart, whereas a Canadian private sector worker is somewhat less than twice as likely to be covered by a collective agreement (table 4.3).[12] These differences in the extent of union organization can be attributed in part to a greater demand for union representation in Canada; Prob(DES_i = 1) is 35 and 20 percent higher in the Canadian public and private sectors, respectively. There is also less unsatisfied demand for union representation in the Canadian private sector than in the U.S. However, it is interesting to note that the amount of unsatisfied demand for unionization is the same in the Canadian and U.S. public sectors. In both sectors, the largest relative intercountry differences are those related to supply conditional on demand; Prob($US_i = 1 | DES_i = 1$) is 77 and 57 percent greater in the Canadian public and private sectors, respectively.

As before, decomposition (4) can be used to indicate the relative importance of demand and supply factors. This decomposition attributes 0.05 (or 29 percent) of the 0.17 private sector differential to the demand side and 0.12 (or 71 percent) to the supply side. In the public sector the contributions of the demand and supply components are 35 and 65 percent, respectively.

Thus the conclusion that about two-thirds of the Canada-U.S. unionization gap is associated with intercountry differences in supply conditional on demand continues to hold when one disaggregates into the public and private sectors.

These general findings also continue to hold after controlling for individual characteristics such as gender, age, and education. These results are shown in tables 4.4 and 4.5. In table 4.4 the dependent variable is DES_i; the estimated

12. Intercountry differences in unionization in the public and private sectors are examined in detail later, using comparable surveys that are representative of the respective labor forces.

Table 4.4 **Probit Model of Demand for Unionization**

Variable	AFL	CFL	Pooled
Constant	−0.14	−0.34	−0.35
	(−0.5)	(−0.9)	(−1.6)
Male	0.13	0.16	0.14
	(1.6)	(1.4)	(2.0)
Age 25–34	0.12	−0.13	0.02
	(0.9)	(−0.7)	(0.2)
Age 35–44	0.14	0.32	0.21
	(1.0)	(1.5)	(1.9)
Age 45–54	0.08	0.22	0.15
	(0.5)	(1.0)	(1.2)
Age 55–64	0.16	0.30	0.21
	(0.9)	(1.1)	(1.4)
Age 65 +	−0.03	−0.35	−0.18
	(−0.1)	(−0.7)	(−0.6)
Some high school	0.28	0.30	0.23
	(1.0)	(0.9)	(1.1)
High school graduate	0.17	0.49	0.31
	(0.7)	(1.5)	(1.6)
Some college	−0.17	0.57	0.13
	(−0.6)	(1.7)	(0.6)
Some university	−0.24	0.34	−0.0
	(−0.8)	(0.9)	(−0.0)
University graduate	−0.30	0.74	0.1
	(−1.1)	(2.2)	(0.3)
Canada			0.33
			(4.7)
N	890	536	1426
Correctly predicted (%)	59	63	59

relationship can thus be interpreted as the demand for unionization. In table 4.5 the dependent variable is US_i (conditional on DES_i); this estimated relationship can thus be interpreted as the supply of unionization function. These demand and supply functions are estimated for each country separately and for the pooled sample. The latter includes a dummy variable for the Canadian observations. The control variables are individual characteristics observed in both surveys (gender, age, and education).[13]

Males are more likely to desire union status in both countries, as is also the case for individuals between 35 and 44 years of age. Otherwise, the demand for collective representation is independent of personal characteristics. When the observations from both countries are pooled, the probability of desiring

13. The age and education groups were adjusted to make them comparable in the two surveys.

Table 4.5 Probit Model of Supply of Unionization

Variable	AFL	CFL	Pooled
Constant	−1.71	−0.02	−1.32
	(−4.1)	(−0.0)	(−4.0)
Male	0.60	0.06	0.39
	(4.7)	(0.4)	(4.0)
Age 25–34	0.62	0.60	0.59
	(3.0)	(2.3)	(3.7)
Age 35–44	0.88	0.60	0.73
	(4.0)	(2.3)	(4.4)
Age 45–54	0.79	1.10	0.89
	(3.4)	(3.4)	(4.8)
Age 55–64	1.33	1.38	1.30
	(4.8)	(3.4)	(5.9)
Age 65+	−5.09	5.59	0.15
	(−0.0)	(0.0)	(0.3)
Some high school	0.70	−0.37	0.17
	(1.7)	(−0.6)	(0.5)
High school graduate	0.51	0.10	0.30
	(1.3)	(0.2)	(1.0)
Some college	0.50	0.35	0.42
	(1.2)	(0.5)	(1.3)
Some university	0.15	−0.17	0.06
	(0.3)	(−0.3)	(0.2)
University graduate	0.74	0.06	0.42
	(1.9)	(0.1)	(1.4)
Canada			0.84
			(8.5)
N	443	339	782
Correctly predicted (%)	65	77	69

unionization is 0.33 higher in Canada than in the United States, a difference that is statistically significant.[14]

The supply of union representation (conditional on demand) depends on two individual characteristics: gender and age. Among those who desire unionization, males are more likely to achieve this status in the United States but not in Canada. Individuals between the ages of 25 and 64 who desire collective representation are more likely to achieve union status than are younger workers (16–24-year-olds). Educational attainment has little impact on the supply of unionization in either country.

The most striking result in table 4.5 is that the probability that a Canadian

14. Adding interaction terms to allow the slope coefficients to differ between Canada and the United States makes little difference to the estimates in table 4.4. Only the university graduate coefficient differs significantly between Canada and the United States.

worker who desires union status will in fact be unionized is 0.84 higher than the equivalent likelihood for an American worker. This finding reinforces the conclusion based on the sample averages in table 4.3: although both the demand for and supply of union representation is higher in Canada, intercountry differences in supply (given the desire for union coverage) are relatively greater than are intercountry differences in demand.

These demand and supply relationships were also estimated separately for the public and private sectors. Appendix tables 4A.1 and 4A.2 contain these estimates. The main finding continues to hold: supply-side differences between Canada and the United States are relatively larger than demand-side differences. These differences are especially large in the private sector. In the pooled sample, the probability of demanding union representation is 0.19 higher in Canada than in the United States (controlling for gender, age, and educational status). In contrast, the probability of being unionized, conditional on desiring union status, is 0.67 higher in the Canadian private sector.

I interpret the results of this demand-supply analysis as providing some—albeit modest—support for the hypothesis that differences between Canada and the United States in the laws governing union organization and collective bargaining, and the administration and enforcement of these laws, together with less overt management opposition to unions in Canada are important factors accounting for the intercountry differential in union coverage. The more favorable legal and administrative environment and less management opposition (itself possibly due to the differences in laws and their enforcement) reduce the cost to workers of union representation, resulting in greater demand even if the underlying preferences of workers on both sides of the border are otherwise identical on average. These same factors also lower the costs to union leaders and organizers of union formation, member representation, and contract administration, thus increasing the supply of unionization. These implications of the hypothesis are consistent with the evidence in this section.

Other explanations of the unionization gap are less easily reconciled with this evidence. Strictly interpreted, explanations based on differences in the structures of the economies and labor forces would imply that intercountry differences in demand and supply would disappear upon controlling for individual and employer characteristics. This clearly does not happen, although admittedly the controls available on a comparable basis are far from comprehensive. Similarly, a pure demand-side explanation (for example, because Canadian workers have stronger underlying preferences for collective forms of representation) is difficult to reconcile with the apparent relative significance of supply considerations (conditional on demand) and the lower excess demand for union coverage in Canada.

The support for the "legal regime/management opposition" view is modest for two reasons. First, the link between the hypothesis and the finding that the intercountry unionization gap is due to greater Canadian demand for and supply of unionization is clearly indirect. Second, the two surveys used in this section differ in several potentially significant ways, as described above. More convincing comparative evidence requires better data.[15] The analysis to which I now turn meets this requirement.

4.4 Structural Explanations

As noted earlier, many of the changes that have been occurring in the structure of the economy and the labor force—away from employment that is predominantly full-time, blue-collar, male, in large firms or enterprises, and in manufacturing or primary industries, toward employment that is increasingly part-time, white-collar, female, in small firms or enterprises, and in service industries—represent shifts from sectors that are typically highly unionized to sectors that have generally been characterized by low degrees of unionization. In the United States there has also been a relative shift of employment away from the highly unionized North to the less unionized South. The only significant development tending to increase the extent of unionization is the relative growth in employment—together with the substantial increase in union density—in the public sector.

Although some studies have concluded that these changes in labor force composition contributed to the decline in unionization in the United States (Dickens and Leonard 1985; Farber 1985, 1990), this "structuralist" view has been challenged because many of the same compositional changes have also occurred in Canada, where union density continued to increase until the mid-1980s (Lipset 1986; Freeman 1988). However, Troy (1990, 1992) has argued that structural changes have indeed led to a decline in private sector unionization in both countries, albeit one that occurred later in Canada because of differences in the timing of key changes in economic structure (e.g., the shift from manufacturing and primary industries to services). Troy's analysis is based on data on unionization by industry—data that have important limitations. This section provides an analysis of the structuralist hypothesis using comparable microdata from both countries. In particular, I examine the extent to which differences in the composition of the respective labor forces can account for intercountry differences in the extent of unionization.

The data come from very similar surveys carried out at the same time (December 1984) in each country. The Canadian data source is the Survey of Union Membership (SUM), carried out as a supplement to the LFS, and the U.S. source is the CPS earnings file, a supplement to the CPS. These data sources were chosen for three main reasons. First, the LFS and CPS are

15. Farber and Krueger (1992) carried out a survey of U.S. workers' attitudes toward union representation. They asked both the CFL and AFL questions and in half the survey randomly reversed the order in which the two questions were asked. They find that the responses are very sensitive to the order in which the questions are asked. These results indicate another reason for caution in interpreting the results of the comparative demand-supply analysis.

monthly household surveys that are very similar in terms of their underlying methodology and structure. Furthermore, the supplements have almost identical questions relating to union membership and collective agreement coverage. For the purposes at hand, collective agreement coverage is the preferred measure of union status and is accordingly used throughout; however, none of the qualitative conclusions would be altered by the use of union membership.

Second, both surveys provide information on whether each paid worker is employed in the private or the public sector. The concept of public sector used here is a broad one—corresponding to whether the employing organization is owned or primarily financed by government—and the two surveys use a very similar methodology for classifying workers into paid public and paid private employment.[16] Later Canadian surveys that provide information on union status (for example, the Labour Market Activity Surveys of 1986–90) do not, unfortunately, provide this information on public-private sector status. The third reason for choosing these sources is that both provide, when the data are appropriately weighted, representative samples of the respective labor forces.[17]

As discussed previously, union status is determined by the decisions made by individual workers, employers, and union leaders and organizers. Let

$$(5) \qquad US_{ij} = 1 \begin{cases} \text{if } y_{ij} > 0, \\ 0 \text{ otherwise,} \end{cases} \qquad j = c,u,$$

where c and u refer to Canada and the United States, respectively, and

$$(6) \qquad y_{ij} = Q_{ij}\, d_j + e_{ij}, \qquad j = c,u.$$

Equation (5) is a reduced-form equation that reflects the combined outcome of demand and supply factors on union status. y_{ij} is an unobserved variable that incorporates the net utility gain of union coverage to worker i (z_i in equation [1]) in addition to influences of employer and union-organizer behavior. Q_{ij} are variables that influence unionization decisions, and d_j is the associated parameter vector. The error term e_{ij} is assumed to be normally distributed, so the parameters d_j can be estimated by a probit model.

The variables available on a comparable basis for both countries are gender, age, part-time employment, public sector employment, occupation, and industry. Table 4.6 reports the sample means of these variables for the two samples, together with the estimated parameters d_j.[18] Excluded from the em-

16. The LFS definition of paid workers (government) is "those who work for a local, provincial or federal government, for a government service or agency, a crown corporation, or a *government owned* public establishment such as a school or hospital" (Statistics Canada 1992b, 12). This coding takes place at the same time as industry and occupation coding. The CPS definition is also based on government ownership. Paid government employees are coded by the interviewer; federal, state, and local employees are identified separately. See Bureau of Labour Statistics, *CPS Interviewers Manual,* item 23E.

17. Unless otherwise noted, the analysis in this paper uses the weighted data.

18. The Canadian sample of 3,995 observations is a one-eighth random subsample of the SUM (after exclusions noted), while the U.S. sample of 4,372 observations is a one-third random subsample of the December 1984 CPS earnings file (after exclusions).

Table 4.6 Determinants of Unionization in Canada and the United States, 1984

	Canada		U.S.		
	Sample Means	Parameter Estimates	Sample Means	Parameter Estimates	Interaction Terms
Constant	1.00	−1.45	1.00	−1.74	0.29
		(−9.1)		(−8.1)	(1.1)
Female	0.45	−0.15	0.47	−0.11	−0.04
		(−2.8)		(−2.0)	(−0.5)
Age 25–34	0.31	0.40	0.30	0.30	0.11
		(5.9)		(3.7)	(1.0)
Age 35–44	0.24	0.53	0.22	0.51	0.02
		(7.2)		(6.1)	(0.2)
Age 45–54	0.15	0.48	0.14	0.64	−0.16
		(5.9)		(7.2)	(−1.3)
Age 55–64	0.08	0.42	0.10	0.33	0.08
		(4.4)		(3.3)	(0.6)
Age 65+	0.005	−0.34	0.03	−0.06	−0.28
		(−0.8)		(−0.3)	(−0.6)
Part-time	0.16	−0.33	0.20	−0.41	0.08
		(−4.7)		(−5.2)	(0.7)
Public	0.23	0.99	0.17	0.94	0.06
		(12.3)		(11.3)	(0.5)
Clerical	0.19	0.40	0.17	0.13	0.27
		(5.2)		(1.6)	(2.4)
Sales	0.07	0.08	0.12	0.04	0.03
		(0.6)		(0.3)	(0.2)
Serving	0.14	0.56	0.14	0.31	0.25
		(6.3)		(3.5)	(2.0)
Primary	0.02	0.57	0.02	−0.41	0.98
		(2.9)		(−1.4)	(2.8)
Processing	0.21	0.96	0.20	0.70	0.26
		(11.9)		(8.7)	(2.3)
Transportation, handling	0.08	0.80	0.09	0.66	0.14
		(8.2)		(6.9)	(1.0)
Manufacturing	0.21	0.40	0.21	0.29	0.11
		(2.7)		(1.4)	(0.4)
Construction	0.04	0.13	0.06	0.09	0.04
		(0.7)		(0.4)	(0.1)
Transportation, communication, utilities	0.09	0.76	0.07	0.79	−0.02
		(4.7)		(3.7)	(−0.1)
Trade	0.16	−0.06	0.21	−0.26	0.20
		(−0.4)		(−1.2)	(0.8)
Finance, insurance, real estate	0.05	−0.53	0.06	−0.59	0.07
		(−2.7)		(−2.3)	(0.2)
Education, health	0.19	1.22	0.21	0.22	1.00
		(7.8)		(1.0)	(3.8)
Other services	0.14	−0.23	0.10	−0.05	−0.18
		(−1.4)		(−0.2)	(−0.7)
Public administration	0.08	0.59	0.05	−0.06	0.65
		(3.3)		(−0.3)	(2.2)
R^2 (Cragg-Uhler)		0.42		0.28	0.42
N		3,995		4,372	8,367

pirical analysis are those who are not paid workers (e.g., the self-employed and unpaid family workers), those not employed in the reference week, and those for whom information on variables of interest was missing.

Although the two labor forces are clearly very similar, some differences are evident. The proportion of females in the labor force is somewhat higher in the United States, as is that of part-time workers. More of the Canadian labor force is under age 55. Public sector employment is substantially higher in Canada (23 percent versus 17 percent in the United States), an aspect examined in more detail below. The occupational distribution of employment is remarkably similar, the only noticeable difference at this level of aggregation being the larger proportion of the U.S. labor force in sales occupations. There are a number of differences in the industrial distribution of employment, although none of these could be described as dramatic. More of the Canadian labor force is employed in transportation, communication, and utilities, public administration, and services, while more of the U.S. labor force is employed in construction and trade.

A number of the estimated parameters are also quite similar across the two countries. However, there are several notable exceptions. The difference in the respective constant terms indicates that the same individual would be 0.29 more likely to be covered by a collective agreement in Canada than in the United States. Public sector workers are much more likely to be unionized in both countries, but the impact of public sector status on the probability of unionization is almost identical in each country. The effects of age, gender, and part-time employment are also very similar in the two countries. However, several of the industry and occupation coefficients differ substantially.

In order to examine these differences more systematically, the two samples were pooled and a Canada dummy (equal to unity for observations from Canada and zero otherwise) was interacted with each of the Q variables.[19] The last column of table 4.6 reports the estimated interaction terms. The only significant differences are in the impacts of the occupational and industrial distributions, the probability of unionization being higher in Canada (other things being equal) in clerical, serving, primary, and processing occupations and in education and health and public administration. Each of these differences is positive; the largest differences are those associated with the coefficients of the education and health industry and of primary occupations.

How much of the Canada-U.S. unionization differential can be attributed to differences in the characteristics of the respective labor forces and how much to differences between the two countries in the likelihood of a worker with the same set of characteristics being unionized? In order to address this question,

19. When the data are weighted, the Canadian observations constitute 14 percent of the pooled sample. For this analysis, it is more appropriate to have equal numbers of observations from each country; thus the weights are scaled so that half of the observations come from each country.

the intercountry gap in the probability of union coverage is decomposed into two terms, one associated with intercountry differences in the characteristics of the respective labor forces, and the second with differences in the impacts of those characteristics on the probability of unionization.[20] Let $h(.)$ denote the value of the standard normal distribution at (.). The estimated probability that individual i of country j is covered by a collective agreement is

$$p_{ij} = h(Q_{ij}\,\hat{d}_j), \qquad j = c,u. \tag{7}$$

The average estimated probability of unionization in each country is given by

$$\bar{p}_j = 1/N_j \sum_i h(Q_{ij}\,\hat{d}_j), \qquad j = c,u, \tag{8}$$

where N_j is the number of observations for country j. Define

$$\bar{p}_o = 1/N_u \sum_i h(Q_{iu}\hat{d}_c). \tag{9}$$

$\bar{p}_o$ is the U.S. union density that would be predicted if each U.S. worker retained his or her unionization-determining characteristics but the impacts of those characteristics on the probability of union coverage were those estimated for Canadians. The intercountry unionization gap can then be decomposed into two terms, the first representing the portion of the gap associated with intercountry differences in characteristics that influence union status and the second associated with differences in the impacts of those characteristics on the probability of union coverage:

$$\bar{p}_c - \bar{p}_u = (\bar{p}_c - \bar{p}_o) + (\bar{p}_o - \bar{p}_u). \tag{10}$$

This decomposition is shown in column 2 of table 4.7. The average predicted union densities equal the actual densities for each country; thus the predicted gap equals the actual gap (0.26). Eighty-five percent of the gap (0.22 of 0.26) is associated with intercountry differences in the parameter vectors, and only 15 percent is associated with intercountry differences in the characteristics of the respective labor forces.

An alternative, and simpler, procedure decomposes the unionization differential at the mean of the data; that is, for the individual with average characteristics for each country (denoted by $\bar{Q}_c$ and $\bar{Q}_u$),

$$\begin{aligned} h(\bar{Q}_c\hat{d}_c) - h(\bar{Q}_u\,\hat{d}_u) = {} & \{h(\bar{Q}_c\,\hat{d}_c) - h(\bar{Q}_u\,\hat{d}_c)\} \\ & + \{h(\bar{Q}_u\,\hat{d}_c) - h(\bar{Q}_u\,\hat{d}_u). \end{aligned} \tag{11}$$

20. The procedures outlined below involve decomposing a nonlinear function in a fashion similar to the Oaxaca type of decomposition of a linear relationship. See Even and Macpherson (1993) and Doiron and Riddell (1993) for details of these procedures and their application to male-female earnings differences.

Table 4.7 Decomposition of the Canada-U.S. Unionization Differential

A. Overall decomposition

	Total Economy			Private Sector			Public Sector		
	Actual[a]	Predicted[b]		Actual[a]	Predicted[b]		Actual[a]	Predicted[b]	
	(1)	(2)	(3)	(1)	(2)	(3)	(1)	(2)	(3)
Canada	0.45	0.45	0.43	0.34	0.34	0.30	0.81	0.81	0.83
United States	0.19	0.19	0.14	0.15	0.15	0.11	0.41	0.41	0.39
Unionization differential	0.26	0.26	0.29	0.19	0.19	0.19	0.40	0.40	0.44
Approximated gap[c]			0.27						
Approximation error			0.02						
Due to differences in		0.04	0.04		0.0	0.0		0.02	0.02
characteristics (%)		(15)	(13)		(0)	(0)		(5)	(5)
Due to differences in impacts		0.22	0.24		0.19	0.19		0.38	0.42
of characteristics (%)		(85)	(87)		(100)	(000)		(95)	(95)

B. Contribution of each variable to the Canada-U.S. unionization differential

Variable	Due to Characteristics	Due to Returns to Characteristics	Due to Both
Constant	0	.088	.088
Age	.006	.005	.011
Gender	.001	−.006	−.005
Part-time	.005	.005	.010
Public sector	.019	.003	.022
Occupation	.002	.052	.054
Industry	.002	.092	.094
Total	.035	.239	.274
Percentage	13	87	100

[a]Sample average using weighted data.

[b]Column 2 predicted using the method shown in equation (7). Column 3 predicted at the mean of the data in each country (method shown in equation [11]).

[c]Based on a Taylor series approximation to equation (11).

The results of this decomposition are shown in column 3 of part A of table 4.7.[21] The conclusions are very similar: 83 percent of the Canada-U.S. unionization gap is attributed to intercountry differences in the parameters affecting the probability of unionization and only 17 percent to differences in the characteristics of the respective labor forces.

Associated with this simpler decomposition is a straightforward procedure

21. Note that this method underpredicts the extent of unionization in both countries. The extent of underprediction is greatest for the United States, so the predicted gap is underestimated. The difference between the two methods is a function of the degree of nonlinearity in the probit function. The U.S. union density is underpredicted more because of the greater degree of nonlinearity in the probit function at low levels of unionization.

for assessing the contribution of each variable.[22] These breakdowns are shown in part B of table 4.7. Although the Canadian labor force has more of each of the characteristics that make unionization likely, the only characteristic that makes a substantial contribution to the gap in union coverage is public sector employment, which accounts for .019 (or 6.9 percent) of the gap.

All of the estimated probit coefficients except gender contribute to a widening of the intercountry gap in union coverage. However, about 85 percent of the gap is associated with three sets of coefficients: industrial composition (34 percent), the constant term (32 percent), and occupational distribution (19 percent). Thus about one-third of the intercountry unionization differential can be accounted for by the fact that an individual with the same characteristics is 0.29 more likely to be covered by a collective agreement in Canada. An additional half (34 percent + 19 percent) of the gap can be attributed to the fact that workers employed in particular industries and occupations in Canada are more likely to be unionized than are U.S. workers with the same personal characteristics employed in those industries and occupations. Finally, almost 7 percent of the gap is associated with the fact that more of the Canadian labor force is employed in the public sector (broadly defined).

In summary, this analysis indicates that the structuralist hypothesis explains very little of the Canada-U.S. unionization differential. Differences in the structure of the respective labor forces account for about 15 percent of the differential; the remaining 85 percent is due to the greater likelihood of union coverage of a Canadian worker with a given set of characteristics. The only structural difference that makes a significant contribution to the unionization gap is the greater extent of public sector employment in Canada, a feature that is now examined in more detail.

4.5 Private versus Public Sector Differences

From part B of table 4.7, the total contribution of the public sector employment variable is .022, or 8.0 percent, of the Canada-U.S. unionization gap. Most of this contribution (6.9 percent) is associated with the larger fraction of Canada's labor force employed in the public sector; the remaining 1.1 percent arises because, other things being equal, Canadian public sector employees are slightly more likely to be unionized than their U.S. counterparts. Despite the evident conclusion that the search for greater understanding of the intercountry unionization gap should be focused elsewhere, there are several reasons why a more detailed examination of public-private sector differences is

22. See Doiron and Riddell (1993). The procedure involves a Taylor series approximation to the left-hand side of equation (11). The approximation error is shown in table 4.7. The Taylor series approximation was evaluated at the mean of the Canadian and U.S. union densities. Evaluating the approximation at either the Canadian or the U.S. level resulted in substantially larger approximation errors.

worthwhile. Perhaps the most important reason is simply that many observers believe that a substantial amount of the unionization differential is associated with intercountry differences in the importance of the public sector and in the relationship between the public sector and unionization.

In addition, in both countries the public sector has been in recent decades the main source of growth in unionization, in contrast to the private sector, where union density has either grown slowly or declined. A full understanding of intercountry differences in the role of collective bargaining requires an analysis of each country's public and private sectors.

Unfortunately, the publicly available data make it difficult to analyze this issue. Data are available on employment and unionization by industry. However, outside of public administration (which is entirely in the public sector in each country), both publicly and privately owned enterprises coexist in many industries—especially in Canada, where federal and provincial governments have numerous Crown corporations operating in industries such as transportation, communications, and natural resource exploration and extraction (Economic Council of Canada, 1986). Researchers have dealt with this problem by making various adjustments to the published data, adjustments that are clearly imperfect.[23]

The problems associated with data on unionization by industry can be overcome by the use of microdata in which both public-private sector status and union status are observed. The two surveys described above (SUM and CPS earnings file) provide comparable measures of union status and public versus private sector employment in the two countries as of December 1984.

Table 4.8 shows the percentage of employed paid workers in the public sector in each country by gender, full-time and part-time employment, occupation, and industry. Overall, 23 percent of paid workers are in the public sector in Canada versus 18 percent in the United States.[24] Public sector employment in Canada is particularly more significant in the transportation, communication and utilities, and finance, insurance, and real estate industries and in the transportation and moving and managerial, professional, and technical occupations. Differences between the two countries in the amount of public sector employment in the education, health, and welfare industries are not large. Table 4.8 also highlights the dangers associated with public versus private sector breakdowns based on industry classifications. In both Canada and the United States, many industries contain a mixture of publicly and privately owned enterprises.

23. For example, Troy (1990) includes all employment in education, health, and welfare services as being in the public sector in Canada. Because many employees in health and welfare services—and to a lesser extent in education—work for private employers, these adjustments probably overstate the size of Canada's public sector. Meltz (1989) also includes all education and health in Canada in the public sector.

24. The tabulations in tables 4.8 and 4.9 are based on the full samples (after exclusions), whereas the tabulations and parameter estimates in table 4.6 are based on random subsamples. Thus small differences in the reported statistics may exist.

Table 4.8 Percentage of Employed Paid Workers in the Public Sector, Canada and the United States, December 1984

	Canada	U.S.
All workers	23	18
Males	22	15
Females	23	20
Full-time	24	18
Part-time	15	14
Occupation		
Managerial, professional, technical	38	32
Clerical	25	24
Sales	3	2
Service	22	22
Primary	12	10
Processing, machining, laborers	9	5
Transportation, moving	23	6
Materials handling	11	10
Industry		
Agriculture	0	3
Forestry, fishing	14	54
Mining	5	0
Construction	0	9
Durable manufacturing	0	1
Nondurable manufacturing	1	0
Transportation	40	24
Communication, utilities	59	15
Wholesale trade	1	0
Retail trade	2	1
Finance, insurance, real estate	8	1
Education, related services	75	80
Health, welfare services	25	20
Other services	1	3
Public administration	100	100

Sources: Tabulated from Statistics Canada, Survey of Union Membership, supplement to the Labour Force Survey, December 1984; and U.S. Bureau of Labor Statistics, CPS earnings file, supplement to the Current Population Survey, December 1984. Excluded from the sample are nonpaid workers (self-employed, unpaid family workers), armed forces, those not employed in the reference period, and observations with missing values for the relevant variables.

Table 4.9 shows the extent of union organization among public and private sector employees by gender, full-time and part-time employment, occupation, and industry. In both countries there are very substantial differences in union density between the public and private sectors. Using the preferred measure of union status (collective agreement coverage), 81 percent of Canadian public sector paid workers are unionized versus 34 percent in the private sector. For the United States the comparable union densities are 41 percent in the public sector and 16 percent in the private sector. Thus in both countries pub-

Table 4.9 **Extent of Union Organization of Government and Private Employed Paid Workers in Canada and the United States, December 1984**

	Percentage of Paid Workers Who Are Union Members				Percentage of Paid Workers Covered by a Collective Agreement			
	Public Sector		Private Sector		Public Sector		Private Sector	
	Canada	U.S.	Canada	U.S.	Canada	U.S.	Canada	U.S.
All workers	74	34	29	15	81	41	34	16
Males	75	40	35	20	81	45	39	21
Females	72	29	23	9	80	37	27	10
Full-time	77	39	32	17	84	46	37	19
Part-time	49	11	15	6	60	16	19	6
Occupation								
Managerial, professional, technical	73	36	24	6	80	42	30	8
Clerical	74	30	19	9	83	37	23	11
Sales	66	11	8	5	72	19	11	6
Service	67	37	21	7	74	42	23	8
Primary	70	21	25	4	73	26	27	4
Processing, machining, laborers	86	39	52	31	89	47	56	33
Transportation, moving	89	42	36	29	92	42	41	30
Materials handling	80	40	50	30	83	41	55	32
Industry								
Agriculture	n.a.	0	2	1	n.a.	0	3	2
Forestry, fishing	63	8	37	0	67	8	40	0
Mining	42	n.a.	34	21	50	n.a.	38	21
Construction	n.a.	39	41	22	n.a.	40	45	23
Durable manufacturing	100	51	50	29	100	56	55	32
Nondurable manufacturing	71	75	47	22	77	86	51	24
Transportation	84	69	39	33	86	73	44	35
Communication, utilities	74	36	59	42	80	51	63	47
Wholesale trade	9	0	14	6	9	0	18	6
Retail trade	60	19	13	6	80	27	16	7
Finance, insurance, real estate	55	14	6	4	63	14	9	5
Education, related services	81	38	44	10	89	46	56	13
Health, welfare services	72	24	53	6	78	28	60	8
Other services	44	13	9	6	45	18	12	7
Public administration	69	29	n.a.	n.a.	78	35	n.a.	n.a.

Sources: See table 4.8.

Note: N.a. means that there were no paid workers (covered or not covered) in the category.

lic sector employees are more than twice as likely as their private sector counterparts to be represented by a union. Even within the same industry or occupation, workers in publicly owned enterprises in both countries are much more likely to be organized than their counterparts in privately owned enterprises. These differences explain the large and highly significant coefficient on public sector status in the unionization equation estimates reported in table 4.6.

Also noteworthy is the finding that the rule of thumb discussed in the context of table 4.2—that a randomly selected Canadian worker is about twice as likely to be unionized as his or her U.S. counterpart—continues to hold when the data are broken down into the public and private sectors. For the public sector as a whole, union density is 81 percent in Canada versus 41 percent in the United States. The comparable statistics for the private sector are 34 percent for Canada and 16 percent for the United States. Thus, although the extent of union organization is higher in each country's public sector, the Canada-U.S. relative unionization differential is the same (i.e., a ratio of approximately two to one) in both the public and private sectors.

Because the determinants of union coverage may differ between the private and public sectors in each country, separate probit models were estimated for the two sectors. The parameter estimates were then used to decompose the intercountry unionization differential by sector into a component associated with differences in the characteristics of the respective labor forces and a component associated with the impacts of those characteristics on the probability of union coverage. These decompositions are shown in part A of table 4.7.[25] In the private sector, all of the intercountry gap in unionization is due to differences in the impacts and none to differences in the characteristics of the respective labor forces. In the public sector, 95 percent of the gap is associated with differences in the estimated probit parameters, and only 5 percent with intercountry differences in characteristics. Thus these results further strengthen the conclusion reached in the previous section that—apart from the greater extent of public sector employment in Canada—differences in the structures of the respective labor forces account for very little of the large intercountry differential in union coverage.

The decompositions for each sector reported in column 3 of part A of table 4.7 were also broken down to show the contribution of each variable, as done for the full sample in part B of table 4.7. In the private sector approximately half of the total gap is attributed to the larger Canadian constant term; about 30 percent is attributed to larger Canadian coefficients associated with particular industries (especially education, health, and welfare) and about 8 percent to larger Canadian coefficients associated with particular occupations (especially primary occupations). In the public sector more than two-thirds of the gap is attributed to the higher constant term in the Canadian probit equation and about one-third to the occupational coefficients, especially clerical, processing, transportation and moving, and materials handling occupations.

In summary, analysis of the public and private sectors separately does not alter the conclusions reached from the analysis of the full samples. Within

25. Estimated parameters for the public and private sectors separately are available on request from me, as are the breakdowns showing the contributions of each variable.

each sector differences in the structural characteristics of the Canadian and U.S. labor forces account for very little of the intercountry unionization gap. Almost all of the differential is due to the greater likelihood of union coverage of a Canadian worker with a given set of characteristics. In each sector, most of the gap can be accounted for by the fact that an employee with the same set of characteristics is much more likely to be covered by a collective agreement in Canada. The remainder of the differential in each sector can largely be attributed to the fact that Canadian workers employed in particular industries and occupations are more likely to be unionized than are U.S. workers with the same personal characteristics employed in the same industries and occupations.

4.6 Social Attitudes toward Unionization

Explanations of the substantial Canada-U.S. gap in unionization must confront the difficult task of distinguishing between endogenous and exogenous forces. For example, beginning with Weiler (1983, 1984), several scholars have identified intercountry differences in the legal framework governing union formation and the practice of collective bargaining as being important contributors to the unionization differential. However, do the laws in each country not simply reflect the underlying values held by the citizens of the respective societies? Canada-U.S. differences in the legal framework governing collective bargaining and in the extent of union organization may thus be jointly endogenous outcomes of fundamental value differences between the two societies.

The thesis that the gap in unionization is due to differences between Canada and the United States in underlying social values has been stated most forcefully by Lipset (1986). It is certainly possible to make a persuasive case that the values and institutions of Canada and the United States differ in important and apparently enduring ways (Lipset 1990). Canadians are more inclined to favor collective forms of organization and state intervention in the economy than are Americans, who place more importance on individual rights and freedoms and free enterprise. On the surface, these apparent differences in social values are consistent with the differences between Canada and the United States in the role played by unions. If underlying social attitudes are an important source, however, why did the Canada-U.S. unionization differential emerge only in the past three decades? Why did the two countries display very similar trends in union density until the 1950s? Clearly Lipset's hypothesis requires a more careful examination.

Comparative evidence on social attitudes toward unions is available from similar public opinion polls in both the United States and Canada. The U.S. data have been used by Lipset (1986) to support the view that postwar changes in American attitudes toward unions are responsible for the decline in union density in that country. In particular, there is a strong correlation between

American attitudes toward unions (as measured by the responses to the question, "In general, do you approve or disapprove of labor unions?") and union density. As can be seen from table 4.10 and figure 4.2, since the early 1950s there has been a steady decline in the percentage of Americans with favorable attitudes toward unions and a steady increase in the percentage who disapprove of unions.

However, inspection of table 4.10 and figure 4.3 reveals that these same trends have occurred in Canada. Indeed, both the percentage who approve or disapprove of unions at each point in time and the changes in these levels over time are remarkably similar in the two countries. A more formal test of this

Table 4.10 Attitudes toward Unions in Canada and the United States, Percentage of Respondents

	Canada		U.S.	
	Favorable	Unfavorable	Favorable	Unfavorable
1949	—	—	62	22
1950	62	14	—	—
1952	60	15	—	—
1953	—	—	75	18
1956	69	12	—	—
1957[a]	—	—	70	16
1958	62	20	—	—
1959	—	—	68	19
1961[a]	66	23	67	20
1962	—	—	64	24
1963	—	—	67	23
1965[a]	—	—	71	19
1967	—	—	66	23
1970	54	30	—	—
1973	—	—	59	26
1975	57	26	—	—
1976	42	36	—	—
1978	46	41	59	31
1979	50	35	55	33
1980	54	30	—	—
1981	—	—	55	35
1982	48	32	—	—
1984	51	35	—	—
1985	—	—	58	27

Sources: Canadian Institute of Public Opinion, *The Gallup Report* (Toronto: various years); Gallup Poll, *The Gallup Report* (Princeton, N.J.: various years).

Notes: For Canada the question posed was, "Generally speaking, do you think that labour unions have been a good thing or a bad thing for Canada" (1950 to 1958 and 1976 to 1985). During the period 1961 to 1975 the question posed was, "In general do you approve or disapprove of labour unions?" For the United States the question posed was, "In general, do you approve or disapprove of labor unions?"

[a]U.S. data are averages of the two surveys conducted in these years.

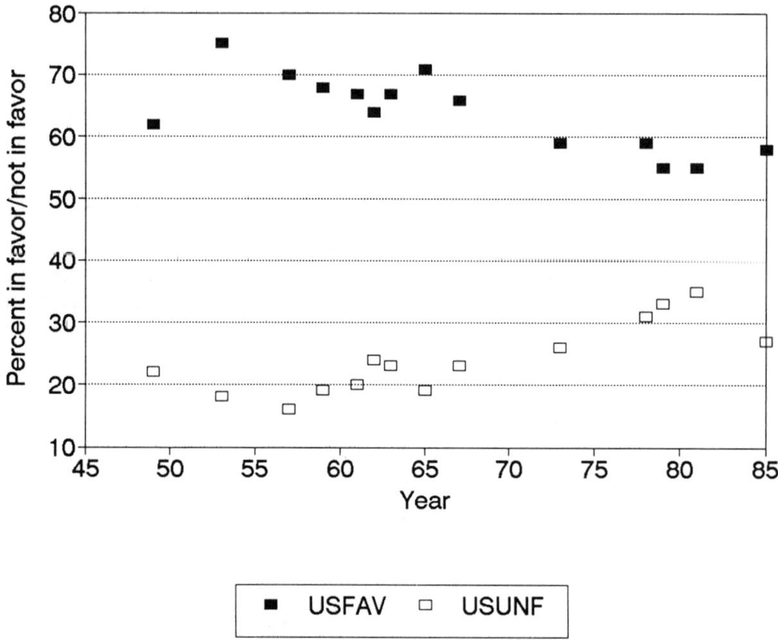

Fig. 4.2 Attitudes toward unions, United States, 1949–85
Sources: See table 4.10.
Note: USFAV = percent in favor, United States; USUNF = percent not in favor, United States.

similarity was carried out by regressing the percentage in favor of unions in each country on a constant term and a time trend. The hypothesis that the responses were drawn from a population with the same attitudes toward unions cannot be rejected.[26] A similar result obtains when the percentage who disapprove of unions is used as the dependent variable.

In summary, although the two societies differ in many ways, Canadians and Americans evidently have very similar attitudes toward unions. Changes in these attitudes during the past four decades have also been remarkably similar in the two countries. Thus there is no empirical support for the view that the

26. The downward trend in favorable attitudes toward unions is actually steeper in Canada than in the United States, although the differences are not statistically significant. The estimated equations are

$$\underset{}{USFAV} = \underset{(13.3)}{92.6} - \underset{(-\,4.2)}{0.43\ TIME}$$

and

$$\underset{}{CANFAV} = \underset{(10.8)}{92.0} - \underset{(-4.3)}{0.53\ TIME},$$

where USFAV and CANFAV are the percentage who approve of unions in the United States and Canada, respectively, and TIME is a time trend. Figures in parentheses are *t*-statistics.

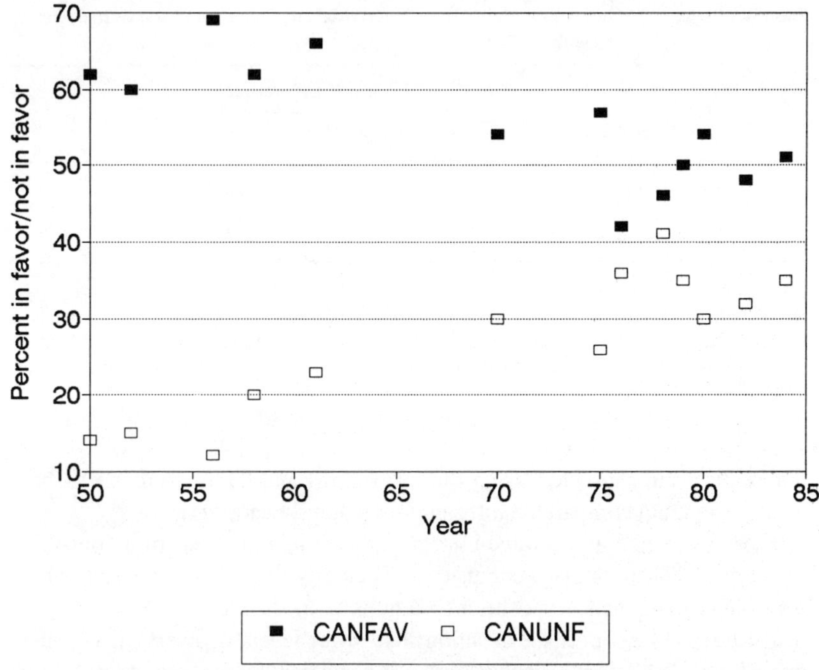

Fig. 4.3 Attitudes toward unions, Canada, 1950–84
Sources: See table 4.10.
Note: CANFAV = percent in favor, Canada; CANUNF = percent not in favor, Canada.

Canada-U.S. unionization differential can be attributed to fundamental differences in social attitudes toward unions and collective bargaining.

4.7 Costs of Unionization to Employers

Several studies have noted that Canada appears to have significantly less overt management opposition to unions in the form of unfair labor practices and significantly more union organizing activity (Freeman 1986; Kumar 1991). The reasons for lower levels of management opposition to unions are not clear, however, especially given the close corporate linkages between the two countries. One view is that the Canadian legal framework and the associated administration and enforcement mechanisms reduce the incentives to oppose unions relative to the United States (Flanagan 1987; Kumar 1991). However, another possible explanation is that unionization is less costly to Canadian employers than to their U.S. counterparts.

Evidence relating to possible intercountry differences in the costs associated with unionization is presented in table 4.11. The union-nonunion wage

Table 4.11 Union-Nonunion Wage Differentials in Canada and the United States, December 1984

	Estimated Differential (%)	
Sector	Canada	U.S.
Total economy	24.0	23.3
Private sector	27.0	27.4
Public sector	7.9	−3.9

Sources: See table 4.8.

Notes: Based on log earnings equations estimated by OLS separately on the covered and uncovered sectors. Differentials are evaluated at the mean of the data in the sector and country. Controls included gender, part-time, age, education, public sector (total economy estimates), industry, and occupation.

differentials are estimated using the 1984 SUM and CPS earnings file; both data sets contain comparable information on hourly earnings.

These estimated union wage impacts indicate that the costs of unionization are very similar in the two countries, particularly in the private sector, where possible management opposition to unions is most relevant. Thus this evidence does not support the position that lower levels of overt management opposition to unions in Canada are due to Canadian unions having less impact on wages than their U.S. counterparts do.

4.8 Conclusions

Canada and the United States displayed similar patterns of union growth from the early 1900s until the mid-1950s. Since that time, trends in unionization have diverged sharply, with union density declining steadily in the United States but growing in Canada until the mid-1980s and subsequently declining modestly. As a consequence, a huge Canada-U.S. gap has emerged in the extent of union organization—so that in recent years the fraction of the Canadian labor force represented by unions has been approximately double that of the United States. The dramatic decline in union strength in the United States and the emergence of a substantial Canada-U.S. unionization differential are important developments affecting these two societies. This paper has been concerned with contributing to our understanding of the causes of these dramatic developments, taking advantage of the "natural experiment" yielded by two countries with not only similar economies but also similar histories of union development and industrial relations systems. To as great an extent as possible I have used data sets that are comparable between the two countries, so that differences in observed outcomes are due mainly to differences in underlying behavior rather than to differences in survey or questionnaire design.

The main findings of this comparative analysis are the following:

1. The intercountry differences in union coverage are pervasive rather than being concentrated in specific sectors of the economy or segments of the labor force. Whether individuals are classified by gender, age, industry, occupation, public or private sector employment, or education, a Canadian worker is approximately twice as likely to be represented by a union as his or her American counterpart.

2. A comparative demand-supply analysis indicates that the gap in unionization can be attributed to the greater likelihood that a Canadian worker who wishes to be represented by a union will in fact be unionized (supply conditional on demand) and to the greater desire for union representation by Canadians. This finding is consistent with the view that differences between Canada and the United States in overt management opposition to unions and the legal framework governing union formation and the practice of collective bargaining contribute to the unionization differential.

3. A comparative microanalysis of union incidence concludes that structural differences in the respective economies and labor forces account for about 15 percent of the intercountry differential in unionization. Eighty-five percent of the differential is attributed to the fact that a Canadian worker with given characteristics is much more likely to be covered by a collective agreement than a U.S. worker with the same characteristics.

4. The only quantitatively important structural difference arises from the fact that the fraction of paid workers employed in government-owned enterprises is about 30 percent higher in Canada than in the United States. In both countries, public sector employees are substantially more likely to be unionized than their private sector counterparts in the same industry or occupation. The greater involvement of publicly owned enterprises in the Canadian economy accounts for about 7 percent of the intercountry differential in union density.

5. There is no empirical support for the hypothesis that the Canada-U.S. gap in union coverage is due to differences between the two countries in the underlying social attitudes toward unions.

6. The impact of unions on wages in the private sector is very similar. Thus intercountry differences in the costs to employers associated with unionization cannot account for differences in the amount of overt management opposition to unions.

On the whole these findings support the hypothesis that much of the Canada-U.S. unionization gap can be attributed to intercountry differences in the legal regime pertaining to unions and collective bargaining and to differences in overt management opposition to unions (itself possibly a consequence of differences in collective bargaining laws and their administration). Only a modest portion of the differential in union coverage is associated with the greater extent of public sector employment in Canada. Other explanations of the differential that have been advanced receive little, if any, support.

Appendix

Table 4A.1 Demand for Unionization in the Public and Private Sectors

	AFL Survey		CFL Survey		Pooled Sample	
Variable	Public	Private	Public	Private	Public	Private
Constant	0.18	−0.48	−1.28	0.31	−0.68	−0.29
	(0.3)	(−1.5)	(−1.6)	(0.6)	(−1.6)	(−1.1)
Male	0.11	0.08	0.08	0.37	0.08	0.17
	(0.6)	(0.8)	(0.3)	(2.6)	(0.6)	(2.1)
Age 25–34	0.19	0.05	0.20	−0.25	0.15	−0.03
	(0.7)	(0.4)	(0.4)	(−1.1)	(0.6)	(−0.2)
Age 35–44	0.08	0.14	0.56	0.11	0.22	0.16
	(0.3)	(0.9)	(1.1)	(0.5)	(0.9)	(1.2)
Age 45–54	0.46	0.03	1.01	−0.08	0.62	0.02
	(1.3)	(0.2)	(1.7)	(−0.3)	(2.1)	(0.2)
Age 55–64	−0.14	0.24	1.37	−0.11	0.30	0.10
	(−0.4)	(1.2)	(1.8)	(−0.3)	(0.9)	(0.6)
Age 65 +	−0.01	−0.18		−0.61	−0.05	−0.34
	(−0.0)	(−0.4)		(−1.0)	(−0.0)	(−0.9)
Some high school	0.30	0.71	1.34	−0.43	0.82	0.24
	(0.5)	(2.2)	(2.0)	(−0.9)	(2.0)	(0.9)
High school graduate	0.08	0.48	1.86	−0.33	0.83	0.22
	(0.2)	(1.6)	(2.9)	(−0.7)	(2.3)	(0.9)
Some college	−0.10	0.07	2.02	−0.32	0.87	−0.05
	(−0.2)	(0.2)	(3.0)	(−0.7)	(2.2)	(−0.2)
Some university	−0.42	−0.04	2.12	−0.58	0.61	−0.22
	(−0.7)	(−0.1)	(2.7)	(−1.1)	(1.4)	(−0.7)
University graduate	−0.15	−0.34	1.76	−0.29	0.66	−0.34
	(−0.3)	(−1.1)	(2.8)	(−0.6)	(1.8)	(−1.3)
Canada					0.65	0.19
					(4.4)	(2.2)
N	216	674	179	338	395	1,012
Currently predicted (%)	62	62	85	58	72	58

Table 4A.2 Supply of Unionization in the Public and Private Sectors

	AFL Survey		CFL Survey		Pooled Sample	
Variable	Public	Private	Public	Private	Public	Private
Constant	−2.12	−1.61	6.24	−0.53	−1.23	−1.22
	(−2.6)	(−2.9)	(0.0)	(−0.7)	(−2.0)	(−2.9)
Male	0.18	0.93	0.24	0.21	0.21	0.63
	(0.7)	(5.8)	(0.9)	(0.9)	(1.2)	(5.0)
Age 25–34	1.41	0.47	−0.12	0.62	0.85	0.47
	(2.5)	(2.0)	(−0.2)	(2.0)	(2.4)	(2.6)
Age 35–44	1.85	0.67	−0.24	0.67	1.05	0.56
	(3.2)	(2.6)	(−0.4)	(2.1)	(2.9)	(2.9)
Age 45–54	1.50	0.62	−0.03	1.41	0.99	0.79
	(2.5)	(2.3)	(−0.1)	(3.3)	(2.6)	(3.6)
Age 55–64	1.97	1.39	−0.23	6.19	1.16	1.51
	(2.9)	(4.1)	(−0.3)	(0.0)	(2.7)	(5.2)
Age 65+	−3.99	−5.4		−6.01	−4.89	0.13
	(−0.0)	(−0.0)		(0.0)	(−0.0)	(0.2)
Some high school	0.26	0.62	−5.6	−0.15	−0.24	0.09
	(0.4)	(1.1)	(−0.0)	(−0.2)	(−0.4)	(0.2)
High school graduate	0.30	0.35	−5.5	0.47	−0.05	0.20
	(0.5)	(0.7)	(−0.0)	(0.7)	(−0.1)	(0.5)
Some college	0.32	0.39	−4.2	0.33	0.46	0.17
	(0.4)	(0.7)	(−0.0)	(0.5)	(0.8)	(0.4)
Some university	0.18	−0.06	−5.5	0.07	−0.11	−0.04
	(0.2)	(−0.1)	(−0.0)	(0.1)	(−0.2)	(−0.1)
University graduate	0.86	0.41	−5.1	−0.09	0.48	−0.01
	(1.4)	(0.7)	(−0.0)	(−0.1)	(0.9)	(−0.0)
Canada					1.02	0.67
					(5.8)	(5.1)
N	133	302	150	181	283	483
Currently predicted (%)	64	69	83	70	73	69

References

Abowd, John, and Henry S. Farber. 1982. Job Queues and the Union Status of Workers. *Industrial and Labor Relations Review* 35 (April): 354–67.

Ashenfelter, Orley, and John Pencavel. 1969. American Trade Union Growth: 1900–1964. *Quarterly Journal of Economics* 83 (August): 434–48.

Chaison, G. N., and J. B. Rose. 1988. Continental Divide: The Direction and Fate of North American Unions. McMaster University, Faculty of Business Working Paper no. 309, September.

Cooke, William. 1985. The Failure to Negotiate First Contracts: Determinants and Policy Implications. *Industrial and Labor Relations Review* 38 (January): 163–78.

Dickens, William, and Jonathan Leonard. 1985. Accounting for the Decline in Union Membership, 1950–1980. *Industrial and Labor Relations Review* 38 (April): 323–34.

Doiron, Denise, and W. Craig Riddell. 1993. The Impact of Unionization on Male-Female Earnings Differences in Canada. *Journal of Human Resources,* forthcoming.

Economic Council of Canada. *Minding the Public's Business.* Ottawa: Minister of Supplies and Services.

Edwards, Richard. 1986. *Unions in Crisis and Beyond: Perspectives from Six Countries.* Dover, Mass.: Auburn House.

Even, William E., and David A. Macpherson. 1993. The Decline in Private Sector Unionism and the Gender Wage Gap. *Journal of Human Resources,* forthcoming.

Farber, Henry S. 1983. The Determination of the Union Status of Workers. *Econometrica* 51 (September): 1417–37.

———. 1985. The Extent of Unionization in the United States. In Thomas A. Kochan, ed., *Challenges and Choices Facing American Labor,* 15–43. Cambridge, Mass.: MIT Press.

———. 1990. The Decline in Unionization in the U.S.: What Can Be Learned from Recent Experience? *Journal of Labor Economics* 8 (January): S75–S101.

Farber, Henry S., and Alan B. Krueger. 1992. Union Membership in the United States: The Decline Continues. Princeton University, Industrial Relations Section, Working Paper no. 306, August.

Flanagan, Robert J. 1987. *Labor Relations and the Litigation Explosion.* Washington, D.C.: Brookings Institution.

Freeman, Richard B. 1985. Why Are Unions Faring Poorly in NLRB Representation Elections? In Thomas A. Kochan, ed., *Challenges and Choices Facing American Labor,* 45–64. Cambridge, Mass.: MIT Press.

———. 1986. Unionism Comes to the Public Sector. *Journal of Economic Literature* 24 (March): 41–86.

———. 1988. Contraction and Expansion: The Divergence of Private Sector and Public Sector Unionism in the United States. *Journal of Economic Perspectives* 2 (Spring): 63–88.

———. 1989. On the Divergence in Unionism among Developed Countries. NBER Working Paper no. 2817. Cambridge, Mass.: National Bureau of Economic Research, January.

———. 1990. Canada in the World Labour Market to Year 2000. In K. Newton, T. Schweitzer, and J. P. Voyer, eds., *Perspective 2000,* 188–98. Ottawa: Economic Council of Canada.

Kochan, Thomas A., Harry Katz, and Robert B. McKersie. 1986. *The Transformation of American Industrial Relations.* New York: Basic Books.

Kumar, Pradeep. 1986. Union Growth in Canada: Retrospect and Prospect. In W.

Craig Riddell, ed., *Canadian Labour Relations,* 95–160. Toronto: Toronto University Press.

———. 1991. Industrial Relations in Canada and the United States: From Uniformity to Divergence. Industrial Relations Centre, Queen's University, Working Paper 1991–2.

Kumar, Pradeep, and Bradley Dow. 1986. Econometric Analysis of Union Membership Growth in Canada, 1935–1981. *Relations Industrielles/Industrial Relations* 41:236–53.

Lipset, Seymour M. 1986. North American Labor Movements: A Comparative Perspective. In Seymour M. Lipset, ed., *Unions in Transition: Entering the Second Century,* 421–52. San Francisco: ICS Press.

———. 1990. *Continental Divide: The Values and Institutions of the United States and Canada.* New York: Routledge.

Meltz, Noah M. 1985. Labor Movements in Canada and the United States. In Thomas A. Kochan, ed., *Challenges and Choices Facing American Labor,* 315–34. Cambridge, Mass.: MIT Press.

———. 1989. Unionism in the Private Service Sector: A Canada-U.S. Comparison. Center for Industrial Relations, University of Toronto, June.

Neumann, George, and Ellen Rissman. 1984. Where Have All the Union Members Gone? *Journal of Labor Economics* 2 (April): 175–92.

Pencavel, John. 1971. The Demand for Union Services: An Exercise. *Industrial and Labor Relations Review* 24 (January): 180–90.

Rose, Joseph, and Gary Chaison. 1985. The State of the Unions: United States and Canada. *Journal of Labor Research* 6 (Winter): 97–111.

Statistics Canada. 1992a. *CALURA Labour Unions 1989.* Ottawa: Statistics Canada.

———. 1992b. *Guide to Labour Force Survey Data.* Ottawa: Statistics Canada.

Strauss, George, Daniel Gallagher, and Jack Fiorito, eds. 1991. *The State of the Unions.* Madison: Industrial Relations Research Association.

Swidinsky, Robert. 1974. Trade Union Growth in Canada, 1911–1970. *Relations Industrielles/Industrial Relations* 29 (July): 435–51.

Troy, Leo. 1990. Is the U.S. Unique in the Decline of Private Sector Unionism? *Journal of Labor Research* 11 (Spring): 111–43.

———. 1992. Convergence in International Unionism, etc.: The Case of Canada and the U.S.A. *British Journal of Industrial Relations* 30 (March): 1–43.

U.S. Department of Labor, Bureau of Labor Statistics, *CPS Interviewers Manual.* Washington, D.C.: Bureau of Labor Statistics.

Voos, Paula. 1984. Trends in Union Organizing Expenditures, 1953–1977. *Industrial and Labor Relations Review* 38:52–63.

Weiler, Paul. 1983. Promises to Keep: Securing Workers' Rights to Self-Organization under the NLRA. *Harvard Law Review* 96:1769–1827.

———. 1984. Striking a New Balance: Freedom of Contract and the Prospects for Union Representation. *Harvard Law Review* 98 (December): 351–420.

5 A Comparative Analysis of Unemployment in Canada and the United States

David Card and W. Craig Riddell

5.1 Introduction

In most countries the unemployment rate is a closely watched indicator of labor market performance. Judged by this standard the performance of the Canadian economy deteriorated sharply in the 1980s. The average decadal unemployment rate rose from 6.7 percent in the 1970s to 9.3 percent in the 1980s. Even more revealing is the increase in Canadian unemployment relative to U.S. Throughout most of the postwar period unemployment rates in the two countries followed very similar trends. This fact is illustrated in figure 5.1, where we show U.S. and Canadian unemployment rates for the past thirty years. Average unemployment rates were nearly equal in the two countries during the 1950s and 1960s, and only slightly higher in Canada in the 1970s. During the 1980s, however, average Canadian unemployment rates were a full 2 percentage points higher.

The emergence of a relative unemployment gap between Canada and the United States has sparked much speculation and research into its causes.[1] Initially many observers argued that the gap reflected the more severe economic downturn in Canada in the early 1980s. Following the longest expansion in the postwar era, however, it is difficult to argue that the unemployment gap is a short-run adjustment phenomenon. In this paper we investigate an alternative "structural hypothesis": that the divergence in unemployment rates reflects an emerging structural difference in the nature of unemployment and

David Card is professor of economics at Princeton University and a research associate of the National Bureau of Economic Research. W. Craig Riddell is professor of economics at the University of British Columbia.

The authors thank Paul Beaudry, Louis Christofides, Lawrence Katz, Stephen Kaliski, and Ian Macredie for their comments and suggestions.

1. See Ashenfelter and Card (1986), Fortin (1986), McCallum (1987), Moorthy (1990), Keil and Symons (1990), and Milbourne, Purvis, and Scoones (1991).

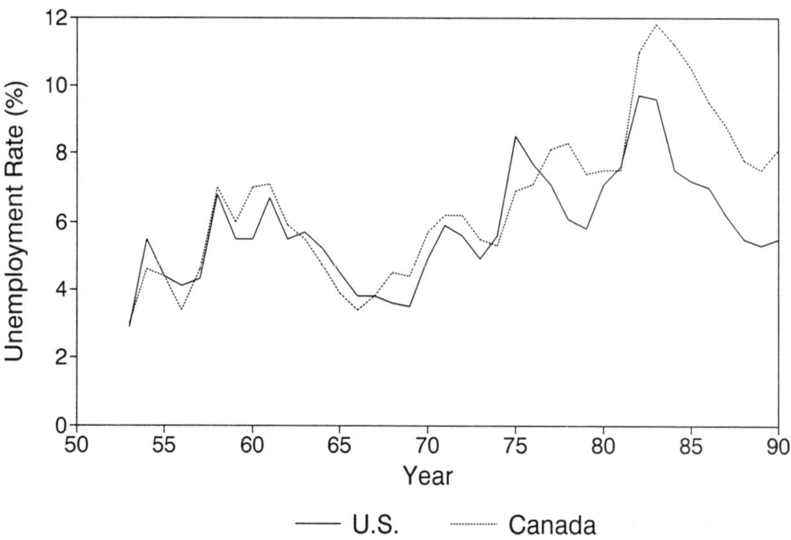

Fig. 5.1 Unemployment rates in the United States and Canada, 1953–90

labor supply in the two countries. To understand this difference we analyze individual employment and unemployment data from the United States and Canada at the beginning and end of the 1980s. Our investigation points to several complementary explanations for the relative growth of unemployment in Canada, including relative changes in the fraction of nonworking time that is reported as unemployment (particularly among women and men with very low levels of labor supply), and relative changes in the overall distributions of working and nonworking time.

Associated with the Canadian-U.S. unemployment gap is an even greater difference in the availability and utilization of income support programs for unemployed workers.[2] An important public policy question is whether the more generous unemployment insurance (UI) system in Canada is causally related to the relative growth in Canadian unemployment. Although we provide no definitive answer to this question, our analysis suggests that the potential availability of UI benefits cannot *by itself* explain the emergence of the gap in unemployment between Canada and the United States. Nevertheless, some of our evidence is consistent with the hypothesis that structural features of the Canadian UI system, including the system of regional extended benefits, contributed to the rise in unemployment in Canada relative to the United States.

2. See Blank and Hanratty (1991) for an analysis of the effects of this difference on the distributions of family income in the two countries. Anderson and Meyer (1993) and Green and Riddell (1993) provide overviews of the unemployment insurance systems in the United States and Canada, respectively.

The research strategy followed in this paper is unabashedly empirical. We regard the emergence of a gap in the unemployment rates of the two countries as a mystery, and sift through the available data for clues. Section 5.2 documents the unemployment gap using aggregate time-series data. Sections 5.3–5.5—the core of the paper—analyze microdata from the two countries before and after the relative rise in Canadian unemployment. Much of the analysis uses a "difference-in-differences" technique to net out any permanent country-specific effects or common time trends in the two countries. At the microlevel, labor market behavior in the two countries is remarkably similar and remarkably stable over time. The most notable relative shift in individual behavior in the two countries concerns the allocation of nonworking time between time spent unemployed and time spent out of the labor force. This conclusion leads us to an investigation in section 5.6 of the income support programs in the two countries. We summarize our findings in section 5.7.

5.2 The Emergence of the Unemployment Gap

Table 5.1 presents a variety of aggregate labor market indicators for the United States and Canada over the 1966–90 period. These data are drawn from very similar household surveys in the two countries—the Current Population Survey (CPS) in the United States and the Labour Force Survey (LFS) in Canada. In particular, the concepts of employment, unemployment, and labor force participation are based on responses to an almost identical battery of questions in the two surveys.[3] We therefore believe that comparisons of U.S. and Canadian labor market data reflect behavioral differences between the two countries, rather than differences in the definitions of labor market status.

The first and fifth columns of the table report the adult civilian populations of the two countries.[4] From the early 1960s to 1980 the adult population grew faster in Canada: 2.16 percent per year versus 1.96 percent per year in the United States. After 1981, growth rates of the adult populations in the two countries slowed to virtually the same rate—1.15 percent per year. The greater relative slowdown in population growth accounts for a slight relative downturn in the economic growth of Canada in the 1980s.

Trends in labor force participation rates show much bigger differences across the two countries. Historically, labor force participation rates were higher in the United States than in Canada. In 1953, for example, the partici-

3. In both countries an individual is counted as employed if he or she did any work in the preceding week or had a job but was absent for reasons of sickness, vacation, and so forth. An individual is counted as unemployed if he or she was available for work during the week and was either laid off from a job and expecting recall, or had looked for work in the preceding month.

4. We present labor market data for the civilian population in each country. Data for the entire population (including active members of the armed forces as employed) are very similar. Note that the adult population is age 15 and over in Canada, and age 16 and older in the United States.

Table 5.1 Population, Labor Force Participation, Employment-Population, and Unemployment Rates, 1966–90

	U.S.				Canada			
	Civilian Population	LFPR	Employment-Population	Unemployment Rate	Civilian Population	LFPR	Employment-Population	Unemployment Rate
1966	128,058	59.2	56.9	3.8	13,083	57.3	55.4	3.4
1967	129,874	59.6	57.3	3.8	13,444	57.6	55.4	3.8
1968	132,028	59.6	57.5	3.6	13,805	57.6	55.0	4.5
1969	134,335	60.1	58.0	3.5	14,162	57.9	55.3	4.4
1970	137,085	60.4	57.4	4.9	14,528	57.8	54.5	5.7
1971	140,216	60.2	56.6	5.9	14,872	58.1	54.5	6.2
1972	144,126	60.4	57.0	5.6	15,186	58.6	54.9	6.2
1973	147,096	60.8	57.8	4.9	15,526	59.7	56.4	5.5
1974	150,120	61.3	57.8	5.6	15,924	60.5	57.3	5.3
1975	153,153	61.2	56.1	8.5	16,323	61.1	56.9	6.9
1976	156,150	61.6	56.8	7.7	16,701	61.1	56.7	7.1
1977	159,033	62.3	57.9	7.1	17,051	61.6	56.6	8.1
1978	161,910	63.2	59.3	6.1	17,377	62.7	57.5	8.3
1979	164,863	63.7	59.9	5.8	17,702	63.4	58.7	7.4
1980	167,745	63.8	59.2	7.1	18,053	64.1	59.3	7.5
1981	170,130	63.9	59.0	7.6	18,368	64.8	59.9	7.5
1982	172,271	64.0	57.8	9.7	18,608	64.1	57.1	11.0
1983	174,215	64.0	57.9	9.6	18,805	64.4	56.8	11.8
1984	176,383	64.4	59.5	7.5	18,996	64.8	57.5	11.2
1985	178,206	64.8	60.1	7.2	19,190	65.3	58.5	10.5
1986	180,587	65.3	60.7	7.0	19,397	65.7	59.4	9.5
1987	182,753	65.6	61.5	6.2	19,642	66.2	60.4	8.8
1988	184,613	65.9	62.3	5.5	19,890	66.7	61.6	7.8
1989	186,393	66.5	63.0	5.3	20,141	67.0	62.0	7.5
1990	188,049	66.4	62.7	5.5	20,430	67.0	61.5	8.1

Notes: Civilian population (age 16 and over in the United States, age 15 and over in Canada) is in thousands. LFPR is the labor force participation rate among the civilian population.

pation rates of U.S. men and women were 86.0 and 34.4 percent, while those of Canadian men and women were 81.0 and 23.6 percent. During the 1960s female participation grew rapidly in Canada, and male participation rates declined more slowly than in the United States, so that by 1975 overall participation rates were nearly identical in the two countries. Interestingly, the much higher unemployment rates in Canada after 1982 did little to dampen Canadian participation rates, which remained slightly above U.S. rates throughout the 1980s.

The relative trend in employment-population rates between the two countries reflects the relative increase in labor force participation in Canada offset by higher Canadian unemployment rates.[5] On net there was an actual increase in the relative employment-population rate in Canada between the 1960s and 1980s. This fact is illustrated in a slightly different way in figure 5.2, where we have plotted the differences in the labor force participation and unemployment rates between the United States and Canada for 1966–90, together with the difference in the "nonemployment" rate. The latter is simply the fraction of the population not working (1 minus the employment-population rate). Although differences in the unemployment and nonemployment rates between Canada and the United States have the same cyclical pattern, they have very different secular trends. The gap in nonemployment actually closed during the 1980s at the same time as the unemployment gap widened.

A comparison of relative employment rates paints a brighter picture of the Canadian labor market in the 1980s than a comparison of unemployment does. Which of these comparisons is preferred depends on one's view of the difference between unemployment and nonparticipation. If the distinction is purely terminological (as suggested by Lucas and Rapping 1970), the employment rate is a better yardstick of labor market performance. If unemployment and nonparticipation are distinct labor market states, however, a comparison of unemployment rates may provide a better index of labor market performance. In any case the increase in relative unemployment in Canada occurred in conjunction with *rising* relative participation and employment, rather than with a relative decline in work activity in the Canadian economy. We return to this point in the following sections.

As noted in the introduction, we have adopted the working hypothesis that the unemployment gap between Canada and the United States cannot be explained as a short-run adjustment phenomenon. Nevertheless, it must be acknowledged that the 1982–83 recession was considerably deeper in Canada. Some evidence of this fact is presented in table 5.2, which shows the changes in real output and employment in the two countries between 1981 and 1982, together with data on earlier trends and subsequent growth rates.[6] Relative to

5. Growth in the employment-population ratio is approximately the difference between growth in the labor force participation rate and the change in the unemployment rate.

6. We present two measures of overall employment growth in each country—one based on household surveys and another based on establishment surveys. The Canadian establishment sur-

Fig. 5.2 Differences in labor market activity rates, Canada minus the United States

Note: LFPR means labor force participation rate.

Table 5.2 Severity of the 1982 Downturn and Extent of the Subsequent Recovery in the United States and Canada

	U.S.			Canada		
		Employment			Employment	
	Real GNP	E-Series[a]	H-Series[b]	Real GNP	E-Series[a]	H-Series[b]
Severity of the 1982 downturn						
Trend growth 1970–81 (% per year)	2.7	2.5	2.4	4.4	3.0	3.0
Growth 1981–82 (%)	−2.6	−1.8	−0.8	−3.3	−3.5	−3.6
1981–82 change relative to trend	−5.3	−4.3	−3.2	−7.7	−6.5	−6.6
Extent of recovery post-1982						
Trend growth 1981–89 (% per year)	3.0	2.2	2.2	3.1	1.4	2.0
1981–89 growth rate relative to 1970–81 growth rate	0.3	−0.3	−0.2	−1.3	−1.6	−1.0

Note: Growth rates are measured as changes in logarithms of series.

[a]Employment as measured by establishment survey. The Canadian establishment survey was revised in 1983 and in 1987. Growth rates are calculated from a spliced series we constructed.

[b]Civilian employment as measured by household survey.

earlier trends, real output fell 5.3 percent between 1981 and 1983 in the United States, and 7.7 percent in Canada. The relative change in employment is similar. After 1983 the growth rates of output and employment returned to their earlier level in the United States but not in Canada. In fact the growth rates of output and employment in the United States and Canada were similar in the 1980s, whereas Canadian growth rates were significantly higher in the 1970s. Although one could argue from this evidence that the Canadian economy failed to fully recover from the 1982–83 recession, we believe a more reasonable hypothesis is that the factors leading to more rapid Canadian growth in the 1960s and 1970s (such as faster adult population growth and faster growth in labor force participation rates) had largely dissipated in the 1980s. The data suggest a return to labor market equilibrium in the late 1980s with permanently higher rates of unemployment in Canada.

Further evidence of a shift in the relation between unemployment and other indicators of labor market equilibrium in Canada is provided in figure 5.3. Here we have plotted a relative version of the classical Beveridge curve relating the unemployment rate to the job vacancy rate. Although true job vacancy data are unavailable for either the United States or Canada, a very similar help wanted index (HWI) is available for both countries.[7] A relative Beveridge curve based on the HWI fits the pre-1982 data for the two countries remarkably well.[8] After 1982, however, the figure suggests a sharp increase in the level of Canadian unemployment relative to the level of job listings. In fact, the excess unemployment during 1983–88 averages 2–3 percentage points—about the size of the unemployment gap between the United States and Canada. Thus a comparison of relative Beveridge curves suggests that the unemployment gap that emerged in the late 1980s resulted from a shift in the unemployment-vacancy relation in Canada, rather than from deficient labor demand.[9]

A similar conclusion emerges from a comparison of the correlations between unemployment and GNP growth in the two countries—the so-called Okun's law relationship. A regression of the unemployment gap between Canada and the United States on the difference in real GNP growth rates and an dummy variable for post-1981 observations shows a relative increase of 2.1

vey has been redesigned twice since 1983, forcing us to splice the available series. Thus the establishment-based employment growth rates in table 5.2 should be interpreted with caution.

7. The HWI is a simple index of the volume of classified newspaper advertisements for help wanted. See Hagar-Guenette (1989) for a brief history of the Canadian HWI and some analysis of its cyclical properties.

8. Interestingly, the country-specific Beveridge curves for 1966–81 show outward-shifting combinations of unemployment and vacancies throughout the 1970s. The curves are stabilized by intercountry differencing.

9. We have also compared the unemployment-vacancy relationship within particular Canadian provinces to the overall U.S. Beveridge curve. These comparisons also show a shift in the unemployment-vacancy relationship in Canada.

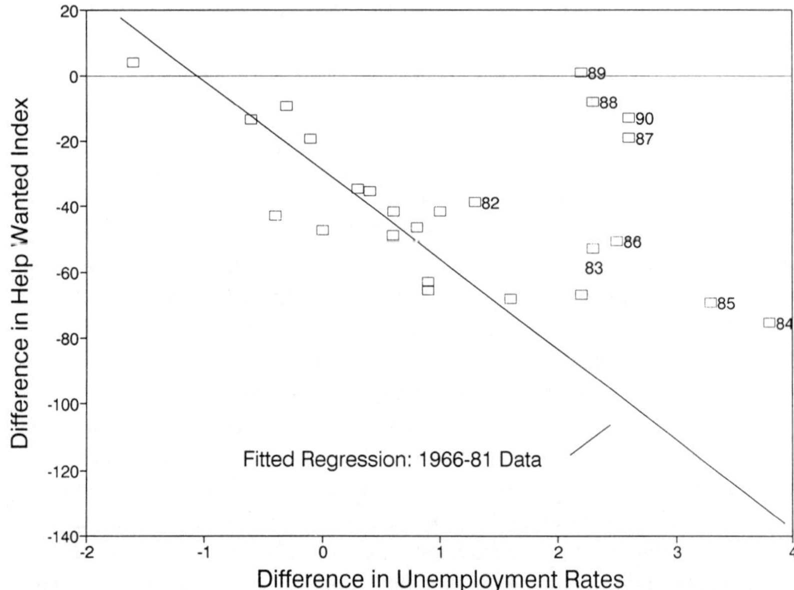

Fig. 5.3 Help wanted and unemployment, Canada minus the United States

percentage points in Canadian unemployment after 1981.[10] Comparisons of both the Beveridge curve and the Okun relationship suggest a structural explanation for the unemployment gap in the late 1980s, rather than a demand-based explanation.

5.3 A Microdata Analysis of Unemployment

We turn to a microdata analysis of employment and unemployment outcomes in the United States and Canada. We use individual-level data to examine changes over the 1980s in the labor market activities of different groups, and to analyze the components of the relative rise in Canadian unemployment. Our comparisons are drawn from CPS and LFS supplements conducted in 1980 and 1987. These surveys contain retrospective data on employment and unemployment experiences in 1979 and 1986, as well as contemporaneous data on labor market activities during the survey week.[11] The

10. The estimated regression is $DU = 0.5 - 0.14 \cdot DG + 2.1 \cdot$ (Post 1981), where DU is the difference in Canadian and U.S. unemployment rates and DG is the difference in real GNP growth rates. The estimated standard error of the relative growth coefficient is 0.08; the estimated standard error of the Post 1981 coefficient is 0.3; and the R^2 of the regression is 0.63. The regression is estimated on annual data for 1954–89.

11. The CPS supplement (the annual demographic file) is conducted as part of the March CPS survey. The LFS supplement (the Survey of Consumer Finances) is conducted as part of the April LFS survey.

1980 surveys pre-date the emergence of the Canada-U.S. unemployment gap and therefore provide a convenient benchmark against which to judge the later data. Although an earlier benchmark might be desirable, limitations in the CPS and LFS make it difficult to extract reliable annual labor force data in earlier surveys.[12]

Table 5.3 provides basic demographic and labor market information on individuals in the four surveys. For the two U.S. surveys and for the later (1987) Canadian survey we present information on both the overall adult population and the subset of family heads.[13] This distinction is necessary because information from the earlier Canadian survey is available only for family heads. Approximately 80 percent of adults in both countries are family heads. This fraction was remarkably stable in the United States over the early 1980s, suggesting that a comparison of changes in the employment and unemployment experiences of family heads will give a reasonably accurate picture of the overall population. Compared to the adult population as a whole, family heads are 3–4 years older and slightly more likely to be female. They also have higher education levels, slightly stronger labor force attachments, and about 10 percent higher average weekly wages.

The age and sex distributions of the population are very similar in the United States and Canada. The U.S. population is better educated: in table 5.3 rows 3 and 4 show that the fraction of individuals with less than high school education is substantially higher in Canada, while the fraction with college or university degrees is lower. The percentage of individuals employed in the survey week (row 5) is also two to three points higher in the United States. Average weeks worked in the previous year are roughly similar in the two countries, however, and average weeks in the labor force in the previous year are actually higher in Canada.[14] The unemployment rate of family heads during the survey week is 1 percentage point higher in Canada in 1980 and 2.5 percentage points higher in Canada in 1987. Compared to the aggregate statistics in table 5.1, the individual microdata show a slightly smaller relative rise in Canadian unemployment.[15]

An alternative measure of unemployment can be obtained from reported weeks of employment and unemployment in the previous year. Simple averages of this "retrospective unemployment rate" (across individuals with posi-

12. The March CPS survey began collecting information on exact weeks worked in the previous year only in 1976. Similar limitations also affect earlier Surveys of Consumer Finances.

13. We define the adult population as age 16–68 in both countries. Our family definition corresponds to the Survey of Consumer Finances definition of "economic families." Our definition of "heads" includes husbands and wives in families where both are present, as well as single heads of either sex.

14. Note that the survey week measures of employment and unemployment in table 5.3 are for a particular month (March in the United States, April in Canada) and do not take account of seasonal adjustment factors.

15. From table 5.1 the gap in overall unemployment rates between Canada and the United States rose from 0.4 percentage points in 1980 to 2.6 points in 1987.

Table 5.3 **Characteristics of Overall Population and Family Heads in the United States and Canada, 1980 and 1987**

	U.S.				Canada		
	All 1987	Heads 1987	All 1980	Heads 1980	All 1987	Heads 1987	Heads 1980
1. Average age	38.2	41.7	37.9	41.6	38.0	41.4	40.6
	(0.1)	(0.1)	(0.1)	(0.1)	(0.1)	(0.1)	(0.1)
2. Female (%)	51.5	52.9	51.8	53.0	50.4	51.8	52.2
	(0.2)	(0.2)	(0.1)	(0.2)	(0.2)	(0.2)	(0.2)
3. Education ≤ 8 years (%)	8.1	8.3	11.2	12.0	14.2	15.6	22.4
	(0.1)	(0.1)	(0.1)	(0.1)	(0.1)	(0.2)	(0.2)
4. Education ≥ 16 years (%)	18.3	21.1	15.0	17.4	11.7	13.3	9.7
	(0.1)	(0.1)	(0.1)	(0.1)	(0.1)	(0.2)	(0.1)
5. Employed (%)	67.1	70.3	64.8	67.9	65.0	66.9	66.1
	(0.2)	(0.2)	(0.1)	(0.2)	(0.2)	(0.2)	(0.2)
6. Unemployed (%)	5.0	4.0	4.7	3.7	7.1	6.5	4.8
	(0.1)	(0.1)	(0.1)	(0.1)	(0.1)	(0.1)	(0.1)
7. In labor force in previous year (%)	77.9	79.0	76.8	77.4	79.8	79.1	76.5
	(0.1)	(0.1)	(0.1)	(0.1)	(0.2)	(0.2)	(0.2)
8. Average weeks work in previous year	33.6	35.7	32.5	34.6	33.7	35.1	34.4
	(0.1)	(0.1)	(0.1)	(0.1)	(0.1)	(0.1)	(0.1)
9. Average weeks in labor force in previous year	35.8	37.6	34.2	36.0	37.6	38.7	36.6
	(0.1)	(0.1)	(0.1)	(0.1)	(0.1)	(0.1)	(0.1)
10. Weeks unemployed (%)[a]	6.7	5.6	5.8	4.7	10.5	9.8	6.3
	(0.1)	(0.1)	(0.1)	(0.1)	(0.1)	(0.1)	(0.0)
11. Average weekly wage ($)	373.3	416.6	242.2	269.2	440.0	483.5	306.9
	(1.4)	(1.6)	(0.7)	(0.9)	(2.1)	(2.5)	(1.4)
12. Heads (%)	80.3	—	80.0	—	80.9	—	—

Sources: U.S. data are from the March 1987 and March 1980 Current Population Surveys. Canadian data are from the 1987 and 1980 Surveys of Consumer Finances (conducted in April). Heads samples include only family heads (see text).

Notes: Standard errors in parentheses. Samples include individuals aged 16–68.

[a]Average fraction of weeks in the labor force spent in unemployment.

[b]In national currencies.

tive weeks in the labor force) are reported in row 10 of table 5.3. For strict comparability with the contemporaneous unemployment rate, the average retrospective unemployment rate should be weighted by each individual's total weeks in the labor force.[16] Weighted averages of the retrospective unemployment rate are slightly lower than the unweighted averages, as shown in table 5.4.

Regardless of weighting, the retrospective data indicate a larger relative

16. In steady state an individual with n weeks in the labor force in the previous year would be in the labor force in any given week with probability $n/52$. This individual's expected contribution to the contemporaneous unemployment rate is $u \cdot n/52$, where u is the probability of unemployment in any week in the labor force (i.e., the individual retrospective unemployment rate).

Table 5.4 Retrospective Unemployment Rates for Family Heads

	U.S.		Canada		Relative Change
	1986	1979	1986	1979	Canada − U.S.
Unweighted	5.6	4.7	9.8	6.3	2.6
Weighted	4.9	3.9	9.3	6.0	2.3

Note: Retrospective unemployment rate is the average fraction of weeks in the labor force spent in unemployment, times 100.

increase in Canadian unemployment than the contemporaneous data does. This difference raises the question of which unemployment measure is "correct." From a measurement perspective, the CPS and LFS questionnaires are very similar. We see no measurement-based explanation for a greater divergence in retrospective unemployment rates. From a behavioral perspective, three factors can cause the retrospective rate to differ from the contemporaneous rate. First, individuals who would be classified as unemployed in a contemporaneous survey may either "forget" their unemployment experience or may consider themselves out of the labor force retrospectively.[17] Second, some discouraged job seekers (who are counted as out of the labor force in the contemporaneous survey) may consider themselves as unemployed in the retrospective survey. To check on the latter phenomenon we examined data on the fractions of discouraged workers in the United States and Canada over the 1980s (see below). We find little change in the relative fraction of discouraged workers in the two countries. A third factor is the timing of the different unemployment measures. The contemporaneous surveys measure unemployment in March (United States) or April (Canada) of 1980 and 1987. The retrospective surveys measure average annual unemployment over 1979 and 1986. Differences in the relative seasonality of unemployment in the two countries, or slight differences in the timing of the 1980 downturn, may potentially account for the greater relative increase in Canadian unemployment indicated by the retrospective data.

A final interesting comparison in table 5.3 is the relative growth of average weekly wages. Average weekly earnings of family heads in the United States rose 43.7 percent between 1979 and 1986. For family heads in Canada the increase was 45.5 percent. Relative to the increase in consumer prices, however, U.S. wage earners fared better: the U.S. price index rose 41.2 percent between 1979 and 1986, while the Canadian index rose 49.4 percent. Thus

17. Levine (1990) presents a detailed comparison of retrospective and contemporaneous unemployment in the United States. His analysis suggests that younger workers, women, and individuals whose main activity in the survey week is not "looking for work" are more likely to underreport unemployment in a retrospective survey. Akerlof and Yellen (1985) suggest that the likelihood of remembering unemployment is proportional to the severity of the unemployment experience. Neither study gives much guidance as to why retrospective Canadian unemployment rates would diverge more than contemporaneous rates.

there was a slight increase in real weekly earnings of U.S. family heads over the 1980s (conditional on working and reporting positive earnings) and a small decrease in the real weekly earnings of Canadian family heads.

Table 5.5 repeats the analysis in table 5.3 for the subset of currently unemployed workers in each survey. In both countries unemployed workers are younger, more likely to be male, and less likely to be family heads than the overall population. All of these contrasts are stronger in the United States. Currently unemployed workers report higher average weeks in the labor force last year than the overall population does (especially in Canada) but substantially lower average weeks of employment. A comparison of the relative wages of unemployed workers to the wages of the overall work force reveals a much bigger wage gap in the United States (20–30 percent) than in Canada (5–10 percent). As with the demographic comparisons, this difference sug-

Table 5.5 Characteristics of Unemployed Workers in the United States and Canada, 1980 and 1987

	U.S.				Canada		
	All 1987	Heads 1987	All 1980	Heads 1980	All 1987	Heads 1987	Heads 1980
1. Average age	31.7	36.7	29.8	35.0	33.6	37.1	36.0
	(0.2)	(0.2)	(0.2)	(0.2)	(0.2)	(0.2)	(0.2)
2. Female (%)	42.5	45.5	42.7	46.4	43.1	46.7	46.5
	(0.7)	(0.9)	(0.7)	(0.8)	(0.7)	(0.9)	(1.0)
3. Education ≤ 8 years (%)	9.5	10.8	11.9	14.1	15.5	17.5	25.5
	(0.4)	(0.5)	(0.4)	(0.6)	(0.5)	(0.7)	(0.8)
4. Education ≥ 16 years (%)	7.9	9.6	5.6	7.4	5.9	6.3	5.4
	(0.4)	(0.5)	(0.3)	(0.4)	(0.3)	(0.4)	(0.4)
5. In labor force in previous year (%)	86.9	89.7	86.9	90.8	94.0	94.7	92.9
	(0.5)	(0.5)	(0.5)	(0.5)	(0.4)	(0.4)	(0.5)
6. Average weeks work in previous year	23.5	26.2	25.7	29.7	22.7	24.0	28.6
	(0.3)	(0.3)	(0.3)	(0.3)	(0.3)	(0.3)	(0.4)
7. Average weeks in labor force in previous year	36.6	39.8	35.6	39.6	43.8	45.5	43.0
	(0.3)	(0.3)	(0.3)	(0.3)	(0.2)	(0.3)	(0.3)
8. Weeks unemployed (%)[a]	35.4	34.5	28.0	25.9	47.1	47.2	33.2
	(0.6)	(0.7)	(0.5)	(0.6)	(0.5)	(0.6)	(0.7)
9. Average weekly wage ($)[b]	268.5	317.0	196.9	230.2	393.0	428.9	297.5
	(4.4)	(5.9)	(2.7)	(3.5)	(13.0)	(17.1)	(7.7)
10. Average length of unemployment spell[c]	13.6	14.5	11.2	11.3	19.2	19.8	0.0
	(0.2)	(0.3)	(0.2)	(0.2)	(0.2)	(0.3)	0.0
11. Heads (%)	64.0	—	62.8	—	73.6	—	—

Sources: See table 5.3.

Notes: Standard errors in parentheses. Samples include individuals classified as unemployed in the survey week.

[a]Average fraction of weeks in the labor force spent in unemployment in the previous year.

[b]In national currencies.

[c]Average duration of the current (interrupted) spell of unemployment.

gests that the incidence of unemployment is more highly concentrated among young and less-skilled workers in the United States than in Canada.

5.4 Analysis of Retrospective Unemployment and Employment

From this general overview we turn to a more detailed analysis of employment and unemployment experiences in the previous calendar year. We begin with a cross-sectional analysis of the components of aggregate unemployment in the United States and Canada in 1986. Table 5.6 contains retrospective labor market information for younger and older and male and female workers in the CPS and LFS surveys. As shown in column 1, the labor force shares of the age-sex groups are very similar in the two countries. Labor force experiences in the previous year, however, differ markedly between the two countries. Most importantly, Canadians in every group report more weeks of unemployment. For women, the extra weeks of unemployment are associated with similar weeks of employment and higher weeks in the labor force. For men, on the other hand, the added weeks of unemployment are associated with lower weeks of employment (1.3 weeks less than U.S. men) and slightly more weeks of labor force attachment (0.6 extra weeks in the labor force relative to U.S. men).

Column 9 shows the ratio of each group's relative share of weeks of unemployment to its relative share of weeks of employment. Two interesting findings emerge from this statistic. First, relative to U.S. women Canadian women generate more unemployment per week of employment. Indeed, Canadian women generate proportionately more unemployment than Canadian men, while the reverse is true in the United States. Second, Canadian youths generate proportionally fewer weeks of unemployment than their U.S. counterparts do.

A final aspect of table 5.6 is the UI recipiency rate, shown in column 10. This is the probability of receiving UI payments in the preceding year among those with positive weeks of unemployment.[18] As is well known, the UI recipiency rate in the United States is low: only about one-quarter of those with unemployment experiences in 1986 report any UI income.[19] The recipiency rate is especially low among youth and women, falling to only 8 percent for 16–24-year-old females. In Canada the overall recipiency rate is close to 60 percent, and recipiency rates are more equal across demographic groups. In combination with the relative patterns of the incidence of unemployment, UI recipiency patterns suggest that the burden of unemployment is more equally distributed in Canada than in the United States. On the one hand, Canadian unemployment is less concentrated among specific demographic groups. On

18. Of course many individuals (particularly in the Canadian survey) report UI recipiency but 0 weeks of unemployment. These individuals are excluded from the recipiency rates in table 5.6.

19. See Blank and Card (1991) and below.

Table 5.6 **Contributions to Overall Unemployment by Various Demographic Groups in the United States and Canada, 1986**

	Share of Labor Force (1)	Average Weeks in Labor Force (2)	Prob of Unemployment (%) (3)	Average Weeks of Unemployment: Conditional (4)	Average Weeks of Unemployment: All (5)	Share Total Unemployment (6)	Average Weeks Worked (7)	Share Total Weeks (8)	Relative Share of Unemployment/ Weeks (9)	Prob UI (%) (10)
				A. United States						
Females	45.9	43.7	14.7	16.2	2.4	40.8	41.3	44.1	0.93	19.4
Males	54.1	47.6	15.7	18.7	2.9	59.2	44.6	55.9	1.06	31.2
Age 25 +	79.8	47.7	12.9	18.5	2.4	70.9	45.3	84.0	0.84	33.3
Age 16–24	20.2	38.1	24.7	15.7	3.9	29.1	34.3	16.0	1.81	10.8
Females 25 +	36.1	45.5	12.5	17.0	2.1	28.4	43.4	36.3	0.78	25.0
Females 16–24	9.9	37.2	23.1	14.6	3.4	12.4	33.9	7.8	1.60	8.3
Males 25 +	43.8	49.6	13.3	19.7	2.6	42.6	47.0	47.7	0.89	39.7
Males 16–24	10.3	39.0	26.2	16.6	4.3	16.6	34.7	8.3	2.01	12.9
All	—	45.8	15.3	17.6	2.7	—	43.1	—	1.00	25.9
				B. Canada						
Females	44.0	45.6	21.5	22.0	4.7	43.3	40.9	42.5	1.02	55.2
Males	56.0	48.2	21.0	23.1	4.9	56.7	43.3	57.5	0.99	61.7
Age 25 +	77.5	49.3	19.3	23.6	4.6	73.5	44.7	82.0	0.90	64.7
Age 16–24	22.5	39.4	28.0	20.2	5.7	26.5	33.7	18.0	1.47	44.9
Females 25 +	33.3	47.7	20.4	23.0	4.7	32.5	43.0	33.9	0.96	59.8
Females 16–24	10.6	38.8	25.0	19.4	4.9	10.8	34.0	8.6	1.26	43.3
Males 25 +	44.2	50.4	18.4	24.2	4.5	41.0	46.0	48.1	0.85	68.7
Males 16–24	11.9	39.8	30.8	20.7	6.4	15.7	33.5	9.4	1.67	46.0
All	—	47.0	21.3	22.6	4.8	—	42.2	—	1.00	58.8

Sources: See table 5.3.

Notes: All tabulations are for individuals who report positive weeks in the labor force during the year. Prob UI is the fraction of individuals with positive weeks of unemployment in the previous year who report receiving UI income in the year.

the other hand, higher UI recipiency rates (especially among youth and women) serve to reduce the individual costs of unemployment.

The comparisons in table 5.6 indicate that unemployment experiences in the United States and Canada differ along both age and sex dimensions.[20] Ideally, we would like to analyze changes over the 1980s in the employment and unemployment outcomes of men, women, youth, and older workers. Unfortunately, 1979 data are only available for family heads in Canada. It is difficult to construct a representative sample of Canadian youth in the earlier survey. In the remainder of the paper we therefore concentrate on measuring changes in the labor market outcomes of family heads in the United States and Canada during the 1980s by sex, making no attempt to disaggregate by age.

Table 5.7 presents means of the labor force outcomes for family heads in the two countries in 1979 and 1986, along with differences between Canada and the United States in the changes between 1979 and 1986 (referred to as difference-in-differences in what follows). Mean weeks of employment, unemployment, and labor force participation are tabulated in two ways: for the subset of individuals in the labor force in the previous year and on a per capita basis. Looking first at the averages for 1979, annual labor force participation rates were higher for men in Canada than in the United States but lower for women. Per capita weeks in the labor force were also higher for male heads in Canada but were about the same for female heads in the two countries. Per capita weeks of employment were lower among Canadian women (by about 1.2 weeks) and higher among Canadian men (by 0.75 weeks).

During the 1980s the participation rates of female heads in Canada grew 2.4 percentage points relative to those in the United States. Average weeks in the labor force also grew significantly for Canadian women. Much of this relative growth took the form of added weeks of unemployment: per capita weeks of employment rose 0.2 weeks faster in Canada than in the United States, while per capita weeks of unemployment rose 1.1 weeks faster in Canada. The relative trends in annual labor supply for female heads are similar to the aggregate trends identified in table 5.1 and figure 5.2. Over the 1980s Canadian women increased both their employment and unemployment weeks relative to U.S. women.

The relative trends for male heads are very different. Per capita weeks of employment fell in both countries during the 1980s, but the fall was bigger in Canada (−2.3 weeks versus −1.0 weeks). This relative loss of employment was counteracted by a small decrease in relative weeks of labor force partici-

20. We have also tabulated the relative contributions of individuals in different industries to unemployment in the two countries in 1986—see appendix table 5A.1. This exercise shows very similar industry shares of employment, weeks in the labor force, and weeks of unemployment in the United States and Canada. We can find no significant role for industry-specific factors in explaining the growth of unemployment in Canada. (See also Ashenfelter and Card 1986, table 7).

Table 5.7 **Labor Force, Employment, and Unemployment during Calendar Year, Family Heads in the United States and Canada, 1979 and 1986**

	Canada		U.S.		Relative Difference,[a]
	1979	1986	1979	1986	1986 − 1979
A. Female heads					
1. Labor force participation rate (%)	61.7	68.1	65.8	69.8	2.4
2. Weeks unemployment | in labor force	3.12	4.84	1.88	2.19	1.41
3. Per capita weeks unemployment	1.93	3.30	1.24	1.53	1.08
4. Employment-population rate (%)	60.7	66.2	64.3	68.3	1.6
5. Weeks employment | in labor force	41.65	42.42	40.92	42.89	−1.20
6. Per capita weeks employment	25.71	28.89	26.92	29.92	0.18
7. Weeks in labor force for labor force participants	44.77	47.26	42.80	45.09	0.20
8. Per capita weeks in labor force	27.67	32.19	28.15	31.46	1.25
9. Retrospective unemployment rate (weighted by labor force weeks)	7.0	10.2	4.4	4.9	2.7
B. Male heads					
1. Labor force participation rate (%)	92.6	90.8	90.5	89.3	−0.6
2. Weeks unemployment | in labor force	2.68	4.35	1.73	2.46	0.94
3. Per capita weeks unemployment	2.48	3.95	1.57	2.20	0.84
4. Employment-population rate (%)	92.0	88.9	90.1	88.5	−1.5
5. Weeks employment | in labor force	47.46	45.90	47.78	47.30	−1.08
6. Per capita weeks employment	43.96	41.69	43.24	42.25	−1.28
7. Weeks in labor force for labor force participants	50.14	50.25	49.51	49.77	−0.15
8. Per capita weeks in labor force	46.44	45.64	44.81	44.45	−0.44
9. Retrospective unemployment rate (weighted by labor force weeks)	5.3	8.7	3.5	4.9	2.0

Sources: See table 5.3.

Note: Based on data for family heads aged 16–68.

[a]The change from 1979 to 1986 in Canada minus the corresponding change in the United States.

[b]The fraction of the population who report any weeks in the labor force during the year.

pation, resulting in a net increase of 0.8 weeks in per capita unemployment among Canadian male family heads.

Retrospective unemployment rates for men and women are shown in row 9 in table 5.7. The retrospective unemployment rate of Canadian women rose 2.7 percentage points faster than the rate for U.S. women, while the relative increase for Canadian men was 2.0 percentage points. Using the fact that the retrospective unemployment rate is a weighted average of rates for different groups, with weights equal to the relative shares of labor force weeks, the overall increase in Canadian retrospective unemployment from 1979 to 1986 can be decomposed into components attributable to male and female heads. This decomposition attributes 45 percent of the relative increase in retrospective unemployment to Canadian women and 55 percent to Canadian men.

The comparisons of annual weeks of employment and unemployment in tables 5.3–5.7 make no allowance for any differences in the weekly hours of workers in the United States or Canada. To check for possible differences, we used information on usual hours per week in the U.S. surveys to construct a full-time/part-time indicator similar to the one in the Canadian surveys.[21] This indicator classifies full-time work as thirty or more hours per week. A comparison of percentages who report usually working full time in the previous year is presented in table 5.8. These tabulations suggest that hours per week are slightly lower for female heads in Canada than in the United States but about the same for males in the two countries. There is no evidence of a major shift in the relative fractions of full-time work during the 1980s. We conclude that the absence of weekly hours information is probably not a major problem for our analysis of changes in relative employment in the two countries.

The data in table 5.7 suggest that the relative increase in unemployment among Canadian women between 1979 and 1986 occurred mainly as a result of a relabeling of nonworking time from "out of the labor force" to "unemployment." A more detailed investigation of this phenomenon is presented in figures 5.4 and 5.5. Figure 5.4 shows the cumulative distribution functions of weeks worked during the year for female heads in Canada and the United States in 1979 and 1986.[22] The plots illustrate the dramatic increases in female employment in both countries over the early 1980s. In 1979, for example, 39 percent of Canadian women and 36 percent of U.S. women reported 0 weeks of work. By 1986 these fractions had fallen to 34 and 32 percent, respectively. At the other end of the distribution, 39 percent of Canadian women and 35 percent of U.S. women reported 52 weeks of work in 1979. By 1986 these fractions had risen to 45 and 43 percent, respectively.

Figure 5.5 shows the average number of weeks in the labor force reported by female heads in the four surveys, conditional on the number of weeks of

21. The Canadian surveys do not provide exact information on hours per week in the previous year, only whether or not the respondent "usually worked full time" in the previous year.

22. Note that we have plotted the distribution function only for 0–51 weeks. The cumulative distribution at 52 weeks is 1.

Table 5.8 **Percentage of Family Heads Working Full-Time in the Previous Year**

	U.S.		Canada		Relative Change
	1986	1979	1986	1979	Canada − U.S.
Female heads	78.7	77.7	74.2	74.5	−1.3
Male heads	94.7	95.2	95.4	96.1	−0.2

Sources: See table 5.3.

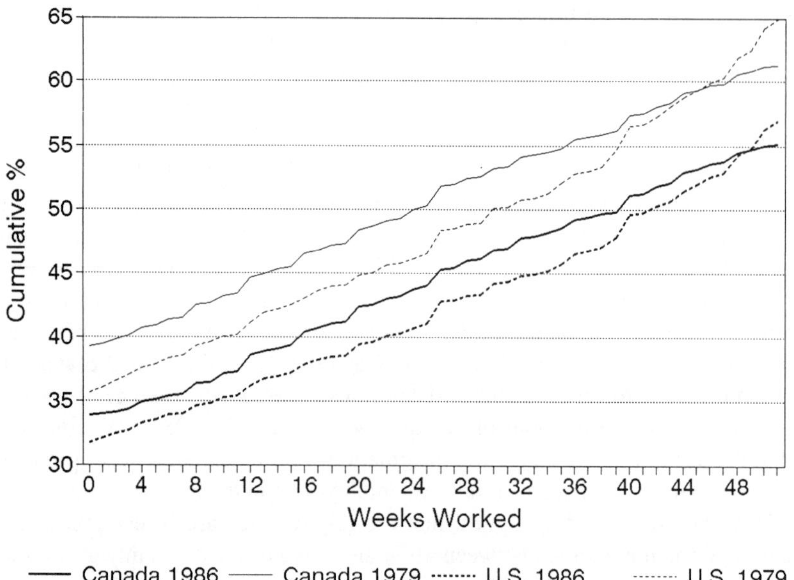

Fig. 5.4 Cumulative distribution of weeks worked, female heads, 1979 and 1986

employment in the previous year. Since weeks in the labor force consist of weeks of employment and weeks of unemployment, average weeks of unemployment are represented by the vertical distance between the forty-five-degree line and the graph. For example, Canadian women with 4 weeks of work in 1979 reported 12.2 weeks in the labor force, while U.S. women reported 8.5 weeks. In 1986 Canadian women with 4 weeks of work reported an average of 20.6 weeks in the labor force while U.S. women reported an average of 10.3 weeks. The increase in reported weeks of unemployment among women with 4 weeks of work was therefore 6.6 weeks greater in Canada than in the United States. Throughout most of the range of weeks worked in the previous year, the graph shows a similar pattern. At every level of annual work experience there was a striking increase in the propensity of Canadian women to report nonworking time as unemployment.

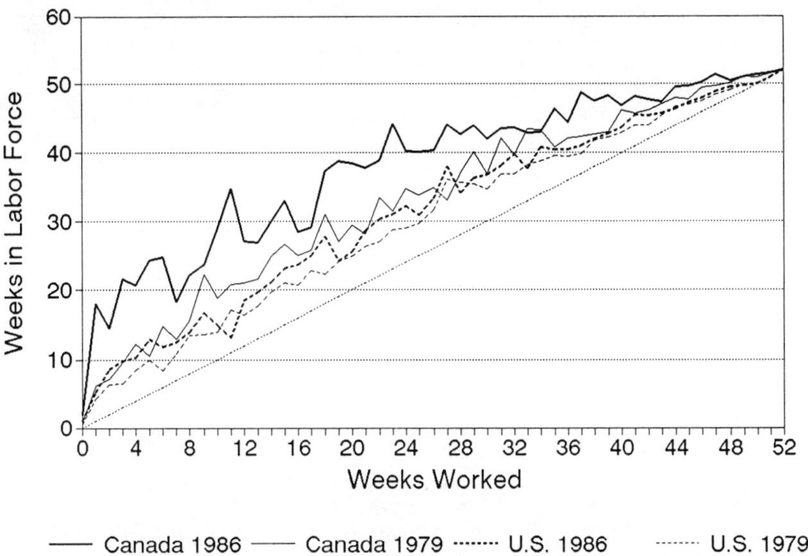

Fig. 5.5 Average weeks in labor force by weeks worked, female heads, 1979 and 1986

This analysis is repeated in figures 5.6 and 5.7 for male family heads. A comparison of the distribution functions of weeks worked indicates a significant relative shift in Canada over the 1980s. In 1979 the Canadian distribution was almost entirely to the right of the U.S. distribution (indicating higher employment levels). The 1986 distribution functions for the two countries are similar in the lower tail but show a substantially larger fraction of Canadian men with 10–26 weeks, and a lower fraction with 40–50 weeks of work.

Figure 5.7 shows the conditional means of weeks in the labor force by weeks of employment in the previous year for male heads in the United States and Canada in 1979 and 1986. Mean weeks of unemployment (conditional on weeks of employment) increased in both countries between 1979 and 1986, with fairly similar relative increases in Canada and in the United States. The most important exception is for men with 0 weeks of employment. For these men, who represent approximately 10 percent of male heads in each country, there was a 3.0-week relative increase in the average number of weeks of unemployment in Canada. Given the size of the group, this relative increase accounts for a large fraction (80 percent) of the overall increase in per capita weeks of unemployment of Canadian men.

A complete decomposition of the relative rise in unemployment in Canada for either sex can be obtained from an identity that expresses the mean per capita weeks of unemployment in either country and either year as a weighted average of the conditional mean weeks of unemployment reported by individuals working different numbers of weeks:

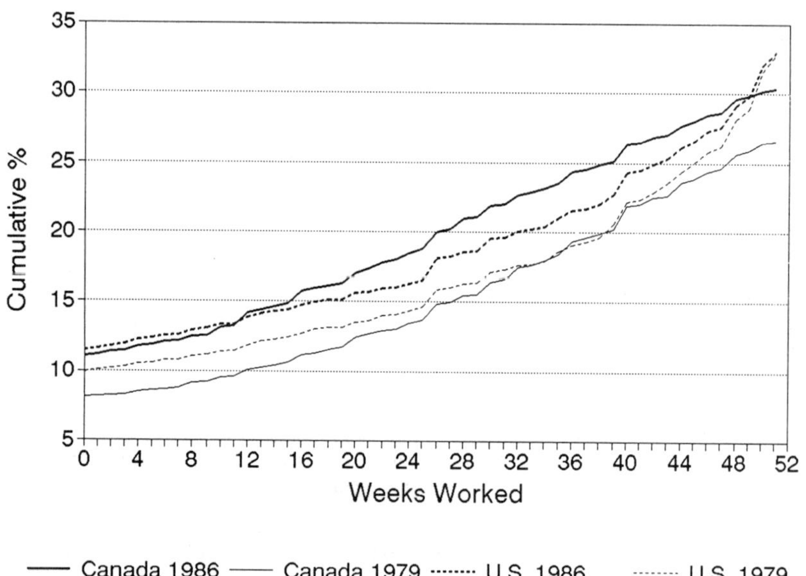

Fig. 5.6 Cumulative distribution of weeks worked, male heads, 1979 and 1986

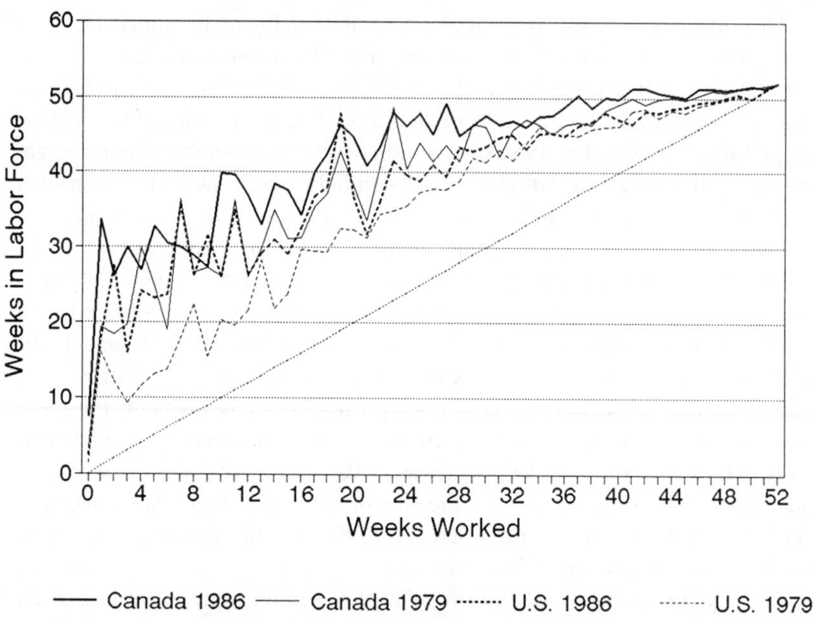

Fig. 5.7 Average weeks in labor force by weeks worked, male heads, 1979 and 1986

$$U_t^j = \sum_{w=0}^{52} P_t^j(w) U_t^j(w),$$

where U_t^j represents mean per capita weeks of unemployment in country j and year t, $P_t^j(w)$ represents the fraction of individuals in country j and year t who worked w weeks ($0 \leq w \leq 52$), and $U_t^j(w)$ represents the mean weeks of unemployment among those who worked w weeks. It follows that the difference-in-differences of average unemployment between Canada and the United States over the 1980s can be written as

$$\begin{aligned} U_2^c - U_1^c - (U_2^a - U_1^a) = \sum_{w=0}^{52} \{ & (U_2^c(w) - U_2^a(w)) \cdot P_2^c(w) \\ & - (U_1^c(w) - U_1^a(w)) \cdot P_1^c(w) + (P_2^c(w) \\ & - P_2^a(w)) \cdot U_2^a(w) - (P_1^c(w) - P_1^a(w)) \cdot U_1^a(w)\}, \end{aligned}$$

where superscripts a and c denote the United States and Canada, respectively, and subscripts 1 and 2 denote 1979 and 1986, respectively. The first two terms on the righthand side represent the effect of relative changes in the mean weeks of unemployment at each level of weeks worked, while the third and fourth terms represent the effect of relative changes in the fractions of workers with each level of weeks worked.[23]

Figures 5.8 and 5.9 display the relative contributions of these two components to the overall relative increase in per capita unemployment in Canada for female and male heads.[24] Looking at the figure for female heads, it is clear that relative changes in the distribution of weeks of employment in the United States and Canada over the 1980s play only a small part in the increase in unemployment. Approximately 90 percent of the increase is attributable to relative increases in unemployment at each level of weeks worked. Among male heads relative changes in the distribution of weeks of employment (i.e., the sum of the third and fourth terms in the above equation) contribute approximately 25 percent of the overall increase in relative Canadian unemployment. The balance is attributable to relative increases in weeks of unemployment conditional on weeks of employment among Canadian men.

As noted above, changes in the number of weeks of unemployment generated by men with 0 weeks of employment are the single most important factor in the rise in unemployment among Canadian men. Women with 0 weeks of work in the previous year also contributed to the overall change in relative female unemployment. There are two interpretations of the relative increase

23. This decomposition is not unique. We have compared results using a decomposition that weights the differences in the conditional means of unemployment by the U.S. probabilities and found no major differences in the inferences.

24. The contributions at each level of weeks are divided by the overall difference-in-differences of per capita unemployment to convert the components into relative shares.

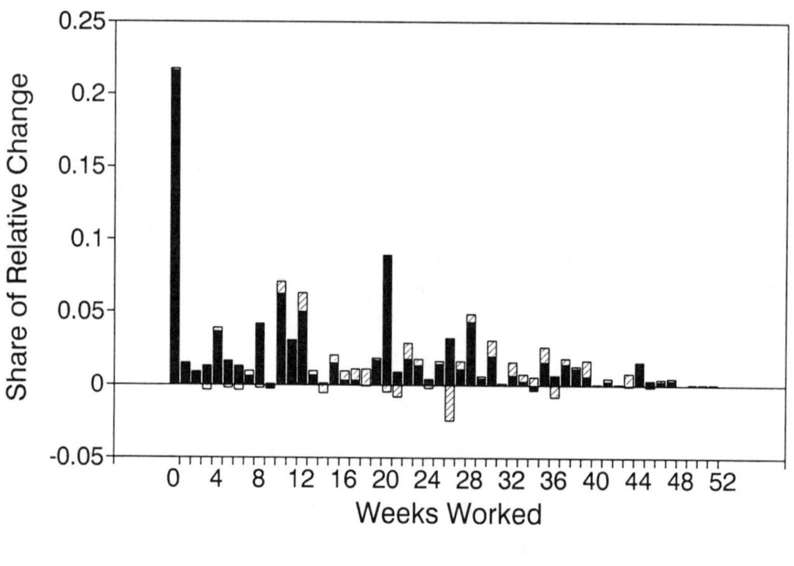

Fig. 5.8 Decomposition of relative growth in unemployment, female heads

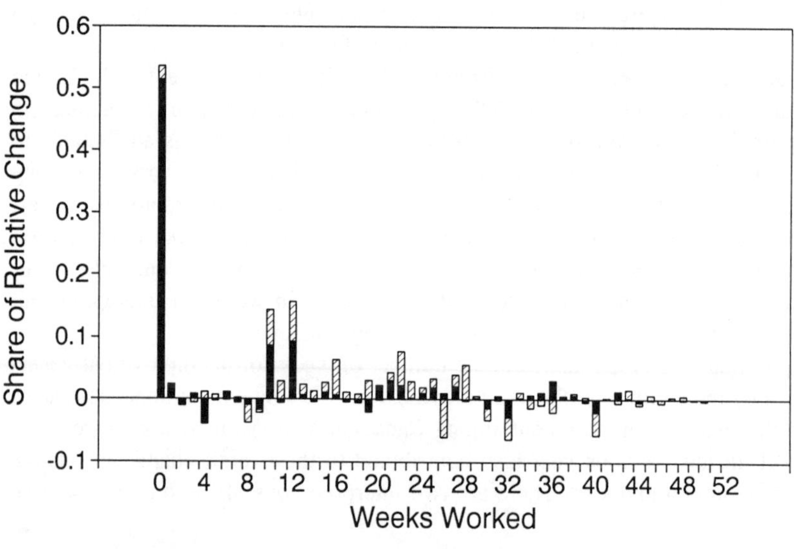

Fig. 5.9 Decomposition of relative growth in unemployment, male heads

in unemployment among these individuals. One possibility is that labor market changes in Canada led to a change in the type of individual with 0 weeks of work (toward a group with more "permanent attachment" to the labor force). An alternative is that, even holding constant the characteristics of individuals with 0 weeks of employment, there was an increase in the fraction of the year reported as unemployment. In an effort to distinguish these hypotheses, we present information on the characteristics of individuals with 0 weeks of work in table 5.9. For both sexes in all four surveys the population who did no work in the previous year (henceforth "nonworkers") mainly comprises two groups: those who were out of the labor force for the entire year, and those who were in the labor force for the entire year. The relative fractions of these two subgroups are shown in rows 2 and 3 of both panels of the table.

Table 5.9 **Weeks of Unemployment and Characteristics of Individuals with 0 Weeks of Work in the Previous Year, 1979 and 1986**

	Canada		U.S.		Relative Difference,[a] 1986 −
	1979	1986	1979	1986	1979
	A. Female heads				
1. Mean weeks unemployment	0.75	1.95	0.51	0.99	0.72
2. 0 weeks unemployment (%)	97.3	94.3	96.0	95.4	−2.4
3. 52 weeks unemployment (%)	0.9	2.9	0.3	1.1	1.2
4. Percentage of total per capita unemployment attributable to women with 52 weeks unemployment	18.3	29.7	8.6	22.8	−2.8
5. Average age	45.5	47.9	46.3	47.1	1.6
6. Education ≤ 8 years (%)	33.4	28.4	19.1	15.2	−1.1
7. Percentage of all female heads with 0 weeks work	39.3	33.8	35.7	31.7	−1.6
	B. Male heads				
1. Mean weeks unemployment	3.53	7.46	1.41	2.38	2.96
2. 0 weeks unemployment (%)	91.7	82.9	95.6	93.1	−6.3
3. 52 weeks unemployment (%)	5.6	12.6	2.0	3.6	5.4
4. Percentage of total unemployment attributable to men with 52 weeks unemployment	18.2	35.3	12.7	18.8	11.0
5. Average age	56.8	55.6	56.0	55.4	−0.7
6. Education ≤ 8 years (%)	51.2	38.0	34.3	24.3	−3.3
7. Percentage of all male heads with 0 weeks work	8.0	11.1	9.9	11.5	1.5

Sources: See table 5.3.

Notes: Samples consist of family heads aged 16–68 with 0 weeks of employment during the year.

[a]The change from 1979 to 1986 in Canada minus the corresponding change in the United States.

The group with 52 weeks of unemployment accounts for a majority of the total unemployment generated by nonworkers and a significant share of total per capita unemployment (see row 4 of each panel). Indeed, the relative increase in the number of Canadian men who report a full 52 weeks of unemployment in the previous year accounts for 40 percent of the relative rise in per capita unemployment in Canada over the 1980s.[25]

It is also interesting to compare the demographic characteristics of nonworkers in the two countries. In both the United States and Canada, nonworking men are about 15 years older than other heads, with an average age over 55. Nonworking heads are also less educated than the overall population. A large fraction of the rising unemployment gap between Canada and the United States is therefore a result of the labor supply behavior of older, less-educated men.[26] The relative rise in long-term unemployment among this group is clearly an important subject for further analysis.

It is also interesting to note the importance of the relative labor supply behavior of individuals with 10 or 12 weeks of employment in figures 5.8 and 5.9. During the 1980s the minimum number of weeks of employment required for eligibility for UI payments in many regions of Canada was 10 or 12 weeks (see below). Evidently, the numbers of men and women reporting 10 or 12 weeks of employment rose faster in Canada than in the United States from 1979 to 1986. In addition there were sizable relative increases in the number of weeks of unemployment declared by workers with 10 or 12 weeks of employment in Canada. For women the 10- and 12-week spikes in figure 5.8 account for 13 percent of the relative rise in Canadian unemployment over the 1980s. For men the 10- and 12-week spikes account for 22 percent of the relative rise in Canadian unemployment.

A final aspect of figure 5.8 is the sharp increase in unemployment among Canadian women with 20 weeks of employment. Amendments to the Canadian UI program in 1979 introduced a minimum eligibility standard of 20 weeks of work for labor force entrants and reentrants (those with limited labor force attachment in the two years prior to their claim). In addition since the early 1970s Canada's unemployment insurance program has offered maternity leave benefits for claimants with at least 20 weeks of employment in the preceding year.[27] Although this requirement did not change in the 1980s, increases in the labor force participation rates of married women might have been expected to increase the number of women adjusting their employment patterns to become eligible for maternity benefits. As with the spikes at 10–

25. Canadian men with 52 weeks of unemployment account for 82–88 percent of unemployment among those with 0 weeks of work. From figure 5.9 the behavior of the 0-weeks group accounts for one-half of the relative rise in unemployment among Canadian men.

26. The falling employment and labor force participation rates of older U.S. men have been a subject of much interest (see Juhn 1992). Corak (1991) has noted the increasing contribution of older men to Canadian unemployment.

27. See Statistics Canada (1984).

12 weeks of work, the importance of the 20-week group in figure 5.8 suggests that Canada's UI program played some role in the rise in Canadian unemployment.

5.5 Analysis of Unemployment during the Survey Week

We turn next to an analysis of unemployment during the survey weeks of the CPS and LFS. A striking conclusion of the retrospective analysis is that much of the relative increase in Canadian unemployment is associated with a reclassification of nonworking time from "out of the labor force" to "unemployment." An important question is whether a similar conclusion emerges from contemporaneously measured labor force data. By using retrospective information on employment last year for individuals in the survey week, it is possible to compare contemporaneous labor force classification probabilities among individuals with different degrees of "attachment" to the labor force.

Table 5.10 gives a breakdown of the contemporaneous labor market activities of male and female household heads in 1980 and 1987. For reference we

Table 5.10 Contemporaneous Labor Market Activity Rates in the United States and Canada, 1980 and 1987

	In Labor Force (%)		Unemployed (%)		$P(U\|N)$[a]		Unemployment Rate	
	All	Heads	All	Heads	All	Heads	All	Heads
				A. Females				
Canada								
1987	62.2	62.2	43.8	43.7	13.9	13.4	9.8	9.4
1980	—	55.1	—	49.2	—	8.7	—	7.7
United States								
1987	62.8	63.5	41.3	39.9	10.0	8.6	6.5	5.4
1980	57.2	47.6	46.7	45.6	8.3	7.1	6.8	5.6
Difference-in-differences[b]	—	1.2	—	0.2	—	3.2	—	1.9
				B. Males				
Canada								
1987	82.1	85.3	26.1	21.8	31.2	32.7	9.9	8.4
1980	—	88.0	—	17.3	—	30.8	—	6.1
United States								
1987	81.9	86.4	24.0	18.2	24.6	25.3	7.2	5.3
1980	82.7	87.4	22.9	16.8	24.5	25.1	6.8	4.8
Difference-in-differences[b]	—	−1.7	—	3.1	—	1.8	—	1.8

Sources: See table 5.3.

Notes: Based on labor market activity during the survey week for individuals aged 16–68.

[a] $P(U|N)$ is the probability that a nonworking individual is classified as unemployed (versus out of the labor force).

[b] The change from 1980 to 1987 in Canada, minus the corresponding change in the United States.

also report the activity rates of all individuals in the two U.S. surveys and the later Canadian survey. To understand the connection between the statistics reported in the table, let $P(U|LF)$ represent the probability of unemployment, given labor force participation (i.e., the conventional unemployment rate); let $P(N)$ represent the unconditional probability of nonemployment; let $P(LF)$ represent the probability of being in the labor force (i.e., the labor force participation rate); and let $P(U|N)$ represent the probability of unemployment given nonemployment. Observe that

$$P(U|LF) = \frac{P(N) \cdot P(U|N)}{P(LF)}.$$

It follows that the logarithm of the unemployment rate is

$$\log P(U|LF) = \log P(N) + \log P(U|N) - \log P(LF).$$

The difference-in-differences of the logarithm of the unemployment rate can therefore be decomposed into components attributable to relative changes in the nonemployment rate, the labor force participation rate, and $P(U|N)$.

Applying this decomposition to female family heads shows that virtually all of the 24 percent relative increase in unemployment in Canada is attributable to the increase in the probability of unemployment, given nonemployment. For male heads, on the other hand, only one-quarter of the 22 percent relative increase in Canadian unemployment is attributable to the rise in $P(U|N)$. The balance is attributable to the proportionally larger increase in nonemployment rates in Canada than in the United States.

A longer-run perspective on these decompositions is provided by figures 5.10 and 5.11. These show aggregate-level differences between Canada and the United States in participation rates, nonemployment rates, and $P(U|N)$ for males and females between 1966 and 1989. Starting in the mid- to late 1970s there was a relative rise in $P(U|N)$ among Canadian women that accounts for virtually all of the relative rise in unemployment. For men there was a similar trend in $P(U|N)$, but the timing is slightly different, with more of the relative increase occurring in the late 1970s and less in the early 1980s. Over the longer run (comparing the 1960s to the 1980s), most of the relative rise in unemployment among Canadian men and women has derived from a relative increase in $P(U|N)$.

One explanation for the relative increase in the probability that nonemployed individuals in Canada are classified as unemployed is that the pool of nonworkers has become "more attached" to the labor force. To check this hypothesis we have assembled data on $P(U|N)$ by weeks of work in the previous year in table 5.11. There was a relative reduction in the number of nonworking female heads with no work experience in the previous year, together with relative increases in each of the categories with 8 or more weeks of work. These patterns suggest some increase in the labor market attachment of female heads in Canada. Nevertheless, changes in the distribution of nonworkers by

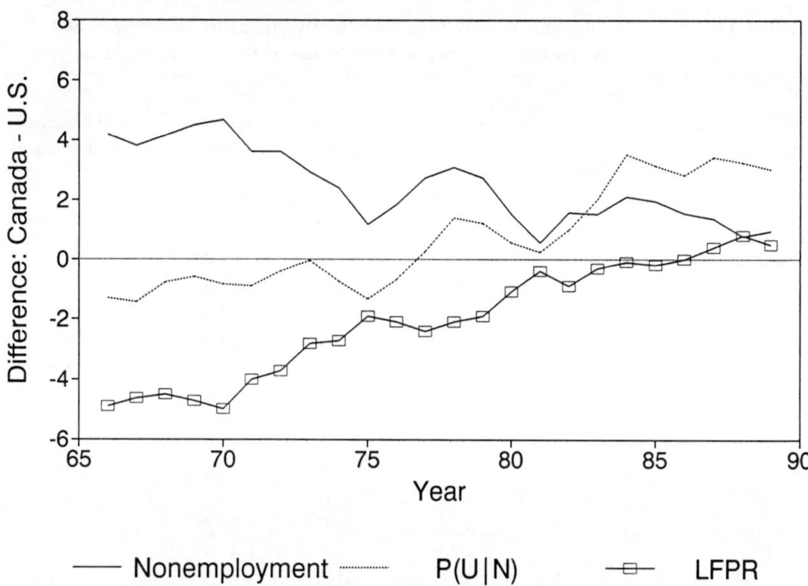

Fig. 5.10 Differences in labor market activity rates of women, Canada minus the United States

Note: LFPR means labor force participation rate.

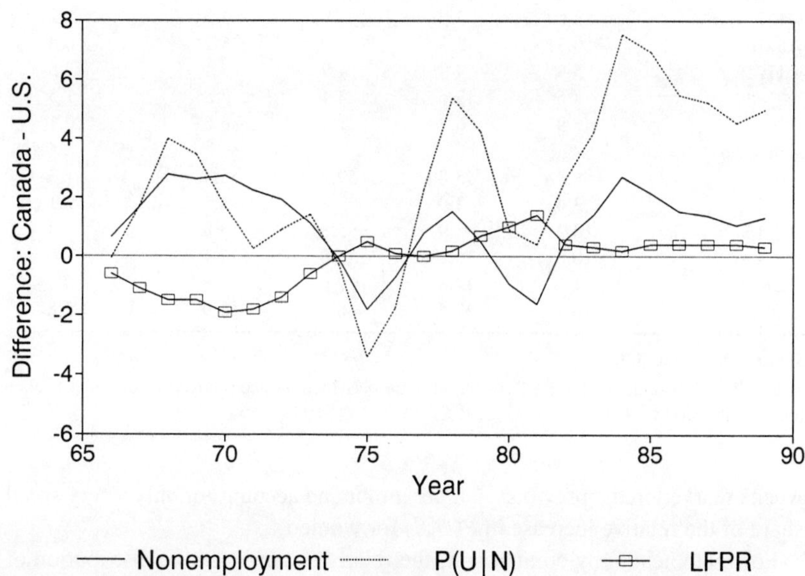

Fig. 5.11 Differences in labor market activity rates of men, Canada minus the United States

Note: LFPR means labor force participation rate.

Table 5.11 Probability of Reporting Unemployment among Nonworkers and Distribution of Nonworkers by Weeks of Work in the Previous Year

Weeks Worked Last Year	Canada 1987	Canada 1980	U.S. 1987	U.S. 1980	Difference-in-Differences
	A. Probability of unemployment among nonworkers (%)				
Female heads					
0	4.3	2.7	3.6	2.4	0.5
1–7	19.8	9.2	14.7	11.3	7.3
8–16	31.0	19.4	17.8	14.7	8.5
17–26	46.7	31.9	21.8	18.6	11.6
27–39	42.5	32.5	30.0	28.6	8.6
40+	48.4	39.7	33.4	29.6	4.8
All	13.4	8.7	8.6	7.1	3.2
Male heads					
0	11.0	5.4	5.7	3.2	3.1
1–7	42.6	30.9	36.0	19.2	−5.1
8–16	47.2	33.6	36.9	25.5	2.2
17–26	55.1	45.7	52.5	43.2	0.2
27–39	59.3	54.7	64.8	66.3	6.1
40+	53.2	60.2	60.2	66.6	−0.5
All	32.7	30.8	25.3	25.1	1.8
	B. Distribution of nonworkers by weeks of work in the previous year (%)				
Female heads					
0	74.4	76.5	76.0	74.8	−3.3
1–7	2.6	3.0	3.9	4.5	0.2
8–16	6.3	5.7	5.0	5.2	0.8
17–26	5.3	4.9	4.9	5.1	0.5
27–39	4.5	3.6	3.1	3.8	1.5
40+	6.9	6.3	7.1	6.6	0.1
Male heads					
0	48.4	43.8	59.7	56.4	1.3
1–7	3.4	3.0	3.8	3.5	0.1
8–16	10.2	8.9	5.8	5.8	1.4
17–26	10.8	10.1	6.8	7.1	1.0
27–39	11.1	12.8	7.6	8.4	−0.9
40+	16.2	21.5	16.5	18.9	−2.8

Sources: See table 5.3.

Notes: Based on individuals aged 16–68 who are classified as unemployed or out of the labor force in the survey week.

weeks worked in the previous year are minor and account for only a very small share of the relative increase in $P(U|N)$ for women.

For male heads, by comparison, the relative changes in the distribution of weeks worked are toward fewer weeks worked in Canada—suggesting that Canadian men became relatively less attached to the work force. This distributional effect was counteracted by significant relative increases in $P(U|N)$

among men with 0 and 27–39 weeks of work in the previous year. The increase in $P(U|N)$ among men with 0 weeks of work in the previous year is especially important because this group constitutes 50–60 percent of nonworking male heads. Indeed, the 3.1-point relative increase in $P(U|N)$ for those with 0 weeks accounts for 80–90 percent of the overall relative increase in $P(U|N)$ among Canadian males. Changes in the relative distributions of previous work experience explain essentially none of the rise in the likelihood of reported unemployment among nonworkers in Canada.

A second possibility is that relative changes in $P(U|N)$ have been driven by relative changes in the characteristics (such as age or education) of nonworkers in Canada and the United States. To examine this hypothesis we estimated linear probability models for $P(U|N)$ by sex, country, and year, including age, education, marital status, and weeks worked last year as control variables. We then carried out an Oaxaca-style decomposition of the relative change in $P(U|N)$ between 1980 and 1987 into a component attributable to relative changes in the mean characteristics of nonworkers in the two countries and another attributable to relative changes in the coefficients of the linear probability models. For both male and female heads this decomposition suggests that relative changes in the demographic characteristics of nonworkers were only a minor factor in the relative rise in Canadian unemployment.

A third explanation for the relative rise in $P(U|N)$ in Canada is that a greater fraction of U.S. workers have become discouraged and withdrawn from the labor force over the 1980s, while their Canadian counterparts have continued to look for work. In both the CPS and the LFS the distinction between unemployed and discouraged workers hinges on self-reported job search effort and is therefore highly subjective.[28] Any change in the fraction of discouraged workers in the United States relative to Canada, however, will lead to a relative change in $P(U|N)$. Akyeampong (1989) presents data on discouraged workers in Canada compiled from supplementary questions in the March LFS survey. Similar data are collected for one-quarter of individuals in the CPS each month and published as annual series in U.S. Bureau of Labor Statistics (1988). Using these sources we have computed unemployment rates for the United States and Canada that include discouraged workers in the count of unemployed workers. The resulting series are graphed in figure 5.12 along with the conventional unemployment rates. The addition of discouraged workers raises unemployment rates in both countries by about 8–10 percent, but leaves the cyclical and trend components of the series unaffected. There is no indication that the relative increase in $P(U|N)$ in Canada over the 1980s has occurred because of a relative change in the fraction of discouraged workers in the United States and Canada.

28. A discouraged worker is an individual who was not working in the survey week and has not looked for work in the previous 4 weeks, but who was available for work and stated that he or she wanted a job. Finally, the individual must give as a reason for not looking that he or she "believes no work is available" (in both the LFS and CPS) or "couldn't find a job" (in the CPS).

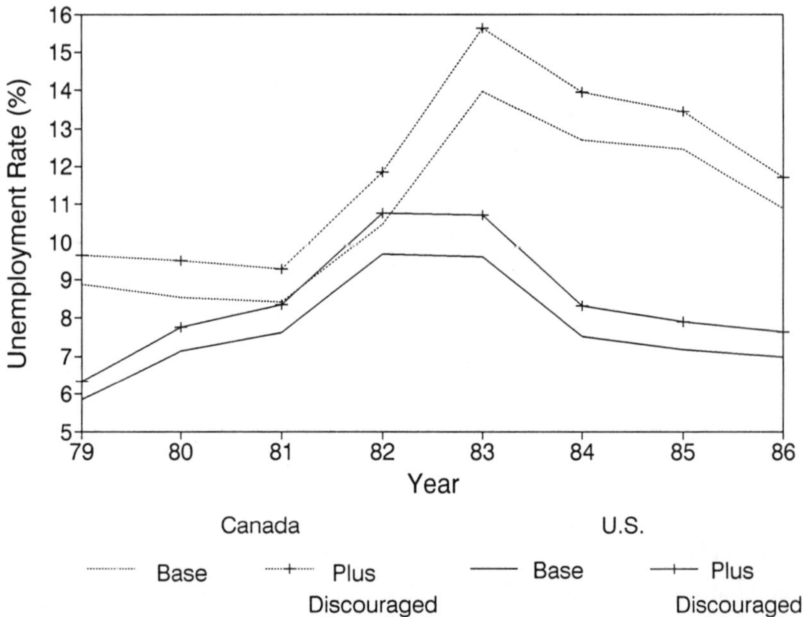

Fig. 5.12 Unemployment rates excluding and including discouraged workers, the United States and Canada

In summary, the results in tables 5.10 and 5.11 reinforce the conclusions from our analysis of retrospective unemployment. Virtually all of the relative increase in female unemployment in Canada is explained by an increase in the propensity of Canadian women to report nonworking time as unemployment. Retrospectively, this is represented by an increase in the number of weeks of unemployment in the previous year reported by women with a given number of weeks of employment. Contemporaneously, it appears as an increase in the conditional probability of unemployment among nonworkers, holding constant the number of weeks worked in the previous year and such variables as age, education, and marital status.

The relative increase in unemployment of Canadian men is a result of similar changes in the propensity to report nonworking time as unemployment, augmented by relative changes in the distribution of employment. Our retrospective analysis indicates that over 50 percent of the relative increase in Canadian male unemployment is attributable to the increase in reported unemployment among men with 0 weeks of work during the year. Contemporaneously, this behavior is reflected in the significant increase in the probability of unemployment among nonworking men with 0 weeks of work in the previous year. A comparison of the distribution of weeks worked among Canadian men shows a relative decrease in full-year employment and a corresponding increase in part-year employment (particularly 10–26 weeks), leading to higher levels of retrospective unemployment and higher rates of contemporaneous nonemployment.

5.6 Unemployment and Unemployment Insurance

The preceding analysis suggests that up to three-quarters of the growth in the unemployment gap between Canada and the United States in the 1980s is attributable to a relative increase in the fraction of nonworking time that is classified as unemployment. For men this increase is particularly strong among individuals with 0, 10, or 12 weeks of employment in the previous year. For women the increases are more evenly distributed across the entire distribution of annual work experience, but also show peaks at 0, 10–12, and 20 weeks of work experience. These patterns are suggestive of a number of hypotheses. Perhaps most obviously, since 1979 the Canadian UI system has provided a relatively strong incentive for individuals with low labor supply characteristics to work at least 10–12 weeks and, in the case of new entrants, reentrants, and women at risk of childbirth, at least 20 weeks. Depending on the region of the country, these thresholds are enough to ensure eligibility for UI benefits for 10–42 weeks. In the United States, on the other hand, UI eligibility requires 20 weeks of work (or the earnings equivalent of 20 weeks of full-time work at the minimum wage) in most states.[29] We conjecture that the more generous UI system in Canada and the changes made to the UI system in the late 1970s have led some Canadians with low–labor force attachment to work just enough to continue collecting UI benefits (i.e., 10, 12, or 20 weeks) and to report their nonworking time as unemployment.

Table 5.12 presents information on the UI programs of the two countries during the 1970s and 1980s. The first two columns of the table give the ratio of the average weekly number of UI recipients in each country to the average weekly count of unemployment. The comparison is striking: the number of active UI claimants is only about one-third as large as the number of unemployed workers in the United States, but is 85 percent or more of the unemployment count in Canada. During the 1980s the ratio fell slightly in the United States but actually rose in Canada, reaching over 100 percent in 1989.

The differences between the United States and Canada in the ratio of UI recipients to unemployed workers reflect three basic differences. First, a larger fraction of unemployed workers in Canada are eligible for benefits. Appendix table 5A.2 presents illustrative calculations of the UI eligibility rate among unemployed individuals in the two countries in 1987. These calculations suggest that the eligibility rate is indeed higher in Canada: 53 percent versus 42 percent in the United States. Second, a relatively large number of

29. See Statistics Canada (1984) and Green and Riddell (1993) for overviews of UI rules in Canada. See U.S. Department of Labor Employment and Training Administration (1989) and Anderson and Meyer (1993) for overviews of UI rules in the United States.

Table 5.12 **Characteristics of UI Systems in the United States and Canada, 1968–88**

	UI Recipients/ Number Unemployed (%)[a]		Weekly UI Benefit/ Weekly Earnings (%)[b]		Average Duration of UI Claims (weeks)[c]	
	U.S. (1)	Canada (2)	U.S. (3)	Canada (4)	U.S. (5)	Canada (6)
1968	33.2	88.6	34.3	24.2	11.6	13.1
1969	32.5	83.6	34.4	26.9	11.4	13.8
1970	37.0	80.1	35.7	27.7	12.3	14.4
1971	41.6	81.4	36.5	28.6	14.4	14.9
1972	35.6	105.9	36.1	41.4	14.0	13.5
1973	32.4	110.3	36.1	42.7	13.4	14.4
1974	39.6	106.5	36.5	42.1	12.7	13.1
1975	51.7	104.0	37.1	41.6	15.7	14.2
1976	41.6	95.9	37.1	40.7	14.9	14.6
1977	37.9	87.7	36.4	40.4	14.2	15.0
1978	34.1	87.6	36.4	41.3	13.3	15.9
1979	34.2	84.9	36.1	37.7	13.1	16.0
1980	37.9	80.8	36.4	38.1	14.9	15.2
1981	34.5	79.3	35.9	36.7	14.5	14.8
1982	37.0	88.9	37.5	36.3	15.9	17.0
1983	30.3	89.3	36.8	36.4	17.5	21.2
1984	25.3	86.0	35.3	39.8	14.3	19.2
1985	27.8	87.7	35.3	40.8	14.3	19.6
1986	28.7	91.9	35.8	42.0	14.6	18.8
1987	27.4	91.8	35.3	43.0	14.6	18.4
1988	27.0	99.8	34.8	43.7	13.7	17.9
1989	28.7	100.9	35.4	44.3	13.2	18.1

[a]The ratio of the average weekly number of UI recipients to the average weekly number of unemployed individuals. UI recipients in the United States include regular and extended benefit recipients and exclude beneficiaries of special programs for exservicemen, federal workers, and railroad workers, as well as recipients of temporary programs.

[b]The ratio of average weekly UI payments to average weekly earnings of insured workers (United States) or averge weekly earnings in the economy (Canada).

[c]Estimated average duration of benefit claims.

individuals who are classified as out of the labor force in the LFS receive UI benefits in Canada (see Levesque 1989). This group includes individuals receiving benefits during periods of training, sickness, and maternity leave, as well as others who are not actively searching for work. Third, take-up rates for benefits may differ between the countries. Blank and Card (1991) estimate that the take-up rate among eligible unemployed workers in the United States is 65–75 percent (it fell sharply in the early 1980s). While no similar estimates are available for Canada, we suspect that the take-up rate is higher.

Columns 3 and 4 of table 5.12 show the ratio of average weekly UI benefits to average weekly earnings in each country.[30] Prior to the revision of the Canadian UI system in 1971, benefits payments were low in Canada relative to the United States. The 1971 act increased the generosity of benefits substantially, to an overall average of just over 40 percent of average weekly earnings. Subsequently the relative generosity of UI payments in the two countries has remained fairly constant, although the data suggest an upward trend in relative payments in Canada during the 1980s.[31] It is important to keep in mind that the ratios in table 5.12 are *not* averages of the replacement rates actually earned by unemployed workers. These will tend to be higher than the rates in the table, since unemployed workers have average earnings that are below the economy-wide average (see tables 5.3 and 5.5).

Columns 5 and 6 show the average duration of benefit claims in the two countries. The maximum duration of regular UI benefits in the United States is 26 weeks; historically, the average potential duration of benefit claims has been relatively constant at 22–23 weeks. Regular benefits are supplemented by so-called extended benefits, which offer up to 13 extra weeks of benefits to claimants in states with relatively high insured unemployment rates, and by ad hoc supplemental benefit programs, which offer additional temporary extended benefit rights. Benefit weeks paid under these programs are not included in the average duration figures for the United States: hence, the figures in table 5.12 understate the rise in average durations associated with previous recessionary periods. Since 1984, however, extended and supplemental benefit programs have been negligible in all states but Alaska.

In contrast to the U.S. case, the average duration figures in table 5.12 for Canada include extended benefit programs, which are a built-in feature of the Canadian UI system. The average duration of Canadian UI claims rose some 30 percent during the 1982–83 recession, reflecting both the availability of longer benefits and slower exit rates from the UI program. The average duration of claims has not fallen back to its pre-1982 level, even as the economy-wide unemployment rate has returned to about the same level as 1979–81. The average duration of (in-progress) unemployment spells in Canada also rose between the beginning and the end of the 1980s. Interestingly, the average duration of unemployment spells in the United States was also higher in 1989 than 1979, even though the U.S. average unemployment rate was slightly lower in 1989 than in 1979.[32]

30. These ratios make no allowance for the tax treatment of UI benefits, which has varied over the period. By 1984 UI benefits were fully taxable in each country. In addition, since 1977 Canadians with income above a certain threshold have been required to pay a surtax on a portion of UI benefits.

31. Statutorily, UI benefits are paid at 60 percent of the claimant's former wage rate in Canada, up to a maximum. In the United States, benefits are paid at rates that average about 50 percent of the former wage, subject to a minimum and maximum rate.

32. In Canada the average duration of (in-progress) unemployment spells was 14.9 weeks in 1979–80 and 17.9 weeks in 1989. In the United States the average duration of unemployment

An important question is whether the Canadian UI system is responsible for the sluggish decline in UI durations, and perhaps the simultaneous rise in relative Canadian unemployment rates. To answer this question, we have used regional extended benefit information for each labor market region in the country, together with a fixed pool of unemployed workers (characterized by their weeks of work in the previous year) to simulate expected maximum benefit eligibility in each year from 1972 to 1989.[33] The fixed unemployment pool consists of all unemployed workers in the 1987 LFS. We use each individual's reported weeks of work in 1986 as an estimate of his or her weeks of work during the UI qualification period. For each year (using data for June as an approximate midpoint) we calculate the maximum weeks of UI that each individual in the unemployment pool could expect in that year in each labor market region. We then weight the averages across regions, using 1981 population weights.

The resulting series of average maximum eligibility weeks is plotted in figure 5.13, along with the average UI claim duration series from table 5.12. Because of the nature of the regional extended benefit formulas, average maximum eligibility tracks the average unemployment rate in the economy very closely. The average duration of UI claims also tracks maximum eligibility until 1985 or 1986. More recently, however, maximum eligibility has returned to its pre-1982 level, while the average duration of UI claims has leveled off. These simulations therefore suggest that the extended benefit rules are not to blame for the high level of UI durations in 1987–89.[34] Rather, high levels of unemployment and longer UI durations have persisted even as the maximum durations of benefits declined in the late 1980s.

Further information on the differences in UI recipiency between the United States and Canada is presented in table 5.13. Here we have used our extracts of family heads in the CPS and the LFS to calculate the fraction of individuals who report receiving UI income in the previous year.[35] As expected from the

spells was 10.8 weeks in 1979 and 11.9 weeks in 1989. (Canadian data are from Statistics Canada, *The Labour Force*, various years; U.S. data are from the 1992 *Economic Report of the President*, table B-39).

33. During the period 1978–90 forty-eight regions were used to administer the extended benefit provisions of the UI system. Eligibility was extended by 2 weeks for each 0.5 percentage-point increase in the regional unemployment rate over and above 4.0 percent, up to a maximum of 32 weeks (see Statistics Canada 1984).

34. Because the simulations assume a fixed pool of unemployed workers in each economic region, the decline in average eligibility between 1983 and 1989 reflects the decline in average unemployment rates experienced in most economic regions of Canada. We are unaware of any changes in the composition of unemployed workers that would offset the decline in maximum UI eligibility displayed in figure 5.13. Indeed, the decline in average weeks worked in the previous year by currently unemployed workers over the 1980s (see table 5.5) suggests that average weeks of maximum eligibility would have fallen *faster* than indicated by the simulations in figure 5.13.

35. A difficulty with these calculations is that the 1979 Survey of Consumer Finances does *not* report person-specific information on UI recipiency, only the number of UI recipients in the family. For families with no UI recipients this is not a problem—we assumed that none of the individ-

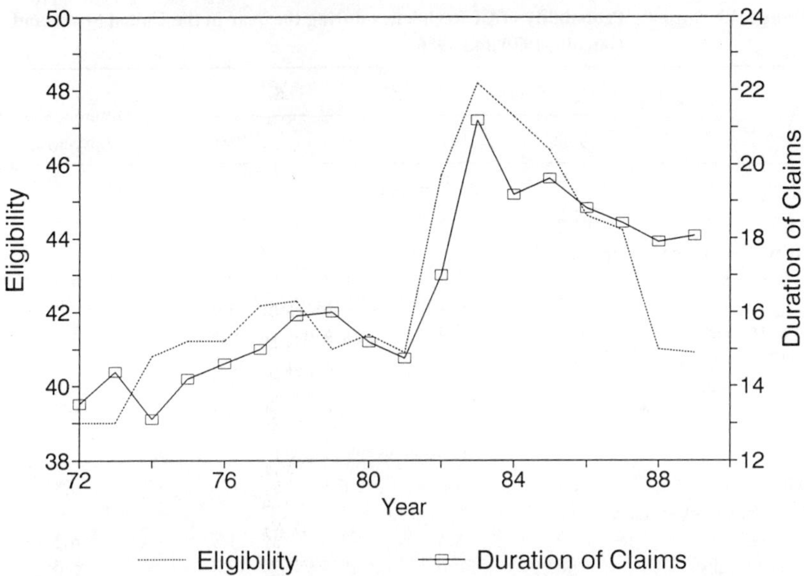

Fig. 5.13 Average weeks of eligibility and average weeks of benefits claimed, Canadian UI system

data in tables 5.6 and 5.12, the probability of UI receipt is uniformly higher in Canada, especially for women. There were substantial relative shifts in UI recipiency rates across the two countries, however, even controlling for weeks of work in the previous year. Inspection of the difference-in-differences in table 5.13 indicates that relative recipiency rates fell in the 1980s for Canadian heads with relatively low annual weeks of work (0 and 1–17 weeks of work). Since individuals (especially men) with 0 weeks of work are a major source of the growing unemployment gap between Canada and the United States, it is difficult to argue that the increase in Canadian unemployment is mainly a result of the UI system. On the other hand, the growth in relative recipiency rates among men and women with 8–16 weeks of work is consistent with the spikes at 10–12 weeks in figures 5.8 and 5.9. Similarly, the growth in relative recipiency rates among female heads with 17–26 weeks of work is consistent with the spike at 20 weeks in figure 5.8. Attributing *all* of the relative increase in unemployment at the 10-, 12-, and 20-week spikes to the UI system, our analysis suggests that at most 22 percent of the relative increase in male un-

uals in the family received UI. For families with two or more UI recipients we assumed that both heads (if present) received UI. For families with two heads and one UI recipient, we allocated UI recipiency to the head with more weeks of unemployment if either head reported positive weeks of unemployment, and to the head with fewer weeks of work if neither head reported any weeks of unemployment.

Table 5.13 **Probability of UI Recipiency during the Year in the United States and Canada, 1979 and 1986**

	Canada		U.S.		
	1979[a]	1986	1979	1986	Difference-in-Differences
		A. Female heads			
All	12.2	13.2	3.9	3.4	1.5
By weeks worked during year					
0 weeks	9.1	2.8	0.3	0.6	−6.6
1–7 weeks	21.8	20.7	4.8	4.4	−0.7
8–16 weeks	30.6	34.4	6.8	6.8	3.8
17–26 weeks	38.8	49.5	11.2	10.5	11.4
27–39 weeks	40.0	48.4	15.3	13.2	10.5
40+ weeks	6.4	11.1	3.9	3.1	5.5
		B. Male heads			
All	14.8	14.6	6.5	6.6	−0.3
By weeks worked during year					
0 weeks	13.9	8.4	1.0	1.7	−6.2
1–7 weeks	40.8	36.6	10.5	12.3	−6.0
8–16 weeks	38.8	50.5	16.6	20.4	7.9
17–26 weeks	52.3	61.6	26.1	28.6	6.8
27–39 weeks	52.2	61.9	33.6	35.7	7.6
40+ weeks	9.7	7.6	4.5	4.2	−1.8

Notes: Probability of UI recipiency is the probability of reporting UI income during the calendar year.

employment and 20 percent of the relative increase in female unemployment is attributable to the Canadian UI system. We regard this estimate as an upper bound on the UI effect. Clearly, a large fraction of the emergent unemployment gap—particularly the component attributable to individuals with very low levels of annual labor supply—remains unexplained.

5.7 Conclusions

We have presented a variety of macroeconomic and microeconomic evidence aimed at discovering the sources of the unemployment gap that emerged between Canada and the United States in the 1980s. We have argued that the long-run persistence of this gap—through more than seven years of economic expansion—suggests a permanent structural difference in the nature of unemployment in the two countries. We have uncovered several important facts that are relevant for the interpretation of the unemployment gap. Most important, higher aggregate unemployment in Canada is not simply a consequence of lower aggregate employment. Indeed, employment-population rates are fairly similar in the two countries and became more similar during the late 1980s. Rather, individuals who are not working in Canada are more likely to be classified as unemployed. Most of the unemployment gap between Canada and the United States at the end of the 1980s is attributable to this propensity.

We have used individual microdata on male and female family heads from 1979–80 and 1986–87 to analyze the components of the relative increase in Canadian unemployment in the past decade. Looking at either contemporaneous or retrospective measures of unemployment, the relative growth of unemployment among Canadian women during the 1980s is attributable to an increase in the likelihood that nonemployment is reported as unemployment. This increase occurred across women with different levels of actual employment experience during the year, with relatively larger shares attributable to women who worked 0, 10–12, and 20 weeks in the previous year. For men, one-half of the relative increase in Canadian unemployment during the 1980s is attributable to the behavior of a single group: those with no weeks of employment during the entire calendar year. During the 1980s there was a sharp increase in the probability that Canadian men with no work experience in the previous year would remain attached to the labor force. Another 20 percent of the relative rise in male unemployment is attributable to the growth in reported weeks of unemployment among Canadian men with 10–12 weeks of employment in the previous year.

An important theme in our study is the role of UI benefits in the emergence of a unemployment gap between the United States and Canada. Unemployed workers are more likely to receive unemployment benefits in Canada than in the United States. This differential widened during the 1980s, as did the relative generosity of UI benefits in Canada and the relative duration of Canadian UI claims. However, an analysis of the regional extended benefit system in Canada suggests that the UI system itself is not the cause of the high level of unemployment at the close of the 1980s. If the same group of workers had entered the pool of unemployment in 1979 as in 1989, our simulations suggest that the average duration of available UI benefits would have been the same. By the same token, UI recipiency rates among men and women with 0 weeks of work actually fell in Canada relative to the United States over the 1980s. The portion of widening unemployment gap accounted for by individuals with 0 weeks of work is clearly not attributable to the Canadian UI system.

Nevertheless, we do find evidence that Canadian workers have increasingly tailored their labor supply behavior to the characteristics of the UI system. Relative increases in the numbers of Canadian men and women reporting exactly 10 or 12 weeks of employment, and relative increases in the weeks of unemployment reported by these workers, account for 13 percent of the relative rise in female unemployment and 22 percent of the relative rise in male unemployment. Similar increases for women with exactly 20 weeks of work account for another 8 percent of the relative rise in female unemployment. UI recipiency rates also increased for Canadian men and women with these labor supply patterns. These findings point to a significant role of the UI system in accounting for the rise in relative Canadian unemployment, although most of the rise in the Canadian-U.S. unemployment gap remains unexplained.

Appendix

Table 5A.1 Industry Shares of Labor Force and Relative Shares of Unemployment and Employment, 1986

	U.S.		Canada	
	Labor Force Share[a] (1)	Relative Share Unemployment/ Employment[b] (2)	Labor Force Share[a] (3)	Relative Share Unemployment/ Employment[b] (4)
Agriculture	2.4	1.27	4.0	0.75
Forestry, fishing, mining	0.9	1.82	2.6	2.17
Nondurable manufacturing	6.9	1.00	8.7	1.04
Durable manufacturing	10.1	0.88	8.1	0.92
Construction	6.1	1.90	5.7	2.15
Transportation, communication, utilities	6.2	0.72	7.3	0.68
Wholesale trade	3.6	0.71	4.3	0.68
Retail trade	15.1	1.10	13.0	0.91
Finance, insurance, real estate	5.9	0.45	5.2	0.55
Health, education, recreation	15.3	0.53	16.7	0.62
Personal services	4.4	1.13	9.5	1.50
Business services	8.7	0.87	7.1	1.15
Public administration	4.1	0.45	7.2	0.76
Currently unemployed	10.5	3.4	—	—
Never worked	—	—	0.7	—

Sources: See table 5.3.

Notes: See notes to table 5.6.

[a]Fraction of all individuals in labor force last year declaring an attachment to industry in the previous year. In the United States, industry is not asked of currently unemployed individuals.

[b]Ratios of the industries' shares of weeks of unemployment in the previous year to the industries' shares of weeks of employment in the previous year.

Table 5A.2 Approximate UI Eligibility Calculations for Currently Unemployed Individuals, 1987

Reason for Disqualification	Unemployed (%)
Canada	
Age 65 or older	0.4
Full-time student	5.7
No work in previous year	20.5
Previous job uncovered	2.7
Unemployed < waiting period	10.5
Worked 1–9 weeks in previous year[a]	7.0
Ineligible (%)	46.8
Eligible (%)	53.2
United States	
Unemployed < waiting period	6.0
Unemployed > maximum duration	24.3
Insufficient earnings/weeks in previous year	30.2
Quit previous job	7.5
Previous job uncovered	0.1
Ineligible (%)	58.3
Eligible (%)	41.7

Sources: Calculations for Canada are based on Levesque (1989). Calculations for the United States are based on Blank and Card (1991).

[a]Ignored by Levesque. Estimate based on weeks of work reported by currently unemployed (excluding full-time students) in 1987 Survey of Consumer Finances.

References

Akerlof, George, and Janet Yellen. 1985. Unemployment through the Filter of Memory. *Quarterly Journal of Economics* 102 (August): 747–73.

Akyeampong, Ernest. 1989. Discouraged Workers. *Perspectives on Labour and Income* 2 (Autumn): 64–69.

Anderson, Patricia, and Bruce Meyer. 1993. Unemployment Insurance in the United States: Lay-off Incentives and Cross-subsidies. *Journal of Labor Economics* 10 (January), forthcoming.

Ashenfelter, Orley, and David Card. 1986. Why Have Unemployment Rates in Canada and the United States Diverged? *Economica* 53 (supplement): S171–96.

Blank, Rebecca, and David Card. 1991. Recent Trends in Insured and Uninsured Unemployment: Is There an Explanation? *Quarterly Journal of Economics* 106 (November): 1157–89.

Blank, Rebecca, and Maria Hanratty. 1991. Responding to Need: A Comparison of Social Safety Nets in the United States and Canada. Working paper, January.

Corak, Miles. 1991. Unemployment Comes of Age: The Demographics of Labour Sector Adjustment in Canada. In Surendra Gera, ed., *Canadian Unemployment.* Ottawa: Economic Council of Canada.

Fortin, Pierre. 1986. Prices, Employment, and Productivity in Canada: A Quick Survey of Facts, Issues, and Evidence. Laval University Department of Economics Discussion Paper.

Green, David A., and W. Craig Riddell. 1993. The Economic Effects of Unemployment Insurance in Canada: An Empirical Analysis of UI Disentitlement. *Journal of Labor Economics* 10 (January), forthcoming.

Hagar-Guenette, Cynthia. 1989. Job Ads: A Leading Indicator? *Perspectives on Labour and Income* 2 (Autumn): 53–62.

Juhn, Chinhui. 1992. Decline of Male Labor Market Participation: The Role of Declining Market Opportunities. *Quarterly Journal of Economics* 107 (February): 79–122.

Keil, M. W., and J. S. V. Symons. 1990. An Analysis of Canadian Unemployment. *Canadian Public Policy* 16 (March): 1–16.

Levesque, Jean-Marc. 1989. Unemployment and Unemployment Insurance: A Tale of Two Sources. *Perspectives on Labour and Income* 1 (Winter): 49–57.

Levine, Phillip. 1990. Contemporaneous vs. Retrospective Unemployment: Through the Filter of Memory or the Muddle of the Current Population Survey? Princeton University Industrial Relations Section Working Paper, October.

Lucas, Robert, and Leonard Rapping. 1970. Real Wages, Employment, and Inflation. In E. S. Phelps, ed., *Microeconomic Foundations of Employment and Inflation Theory.* New York: Norton.

McCallum, John. 1987. Unemployment in Canada and the United States. *Canadian Journal of Economics* 20 (1987): 802–22.

Milbourne, Ross, Douglas Purvis, and W. David Scoones. 1991. Unemployment Insurance and Unemployment Dynamics. *Canadian Journal of Economics* 23 (November): 804–26.

Moorthy, Vivek. 1990. Unemployment in Canada and the United States: The Role of Unemployment Insurance Benefits. *Federal Reserve Bank of New York Quarterly* 14: 48–61.

Statistics Canada. 1984. *Unemployment Insurance 1984.* Statistics Canada Health Division Social Security Section, Social Security National Programs, vol. 2. Ottawa: Ministry of Supply and Services.

U.S. Department of Labor. Bureau of Labor Statistics. 1988. Labor Force Statistics Derived from the Current Population Survey, 1947–1987. Bureau of Labor Statistics Bulletin 2307. Washington, D.C.: GPO.

U.S. Department of Labor. Employment and Training Administration. 1989. Comparison of State Unemployment Insurance Laws. Washington, D.C.: U.S. Department of Labor.

6 Responding to Need: A Comparison of Social Safety Nets in Canada and the United States

Rebecca M. Blank and Maria J. Hanratty

6.1 Introduction

The United States and Canada share similar populations and similar macroeconomic environments. Yet each has chosen a different set of policies to address the problem of poverty. Canada has a tradition of universal non-means-tested programs that is almost entirely absent in the United States. In addition, Canada's means-tested programs maintain broader eligibility and more generous benefit payments than those of the United States. Preliminary evidence suggests that Canadian institutions have been more successful than U.S. institutions in eliminating poverty: although the United States has slightly higher average incomes than Canada, Canada has substantially lower poverty rates of families with children. In 1986, the poverty rate of single-parent families with children was 32.3 percent in Canada compared to 45.3 percent in the United States; the poverty rate of two-parent families with children was 5.2 percent in Canada and 6.8 percent in the United States.[1]

This paper examines the extent to which the differences in social welfare institutions can explain the different poverty outcomes in the two countries. In particular, we ask what would be the impact of adopting Canadian antipoverty programs in the United States, and U.S. antipoverty programs in Canada.

Rebecca M. Blank is an associate professor at Northwestern University in the Department of Economics and the School of Education and Social Policy, a research faculty member of the Center for Urban Affairs and Policy Research at Northwestern University, and a research associate of the National Bureau of Economic Research. Maria J. Hanratty is an assistant professor in the New York State School of Industrial and Labor Relations at Cornell University.

The Donner Foundation provided much of the funding for this research. Kristin Butcher and Jon Jacobsen provided excellent research assistance. The authors thank Lawrence Katz, Richard Freeman, Joshua Angrist, and members of the NBER–Donner Foundation Canada–United States Comparative Social Policy Project for useful comments.

1. These are poverty rates for nonelderly families, based on the U.S. definition of poverty. See section 6.3.1 for details on their computation.

We simulate the potential impact of running Canadian transfer programs in the United States and vice versa by applying institutional rules on program eligibility and benefit levels to microdata from each country, allowing for a range of labor supply and participation responses. We also use these simulations to estimate participation rates among different population groups, and to document the extent of regional variation in program generosity. This paper focuses on program differences in 1986 between the United States and Canada; a description of comparative poverty rates over time between these two countries can be found in Hanratty and Blank (1992).

Our results indicate particularly dramatic differences in the impact of the two systems on the poverty rates of single parents with children. The poverty rate of single-parent families would decline from 43 percent to 16 percent if the United States adopted the "mean" Canadian program, assuming Canadian participation rates were duplicated in the United States. Assuming 100 percent participation rates, poverty among this group would nearly disappear. These results are not very sensitive to a range of assumed labor supply elasticities.

Not surprisingly, our results also suggest that transfer expenditures would increase substantially if the United States were to adopt the Canadian transfer system. Our estimates imply that total U.S. transfer expenditures would be two to three times higher under the Canadian transfer system, depending on the assumed labor supply elasticities and participation rates.

This paper is divided into four sections. The first section describes the key Canadian and U.S. social welfare programs. Because we were unable to find a detailed comparison of these programs elsewhere in the literature, we include a lengthy description here. The reader who is primarily interested in the simulation results may turn to table 6.1 for a quick summary of the transfer programs and then skip to section 6.3. Section 6.3 presents information on the demographic characteristics and income sources of families in the two countries. Section 6.4 presents the simulation results. Section 6.5 summarizes and concludes the paper.

6.2 Comparing Antipoverty Programs in the United States and Canada

6.2.1 Introduction

This paper is concerned with transfer programs for nonelderly, nondisabled individuals and families in the United States and Canada. Because of data availability, we focus on the year 1986.[2] The key programs that this paper

2. An extensive description of the legislative rules on eligibility and benefits by program and across provinces was not available in Canada until 1985, with an update for 1986. See Canada Department of National Health and Welfare (1986, 1988).

Table 6.1 **Transfer Programs in 1986, Nonelderly, Nonhealth Related (in 1986 U.S. dollars)**

A. Canadian Transfer Programs

Unemployment insurance (UI)

Available to unemployed workers for at least 42 weeks. As provincial unemployment rises, weeks rise to a maximum of 50 (received by most workers in 1986). Federal government determines all eligibility rules and benefits. Replaces 60 percent of weekly earnings up to a maximum of $396/week. Must have worked more than 14 weeks in past year and/or earned more than $74/week.

Family Allowance (FA)

Available to all families with children under 18; no means testing. Provides $303/child/year. Two provinces have variations.

Social Assistance (SA)

Available to low-income families and inviduals. Eligibility and benefits determined and run by province; grant levels, deductions, and tax rates vary widely by province. Grant supplements often available "at discretion of local office." Work programs included in some provinces. (Three provinces—Nova Scotia, Ontario, and Manitoba—have a "two-tier" system in which the municipalities determine eligibility and benefit rules for particular groups of applicants.) Population-weighted average provincial grant for single nondisabled individual with no countable income on long-term assistance is $266/month (lowest province is $171; highest province is $524). For a single parent with two children it is $627/month (lowest province is $594; highest province is $922).

Child Tax Credit (CTC)

Available to lower-income families with children under 18. Maximum credit of $363/year/child. Available to all families with $18,800 or less income. Breakeven income level for a household with one child is $26,064. Credit refundable to those without tax liabilities.

B. United States Transfer Programs

Unemployment Insurance (UI)

Available to unemployed workers for up to 26 weeks. (At very high state unemployment levels, the federal extended benefit [EB] program supplements state programs with additional weeks of benefits; only one state received EB in 1986.) Eligibility requirements as well as benefit levels are set by the states and vary significantly. Most states have either minimum weeks or minimum earnings requirements for eligibility. the population-weighted state average replacement rate is 64.2 percent in 1986, with an average maximum benefit of $184/week. (Lowest state is $115; highest state is $310.)

Aid to Families with Dependent Children (AFDC)

Primarily available to single-parent households, although some states allow two-parent households to receive AFDC, typically with stricter eligibility requirements. States set some eligibility rules and set benefit levels. The federal government determines other eligibility rules and sets the tax rate. A tax rate on earnings of 66 percent applies for the first four months of recipiency and rises to 100 percent thereafter. The population-weighted state average benefit for a family of one adult and two children with no countable income is $368/month. (Lowest state is $118; highest state is $740. This is an outlier; the next highest state pays $583/month.)

Food stamps

An in-kind program that provides "coupons" that can be used to purchase food. Generally agreed to be the equivalent of a cash grant for most recipient families. Eligibility and benefits set at the federal level. Maximum food stamps available to a family of three with no countable income is $211/month.

Earned Income Tax Credit (EITC)

Available to low-income families with children under age 18 and with earned income. Does not vary with family size. As earnings rise, credit increases to a maximum of $550 between $5,000 and $6,500 in earned income, and then declines to zero at $11,000. Credit refundable to those without tax liabilities.

deals with are outlined in table 6.1. A history of the relevant legislative changes in these programs from the mid-1960s to the mid-1980s is provided in appendix A.[3]

We do not include medical insurance programs in our analysis because there is no information in our microdata for either the United States or Canada on medical needs or insurance usage. The result of this omission is to consistently underestimate the extent of public assistance in Canada relative to the United States. Canada's national health insurance program covers the entire population. In the United States, insurance among the nonelderly is largely privately provided by employers. Public medical assistance is available to some low-income households through the Medicaid program, but 39.6 percent of poor families in the United States are uninsured in 1986.[4]

All dollar values are denominated in U.S. dollars. To convert Canadian dollars we use an index based on the 1985 OECD estimate of purchasing power parity for consumption goods.[5] This measures the ratio of the number of Canadian dollars to U.S. dollars required to buy the same market basket of goods in each country.

This paper uses data on the ten major Canadian provinces. In the United States, we include the fifty states and the District of Columbia.

6.2.2 The Programs

Unemployment Insurance

Both Canada and the United States operate unemployment insurance (UI) programs that offer payments to individuals who have involuntarily lost their jobs. In Canada, the UI program is a national program, available to most unemployed workers.[6] The weekly UI benefit is set at 60 percent of the average weekly earnings during the weeks worked in the past twenty weeks, to a maximum of $396 per week. The duration of UI payments varies with both the weeks worked in the previous year and the regional unemployment rate. In 1986, the maximum UI duration was fifty weeks in all provinces.

In the United States, the UI program is entirely state run, which means that program rules differ significantly across states. Most states have requirements

3. For a review of the existing literature on the economic and behavioral effects of transfer programs, see Ismael (1987) or Vaillancourt (1985) for Canada and Danziger and Weinberg (1986) for the United States. For a comparative discussion of historical poverty issues in both countries, see Leman (1980).

4. See Chollett (1988). The Medicaid program in 1986 primarily covered families or individuals who were eligible for Aid to Families with Dependent Children or Supplemental Security Income.

5. OECD (1987). This is adjusted to 1986 using the relative inflation rates based on the U.S. GNP implicit price deflator for consumption and the Canadian GDP implicit price deflator for consumption. This gives a conversion rate of 1.25 U.S. dollars per Canadian dollar in 1986.

6. Workers who have less than ten to fourteen weeks of insurable employment in the previous year, or who work less than fifteen hours/week, or who earn less than 20 percent of maximum weekly insurable earnings are not covered by the UI program.

(stricter than those in Canada) that an individual work either a minimum number of weeks or earn a minimum amount on the job to qualify for UI. UI payments on average are set at 64.2 percent of previous weekly earnings; the maximum state payment averages $184/week. UI payments are available for only twenty-six weeks in most states, as opposed to fifty in Canada. As a result of these differences, a lower percentage of the unemployed receive UI in the United States than in Canada: in 1986, 59 percent of the unemployed received UI in Canada, while only 28 percent of the unemployed received UI in the United States.[7]

Public Assistance to the Poor

The primary means-tested assistance program in Canada is Social Assistance (SA), which provides cash assistance to low-income families and individuals. This program is funded jointly by the federal and provincial governments, but it is run almost entirely at the provincial level.[8] Provinces set eligibility standards and benefit levels, which vary widely.[9] Unlike the United States, this program does not exclude individuals from the program because of their family composition. However, benefit levels do vary by family composition: the maximum payment for single individuals is $266/month, while it is $627/month for a single parent with two children.[10]

In the United States, assistance to the poor is divided between two programs: Aid to Families with Dependent Children (AFDC) and food stamps. AFDC provides cash assistance to (primarily) single-parent families.[11] This program is run jointly by the states and the federal government. AFDC maximum benefits in the United States are substantially lower than SA maximum benefits for single-parent families in Canada. The population-weighted state average maximum benefit for a single parent with two children is $368/month in 1986, less than 60 percent of Canada's level.

7. The U.S. figure is from Blank and Card (1991), while the Canadian figure is from Card and Riddell (chap. 5 in this volume).

8. Federal regulations for SA under the 1966 Canada Assistance Plan impose two requirements: provinces cannot impose residency requirements and eligibility must be based on a needs test (rather than an income test). Quebec has opted out of the Canada Assistance Plan and runs its own SA program, with special cost-sharing arrangements with the federal government.

9. In three "two-tier" provinces (Nova Scotia, Ontario, and Manitoba), SA benefits and eligibility are determined at the municipal level for certain categories of recipients. In Ontario, for example, municipal governments are responsible for all individuals who are determined to be employable, while the provincial government provides support to those unable to work. The benefit levels reported for municipally run programs refer to the largest city in the province.

10. We use the benefit levels provided by the Canada National Council of Welfare (1987). The levels we use assume that any single individual or two-parent family would be classified by the province as employable, while single-parent families would be considered unemployable (except in Alberta or British Columbia, where only single parents with extremely young children are considered unemployable).

11. In 1986, twenty-eight states allowed some two-parent families to receive AFDC, although eligibility standards were typically stricter. Over 90 percent of the AFDC caseload has always been female-headed families. In 1990, all states were required to provide AFDC to eligible two-parent households.

The food stamp program provides monthly vouchers redeemable for grocery items to low-income families and individuals. Food stamp benefits and eligibility are entirely set at the federal level, with uniform national benefits. In contrast to AFDC, food stamps are available to any household below a certain income level, regardless of household composition. Thus single individuals or two-parent households who cannot receive AFDC can receive food stamps. The maximum food stamp payment is $80/month for a single individual and $211/month for a family of three in 1986.

Tax Credits

In addition to cash and in-kind assistance, both countries also run tax credits for low-income households with children. The Canadian Child Tax Credit (CTC) is a refundable tax credit for families with children. The CTC provides $363/year/child for households with annual incomes below $18,800, declining to zero at $26,064 in income.

The U.S. Earned Income Tax Credit (EITC) is a refundable tax credit available to working families with children. As earnings increase, the tax credit increases to a maximum of $550 between $5,000 and $6,500 in earnings, and declines to zero at $11,000. Unlike the CTC, the EITC is not prorated by the number of children. In addition, families must have earnings in order to receive the EITC.[12]

Universal Benefits

In Canada, there is one program that has no counterpart in the United States. This is a universal benefit program for all families with children under 18, called Family Allowance (FA). FA is paid by the federal government and provides $303/child/year to all Canadian families, regardless of income level.[13]

6.2.3 Institutional Differences in Canadian and U.S. Antipoverty Programs

This section highlights some of the primary conceptual differences in the way the U.S. and Canadian antipoverty programs are designed.

Program Extensiveness

Canada's safety net is far more extensive than the U.S. system, both in population coverage and benefit levels. There are at least three dimensions of comparison.

12. Other tax differences between the countries also clearly affect the well-being of the poor, although these two tax credits are the primary piece of the tax system in each country designed to assist only low-income households. For a fuller discussion of tax differences see Kesselman (1992).

13. Quebec does not participate in the national FA program, but established its own system of FA levels, which increase as family size rises. Alberta also runs a slightly altered FA program.

First, there are differences in the extent of *means testing* between the two countries. In Canada, there is a tradition of universal social transfer programs, along the model prevalent in many European countries. Thus, Canada runs a universal health insurance program, a universal Old Age Security pension, and provides universal per-child payments (FA) to all households with children. Households receive similar benefits from these programs regardless of their other income. In the United States, there are no purely universal programs; means testing occurs in every public program to at least some extent.[14] This tradition of universal programs gives a flavor to Canadian discussions of antipoverty policy that is not found in the United States.[15]

Second, due to differences in *categorical eligibility requirements,* a greater share of single individuals and two-parent families are eligible for transfers in Canada than in the United States. Although Canadian SA benefits and eligibility vary significantly across household types, most provinces provide some cash assistance to all households if they are poor enough. In contrast, cash assistance in the United States is largely limited to single-parent families.[16]

Third, Canada's programs generally have higher *benefit levels.* As table 6.1 indicates, both the average UI maximum weekly payment and the average SA maximum payment are substantially higher in Canada than in the United States. Even in the least-generous province in Canada, the SA benefit level for single-parent families exceeds the maximum low-income transfers (AFDC and food stamps) available in all states except Alaska.

Because of both the broader eligibility and greater generosity of the UI system in Canada, this program is much more important as an antipoverty program than in the United States. In Canada, most nonworking households with an employable family member will receive UI rather than SA, so that while the availability of SA to all household types suggests that this program would be used more broadly than AFDC, in reality SA recipients tend to look much more like AFDC recipients (women with small children or families with long-term employment problems) than the program rules suggest.

Program Control and Government Structure

Canada and the United States both have a federalist system of government, in which legislative authority is shared between the federal and state govern-

14. For instance, although most U.S. workers are eligible for Social Security after retirement, the amount received depends upon the level of earnings.

15. For instance, in the United States one of the proposals often made by welfare reform advocates is a minimum income program (negative income tax), which would provide similar levels of economic support to all households below a given income level. Such a program was supported in the recent U.S. Catholic Bishops' statement on economic justice. In contrast, the Canadian Bishops released their own statement in 1988 in which they explicitly rejected a minimum income program and called instead for full employment, coupled with improved social insurance and extended universal services. Means-tested programs were criticized as divisive, stigmatizing the poor (Canadian Conference of Catholic Bishops, 1988).

16. Some states provide very limited cash assistance to single individuals through a program known as General Assistance.

ments. There are notable differences in the decision-making structure for social assistance programs in the two countries, however. The UI system is entirely state-run in the United States, while it is a federal program in Canada. By contrast, the SA program is largely controlled by the provinces in Canada, while both states and the federal government determine AFDC rules in the United States. Both countries divide the costs of AFDC/SA programs between the federal and state/provincial governments. While the federal government establishes key categorical and financial eligibility criteria for the AFDC program in the United States, however, the Canadian federal government exerts almost no influence over eligibility rules or benefit criteria for the SA program.

Canada's SA program also allows more discretion to caseworkers than does the U.S. AFDC program. This occurs in part because little public information is available on eligibility and benefit rules in Canada. For example, a full description of provincial eligibility and benefit rules was not available in Canada until 1986, whereas the U.S. federal government has been publishing descriptions of state AFDC program rules for over two decades.[17] It also occurs because SA program rules explicitly give greater discretion to the caseworker. For example, SA benefit levels often depend on a detailed itemization of a household's need for goods such as food, housing, or medical care. The SA caseworker is in charge of this needs assessment, and can provide quite different benefits to families of the same size in the same city, depending on such things as their housing situation and the ages of their children.

This difference between the two systems is striking. Discretionary benefits are almost inconceivable in the United States, where watchdog groups demand that publicly known, uniform regulations be applied to all applicants. In Canada, there appear to be greater trust in the decisions and competence of government employees and a willingness to grant decision-making authority to government caseworkers.[18]

Work Incentives

Both the United States and Canada currently offer only modest financial incentives for public assistance recipients to enter the work force. The U.S. AFDC program disregards 33 percent of earnings for the first four months on welfare, but taxes earnings at 100 percent afterwards. Many states allow deductions for transportation, child-care, or other work expenses, thus lowering the effective tax rate. The U.S. food stamp program disregards 24 percent of

17. In the United States, there has been an ongoing public debate over whether individuals who should receive assistance are being turned away and whether individuals who shouldn't receive assistance are being accepted. Concern over both of these issues (often by quite different groups) has created a demand for public information on AFDC regulations.

18. This is consistent with both Leman's (1980) and Lipset's (1990) argument that Canadians are more deferential to authority, giving political leaders greater independence than in the United States.

earnings, after a standard deduction of $98/month plus deductions for childcare, shelter costs, and medical expenses.

In Canada, as in the United States, financial work incentives in the SA program are limited. In 1986, the provincial programs offered a mean earnings deduction of $117/month plus a 12 percent disregard on any additional earnings. However, there is substantial variability in financial incentives across provinces. Earnings deductions vary from zero (Prince Edward Island) to $224/month (Quebec). The additional tax rate on earnings ranges from 100 percent in five provinces to 70 percent (Manitoba).[19]

Both Canada and the United States have moved toward combining job programs with welfare as an alternate method of encouraging work.[20] However, the system of mandated work programs found in the United States is clearly not yet acceptable in Canada: recently, the federal government aborted an attempt by Alberta to mandate work for welfare. The federal government claimed this plan violated federal regulations requiring provinces to assist all families in need.

6.3 The Effect of Transfers on Poverty

6.3.1 The Data

This section uses microdata from the United States and Canada to investigate the role that transfer income plays in the economic well-being of various groups among the poor in each country. The U.S. data come from the March 1987 Current Population Survey (CPS), which provides information on income and work behavior for over 50,000 families during 1986. The Canadian data come from a very similar survey, the April 1987 Survey of Consumer Finances (SCF), which surveys over 30,000 families and asks about their income and labor market experiences in 1986.

We use data for all families that are headed by an individual between the ages of 18 and 60 who is neither retired, in school, or disabled. The resulting samples contain 44,568 family observations for the United States and 22,074 family observations for Canada. (Throughout this paper, we use the word *family* to refer to single individuals living alone as well as related individuals living together.)

In both countries, we use what Canada defines as "census families" rather than "economic families." An economic family consists of all related individuals who live in the same household. A census family consists of all married or single individuals and any unmarried children that live together. Thus, a three-generation household will contain two census families but only one eco-

19. For further discussion of this issue, see Banting (1987) or the Evans and McIntyre article in Ismael (1987).

20. See Gueron (1990) for a description of U.S. programs.

nomic family. We focus on census families because most transfer programs determine eligibility and benefit levels at the census family level. In addition, the formation of economic families is typically assumed to be endogenous to public assistance benefits; the lower are benefit levels, the more likely that multiple census families will live together and pool income.[21]

We compare income and poverty status across a variety of subpopulation groups in the tables discussed below. We distinguish between households with single and married heads, with and without children. We also distinguish between the poor, whose income falls below the official poverty line, the near poor, whose income is between one and two times the poverty line, and the upper income, whose income is over two times the poverty line. (Note that 70 percent of the population is included in the upper-income category for both countries.) In addition, we look separately at the white, black, and Hispanic populations in the United States and at the English- and French-speaking populations in Canada.[22]

We calculate poverty rates using both the U.S. and Canadian definitions of poverty. The U.S. poverty line is based on a 1964 calculation of need that uses the cost of a minimally adequate food budget as its basis. It varies with family size. In contrast, the Canadian "low-income cutoff" measures the average income level at which a family spends more than 58.5 percent of their income on food, clothing, and shelter. It varies with family size and city size.[23] Appendix table 6B.1 presents the U.S. poverty thresholds and the Canadian low-income cutoffs for 1986 in U.S. dollars. The Canadian poverty thresholds lie uniformly above the U.S. thresholds. A family of four is considered poor in the United States at $11,203, while the equivalent low-income cutoff in a large urban area in Canada is $17,330.

Table 6.2 provides information on the comparative populations in the United States and Canada. The primary message of table 6.2 is that these two countries have similar populations with respect to demographic and household characteristics. In fact, within groups that have higher average incomes, there are almost no notable differences. There are three areas of difference, however, noticeable among lower-income households. First, Canadians have fewer female households heads. Only 47 percent of Canadian poor families

21. We experimented in some initial calculations with the economic family definition rather than the census family definition and found results that were largely comparable to those reported here; poverty counts were slightly lower in both countries, with the United States being more affected. In both countries, official poverty counts are based on economic families and thus will differ from our calculations.

22. The SCF in Canada has no information on racial or ethnic background. The English- and French-speaking populations are identified by a question that asks about the mother tongue of a family. Twelve percent of the Canadian population identifies a language other than English or French as their mother tongue. In the tabulations along this dimension, this group is excluded.

23. See Ruggles (1990) for a full description of how the U.S. poverty line has been calculated; see Wolfson and Evans (1989) for a description of how the Canadian low-income cutoffs are calculated.

Table 6.2 Population Comparisons, United States versus Canada, 1986

	Total Population		Poor[a]		Near Poor[a]		Upper Income[a]	
	U.S.	Canada	U.S.	Canada	U.S.	Canada	U.S.	Canada
Population (%)	100.0	100.0	13.5	11.8	16.7	18.2	69.8	70.0
Married (%)	55.3	61.8	21.9	28.2	46.7	51.3	64.0	70.2
Years of education[b]	13.0	12.5	11.3	11.4	12.0	11.8	13.6	12.9
Age of head	37.6	37.7	32.6	35.7	34.8	35.9	39.3	38.4
Working heads (%)	91.4	90.1	59.7	49.8	92.6	87.1	97.5	97.7
Female heads (%)[c]	29.5	21.1	62.0	46.7	36.5	29.0	21.4	14.8
Persons in household	3.0	2.9	3.5	2.8	3.3	3.0	2.9	2.8
Families in household	1.2	1.2	1.5	1.3	1.3	1.2	1.2	1.1
	Single, No Children		Single, Children		Married, No Children		Married, Children	
	U.S.	Canada	U.S.	Canada	U.S.	Canada	U.S.	Canada
Population (%)	32.5	32.5	12.2	7.3	21.1	18.8	34.2	41.4
Married (%)	—	—	—	—	100.0	100.0	100.0	100.0
Years of education[b]	13.2	12.7	12.0	12.0	13.0	12.4	13.1	12.5
Age of head	35.5	35.1	33.1	36.5	44.3	40.5	37.1	38.6
Working heads (%)	91.7	87.1	72.3	68.9	93.8	92.1	96.6	95.4
Female heads (%)[c]	46.8	45.4	88.2	86.9	7.7	0.0	5.6	0.0
Persons in household	1.9	1.8	3.6	2.9	2.5	2.1	4.2	4.0
Families in household	1.5	1.5	1.4	1.1	1.1	1.0	1.0	1.0

Note: Based on census families, heads aged 18–60.

[a]Based on U.S. poverty lines.

[b]The Canadian data reports education only in discrete intervals. Shown are interpolated midpoints. In addition, Ontario requires thirteen years for high school graduation, whcih increases the difficulty of comparing years of education between Canada and the United States.

[c]In Canada, if a male adult is present, he is considered the household head, therefore no married couples are female-headed. In the United States, the household head is self-reported.

are female-headed, in contrast with 62 percent of U.S. poor families. Second, Canadians have fewer families per household and fewer persons per household, particularly among the poor and among single parents with children. This may reflect the lower levels of public assistance in the United States, which are likely to lead more nuclear (census) families to live together and pool income. Third, fewer Canadian households are working than in the United States, particularly in lower-income households. In part, this reflects a higher unemployment rate in Canada in 1986.[24] It may also reflect more generous transfer income payments, which allow families to survive without earnings.

24. Canada's unemployment rate for civilian workers was 9.5 percent in 1986, while the U.S. unemployment rate was 7.0 percent.

6.3.2 Income Sources and Poverty Rates in the United States and Canada

Table 6.3 shows how income sources and total incomes compare in the United States and Canada, by household composition and by income group. We highlight four major issues.

First, while Canada's average total income is lower than that of the United States,[25] disadvantaged groups have higher incomes in Canada than in the United States. Poor families have average total incomes of $4,921 in Canada, while they have incomes of $4,789 in the United States; income levels among the near poor are also very similar in each country. Single-parent families have higher incomes in Canada than in the United States. In analysis not shown here, we also verify that income among the French-speaking minority in Canada is only slightly lower than among the English-speaking majority. In contrast, income among nonwhites in the United States is far below that of whites.

Second, the principal reason for higher total income among disadvantaged groups in Canada is higher transfer income. Poor, near-poor, and single-parent family earnings are no higher in Canada, but transfers are substantially higher. In fact, all groups of Canadians receive more transfer income; on average Canadians receive 6.0 percent of their income from government transfers, while Americans receive only 2.4 percent.

Third, single-parent families have remarkably similar earnings levels in both countries. This finding is of interest since, as we shall verify below, these families are major users of public assistance in both countries. Thus, there seems to be little evidence in these initial tabulations to suggest that the more generous SA program in Canada has caused more single-parent families to drop out of the labor force. In fact, among the poor in each of the four household types shown at the bottom of table 6.3, it is poor single-parent families who are most similar in their work behavior in both countries.

Table 6.4 shows the percentage of poor, near poor, and upper income, using both the U.S. and the Canadian definitions of poverty for each population subgroup.[26] We also present a poverty gap measure based on the U.S. poverty line. The poverty gap is defined as the average difference between the income of the poor and the poverty line. Whereas the poverty rate measures the number of individuals below a fixed line, the poverty gap measures how far on

25. Note that these tables compare the pretax, posttransfer income levels of both countries. Since Canada has more extensive transfer payments on average, it also is likely to have higher taxes. Thus, if one were to compare the posttax and posttransfer income distributions, one would likely find even greater differences in average income.

26. In tabulating household income in tables 6.4 and 6.5, we include CTC income for Canadian households that report receiving it, but we exclude the EITC among U.S. households because we have no reported data on EITC receipt. Table 6.3 indicates that simulated EITC amounts (which assume 100 percent take-up) are extremely small. In the simulations that follow, the simulated EITC amounts are included in income for U.S. households.

Table 6.3 Income Sources, United States versus Canada, 1986 (in 1986 U.S. dollars)

	Total Population		Poor[a]		Near Poor[a]		Upper Income[a]	
	U.S.	Canada	U.S.	Canada	U.S.	Canada	U.S.	Canada
Earnings	28,292	23,884	2,592	1,950	11,655	9,880	37,237	31,432
Head	21,401	18,217	2,210	1,729	9,665	8,368	27,916	23,714
Spouse	5,445	4,874	259	177	1,535	1,236	7,383	6,657
Government transfers	730	1,622	1,818	2,731	912	2,349	477	1,236
AFDC/SA	172	358	987	1,824	195	538	10	51
FA	—	249	—	233	—	318	—	233
Food stamps	86	—	504	—	90	—	4	—
UI	241	730	125	389	288	1,056	252	707
Total income	30,978	26,877	4,789	4,921	13,370	12,989	40,251	34,398
Tax credit[b]	20	130	98	267	36	295	1	32

	Single, No Children		Single, Children		Married, No Children		Married, Children	
	U.S.	Canada	U.S.	Canada	U.S.	Canada	U.S.	Canada
Earnings	18,199	13,846	10,734	10,770	40,043	29,241	36,868	31,659
Head	17,066	13,846	9,857	9,343	25,720	19,580	26,960	22,604
Spouse	—	—	—	—	11,598	9,661	8,753	7,392
Government transfers	446	1,006	2,064	3,073	592	1,366	610	1,967
AFDC/SA	49	340	1,014	1,673	12	187	88	217
FA	—	2	—	418	—	2	—	525
Food stamps	27	—	447	—	9	—	59	—
UI	180	418	126	526	293	827	308	969
Total income	20,217	15,796	14,239	15,296	43,973	32,672	39,130	35,000
Tax credit[b]	—	—	98	389	—	—	23	246

Note: Based on census families, heads aged 18–60.

[a]Based on U.S. poverty lines.

[b]Since there is no information on EITC in the U.S. CPS, this is imputed assuming a 100 percent take-up rate. The Canadian CTC is based on reported data. Tax credits are not included in total income.

average most individuals are below that line, providing a measure of well-being among the poor.

Using the U.S. definition of income, table 6.4 indicates that the overall poverty count is 13.5 percent for the United States, while it is 11.8 percent in Canada. In Canada, however, the percentage that is near poor is greater than in the United States, so that the percentage of upper income is virtually identical in the two countries. The poor in Canada also have substantially smaller poverty gaps than in the United States among every group in table 6.4, implying that poverty is not only lower but that it is also less extreme in Canada.

Single individuals in Canada and married couples without children have

Table 6.4 Income Needs, U.S. versus Canada, 1986 (in 1986 U.S. dollars)

	Total Population		Canada—Language		U.S.—Race		
	U.S.	Canada	English	French	White	Black	Hispanic
U.S. poverty definition							
Poor (%)	13.5	11.8	10.8	14.2	9.9	30.2	25.3
Near poor (%)	16.7	18.2	17.6	19.2	14.8	22.4	28.1
Upper income (%)	69.8	70.0	71.5	66.6	75.3	47.3	46.6
Poverty gap[a]							
Poor	3,702	2,528	2,644	2,042	3,479	4,107	3,867
Canadian definition							
Poor (%)	20.6	18.3	16.5	21.8	15.7	41.2	40.2
Near poor (%)	26.2	30.0	29.2	31.1	25.4	28.2	31.8
Upper income (%)	53.2	51.7	54.3	47.1	58.8	30.7	28.0

	Single, No Children		Single, Children		Married, No Children		Married, Children	
	U.S.	Canada	U.S.	Canada	U.S.	Canada	U.S.	Canada
U.S. poverty definition								
Poor (%)	15.5	19.9	45.3	32.3	2.8	4.1	6.8	5.2
Near poor (%)	18.4	22.0	24.4	28.8	7.8	9.4	17.9	17.3
Upper income (%)	66.0	58.1	30.3	38.8	89.5	86.5	75.3	77.5
Poverty gap[a]								
Poor	3,017	2,341	4,172	2,519	3,374	2,430	4,152	3,142
Canadian definition								
Poor (%)	23.1	28.8	59.0	47.7	5.5	6.7	13.8	10.2
Near poor (%)	26.8	29.8	25.8	33.3	15.2	17.7	32.6	35.0
Upper income (%)	50.0	41.3	15.2	19.0	79.3	75.5	53.6	54.8

Notes: Based on census families, heads aged 18–60.

Poor is below poverty line; *near poor* is between one and two times poverty line; *upper income* is greater than two times poverty line.

[a]The poverty gap is defined as the average difference between the incomes of the poor and the poverty line. We report estimates based on the U.S. poverty line.

uniformly higher poverty and near-poverty counts than in the United States. Single parents, however, are much less likely to be poor in Canada; the poverty rate among this group is 32 percent in Canada, while it is 45 percent in the United States.

Table 6.5 investigates the extent to which government transfers move families out of poverty, by comparing poverty rates based on pretransfer family income with poverty rates based on total (posttransfer) family income. Of course, this only approximates the effect of transfers, since it assumes that transfers do not affect other sources of income. If transfers cause families to work less, table 6.5 will overestimate the extent of pretransfer poverty that would result in the absence of transfers.

Table 6.5 **Pre- versus Posttransfer Poverty, Using U.S. Poverty Definitions, 1986 (in 1986 U.S. dollars)**

	Total Population		Canada—Language		U.S.—Race		
	U.S.	Canada	English	French	White	Black	Hispanic
Poor (%)							
Pretransfer	15.4	17.5	15.8	21.9	11.5	33.3	28.8
Posttransfer	13.5	11.8	10.8	14.2	9.9	30.2	25.3
Difference	1.9	5.7	5.0	7.7	1.6	3.1	3.5
Poverty gap							
Pretransfer	5,255	4,825	4,774	4,975	4,627	6,376	5,886
Posttransfer	3,702	2,528	2,644	2,042	3,479	4,107	3,867
Difference	1,553	2,297	2,130	2,933	1,148	2,269	2,019

	Single, No Children		Single, Children		Married, No Children		Married, Children	
	U.S.	Canada	U.S.	Canada	U.S.	Canada	U.S.	Canada
Poor (%)								
Pretransfer	17.4	26.1	50.5	46.6	3.7	7.5	8.2	10.2
Posttransfer	15.5	19.9	45.3	32.3	2.8	4.1	6.8	5.2
Difference	1.9	6.2	5.2	14.3	0.9	3.4	1.4	5.0
Poverty gap								
Pretransfer	3,561	3,817	6,953	6,584	3,802	4,227	5,342	5,619
Posttransfer	3,017	2,341	4,172	2,519	3,374	2,430	4,152	3,142
Difference	544	1,476	2,781	4,065	428	179	1,190	2,477

Note: Based on census families, heads aged 18–60.

Table 6.5 indicates that the Canadian transfer system is substantially more effective than the U.S. transfer system in raising people out of poverty. Canada's overall pretransfer poverty rate is about 2 percentage points higher than the United States', but its posttransfer poverty rate is 2 percentage points lower. This pattern is particularly strong for families with children: transfers reduce poverty rates of single-parent families by 14 points in Canada as opposed to 5 points in the United States, and they reduce poverty rates of two-parent families with children by 5.0 points in Canada as opposed to 1.4 points in the United States. Even more striking is the impact on poverty gaps: transfers reduce the poverty gap of single-parent families by 62 percent in Canada as opposed to 40 percent in the United States.

The results of this section indicate that Canadian families on average are worse off than U.S. families in terms of total income, but that the poverty rate and poverty income gap is lower in Canada, indicating that the poorest in Canada are better off than in the United States. Much of this difference is due to a more extensive government transfer system. Single individuals and married couples without children have both lower incomes and higher poverty rates in Canada than in the United States; however, the more extensive Canadian transfer system substantially moderates these differences. Single parents with children are strikingly better off in Canada than in the United States. They start out with more income before transfers and receive extensive transfer assistance, leading to much lower poverty rates.

6.4 Simulating the Effects of Antipoverty Programs

Section 6.3 indicates that the Canadian transfer system is apparently more effective than the U.S. system in moving families out of poverty. However, it is possible that this difference results from differences in the pretransfer income distributions across the two countries rather than from differences in transfer program rules. For example, if the income levels of the pretransfer poor are closer to the poverty threshold in Canada than in the United States, then the same level of transfer payments could have a greater impact on poverty in Canada.

In this section, we measure the impact of the transfers more directly, by conducting simulations of the transfer systems in each country. We address three issues: First, what are the estimated take-up rates for each of the transfer programs in the two countries? Second, how does transfer-program generosity vary across states and provinces in each country? Third, what would be the impact on poverty rates and program costs of implementing Canadian antipoverty programs in the United States and vice versa?

6.4.1 Simulation Methodology

To simulate the impact of Canadian and U.S. transfer programs, we apply state- and province-specific eligibility and benefit rules to microdata from each country to estimate transfer eligibility and benefits among a random sample of the population. We use the published sources listed in appendix C to determine program parameters. This appendix also includes a detailed description of our simulation methodology. Our microdata sources are the March CPS for 1987, and the April SCF for 1987, described above. As noted before, we restrict our sample to families that are headed by an individual between the age of 18 and 60 who is not retired, in school, or disabled.

The most difficult program to simulate with our data is the UI program. In both countries, UI benefits and eligibility depend upon the average weekly earnings and the duration of employment during a base period prior to the unemployment spell. Unfortunately, our data contain information about employment and earnings for only one year (1986) and not for the complete base period. In fact, if an individual began a spell of unemployment at the start of the calendar year, we would not observe any data from their base period. We proxy base period earnings and employment with reported weekly earnings and weekly hours of work while employed in 1986. This is at best a rough approximation, since, for many individuals whose unemployment spell occurred early in 1986, this means using data from employment spells that occurred *after* the unemployment spell rather than before it.[27]

A second area of concern is the accuracy of our simulated estimates for the SA program. As discussed above, eligibility and benefit levels in the SA program are not as standardized as in AFDC. This makes it difficult to duplicate the SA benefit and eligibility determination process faced by any particular family. We use provincial information on the benefits available to a typical family, which may be inaccurate for some households.

Appendix D contains a comparison of simulated and reported income sources for each of the transfer programs included in the simulation and a brief discussion of the accuracy of the simulation. This analysis shows a fairly high degree of consistency between reported and simulated benefits. For the UI programs in both countries, the simulation classifies between 85 and 95 percent of the cases correctly. For other programs, the range of correct estimates falls within the 90th percentile.

In sections 6.4.2 and 6.4.3, we present results from our base simulations, which assume 100 percent participation and zero labor supply responses. In sections 6.4.4 and 6.4.5, we present a range of estimates that allow for variation in participation rates and labor supply elasticities.

6.4.2 Estimated Take-up Rates in U.S. and Canadian Transfer Programs

In table 6.6, we present estimates of the take-up rates for each of the key transfer programs in both countries. The take-up rate is defined as the ratio of the number of families who reported positive transfer incomes to the number who had either simulated or reported transfer income greater than zero.[28] It is intended to measure the share of eligible families who participate in transfer programs. This number will be a biased estimate of the true participation rate of eligible families to the extent that transfers are underreported in our microdata and that our simulations inaccurately predict eligibility. Since the undercounts of both AFDC and SA income in our microdata are sizable,[29] the low

27. Average weekly earnings received after a spell of unemployment may tend to be lower than those reported in the base period, during which a worker was continuously employed on his or her previous job. This could lead us to underestimate UI eligibility and benefits levels. However, since we know nothing about the duration of previous employment and do not impose any restrictions on UI eligibility based on this duration, we may overestimate eligibility.

28. The take-up rates in table 6.7 are calculated as the ratio

$$\frac{(\text{Sim} > 0, \text{Actual} > 0) + (\text{Sim} = 0, \text{Actual} > 0)}{(\text{Sim} > 0, \text{Actual} > 0) + (\text{Sim} > 0, \text{Actual} = 0) + (\text{Sim} = 0, \text{Actual} > 0)},$$

where the numerator is the share of the population who report receiving transfers, and the denominator is the share of the population either simulated to be eligible or actually receiving transfers. Note that one could estimate an alternative take-up rate that excluded the "errors" in the simulation (Sim = 0, Actual > 0) from both numerator and denominator. These alternative take-up rates are slightly lower than those reported here, but the relative patterns across groups and programs are largely identical.

29. The SCF documentation for 1987 indicates that the undercount is fairly small for the CTC (4 percent) and the FA program (6 percent). It reports undercounts of 47 percent for SA and other

Table 6.6 Estimated Take-up Rates

	U.S.			Canada			
	Unemployment Insurance	Food Stamps	AFDC	Unemployment Insurance	Family Allowances	Social Assistance	Tax Credit
Total population	57.9	46.1	74.5	81.9	97.4	59.5	88.8
Single, no children	51.0	34.2	—	73.2	—	54.7	—
Single, children	45.0	60.3	71.6	79.0	97.6	71.1	88.8
Married, no children	62.5	30.9	—	82.6	—	74.1	—
Married, children	63.4	40.5	69.7	86.3	97.3	51.4	88.9
Poor[a]	37.9	45.6	72.5	74.3	95.9	58.4	94.9
Near poor[a]	51.2	41.6	81.6	80.3	97.2	54.2	89.5
Upper income[a]	65.4	—	—	83.6	97.5	—	87.7
White	60.0	39.6	72.1	—	—	—	—
Black	48.9	60.6	80.2	—	—	—	—
Hispanic	52.3	46.2	70.3	—	—	—	—
English	—	—	—	79.2	97.5	53.5	90.6
French	—	—	—	87.9	97.4	76.8	88.2

Note: Take-up rates calculated as the ratio of all those who receive income from a program, divided by all those who either are estimated as eligible and/or receive income from a program.

[a]Based on U.S. poverty lines.

estimated take-up rates in both programs are at least partially explained by underreporting of transfer income.

The first point to notice in table 6.6 is that take-up rates in most programs are well below 100 percent. Estimated take-up rates for the United States range from a low of 46 percent for the food stamp program,[30] to 58 percent for the UI program,[31] to 75 percent for the AFDC program.[32] In Canada, the SA program has a low take-up rate of 60 percent, while the UI take-up rate is higher at 82 percent. Canada's CTC and FA program have high participation rates of 89 percent and 97 percent, respectively.

Second, it is evident from table 6.6 that there is no consistent pattern between program generosity and benefit levels. The take-up rate in Canada's UI program is 82 percent, while the take-up rate for the less-generous UI program

provincial assistance programs, and 22 percent for the UI program. In 1983, the U.S. CPS undercount was 24 percent for UI and 24 percent for AFDC (U.S. Bureau of the Census, *Current Population Reports, Series P-60,* no. 103).

30. Our estimated 46 percent participation rate in food stamps is not too far from the GAO estimate (U.S. General Accounting Office, 1988b, fig. 2.1) of 44 percent for 1986. Both of these estimates are lower than a variety of estimates derived from studies done in the late 1970s. For a summary of these, see U.S. General Accounting Office (1988a), table 2.2.

31. This estimate for the United States is below the estimated take-up rate for UI in 1986 of 67.3 percent by Blank and Card (1991) and probably reflects the less adequate data available for our eligibility imputations. We do not know of any existing estimate of Canadian UI take-up.

32. These take-up rates for AFDC are quite close to other estimates for earlier in the 1980s by Ruggles and Michel (1987), who estimate an AFDC participation rate of 78 percent for 1984.

in the United States is 58 percent. By contrast, the estimated take-up rate for SA is lower than the estimated take-up rate for AFDC, even though SA is a substantially more generous program than AFDC. This result is not surprising, since the correlation between take-up rates and benefit levels is determined by two conflicting relationships: as benefits increase, more individuals will participate in the program; however, as more individuals participate in the program, program administrators may cut back on benefits.

An alternative way of investigating the relationship between take-up rates and benefit levels is to look at the correlation across more and less generous states and provinces. In the United States, the correlation coefficient between the AFDC benefit level in a state and our estimated state take-up rate is 0.152.[33] The correlation between state maximum UI benefit levels and state-specific UI take-up rates is 0.359. In Canada, the correlation coefficient between the SA benefit level for single parents and the estimated provincial take-up rate for SA is −0.591.[34] None of these results provide strong support for the theory that higher take-up rates occur in more generous programs.

6.4.3 Simulation Results for U.S. and Canadian Programs

Table 6.7 presents the results from our base simulations, which assume zero labor supply responses and 100 percent participation rates. For each simulation, table 6.7 reports total family income, the percentage of income received from government transfers, the share of families receiving each type of transfer, the estimated dollars received, and the resulting poverty count and poverty gap. The top of the table shows a series of simulations on U.S. data and the bottom shows a series of simulations on Canadian data.

Column 1 shows actual transfers reported in the CPS or the SCF. Column 2 shows simulated transfers, estimated using the mean (population-weighted) U.S. program parameters for U.S. microdata and mean Canadian parameters for Canadian microdata. These results are almost identical to simulations that apply the rules specific to each state or province. Thus, we do not present these latter simulations here.

For the United States, simulated average total income is $31,134, with 2.8 percent from transfers. This is only slightly above the reported average income of $30,998. The biggest effect of the simulation is to double the share of the population receiving food stamps, from 7.6 percent (reported) to 14.7

33. There is a lot of noise in the state estimates of take-up rates, because of small numbers of observations in low-population states. This would tend to reduce the correlation coefficient. The state sample ranges from 354 observations (Wyoming) to 4,077 (California), but a much smaller number in each state are estimated to be eligible for any of the programs. The province sample ranges from 596 observations (Prince Edward Island) to 4,128 (Ontario).

34. The negative relationship between benefit levels and participation rates in Canada may be related to program structure: in Canada's SA program, provinces can choose both eligibility rules and benefit levels. Thus, provinces may choose to restrict eligibility for SA, in order to give out more generous benefits. If we imperfectly simulate these eligibility restrictions in our microdata, we may report lower participation rates in the more generous provinces.

Table 6.7 Simulation Results, Total Population (in 1986 U.S. dollars)

		U.S. Programs			Canadian Programs		
	Actual (1)	Mean[a] (2)	High[b] (3)	Low[c] (4)	Mean[a] (5)	High[b] (6)	Low[c] (7)
		U.S. data					
Income ($)	30,998	31,134	31,236	31,012	31,792	31,965	31,531
Government transfers (%)	2.4	2.8	3.2	2.5	4.9	5.4	4.1
Receiving (%)							
Food stamps/FA	7.6	14.7	14.4	14.7	46.4	46.4	46.4
AFDC/SA	5.1	4.5	6.8	3.4	13.2	14.4	9.9
UI	11.8	14.5	15.1	15.4	13.6	13.6	13.6
EITC/CTC	6.8	6.8	6.8	6.8	21.7	21.7	21.7
Received ($)							
Food stamps/FA	1,132	1,260	902	1,495	554	554	554
AFDC/SA	3,356	3,663	5,123	1,321	4,586	5,414	3,463
UI	2,045	1,963	1,728	1,614	2,397	2,397	2,397
EITC/CTC	293	293	293	293	575	575	575
Poor, U.S. definition (%)	13.2	12.6	11.5	12.6	6.1	5.5	11.3
Poverty gap	3,683	2,767	1,957	3,411	1,618	1,567	2,301

		Canadian Programs			U.S. Programs		
	Actual	Mean[a]	High[b]	Low[c]	Mean[a]	High[b]	Low[c]
		Canadian data					
Income ($)	26,877	27,069	27,198	26,833	26,318	26,270	26,206
Government transfers (%)	6.0	6.7	7.1	5.9	4.0	3.9	3.6
Receiving (%)							
FA/Food stamps	43.6	43.3	43.3	43.3	14.6	14.6	14.8
SA/AFDC	8.7	12.8	13.6	13.6	0.3	0.3	0.1
UI	23.8	20.5	20.5	20.5	21.6	22.2	22.2
CTC/EITC	23.6	18.7	18.7	18.7	5.5	5.5	5.5
Received ($)							
FA/Food stamps	570	559	559	559	1,409	1,399	1,415
SA/AFDC	4,131	4,028	4,765	2,976	2,726	4,582	897
UI	3,070	3,270	3,270	3,270	2,545	2,234	1,991
CTC/EITC	553	526	522	526	289	289	289
Poor, U.S. definition (%)	11.8	8.8	8.3	12.9	13.4	13.4	13.6
Poverty gap	2,528	1,770	1,704	2,468	3,422	3,398	3,415

[a]Based on population-weighted average state/province program rules.
[b]Based on Vermont program rules for the United States and Saskatchewan rules for Canada.
[c]Based on Alabama program rules for the United States and New Brunswick rules for Canada.

percent (simulated). This reflects the low estimated take-up rates for food stamps among eligible families. (Recall that these initial simulations assume 100 percent participation.) Because of the higher transfer income levels, the simulated poverty rate is 0.6 points lower than the reported poverty rate of 13.2, and the poverty gap is over $900 smaller than the reported gap of $3,683. In Canada, the results of using simulated rather than reported income are similar in magnitude: the share of government transfers rises from 6.0 to 6.7 percent, the poverty rate (U.S. definition) falls from 11.8 to 8.8 percent, and the poverty gap falls by about $750.

To document the range of variation in transfer programs within each country, we apply the rules from the most generous state or province, and those from the least generous state or province to the entire country. These results are shown in columns 3 and 4. In the United States, we use the programs from Vermont (most generous) and Alabama (least generous),[35] while in Canada, we use Saskatchewan (most generous) and New Brunswick (least generous).[36]

Of course, the results from these simulations cannot be interpreted literally as the expected results of such a legislative change, since the only variables that are allowed to change in the simulations are government transfer income. If individuals decrease their labor supply in response to an increase in transfers, these simulations will overstate the impact of moving to a more generous program. These simulations do, however, provide an indication of the magnitude of variation between antipoverty programs.

Our simulations suggest that, if the United States adopted the Vermont transfer system (and no other income sources changed), poverty would fall from 12.6 percent (as simulated on mean U.S. programs) to 11.5 percent and the poverty gap would fall by $810. If it adopted the Alabama transfer system, poverty would remain at 12.6 percent, but the poverty gap would increase by $644.

Similar simulations suggest that if Canada were to adopt its most generous provincial program, poverty rates would decrease from 8.8 to 8.3 percent and the poverty gap would decrease slightly. If it adopted its least generous provincial program, poverty would increase to 12.9 percent and the poverty gap would increase substantially. While the most generous Canadian program re-

35. We select these states on the basis of AFDC maximum benefit payments. Vermont is used as the most generous state, even though Alaska has a substantially higher AFDC benefit level, because Alaska's level is so far above all other states that it is perhaps best treated as an outlier. It is important to note that these are not the most and least generous states with respect to UI payments, although Vermont is among the more generous UI states and Alabama is among the least generous UI states. A clear ranking of UI generosity would be difficult to determine among U.S. states, since states set both eligibility criteria and benefit levels. In a number of states, broader eligibility is offset by lower maximum benefit limits or vice versa.

36. These provinces are ranked on the basis of payments to single parents. New Brunswick is also the least generous to married couples and is the second least generous to single individuals (Quebec pays less). Saskatchewan is also most generous for married couples but ranks in the middle with regard to generosity to single individuals.

sults in poverty counts in that country well below the U.S. poverty counts, the least generous provincial program results in Canadian poverty counts that are quite comparable to those in the United States.

These results suggest that program variation has a more dramatic impact on poverty rates in Canada than in the United States: there is a 4.6-point difference in poverty rates between the best and worst Canadian simulation, but only a 1.1-point difference between U.S. simulations. This is because Canada's most generous province has benefit levels high enough to bring a large share of the poor over the poverty line, while no U.S. states have benefit levels high enough to have a sizable impact on poverty. Thus, although AFDC benefit levels vary far more than Canadian SA benefit levels in percentage terms, variations in AFDC benefit levels have a much smaller impact on poverty.

Columns 5–7 investigate the effect of applying the mean Canadian program rules in the United States, and the mean U.S. program rules in Canada. Note that in comparing the impact of moving from one country's transfer system to the other's, the appropriate comparison is between the simulated impact of the new program and the simulated impact of the existing program. In both countries the effect is dramatic. In the United States, shifting from the mean U.S. plan to the mean Canadian plan would reduce the poverty rate from 12.6 percent to 6.1 percent and decrease the poverty gap from $2,767 to $1,618. Even the least generous provincial transfer system achieves a lower poverty rate than the most generous U.S. state transfer system, although the poverty gap would be somewhat higher. If the United States adopted Saskatchewan programs, poverty rates would plummet to 5.5 percent, and the poverty gap would fall to $1,567. Thus, the Canadian provincial programs appear to provide substantially greater transfer income and have much stronger antipoverty effects than any existing U.S. state programs.

In Canada, application of U.S. programs has the opposite effect. Poverty rates rise and government transfers fall. The best U.S. transfer system, from Vermont, produces a poverty rate and poverty gap lower than in the least generous province, but well below the mean of Canadian programs.

Table 6.8 examines how these results vary among different subgroups in the United States; table 6.9 repeats this analysis for Canada. The most striking result in table 6.8 is the dramatic impact of Canadian programs on the poverty rates of single-parent families with children. This is of particular interest, given the enormous public concern in the United States with the high poverty rate of these families. As table 6.8 shows, under the mean U.S. program the simulated poverty rate for single-parent families is 43 percent and the poverty gap is $2,628. Even if all states adopted the generous transfer programs of Vermont, the poverty rate would decrease to only 36 percent, although the poverty gap would fall to $1,293. In contrast, the simulated effect of the Canadian programs on this group is astounding. The average Canadian transfer program would decrease poverty to 2.4 percent. If the generous Saskatchewan plan were implemented, poverty among single-parent families would almost

Table 6.8 **Simulation Results, U.S. CPS Data (in 1986 U.S. dollars)**

		U.S. Programs			Canadian Programs		
	Actual (1)	Mean[a] (2)	High[b] (3)	Low[c] (4)	Mean[a] (5)	High[b] (6)	Low[c] (7)
Poor (%)	13.2	12.6	11.5	12.6	6.1	5.5	11.3
Poverty gap	3,683	2,767	1,957	3,411	1,618	1,567	2,301
Single, no children							
Poor (%)	15.5	15.2	15.2	15.2	15.3	15.3	15.3
Poverty gap	3,017	2,597	2,586	2,571	1,710	1,591	2,513
Single, children							
Poor (%)	43.7	43.4	36.5	43.4	2.4	0.1	34.5
Poverty gap	4,197	2,628	1,293	4,197	691	811	1,859
Married, no children							
Poor (%)	2.8	2.4	2.4	2.4	2.6	2.6	2.6
Poverty gap	3,374	2,731	2,714	2,651	1,835	1,368	3,009
Married, children							
Poor (%)	6.5	5.4	4.7	5.4	0.9	0.0	4.5
Poverty gap	4,040	3,627	1,627	3,609	661	179	2,568
White							
Poor (%)	9.7	9.2	8.3	9.2	5.2	4.8	8.1
Poverty gap	3,457	2,647	1,967	3,070	1,600	1,548	2,256
Black							
Poor (%)	29.7	28.8	26.5	28.7	10.9	9.3	25.9
Poverty gap	4,101	2,933	1,988	3,971	1,745	1,678	2,377
Hispanic							
Poor (%)	24.7	23.5	21.9	23.4	8.9	7.2	21.8
Poverty gap	3,834	2,950	1,856	3,757	1,478	1,473	2,340

[a]Based on population-weighted average state/province program rules.

[b]Based on Vermont program rules for the United States and Saskatchewan rules for Canada.

[c]Based on Alabama program rules for the United States and New Brunswick rules for Canada.

disappear, to less than 1 percent. This is because the Canadian transfers available to single women with children are large enough to bring these families up to the U.S. poverty line, assuming that all eligible persons participated.

Because participation rates on these programs are substantially below 100 percent, expected poverty rates among female-headed families may be higher, as the analysis in section 6.4.4 indicates. These simulations also do not include any labor supply responses; however, the analysis in section 6.4.4 indicates that these results hold for a wide range of assumed labor supply elasticities. Moreover, as our data in table 6.2 indicate, since the earnings of single-parent families in Canada are quite comparable to those of families in the United States, there is little evidence that transfer programs have induced large reductions in work effort in Canada.

Table 6.9 Simulation Results, Canadian SCF Data (in 1986 U.S. dollars)

		Canadian Programs			U.S. Programs		
	Actual (1)	Mean[a] (2)	High[b] (3)	Low[c] (4)	Mean[a] (5)	High[b] (6)	Low[c] (7)
Poor (%)	11.8	8.8	8.3	12.9	13.4	13.4	13.6
Poverty gap	2,528	1,770	1,704	2,468	3,422	3,398	3,415
Single, no children							
Poor (%)	19.9	21.3	21.3	21.3	21.3	21.4	21.4
Poverty gap	2,341	1,814	1,730	2,692	2,870	2,856	2,840
Single, children							
Poor (%)	32.3	3.1	2.8	33.0	40.2	38.8	40.4
Poverty gap	2,519	1,911	1,440	1,607	4,380	4,369	4,493
Married, no children							
Poor (%)	4.1	5.3	5.3	5.3	5.1	5.2	5.2
Poverty gap	2,430	2,083	1,658	3,402	3,098	3,074	3,038
Married, children							
Poor (%)	5.2	1.7	0.4	6.3	6.3	6.4	6.5
Poverty gap	3,142	828	1,186	2,317	3,926	3,894	3,854
English							
Poor (%)	10.8	7.4	7.1	11.4	12.1	12.0	12.2
Poverty gap	2,644	1,710	1,650	2,323	3,320	3,296	3,320
French							
Poor (%)	14.2	12.2	11.2	16.6	16.9	16.9	17.1
Poverty gap	2,042	1,846	1,771	2,623	3,594	3,570	3,571

[a]Based on population-weighted average state/province program rules.

[b]Based on Vermont program rules for the United States and Saskatchewan rules for Canada.

[c]Based on Alabama program rules for the United States and New Brunswick rules for Canada.

Our simulations also indicate that Canada's programs would have a sizable impact on the poverty rates of two-parent families with children. Moving from the mean program in the United States to the mean program in Canada would decrease the two-parent family poverty rate from 5.4 points to 0.9 points, while the poverty gap would decrease from $3,627 to $661. Under Canada's best provincial plan, the poverty rate would decrease to 0.0 percent and the poverty gap would decline to $179.

Note that, while there is a dramatic difference in the simulated impact of U.S. and Canadian programs on families with children, the differences for two-parent families without children and single individuals are fairly small. Moving from the mean U.S. to the mean Canadian program has a negligible impact on poverty rates for single individuals and two-parent families without children, although the poverty gap does decrease. This reflects the lower level of transfer assistance available to these groups in both countries.

The results in table 6.9, which are based on the Canadian population, generally mirror the effects discussed above. This is not surprising, given the similarities of the U.S. and the Canadian populations.

6.4.4 Adjusting for Labor Supply Responses and Program Participation

The above analysis assumes 100 percent participation rates and zero labor supply responses. In this section, we estimate the impact on the U.S. population of moving from the current U.S. programs to the mean Canadian program, allowing for a range of labor supply elasticities and for incomplete program participation. This enables us to test whether our results are robust to other behavioral assumptions.

We compare estimates of U.S. poverty rates and poverty gaps with Canadian programs, assuming 100 percent program participation and assuming lower participation rates. In the latter case, we use the estimated participation rates by family type for Canada shown in table 6.6 and assume these same participation rates would occur in the United States if the Canadian programs were adopted. As discussed above, observed participation rates should produce overestimates of poverty rates, due to underreporting of transfer income.

To simulate the potential changes in work effort that may result from adopting the average Canadian means-tested programs, we use a range of income and substitution elasticity estimates from the Seattle-Denver negative income tax experiments reported in Keeley (1981).[37] To simulate the impact of changes in the UI system, we rely on estimates from the UI duration literature.[38] We assume that the change in labor supply induced by the change in transfer systems is small enough that wages in the low-wage labor market remain relatively constant. Thus, we use the current wage as a measure of the wage that would prevail under the new transfer system. Our methodology for these labor supply and program participation adjustments is explained in more detail in appendix E.

The results, shown in table 6.10, indicate that our poverty rate estimates and poverty gap estimates are surprisingly robust to the impact of changing labor supply elasticities. For all family types, the impact of different labor supply elasticities is quite small. The participation rate assumptions appear to have a larger impact: using Canadian participation rates rather than assuming 100 percent participation increases the estimated U.S. poverty rate under the Canadian system from 6 percent to 9 percent for all families, and from 2 percent to 16 percent for single-parent families. Note, however, that the estimated reduction in poverty from adopting the Canadian system is still substantial: poverty rates of all families decline from 13 percent under the U.S. programs to 9 percent under the Canadian programs, while poverty rates for single-

37. The low-, medium-, and high-income and substitution elasticities for annual hours worked for male heads are (.04, −.14), (.12, −.21), and (.30, −.30); for wives they are (.18, −.14), (.24, −.24), and (.67, −.77); and for female heads they are (.07, −.13), (.17, −.24), and (.36, −.80). These elasticities are larger than those presented in Moffitt and Kehrer (1981).

38. We use estimates from Moffitt and Nicholson (1982) and Katz and Meyer (1990).

Table 6.10 **Simulated Impact in the United States of Mean Canadian Program under Range of Labor Supply Elasticities and Participation Rates**

	100% Participation		Estimated Take-up Rates[b]	
Elasticities[a]	Poverty Rate	Poverty Gap	Poverty Rate	Poverty Gap
All families				
Low	6.2	1,624	9.4	3,162
Medium	6.2	1,641	9.5	3,171
High	6.3	1,698	9.5	3,197
Single, no children				
Low	15.4	1,713	16.0	2,521
Medium	15.5	1,733	16.2	2,522
High	15.5	1,800	16.2	2,548
Single, children				
Low	2.4	702	15.8	3,911
Medium	2.5	693	15.9	3,952
High	2.5	701	16.2	3,989
Married, no children				
Low	2.6	1,862	2.7	3,767
Medium	2.5	1,912	2.8	3,756
High	2.8	1,978	2.8	3,731
Married, children				
Low	0.9	666	5.1	4,050
Medium	1.0	665	5.1	4,065
High	1.1	669	5.0	4,104

[a]See footnote 37 for assumed elasticities for high, medium, and low cases.
[b]Estimated take-up rates are based on estimates for Canada reported in table 6.6.

parent families decline from 43 percent to 16 percent. The poverty rate of two-parent families decreases more moderately. This is in part because the greater generosity of the Canadian programs is offset by the lower participation rate in SA than in AFDC for this group.

6.4.5 Expenditures under U.S. and Canadian Transfer Systems

Given the substantial differences in the simulated impact of the U.S. and Canadian transfer systems on poverty, it is of interest to ask how program expenditures would differ under the two systems. While it is difficult to estimate the total increase in spending under each program since we have little information on administrative expenditures, we can calculate the total cost of transfer payments. As before, it is more appropriate to compare results from different simulations, rather than to compare simulated with actual expenditures. However, actual expenditures are included for the reader's interest.

Table 6.11 presents the total transfer spending under each of the simulations discussed above. For each simulation, we estimate spending assuming 100

Table 6.11 **Change in U.S. Transfer Spending under Mean Canadian Program (in billions of dollars)**

	100% Participation	Estimated Take-up Rates[a]
Reported U.S. expenditures = $35.9 billion		
Simulated U.S. expenditures with U.S. programs	46.6	28.3
Simulated U.S. expenditures with mean Canadian programs[b]		
Zero elasticities	91.0	67.9
Low elasticities	97.5	75.0
Medium elasticities	102.6	79.7
High elasticities	109.6	81.1

[a]Take-up rates for Canadian programs based on estimated Canadian participation rates reported in table 6.6. Take-up rates for U.S. programs based on actual participation, reported in the microdata.

[b]See footnote 37 for assumed elasticities for high, medium, and low cases.

percent take-up rates, and we recalculate spending using the take-up rates prevalent in each country, which are shown in table 6.6.[39] We present estimates for a range of labor supply responses to the change in welfare policy.

With full participation, the simulated cost of U.S. benefit payments for the U.S. population would be $46.6 billion; Canadian transfer programs would cost from $91.0 billion to $109.6 billion, or about 2.0 to 2.4 times the cost of U.S. programs. At current take-up rates, in contrast, the cost of the Canadian programs would range from $67.9 billion to $81.1 billion, or about 2.4 to 2.9 times the cost of current U.S. programs.

In evaluating the impact of this increase in expenditures, two points are important. First, to evaluate the impact of these programs on family incomes, one must consider both the additional transfers and the additional taxes generated by the program. For example, the net impact of the FA program on most families may be minimal, since they will receive an increase both in taxes and in transfers as a result of the program. In table 6.12, we present some simple calculations that are illustrative of the change in the posttax, posttransfer income distribution that might result from moving to the Canadian programs. We assume that all non-UI programs are financed by a proportional increase in the federal income tax. We ignore any deadweight loss that may result from the additional taxes. We do not attempt here to examine the

39. Table 6.11 uses the estimated take-up rates for existing programs to estimate expected costs in new programs, even though the benefit and eligibility rules change across programs. This is clearly inaccurate, but unfortunately we have no information on how take-up rates might change as program parameters change. For this reason, looking at the relative cost differences between different simulations that assume a 100 percent take-up rate might be more informative.

Table 6.12 Change in U.S. Taxes and Transfers under Mean Canadian Program by Family Income Quintile

	Change in Transfers				
Quintile	UI ($)	Non-UI ($)	Average Tax Rate	Change in Taxes ($)	Change in Income ($)
1	225.5	1,731.4	0.000	0.0	1,956.9
2	105.9	316.8	0.035	91.4	331.3
3	78.9	164.2	0.067	273.4	−30.3
4	46.0	108.9	0.090	511.2	−356.3
5	32.5	68.2	0.156	1,512.9	−1,412.2

Notes: This table provides an estimate of the change in taxes and transfers resulting from a change from the mean U.S. to the mean Canadian transfer program, assuming observed U.S. and Canadian participation rates and zero labor supply adjustments. We assume that all non-UI transfers are financed by a proportionate increase in the income tax, and we ignore any deadweight loss resulting from change in taxes or transfers. All dollar values presented in annual per capita basis. Quintiles represent ranking of pretransfer, pretax incomes divided by poverty level. Average tax rate information is drawn from U.S. House of Representatives (1990). This source gives average tax rates by posttransfer rather than pretransfer income distribution. However, in only 3 percent of the cases do families change rankings when moving from pretransfer to posttransfer definition. This source reports a negative tax rate for the bottom quintile, due to the EITC. We assume that the tax rate for this group is zero, because we have already accounted for the EITC in our simulations.

distribution of taxes resulting from the change in the UI program; the incidence of these taxes is beyond the scope of the current study.

Columns 1 and 2 of table 6.12 represent the increase in UI and non-UI transfers ranked by pretransfer family income quintiles.[40] Column 3 indicates average income tax rates by income quintile.[41] Column 4 represents the change in taxes resulting from the program, and column 5 represents the change in income.

This table clearly shows that the net income gains from these programs are concentrated among the bottom quintile of families: the bottom two quintiles have increases in average posttax, posttransfer incomes of $1,957 and $331, respectively, while the top quintiles have net income declines. This table also suggests that the increase in UI expenditures is more evenly spread across the income distribution than the increase in the non-UI programs is.

The second point to consider in evaluating the impact of the additional expenditures is the efficiency costs of raising the additional tax revenue needed to finance the programs. In this case, the total rather than the net increase in

40. We divide pretransfer family incomes by the poverty level, to adjust for family size. These computations assume the observed participation rates by family type in the United States and Canada, and zero labor supply response.

41. The effective tax rates are reported in U.S. House of Representatives (1990), table 99 for the year 1985, and are based on the Congressional Budget Office Tax Simulation Model. They are based on posttransfer rather than pretransfer income quintiles. However, in our sample the pre- and posttransfer income quintiles are quite similar: only 3 percent of all families shifted quintiles as a result of transfers.

expenditures is the relevant metric, because this indicates the extent to which marginal tax rates will have to be altered to raise additional revenue. The excess burden can be substantial. For example, Ballard, Shoven, and Whalley (1985) estimate that the deadweight loss of raising an additional dollar of tax revenue can range from $0.33 to $0.48. This would imply an excess burden from the increased taxation of 0.3 percent to 0.7 percent of GNP, assuming estimated take-up rates.[42]

6.5 Conclusions

This paper has demonstrated that the Canadian transfer system is far more extensive than the U.S. system. It offers both higher benefit levels and broader eligibility than the U.S. system. As a result, Canadian transfer programs offer far more protection against poverty. Our simulations suggest that the Canadian system would generate substantially lower poverty rates and lower poverty gaps in the United States than the current U.S. system.

The primary group that would benefit from the adoption of the Canadian antipoverty system is families with children. Our simulations suggest that poverty among both single-parent and two-parent families with children would decline dramatically if the United States adopted the average Canadian antipoverty transfer program. This result is striking, given the enormous public concern in the United States over the high poverty rates of children. Our simulations further indicate that this change would increase program expenditures: total U.S. transfer spending would increase by two to three times under the mean Canadian transfer program.

There are limits to the extent to which such cross-country comparisons provide useful policy information. The substantially more costly Canadian programs may be entirely infeasible in the U.S. political context. In addition, Canada has a *system* of antipoverty programs; transplanting only some parts of that system to another country may produce very different results. At a minimum, however, the results of this paper indicate that there is nothing inherently unchangeable in the current poverty rates among women and children in the United States. They are, at least in part, a result of the policy choices that we have made. Canada's different choices have produced different results.

The discussion in this paper has suggested a variety of avenues for further research. A primary question is why Canada and the United States have adopted such different transfer systems. The Canada-U.S. case is interesting, because it appears to contradict standard theories that hold that regional control of welfare programs should lead to underprovision of welfare benefits.[43]

42. Note that, to compute the total excess burden of the program, one would also have to consider the impact of the additional transfer payments.

43. See Brown and Oates (1987) for a summary of this literature.

As noted above, this does not appear to be the case in Canada, since the Canadian SA program is both more decentralized and more generous than the U.S. AFDC program.

In addition, it would be of interest to exploit the variation in program rules across the two countries to study the behavioral effects of transfer programs. For example, while the AFDC program imposes the same tax rate across all U.S. states, tax rates vary substantially across provinces under the SA program. One could examine whether these different tax rates have caused different labor supply responses across Canadian provinces. Alternatively, one could test whether the different treatment of one- versus two-parent families in the two countries has had a significant effect on family formation. These studies would provide an interesting supplement to the wide variety of such studies in the United States focusing on AFDC.

Appendix A
Chronology of Selected Social Service Legislation

Canada

1966 Canada Assistance Plan. Created the current system of Social Assistance programs within the provinces.
Medical Care Act. Established national health insurance.

1971 Unemployment Insurance Act. Extended coverage from 80 to 96 percent of the labor force. Reduced required weeks of covered employment for eligibility. Increased maximum benefits from 50 to 75 percent of average earnings for persons with dependents and from 40 to 66 percent for persons without dependents.

1973 Family Allowance Act. Replaced previous family assistance program and youth allowance act, and created the Family Allowance program. Set monthly payments at $12 per child in 1973 and $20 per child in 1974. Provided for indexation of family allowance benefit to inflation using the CPI.

1975 Unemployment Insurance Amendments. Reduced maximum unemployment insurance benefit to 66 percent of earnings.

1977 Amendments. Increased weeks of employment required to qualify for UI from 8 to between 10 and 14 weeks, depending on the regional unemployment rate. Maximum benefit duration decreased from 51 to 50 weeks.

1978 Unemployment Insurance Amendments. Required 20 weeks of employment in prior year for new entrants to labor force. Required higher entrance requirement for repeaters (one additional week of covered employment for each week of benefits received up to a maximum of 20 weeks). Maximum benefits reduced from 66 to 60 percent.

Child Tax Credit. Established refundable national income tax credit for families with children.

Family Allowance Amendment. Reduced monthly family allowance rate for 1979 to $20 per child from $25.68 in 1978. Retained annual escalation from 1979 onward.

1982 Family Allowance Amendment. Limited indexation of family allowances.

1986 Family Allowance Amendment. Further limited indexation of family allowances.

Source: Health and Welfare Canada 1987.

United States

1964 Food Stamp Act. Established national food stamp program, with optional state participation.

1965 Medicaid Act. Established public health insurance for AFDC recipients.

1967 Aid for Families with Dependent Children Amendments. States must disregard the first $30 of earnings and one-third of the remainder in determining benefit levels.

1970 Unemployment Insurance Amendments. Provided a federal extended benefits program for workers who exhaust state unemployment insurance benefits in states with high insured unemployment rates. Expanded coverage of the unemployment insurance system.

1971 Food Stamp Amendments. Required benefits large enough to purchase nutritionally adequate diet. Established national eligibility standards.

1972 Supplemental Security Income Program. Replaced programs for federal/state old-age assistance, aid to the blind, and aid to the permanently and totally disabled.

1973 Food Stamp Amendments. Expanded food stamp program. Provided for semiannual adjustment of food stamp allotments. Broadened classes of people eligible.

1975 Earned Income Tax Credit. Established for working families with children.

1976 Unemployment Insurance Amendments. Extended unemployment insurance coverage to state, local, and nonprofit employees.

1977 Food Stamp Amendments. Eliminated purchase requirement, so families received only bonus portion of coupon at no cost. Eligibility standards tightened.

1978 Unemployment Insurance Amendments. Provided for federal taxation of unemployment insurance benefits.

1980 Food Stamp Amendments. Benefits updated on annual rather than semiannual basis. Restricted eligibility of students.

1981 Major Transfer Reductions. Limited $30 and one-third income disregard under AFDC program to four months. Set eligibility cap on gross income, at 150 percent of state-determined standard of need. Limited total assets to $1,000.

Gross income eligibility limit established for food stamp program. Earnings deduction lowered to 18 percent. Postponed increases in benefit levels until October 1982.

Decreased income deductions for supplemental security income program, from $60 of earned and unearned income and $195 of earned income to $20 and $65, respectively.

Eliminated the national trigger in the extended benefits program of unemployment insurance. Prohibited payment of extended benefits to an individual with fewer than 20 weeks of work in base period.

1984 Aid to Families with Dependent Children Amendments. Gross income cap on eligibility raised to 185 percent of state standard of need. $30 disregard extended from four to twelve months. States must disregard first $50 of child-support collections per month.

1988 Family Support Act. Required all states to establish Aid to Families with Dependent Children programs for eligible two-parent families. Required all states to run education, training, and employment programs for work-eligible AFDC recipients, with mandatory participation.

Sources: U.S. House of Representatives 1990; U.S. Department of Health and Human Services 1988; U.S. Department of Labor 1986.

Appendix B

Table 6B.1 1986 U.S. Poverty Line and Canadian Low-Income Cutoff (in 1986 U.S. dollars)

Family Size	U.S. Poverty Line	Canadian Low-Income Cutoffs by Size of City				
		500+K	100–499K	30–99K	<30K	Rural
1	5,701	8,521	8,093	7,592	7,019	6,302
2	7,372	11,242	10,671	9,956	9,237	8,236
3	8,737	15,039	14,252	13,320	12,390	11,028
4	11,203	17,330	16,470	15,397	14,322	12,749
5	13,259	20,194	19,122	17,832	16,614	14,825
6	14,986	22,057	20,839	19,479	18,118	16,185
7	17,049	24,278	22,988	21,485	19,980	17,832

Notes: The U.S. CPS data do not contain information on city size. All calculations in this paper that apply the Canadian low-income cutoffs to U.S. data collapse the five-city size breakdowns into three categories. All U.S. individuals reporting that they live in an SMSA are given a low-income cutoff based on the mean of the two largest city size categories. All individuals reporting that they do not live in an SMSA but are not on a farm are given a low-income cutoff based on the mean of the third and fourth largest city size categories. All individuals on farms are given the rural low-income cutoff.

Appendix C
Calculating Simulated Government Transfers on U.S. and Canadian Data

Simulating U.S. Programs

Food Stamps. Rules for food stamp eligibility and benefit levels are taken from U.S. House of Representatives (1986), appendix G. Separate calculations are made for Alaska and Hawaii, where program rules vary.

AFDC. Rules for AFDC need standards and benefit maximums by family size by state, and state rules for payment of benefits are from the U.S. House of Representatives (1986), section 8. Eligibility is determined by whether total family income is less than 1.85 times the state need standard. AFDC for eligible two-parent households is calculated in the states that allow such payments. Benefit amounts are adjusted for child-support deductions (allowable up to $600/year), based on reported child-support income. Benefits also adjusted by earnings deductions, including the deduction for work expenses of up to $625/year and the standardized earnings deduction of $30/month. Because we have no information on how long a recipient has been in the program, we use the 100 percent tax rate for earnings, which is effective after four months on the program.

Unemployment Insurance. Information on waiting periods, minimum and maximum earnings limits, and minimum and maximum benefit payments were provided by Blank and Card (1991), who collected this information from the U.S. Department of Labor, *Comparison of State Unemployment Insurance Laws* (various years). Maximum duration is set to twenty-six weeks except for Massachusetts and Washington, which have a duration of thirty weeks, and Alaska, which is on the federal extended benefits program and has a maximum of thirty-nine weeks. Replacement rates are calculated for each state as the average of the ratio of minimum benefits to minimum earnings and the ratio of maximum benefits to maximum earnings. Separate calculations on UI eligibility and benefits are made for both head and spouse (if present) for each household in the simulation.

EITC. Rules for the EITC taken from the U.S. House of Representatives (1986), section 10.

Simulating Canadian Programs

Family Allowance. Information on eligibility and benefit levels from Canada Department of National Health and Welfare (1986, 1988), chapter 3. Alternative calculations are made for Alberta and Quebec, where provincial variations in the program occur.

Social Assistance. Provincial rules for eligibility and benefit payment determination are from the Canada Department of National Health and Welfare (1986, 1988), chapter 4. Benefit levels for nondisabled single individuals (employable), nondisabled married couples with children (employable), and nondisabled single parents with children (nonemployable) were taken from Canada National Council of Welfare (1987), table 5. See that publication for the assumptions by which these benefit levels were developed. Benefit levels for other family sizes were interpolated as follows: We have information on benefits for a single individual ($B1$), a single parent with one preschool child ($B2$), and a married couple with two school-age children ($B3$). We assume benefits for single-parent families are equal to $B2$ + (Number of children − 1) * ($B3$ − $B2$)/2. We assume benefits for married families are equal to $B3$ + (Number of children − 2) * ($B3$ − $B2$)/2. These linear interpolations are probably least accurate for large families. The Work Income Supplement Program in Quebec is included as part of SA for the province, as is the Family Income Plan for Saskatchewan and the Child-Related Income Support Program for Ontario. The Work Incentive Program for Ontario is not included, since the 1985 data indicate less than 2 percent of the caseload participates in this program.

Unemployment Insurance. The eligibility, duration, and benefits information for UI in Canada is taken from the Canada Department of National Health and Welfare (1986, 1988), chapter 8. Durations by province are based on 1986 unemployment rates in each province. Separate calculations on UI eligibility and benefits are made for both head and spouse (if present) for each household in the simulation.

Child Tax Credit. Rules for calculating eligibility and tax credit amounts described in the Canada Department of National Health and Welfare (1986, 1988), chapter 3.

Appendix D
Comparing Simulated and Reported Transfer Income

Table 6D.1 compares our 1986 simulations with the reported income sources in our microdata. We report cases where our simulations agree with reported benefits (Sim > 0, Actual > 0; Sim = 0, Actual = 0) and cases where our simulations do not agree with reported benefits (Sim > 0, Actual = 0; Sim

Table 6D.1 Accuracy of Simulations

	U.S.	Canada
UI benefits		
Percentage (sim > 0, actual > 0)	6.0	15.3
Percentage (sim = 0, actual = 0)	79.6	70.9
Percentage (sim > 0, actual = 0)	8.6	5.2
Percentage (sim = 0, actual > 0)	5.8	8.5
Minimum percentage correct	85.6	86.2
Maximum percentage correct	94.2	91.4
Actual/simulation (sim > 0, actual > 0) ($)	1.39	1.53
AFDC/SA benefits		
Percentage (sim > 0, actual > 0)	3.3	6.3
Percentage (sim = 0, actual =0)	93.1	85.4
Percentage (sim > 0, actual = 0)	1.8	5.9
Percentage (sim = 0, actual > 0)	1.8	2.4
Minimum percentage correct	96.4	91.7
Maximum percentage correct	98.2	97.6
Actual/simulation (sim > 0, actual > 0) ($)	1.24	2.09
Food stamps/FA benefits		
Percentage (sim > 0, actual > 0)	5.9	42.1
Percentage (sim > 0, actual > 0)	83.6	55.2
Percentage (sim > 0, actual = 0)	8.8	1.2
Percentage (sim = 0, actual > 0)	1.7	1.5
Minimum percentage correct	89.5	97.3
Maximum percentage correct	98.3	98.5
Actual/simulation (sim > 0, actual > 0) ($)	1.04	.99
EITC/CTC		
Minimum percentage correct	n.a.[a]	89.0
Maximum percentage correct		92.0
Actual/simulation (sim > 0, actual > 0) ($)		2.66

[a]The data contain no information on actual receipt of the EITC in the United States.

= 0, Actual > 0). We also report the ratio of reported to simulated benefits among the subgroup of individuals who have both nonzero simulated and nonzero reported transfers.

There are three reasons why our simulations might predict positive transfer payments while reported benefits are zero. First, the simulations may correctly predict eligibility, but the individual may choose not to participate in the program. Second, the individual may choose to participate in the program but not to report transfer income. Finally, the simulation may inaccurately predict eligibility. Thus, it is clear that the case (Sim > 0, Actual = 0) does not necessarily indicate an error in the simulation procedure. In contrast, the simulation is in error in all cases where it indicates that no eligibility occurs and the data indicate that the individual received the program (Sim = 0, Actual > 0). Table 6D.1 indicates a range for the number of correctly classified individuals, where the minimum is the share of cases in which both the simulated and actual data agree, and the maximum is that share plus the share in which the simulation shows eligibility but the actual data shows no receipt.

The simulation accuracies shown in the table are quite good. For the UI programs in both countries, the simulation classifies between 85 and 95 percent of the cases correctly. For the other programs, the range of correct estimates falls almost entirely within the 90th percentile. Not surprisingly, the program with the lowest error in eligibility classification (and in benefit levels) is the Canadian FA program, which has the simplest set of national rules.

The simulated and reported benefit payment levels are very close for the food stamp program in the United States and for the FA program in Canada. For other programs, the simulation consistently underpredicts benefit payments. In the case of UI, there appears to be no particular pattern to this benefit underprediction across groups, and it probably reflects the fact that benefits are being estimated from wages reported during 1986, which, as noted above, are probably underestimates of base period wages. In the case of AFDC, the undercount is concentrated among married couples with children. This may in part be due to the fact that the reported AFDC income category in the CPS includes some other sources of public assistance income (such as foster-care payments) that are more likely to be received by married couples. SA benefits are most seriously underestimated, with reported benefits double the simulated benefits. Among single parents, the SA estimates are fairly accurate. The major errors arise in the estimated SA benefits among single individuals and married couples without children. We suspect that this may because we incorrectly classify individuals as employable who in fact would be classified as unemployable.

In any case, the results in this table are generally reassuring. They indicate that the simulation results are reasonable and not too different from the reported data. The eligibility estimates appear to be quite good, while the benefit estimates somewhat underestimate actual receipt.

Appendix E
Adjusting for Labor Supply Changes and Program Participation

The following is a brief outline of the methodology used to adjust for labor supply changes and incomplete program participation, in simulating the impact of adopting the mean Canadian program in the United States. We present separate methods for the case where a family receives UI and for the case where they receive non-UI programs. A family is assumed to receive UI only when their total income from UI would exceed that available under SA or UI.

Non-UI Case

Determining Program Parameters

We use the simulation methodology described in appendix C to characterize the potential transfer income received by each household under both the U.S. and Canadian systems, in terms of the following equation:

$$B = G - tY,$$

where B is total transfer income, G is the guaranteed income at zero earnings, Y is total earnings, and t is the tax rate on earnings.

The values of B and t will vary depending on the family's earnings. For example, a family with income greater than the break-even income level of G/t will have a guarantee and a tax rate of zero.

For existing U.S. programs, we can use the observed earnings level of each family to determine which values of G and t apply to them. For Canadian programs, we compute possible values of G and t, both in the case where the family participates and where they do not participate in SA. We then use the procedure described next to determine which budget segment they will select.

Determining Program Participation

Opting-in Income. Some families who have incomes above the break-even level G/t under the more generous Canadian system may reduce their income in order to qualify for assistance. A family will choose to participate in the program as long as the additional nonwage income received from the transfer program is enough to compensate them for the loss in utility from the higher tax rate on earnings imposed by the transfer program. Ashenfelter (1978) has derived the income level at which families will decide to enter the program, by using a Taylor series approximation of the expenditure function for program participants around the nonparticipant equilibrium. We use these equations to determine the opting-in income level:

$$\text{YOPT} = \{G - tN\}/\{t(1 - .5te)\} \qquad \text{(one worker)},$$

and

$$\text{YOPT} = \{G - tN\}/\{t(1 - .5t(e_{11}\Theta_1 + e_{22}\Theta_2))\} \qquad \text{(two workers)},$$

where G is the guarantee; t is the tax rate; N is nonlabor, nonwelfare income; e, e_{11}, and e_{22} are compensated elasticities of substitution; and Θ_1 and Θ_2 are the shares of total wages received by the husband and wife in total family earnings. (We assume cross-elasticities are zero in this case.)

Adjustment for Incomplete Participation. To estimate the impact of U.S. programs under incomplete participation, we assume that a family is a program participant only if they report that they receive transfer income in the microdata. For the EITC, where we have no information available on participation in the microdata, we randomly assign a fraction of the population to participant status. We assume that the total participation rate for this program is the same as reported for the Canadian CTC in table 6.6.

To estimate the impact of implementing Canadian programs in the United States, we assume that the U.S. participation rate for each program will be the same as reported for Canada in table 6.6. In addition, we assume that families who indicate that they participate in U.S. programs will be more likely to participate in comparable Canadian programs. Thus, if a family reports that it participates in the U.S. UI program, we assume that it will also participate in the Canadian UI program. If it participates in the U.S. AFDC program or if it is a family without children and it participates in food stamps, we assume that it participates in SA. We then randomly assign some of the remaining families who are eligible for Canadian programs to participant status, in order to reconcile the U.S. participation rates with the participation rates reported for Canada in table 6.6.[44]

Determining Labor Supply Response, Given Participation Status

Slutsky Equations. Above we derive the values of each family's guarantee level and tax rate under both the U.S. and the Canadian systems. We then compute the implied change in labor supply using the Slutsky decomposition:

$$\begin{aligned}\%\Delta\text{Hours} &= e\ (\%\Delta\text{Wage}) + b\ (\%\Delta\text{Income}) \\ &= e(t_1 - t_2)/(1 - t_1) + b\{H(t_1 - t_2)W + (G_2 - G_1)\}/Y,\end{aligned}$$

where e is the compensated elasticity of substitution; b is the income elasticity; t_1 and t_2 are the tax rates and guarantee under the U.S. and Canadian systems, respectively; G_1 and G_2 are the guarantees under the U.S. and Canadian systems; H, Y, and W are hours, total income, and the wage rate under the U.S. system. In the two-worker case this generalizes to

$$\begin{aligned}\%\Delta\text{Hours}_i = {} & e_i(t_1 - t_2)/(1 - t_1) + b_i\{H_h(t_1 - t_2)W_h + \\ & H_w(t_1 - t_2)W_w + (G_2 - G_1)\}/Y, \qquad i = h,w,\end{aligned}$$

where h and w index the husband and wife. Note that we again assume cross-elasticities are zero.

Labor Supply Elasticities. We use a range of estimates of income and substitution elasticities from the Seattle-Denver negative income tax experiment. We use the minimum, mean and maximum income and substitution elasticities reported in Keeley (1981). For male heads, these elasticities are

44. For the case of married couples with children, the participation rate is actually higher for AFDC than for SA. Thus, we randomly assign a fraction of those who report AFDC income to nonparticipant status under the SA program.

(.04, − .14), (.12, − .21), and (.30, − .30); for wives they are (.18, − .14), (.24, − .24) and (.67, − .77); and for female heads they are (.07, − .13), (.17, − .24), and (.36, − .80).

UI Case

For the case where a family member is eligible for UI under either the U.S. or the Canadian program, we characterize their potential UI benefits in terms of the benefit replacement rate (weekly UI payment over the weekly wage) and the maximum weeks of UI payments. We then apply results from Katz and Meyer (1990) and from Moffitt and Nicholson (1982) that estimate the impact of these two parameters on the duration of unemployment.

Katz and Meyer estimate that a 10 percent increase in the benefit replacement rate will increase mean unemployment duration by 1.5 weeks, while Moffitt and Nicholson estimate an increase of 1.0 weeks for males and 0.8 weeks for females. The estimated impact of a 1-week increase in maximum duration of UI is 0.2 weeks for Katz and Meyer and 0.1 weeks for Moffitt and Nicholson. Note that this approach considers the impact of the UI program only on the duration of unemployment spells. It does not account for the impact of UI on the rate at which individuals enter unemployment, or for its impact on the rate at which individuals move from out of the labor force to employment.

This approach is not entirely satisfactory, since it does not integrate the UI program with other transfer programs. We also tried an approach that parameterized the UI program as a means-tested program with a guarantee equal to the UI payment, and a tax rate of 100 percent (on the unemployed worker), and then applied the methodology described for the non-UI case. This approach did not yield substantially different results, so we do not report them here.

References

Ashenfelter, Orley. 1978. The Labor Supply Response of Wage Earners. In *Welfare in Rural Areas: The North Carolina–Iowa Maintenance Experiment,* ed. J. L. Palmer and J. A. Pechman. Washington, D.C.: Brookings Institution.

Ballard, Charles L., John B. Shoven, and John Whalley. 1985. General Equilibrium Computations of the Marginal Welfare Costs of Taxes in the United States. *American Economic Review* 75 (March): 128–38.

Banting, Keith G. 1987. *The Welfare State and Canadian Federalism.* 2nd edition. Kingston, Ontario: McGill–Queens University Press.

Blank, Rebecca M., and David E. Card. 1991. Recent Trends in Insured and Uninsured Unemployment: Is There an Explanation? *Quarterly Journal of Economics* 106 (November): 1157–89.

Brown, Charles C., and Wallace E. Oates. 1987. Assistance to the Poor in a Federal System. *Journal of Public Economics* 32 (April): 307–30.

Canada Department of National Health and Welfare. 1986. *Inventory of Income Security Programs in Canada: July 1985*. Ottawa: Department of National Health and Welfare, September.

———. 1988. *Inventory of Income Security Programs in Canada: Recent Initiatives and Statistical Update as of January 1987*. Ottawa: Department of National Health and Welfare, February.

Canada National Council of Welfare. 1987. *Welfare in Canada: The Tangled Safety Net*. Ottawa: National Council of Welfare, November.

Canadian Conference of Catholic Bishops. 1988. A Statement on Social Policy. *Dissent* 35 (Summer): 314–21.

Chollet, Deborah. 1988. *Uninsured in the United States: The Nonelderly Population without Health Insurance, 1986*. Washington, D.C.: Employee Benefit Research Institute.

Danziger, Sheldon H., and Daniel H. Weinberg. 1986. *Fighting Poverty: What Works and What Doesn't*. Cambridge, Mass.: Harvard University Press.

Gueron, Judith M. 1990. Work and Welfare: Lessons on Employment Programs. *Journal of Economic Perspectives* 4 (Winter): 79–98.

Hanratty, Maria J., and Rebecca M. Blank. 1992. Down and Out in North America: Recent Trends in Poverty Rates in the U.S. and Canada. *Quarterly Journal of Economics* 107 (February): 233–54.

Health and Welfare Canada. 1987. *Chronology of Selected Federal Social Security Legislation since 1918*. Ottawa: Department of National Health and Welfare.

Ismael, Jacqueline S. 1987. *The Canadian Welfare State: Evolution and Transition*. Edmonton: University of Alberta Press.

Katz, Lawrence F., and Bruce D. Meyer. 1990. The Impact of the Potential Duration of Unemployment Benefits on the Duration of Unemployment. *Journal of Public Economics* 41 (February): 45–72.

Keeley, Michael. 1981. *Labor Supply and Public Policy: A Critical Review*. New York: Academic Press.

Kesselman, Jonathan R. 1992. Income Security via the Tax System: Canadian and American Reforms. In *Canada-U.S. Tax Comparisons,* ed. J. Shoven and J. Whalley. Chicago: University of Chicago Press.

Leman, Christopher. 1980. *The Collapse of Welfare Reform: Political Institutions, Policy, and the Poor in Canada and the U.S.* Cambridge, Mass.: MIT Press.

Lipset, Seymour M. 1990. *Continental Divide: The Values and Institutions of the United States and Canada*. New York: Routledge.

Moffitt, Robert, and Kenneth Kehrer. 1981. The Effect of Tax and Transfer Programs on Labor Supply: The Evidence from the Income Maintenance Experiments. In *Research in Labor Economics,* vol. 4, ed. Ronald Ehrenberg. Greenwich, Conn.: JAI Press.

Moffitt, Robert, and Walter Nicholson. 1982. The Effect of Unemployment Insurance on Unemployment: The Case of Federal Supplemental Benefits. *Review of Economics and Statistics* 64(1): 1–11.

Organization for Economic Cooperation and Development (OECD). 1987. *Purchasing Power Parities and Real Expenditures*. Paris: Organization for Economic Cooperation and Development.

Ruggles, Patricia. 1990. *Drawing the Line*. Washington, D.C.: Urban Institute Press.

Ruggles, Patricia, and Richard C. Michel. 1987. Participation Rates in the Aid to Families with Dependent Children Program: Trends for 1967 through 1984. Washington, D.C.: Urban Institute Report, April.

U.S. Bureau of the Census. 1983. *Current Population Reports, Series P-60*. No. 103. Washington, D.C.: GPO.

U.S. Department of Health and Human Services. Social Security Administration. 1988. *Social Security Bulletin: Annual Statistical Supplement*. Washington, D.C.: GPO.

U.S. Department of Labor. 1986. *Fifty Years of Unemployment Insurance: A Legislative History: 1935–1985*. Unemployment Insurance Service Occasional Paper 86-5. Washington, D.C.: GPO.

U.S. General Accounting Office. 1988a. *Food Stamps: Examination of Program Data and Analysis of Nonparticipation*. Washington, D.C.: U.S. General Accounting Office.

———. 1988b. *Food Stamps: Reasons for Nonparticipation*. Washington, DC: U.S. General Accounting Office.

U.S. House of Representatives. Committee on Ways and Means. 1986, 1990. *Background Material and Data on Programs within the Jurisdiction of the Committee on Ways and Means*. Washington, D.C.: U.S. Government Printing Office.

———. 1990. *Overview of Entitlement Programs: 1990 Green Book*. Washington, D.C.: GPO.

Vaillancourt, Francois. 1985. *Income Distribution and Economic Security in Canada*. Toronto: University of Toronto Press.

Wolfson, M. C., and J. M. Evans. 1989. Statistics Canada's Low-Income Cutoffs: Methodological Concerns and Possibilities. Statistics Canada Discussion Paper.

7 The Distribution of Family Income: Measuring and Explaining Changes in the 1980s for Canada and the United States

McKinley L. Blackburn and David E. Bloom

7.1 Introduction

It is now well known that income inequality increased substantially in the United States during the 1980s. Why it increased and whether the trend will continue are still questions that are much debated. Less concern seems to have been devoted to changes over time in inequality in Canada, although this is changing. Yet, with few exceptions, researchers have not attempted to compare trends in income inequality and its correlates between the two countries. Such a comparison could help identify the forces responsible for observed patterns in inequality for the two countries. Indeed, Canada and the United States seem to be particularly appropriate for making cross-national inequality comparisons, since the two countries are fairly similar in the extent of the welfare state, the lack of a centrally controlled wage-setting mechanism, and the nature of the family.

It is inherently difficult to draw conclusions from international comparisons of inequality. As has been pointed out by Lydall (1978), for example, differences across countries in how data are collected, or in any quality-control adjustments that are made by statistical agencies that collect the data, can generate misleading differences in measured inequality. Nevertheless, much use has been made of compilations of inequality measures for several countries, for example, those collected in Jain (1975), despite the fact that there are differences across countries in the income concept being applied, in the definition of an income-receiving unit, and in population coverage (see van

McKinley L. Blackburn is assistant professor of economics at the University of South Carolina. David E. Bloom is professor of economics at Columbia University and a research associate at the National Bureau of Economic Research.

Helpful comments and suggestions were provided by Gary Burtless, Martin Dooley, Garnet Picot, and Robert Plotnick. This paper was written while the authors were visiting scholars at the Russell Sage Foundation.

Ginneken and Park 1984). In our view, the preferred method of making such cross-national inequality comparisons is to use comparably collected microdata—which we believe are available for the United States and Canada—and to make adjustments so that the underlying concepts that define an income distribution are as close as possible in the two countries. In this paper, we make such a comparison for the distributions of family income and individual earnings in Canada and the United States in 1979 and 1987.

While a discussion of the literature on recent changes in income and earnings inequality in the United States is available (see Beach 1989; Blackburn and Bloom 1987), we are not aware of any such summary for Canada. Section 7.2 of the paper provides such a review. Section 7.3 discusses our approach to comparing income distributions across countries and over time and presents our empirical results for the distribution of family income. Section 7.4 continues the analysis by focusing on the determinants of changes in the dispersion of earnings among males in the two countries. Section 7.5 summarizes our findings.

7.2 A Review of Studies of the Distribution of Income in Canada

Several recent studies have focused on the topic of changes in the level of economic inequality in the United States. The prime questions of interest have been the following: Is there any evidence of an increasing (or decreasing) trend in the level of inequality? If so, what factors can explain the trend? For the most part, these studies can be separated into those that have family income inequality as their focus and those that analyze individual earnings inequality. (One exception is Blackburn and Bloom 1987, which analyzes both.) It is apparent from these studies that income inequality among families has been increasing, at least since the 1960s (see Blackburn and Bloom 1987; Levy 1988). The reasons that have been proposed to explain this trend include changes in the distribution of family size, the increase in the percentage of families with female heads, and the increased labor force participation rate of women, as well as the commonly suspected changes in the distribution of individuals' earnings. Blackburn and Bloom (1987) argue that the distinction between family income and individual earnings inequality is important over the period because changes in the individual earnings distribution are only part of the explanation for rising family income inequality. Studies of earnings inequality find an upward trend for males (but not for females or for all earners) that seems to have steepened in the 1980s (see Blackburn and Bloom 1987; Karoly 1988; Burtless 1990). Shifts in the demographic and industrial composition of the male working population have been suggested as possible explanations for the increase in male earnings inequality, though the evidence suggests that the increase is largely attributable to changes in the "structure" of wages, that is, changes in the returns to education and experience, and changes in the mean level of earnings within industries (e.g., see Juhn, Murphy, and Pierce 1989; Blackburn 1990).

Many of the issues noted above have also arisen in connection with recent work on the distributions of earnings and income in Canada. As in the United States, there appears to have been an upsurge of academic interest in these topics in the 1980s, and many of the same hypotheses to explain inequality changes have been considered in both countries. In this section, we briefly review the recent literature on inequality (and average income) trends in Canada. Appendix table 7A.1 further details selected aspects of these studies.

One of the earliest studies of Canadian income inequality is Henderson and Rowley (1977). In a detailed analysis using data from the Survey of Consumer Finances (SCF), these authors discovered a slight upward trend in the inequality of total family income over the years 1965–73. Since their empirical analysis suggests that income inequality is higher among smaller families and since family size declined in Canada in the years under study, they point to changes in family size as one of the major reasons for the increase. They also find that the decline in the percentage of families with at least one male earner, presumably due to both an increase in female-headed families and a decline in the rate of male labor force participation, is important to the increase, since families with no male earners have higher measured inequality.

Subsequent studies of family income inequality in Canada have also pointed to family-size and labor force participation rate changes as contributing to movements over time in the level of inequality.[1] Wolfson (1986) extends the time period studied by Henderson and Rowley to 1983; his results suggest that inequality increased in the late 1960s, decreased over the 1970s, and began to increase again in the early 1980s. Like Henderson and Rowley, he finds changes in the size and structure of families to be an important contributor to increased inequality; he also points to the rise in female labor force participation as another factor leading to increased inequality. He explains the fall in inequality over the 1970s in terms of the increases in both transfer and investment income as a percentage of total family income, since increases in both appear to have an equalizing effect on the family income distribution.

Dooley (1988) analyzes changes in the prevalence of low-income status in Canada from 1973 to 1986. Low-income status is similar to the official definition of poverty in the United States. Like changes in poverty rates in the United States, changes over time in the proportion of individuals that are in families classified as low-income can result from changes in the mean of the income distribution or from changes in the level of inequality characterizing the distribution.[2] Dooley finds that the low-income proportion fell from 1973 to 1979—due both to a decline in inequality and to an increase in the average level of real family income—but increased from 1979 to 1986 (although not

1. As alluded to earlier, this contrasts somewhat with the U.S. literature, which often treats changes in family income inequality as mainly reflective of changes in the earnings distribution for working males.

2. The low-income proportion could also change over time if the real value of the low-income cutoff levels changed; however, Dooley applies the 1986 values of the cutoffs to data from all of the years that he considers.

for the elderly, for whom it continued to decrease). Dooley attributes the fall in low-income percentages in the 1970s to declines in family size, increases in the level of government transfer payments, and increases in the level of wives' earnings;[3] the increase in the incidence of low income in the 1980s is argued to be related to the decline in the real value of husbands' earnings, especially among younger adults. Dooley (1989) focuses on the low-income status of children, finding that declining family size and increasing educational attainment of family heads are most important to the decline in the 1970s in the percentage of children in low-income families.[4]

McWatters and Beach (1990) present measures of both average family income and family income inequality for the years 1965–87. Like earlier studies, the figures they report suggest increasing inequality in the late 1960s and falling inequality in the 1970s. Their numbers also suggest that inequality was higher in 1984 than in 1979, but that it declined from 1984 to 1987. On the basis of time-series regressions of quintile shares on various aggregate-level variables, McWatters and Beach show that family income inequality is negatively associated with the rate of male labor force participation and positively associated with the rate of female labor force participation.

Compared to the literature pertaining to U.S. inequality trends, Canadian analyses have paid more attention to changes in the family income distribution and less attention to changes in the distribution of individual earnings. We are aware of only four recent studies for Canada focused on trends in the distribution of individual income or earnings. The study by Buse (1982) uses microlevel data from individual income tax returns to study individual income inequality from 1947 to 1978. Although changes in the definition of income over the period cloud his inferences somewhat, Buse finds an upward trend in inequality over the period as a whole. His time-series regressions also suggest that the overall labor force participation rate is a strong negative correlate of inequality.

While Dooley (1986) does not focus on earnings inequality per se, he does consider the extent to which there have been changes in the relationship between annual earnings and two individual characteristics: age and education. His findings suggest a relatively stable age-earnings relationship in the 1970s, and a large decline in the estimated return to schooling in the early 1970s. This latter finding parallels the results of Freeman (1976) for the United States. Both authors suggest that the phenomenon of generational crowding can explain some (but not all) of the decline in the return to schooling that they document.

In his 1987 paper, Dooley focuses on how earnings inequality among Ca-

3. The family-size effect likely works through increasing mean incomes within family-size categories, since (as mentioned above) other research using the same data finds that in Canada inequality tends to be higher among smaller families.

4. Changes in educational attainment were not studied as a contributor to changes in low-income incidence in Dooley (1988).

nadian men changed from 1971 to 1982. Focusing on seven years from that period, his results reveal no clear trend in the inequality of weekly earnings, or the inequality of annual earnings among full-time, year-round workers. Within age/education groups, however, he finds increases in earnings inequality among less-educated, younger males and declines in inequality among more-educated, older males. Regression results suggest that the unemployment rate was an important factor associated with increased earnings inequality (for some groups) over this period.

Myles, Picot, and Wannell (1988) also study changes in the distribution of individual earnings. They find that from 1981 to 1986 there was an increase in the percentage of male workers in low-wage jobs. However, they also find evidence of an increase in the employment share of what might be described as the upper middle portion of the hourly earnings distribution, so that the change in inequality over the period is not clear. They perform a shift-share analysis that suggests that industry and occupational changes played only a small role in the observed changes in the wage distribution.

To summarize the existing Canadian evidence (which tends to be more consistent across studies than the evidence for the United States), Canada appears to have experienced two periods of increasing family income inequality over the last twenty-five years: the late 1960s and the early 1980s. Prior to 1980, there were large increases in real incomes and corresponding declines in poverty rates; since 1980, there has been some reversal of these trends. The decline in family size in Canada is a factor that leads to higher inequality and, somewhat paradoxically, to lower poverty rates, while the increase in female labor force participation is found to be positively associated with the level of inequality. The evidence that is available on earnings distributions provides little indication of a significant trend in earnings inequality.

With the exception of Buse, and Myles, Picot, and Wannell, all of the studies we surveyed use the SCF as their source of data. As noted by Dooley (1986), one problem with using the SCF for this purpose is that, prior to 1977, Statistics Canada did not make available public use samples with information on income nonrespondents. Since 1977, however, they have imputed income values for nonrespondents to the income questions. With the Current Population Survey (CPS) in the United States, imputed incomes are provided over the entire history of the public use samples. With the CPS, it is clear that the characteristics of income nonrespondents tend to be different from those of income respondents (e.g., Lillard, Smith, and Welch 1986), so that the omission of income nonrespondents in the Canadian data before 1977 might seriously bias inequality comparisons between the pre- and post-1977 samples.[5]

5. This observation suggests that the studies of Canadian income inequality reviewed above (which all use the SCF) may have biased estimated of the change in inequality over the late 1970s. It would be useful to know if using only nonimputed incomes for the Canadian analysis after 1977 would change any conclusions regarding the level of inequality, but there are unfortunately no imputation flags in the Canadian public use samples.

For this reason, our use of the SCF is limited in this paper to the study of patterns and trends in the 1980s.

7.3 Welfare Comparisons for Families in Canada and the United States

7.3.1 Making Welfare Comparisons

For a population of n individuals, let $y_1, y_2, \ldots, y_n$ be the associated incomes subscripted such that $y_1 \leq y_2 \ldots \leq y_n$. The Lorenz-curve function is defined as

$$L(i/n) = \sum_{j=1}^{i} (y_i/n\bar{y}) \qquad \text{for } i \leq n, \tag{1}$$

where $\bar{y} = \sum_{j=1}^{n} (y_i/n)$. In addition to the Lorenz curve, there are also numerous scalar indices that are commonly used to make inequality comparisons between two distributions. Many of the indices, including those used in this section of the paper, satisfy the following property: if the Lorenz curve for one distribution lies above the Lorenz curve for a second distribution at one or more points and never lies below it at any other point, then the inequality index will be lower for the first distribution than for the second. However, the converse does not hold.[6] In what follows we measure inequality using the mean logarithmic deviation (MLD),

$$\text{MLD} = \sum_{i=1}^{n} \log(\bar{y}/y_i)/n;$$

the entropy index (E),

$$E = \sum_{i=1}^{n} [y_i \log (y_i/\bar{y})]/(n\bar{y});$$

and the Gini coefficient (G),

$$G = \sum_{i=1}^{n} \sum_{j=1}^{n} | y_i - y_j | /(n^2\bar{y}).$$

Atkinson (1987) was one of the first economists to consider the relation between inequality and social welfare. He showed that under fairly minimal

6. In section 7.4, we use the variance of logarithms as a measure of inequality since it possesses a convenient decomposition property (outlined in that section). Although it is widely used, the variance of logs does not satisfy the Lorenz-curve property.

assumptions income distributions could be compared in terms of their implied levels of social welfare on the basis of the location of their corresponding Lorenz curves. In particular, if the Lorenz curve for one distribution lies above the Lorenz curve for a second distribution at one or more values of the ordinate, and if the first distribution's Lorenz curve never lies below that of the second, then the first distribution has (lower inequality and) higher social welfare than the second. Two key assumptions underlie this result: (1) social welfare increases whenever the income received by any member of society increases; and (2) social welfare is a strictly quasi-concave[7] function of all individual incomes.[8] If the Lorenz curves for the two income distributions cross, nothing can be said about the relative social welfare associated with the two distributions without imposing additional structure on the social welfare function.

The usefulness of Atkinson's result is diminished by two important properties of the social welfare interpretation of Lorenz-curve comparisons. As can be seen from equation (1), the Lorenz curve will be the same for two distributions if either of the following is true: (1) one of the distributions is an n-fold replication of the other distribution; or (2) one distribution consists of incomes from the other distribution all multiplied by a common factor. This property suggests that Lorenz curves can be used to compare the "inequality" levels of income distributions, even if those distributions have different numbers of individuals or different mean incomes. These inequality comparisons lose any social-welfare interpretation, however, since social welfare is by assumption an increasing function of all incomes.

These limitations of Lorenz-curve comparisons can be circumvented by making comparisons of both the mean level of income and the level of income inequality. For example, if the mean of one distribution is higher and its inequality (in the Lorenz-curve sense) is lower, then the social welfare of that distribution must be higher (given the earlier assumptions); likewise, if the mean is lower and inequality is higher, social welfare must be lower. But this procedure is inconclusive when the mean and inequality move in the same direction. Fortunately, Shorrocks (1983) and Kakwani (1984) have extended the Atkinson result to comparisons of income distributions with different mean incomes. The structure of their result is similar to that of Atkinson: given the same assumptions about the social welfare function, one distribution

7. Strict quasi-concavity implies that the social welfare of the average of any two income distributions will be higher than the social welfare of at least one of the two distributions being averaged. Atkinson actually made a more restrictive assumption about social welfare than quasi-concavity: he assumed social welfare was the sum of individual strictly concave utility functions that were identical for all individuals. The less-restrictive result referred to here is from Dasgupta, Sen, and Starrett (1973), who show that the result holds assuming strict Schur concavity of the social welfare function (a less restrictive assumption than strict quasi-concavity).

8. Symmetry across income units in the aggregation of incomes into social welfare is also assumed.

corresponds to a higher level of social welfare than another if and only if its generalized Lorenz curve (GLC) lies above the other distribution's GLC at all ordinates, where the GLC is defined simply as the Lorenz curve multiplied by the mean income, that is,

$$\mathrm{GL}(i/n) = \sum_{j=1}^{i} (y_j/n) \qquad \text{for } i \leq n.$$

GLC comparisons are identical to the following sort of comparison: at the qth n-tile of the population for both distributions, compute the average income of all individuals with incomes less than y_q; if this average income is higher for all q for one of the distributions, then that distribution must have a higher level of social welfare.[9]

In section 7.3.2, we compare family income distributions in 1979 and 1987, for Canada and the United States, on both an inequality and a welfare basis. For meaningful welfare comparisons (e.g., for comparing GLCs) it is necessary to express incomes for different years in an identical year's currency. To this end, all incomes are expressed in 1987 U.S. dollars, correcting for inflation in the United States using the GNP personal consumption expenditure (PCE) deflator, for inflation in Canada using the consumer price index (CPI), and for the exchange from Canadian into U.S. dollars using a 1980 purchasing power parity measure provided by the OECD. Since the most tenuous part of these adjustments relates to the OECD measure of purchasing power parity, the comparisons of average income across countries should be interpreted cautiously.[10] Alternatively, the comparisons that we consider most

9. GLC comparisons can also be thought of in the following way. Suppose an expected-utility-maximizing individual has a choice between two probability distributions for determining his or her income. Assume that the individual's utility function is increasing and quasi-concave in income. Provided that the GLCs associated with the two distributions do not cross, the individual will choose the probability distribution with the higher GLC. If the GLCs do cross, our assumption about the utility function does not yield a certain prediction about which distribution he or she would choose.

The method of comparing distributions through GLCs corresponds identically to the criterion for second-order stochastic dominance that has been suggested in the finance literature (e.g., see Hadar and Russell 1974). It is also possible to compare income distributions on the basis of the criterion for first-order stochastic dominance, which would be appropriate if the restriction to quasi-concave welfare functions were not desirable. The first-order criterion is that the cumulative distribution function for one distribution lie below the cumulative distribution function for a second distribution in order for the first distribution to have higher welfare. The condition for first-order stochastic dominance is stronger than the second-order condition, in the sense that, if the first-order condition holds, then the second-order condition must also hold, while the converse is not true. Since the assumption of quasi-concavity does not seem overly restrictive to us, we focus primarily on GLC comparisons in our empirical work, although we do make some use of first-order comparisons.

10. For instance, if we used the purchasing power parities implicit in the tables provided in Summers and Heston (1988), the average incomes that we report for Canada in section 7.3.2 would be somewhat lower.

informative are those relating to how the U.S. and Canadian income distributions are changing differently over time.

7.3.2 Results

Comparisons of changes in income inequality across countries are more informative when the data from the countries are more similar—both in the kinds of income information collected and in the way in which the population being sampled is defined. In this section we use the CPS for the United States and the SCF for Canada to study the distribution of family income. These data sources provide information for nationally representative samples of the population of families in the United States and Canada, and both employ similar definitions of the family—two or more related persons living together (using the "economic" family concept for Canada). Both data sets also include information on individuals who live alone or with others to whom they are not related. These individuals are included in our analysis and treated as separate families. Total income also has a similar definition in the U.S. and Canadian data—cash income received over the preceding calendar year, excluding capital gains and any lump-sum payments received. Although several sources of income tend to be underreported in both surveys—in particular, some government transfer payments and investment income—the extent of underreporting appears to vary little across countries (and over time within countries). Both surveys also have upper limits on the amount of income from a particular source that can appear in the public use samples; we recoded incomes for some of the surveys so that all samples used would have the same top code for incomes ($50,000 in 1979 U.S. dollars). For both countries, we use data collected in 1980 and 1988, so that we have income information for 1979 and 1987.

One problem that naturally arises in measuring family income inequality relates to the fact that families of different sizes and compositions may require different amounts of income to be equally well-off.[11] We handle this problem in two ways: first, in addition to focusing on the distribution of total family income, we analyze a distribution of income that is standardized for family size and composition, that is, "equivalent" income; second, we classify all families into one of eight demographic types, our assumption being that all families of a particular type have roughly equal income needs. The eight family types are male unrelated individuals, female unrelated individuals, unmarried females living only with one child (under age 18), unmarried females living only with two or more children, married couples living with no children (or any other related individuals), married couples living only with one child,

11. For example, a distribution where all one-person families receive $10,000 and all two-person families receive $15,000 may be preferable to a distribution where all families receive the average income, although the latter distribution would be considered more equal if no account were taken of family size.

married couples living only with two or more children, and all other families. Disaggregating the data in this manner allows us to examine whether inequality or welfare is changing differently within these relatively homogeneous demographic groups.

The distribution of families according to demographic type is reported in the top panel of table 7.1 for the United States and Canada in 1979 and 1987.[12] The family breakdown is quite similar in both countries, the primary difference being that U.S. families are more likely to be female-headed and less likely to consist of married couples with two or more children. Our hope was to capture most of the families in the first seven categories, since comparisons of changes in inequality or welfare among families in the "other" category—families with children over 18, or with aunts, uncles, grandparents, and so forth—are less valid because the types of families that fall into this category can be quite varied. But, somewhat to our dismay, roughly one-fifth of the families in any year fall into the "other" category.

During the 1980s, the only family type that clearly grew in both countries was males living without relatives; female-headed families and females living without relatives increased their share in the United States but not in Canada, where there were instead sizable increases in the percentage of families classified as married couples with no children and as "other." The middle panel of table 7.1 reveals that the growth of unrelated individuals as a percentage of all families has been due to both more formerly married and more never-married individuals living without relatives. The increase in female-headed families in the United States has been almost entirely due to an increase in families headed by never-married females. The bottom panel shows that two-earner families have increased in both countries (and especially in Canada) among married couples with children. The relatively large growth in female-headed families and unrelated individuals in the United States led to the average number of earners per family actually falling in the United States from 1979 to 1987, in contrast to Canada, where the average increased.

Estimates of average total family income for each of the family types and for all families are reported in table 7.2. Among all families, total income grew at an annual rate of 0.7 percent in Canada and at a rate of only 0.4 percent in the U.S. Income grew for almost all family types in both countries, the exceptions being female-headed families with two or more children and "other" families in the United States. Married couples with children and families with female heads (with or without children) experienced the largest growth in average income in Canada, while females living alone and married-couple families had the highest income growth in the United States.[13] In both

12. Although the family distribution is actually measured at the time of the survey (i.e., 1980 and 1988), in order to minimize confusion we will refer to these family distributions as being for 1979 and 1987.

13. Using Canadian census data for 1980 and 1985, Dooley (1990) does not find an increase in average income for lone females with children, though he does report an increase in average

Table 7.1 Descriptive Statistics for the Family Population

	U.S.		Canada	
Variable	1979	1987	1979	1987
Family-type group (%)				
Lone male	13.7	15.6	13.0	14.1
Lone female	16.8	18.0	16.5	16.5
Female/1 child	2.3	2.7	1.7	1.6
Female/2+ children	3.0	3.1	1.5	1.6
Married/0 children	21.3	20.5	19.7	21.1
Married/1 child	8.2	7.5	8.9	7.4
Married/2+ children	15.0	13.3	19.0	16.5
Other	19.7	19.4	19.7	21.2
Families with head widowed, divorced, or separated (%)				
All families	26.6	28.0	19.2	19.8
Lone male	42.9	42.2	30.4	32.5
Lone female	64.8	63.2	51.6	51.5
Female/1 child	74.5	66.7	73.9	59.2
Female/2+ children	80.0	69.9	85.0	80.3
Married/0 children	—	—	—	—
Married/1 child	—	—	—	—
Married/2+ children	—	—	—	—
Other	29.1	32.4	21.2	21.5
Families with 2+ earners (%)				
All families	39.0	37.5	40.7	44.3
Lone male	—	—	—	—
Lone female	—	—	—	—
Female/1 child	6.6	7.7	6.5	8.3
Female/2+ children	11.5	9.0	9.1	10.9
Married/0 children	44.2	44.4	48.1	48.3
Married/1 child	69.6	76.0	66.3	77.1
Married/2+ children	60.8	68.5	55.0	71.7
Other	72.1	70.2	74.2	76.5
Average number of earners	1.34	1.29	1.27	1.43

Notes: The family population definition includes unrelated individuals—individuals living alone or with individuals to whom they are not related—as separate families. Children are defined as anyone under the age of 18. Sample weights were used in calculating all figures reported in tables 7.1–7.7

countries, income growth was most rapid among families with no earners, while families with only one earner experienced the slowest income growth over the period.

Table 7.3 examines the sources of total family income and the strength of

transfers received by such families. Whether this difference in findings is due to different ways in which the data were collected or handled or to differences in the specific years being studied is not clear.

Table 7.2 **Average Total Family Income (in 1987 U.S. dollars)**

	U.S.			Canada		
Population Group	1979	1987	Growth Rate (%)[a]	1979	1987	Growth Rate (%)[a]
All families	27,043	28,026	0.4	26,438	28,066	0.7
Among family type						
Lone male	18,021	19,137	0.8	16,281	16,601	0.2
Lone female	11,846	14,000	2.1	11,679	13,398	1.7
Female/1 child	13,181	13,497	0.3	11,633	13,039	1.4
Female/2+ children	12,144	11,522	−0.7	12,789	14,336	1.4
Married/0 children	30,231	32,022	0.7	28,123	29,675	0.7
Married/1 child	33,314	36,759	1.2	31,745	34,533	1.1
Married/2+ children	34,992	36,936	0.7	32,921	36,026	1.1
Other	38,037	37,996	−0.0	37,451	39,149	0.6
Number of earners						
0	10,836	12,466	1.8	9,246	12,801	4.1
1	22,836	23,244	0.2	21,639	21,527	−0.1
2	36,501	39,145	0.9	35,633	37,018	0.5
3+	48,851	50,561	0.4	47,250	48,324	0.3

Notes: The conversion to 1987 U.S. dollars used the GNP PCE deflator for the U.S., the Canadian CPI reported in the *Year Book of Labor Statistics, 1987* (Geneva: International Labour Office), and the purchasing power parities developed by the OECD. Total family income includes cash income for all family members, excluding capital gains and one-time lump-sum receipts. Income figures were top coded at 50,000 1979 US dollars.

[a]These are estimated annual (exponential) growth rates, calculated using the 1979 and 1987 endpoints.

Table 7.3 **Components of Total Family Income**

	U.S.		Canada	
	1979	1987	1979	1987
Percentage of income from				
Total family earnings (TFE)	82.9	81.0	83.8	79.7
Property income (PI)[a]	5.7	7.0	5.8	5.3
Transfer income (TI)[b]	11.4	12.0	10.4	15.1
Correlation between				
TFE and PI	0.040	0.036	0.013	0.015
TFE and TI	−0.423	−0.434	−0.414	−0.453
PI and TI	−0.133	−0.094	−0.063	−0.020

[a]Property income consists of interest and dividend income but does not include private pension income.

[b]Transfer income includes both government cash transfers and some private cash transfers (e.g., alimony and child support), as well as government and private pension income.

their association within families. Income is divided into three sources: total family earnings, property income, and transfer income.[14] One relevant fact evident from table 7.3 is that, while transfer income increased as a percentage of total family income in both countries, the increase in transfers was especially large in Canada. The share of income from property sources increased in the United States, while the share coming from total family earnings decreased in both countries. The only notable change in the correlations between sources of income was the increased absolute value of the negative correlation between transfer income and total family earnings in Canada, suggesting that transfer income became more redistributive in Canada from 1979 to 1987.

One limitation of using statistics for average total family income (reported in table 7.2) to study changes over time in the average level of economic well-being is that these statistics essentially double-count the contribution of transfers. This is because total family income is a pretax, posttransfer measure of income. For instance, an economy that experiences no growth in factor income, but increases the amount of money (frictionlessly) transferred through the government (and therefore the rate of taxation in order to finance the increased transfers), will record an increase in average total family income (as it is measured in table 7.2), even though there has been no change in the average well-being of families. Such double-counting is likely to influence substantially our inferences about average income growth, since transfer income increased in both the United States and Canada during the 1980s. To circumvent this problem, we measured factor income only (i.e., earnings plus property income) in recalculating average income for the economy as a whole. With this measure, we find that average family income growth was actually higher in the United States (0.18 percent per annum) than in Canada (0.08 percent per annum) from 1979 to 1987, showing that almost all of the growth in average income observed in table 7.2 for Canada and about half of the increase for the United States was due to increased transfers. Also, using factor income only shows average income to be roughly $500 higher in the United States than in Canada in 1987 (rather than being roughly equal in the two countries, as table 7.2 suggests).

Table 7.4 presents Lorenz-curve coordinates for the distribution of total family income (including transfer income) among all families and within family types. Comparisons of Lorenz curves are made at quintile points of the income distributions.[15] Among all families in the United States, the Lorenz

14. There is likely to be some misclassification of income in table 7.3 (if income from privately held pensions is considered property income), since a lack of detail in the public use samples made it necessary to include all pension income as part of transfer income. Note also that property income is underreported by 40 to 55 percent in both surveys.

15. Strictly speaking, the curves should be compared at every point available in order to determine whether they cross. However, a comparison of selected curves at decile (and finer) levels indicates that our substantive conclusions are not sensitive to the fineness of the comparison.

Table 7.4 **Lorenz-Curve Coordinate at Quintile Points, for Total Family Income**

Family Type	U.S. 1979	U.S. 1987	U.S. Δ[a]	Canada 1979	Canada 1987	Canada Δ[a]
All families						
First quintile	.039	.035		.043	.048	
Second quintile	.139	.131		.151	.156	
Third quintile	.310	.298	+	.331	.330	?
Fourth quintile	.568	.558		.590	.585	
Lone male						
First quintile	.035	.031		.043	.046	
Second quintile	.133	.124		.140	.147	
Third quintile	.302	.283	+	.316	.312	?
Fourth quintile	.554	.536		.573	.567	
Lone female						
First quintile	.045	.040		.052	.062	
Second quintile	.143	.132		.149	.173	
Third quintile	.297	.283	+	.297	.326	–
Fourth quintile	.539	.528		.549	.566	
Female/1 child						
First quintile	.039	.031		.048	.070	
Second quintile	.142	.115		.155	.183	
Third quintile	.319	.270	+	.326	.335	–
Fourth quintile	.581	.527		.573	.584	
Female/2 + children						
First quintile	.045	.038		.047	.074	
Second quintile	.152	.125		.158	.199	
Third quintile	.313	.266	+	.313	.356	–
Fourth quintile	.558	.502		.546	.583	
Married/0 children						
First quintile	.058	.059		.062	.071	
Second quintile	.175	.175		.179	.189	
Third quintile	.351	.351	–	.365	.363	?
Fourth quintile	.603	.603		.619	.609	
Married/1 child						
First quintile	.076	.066		.080	.078	
Second quintile	.216	.198		.229	.220	
Third quintile	.405	.385	+	.421	.410	+
Fourth quintile	.647	.633		.661	.651	
Married/2 + children						
First quintile	.076	.067		.083	.085	
Second quintile	.220	.203		.234	.233	
Third quintile	.408	.391	+	.424	.422	?
Fourth quintile	.647	.637		.660	.660	
Other						
First quintile	.057	.051		.068	.072	
Second quintile	.181	.169		.203	.205	
Third quintile	.369	.353	+	.393	.392	?
Fourth quintile	.628	.620		.645	.644	

Note: The numbers reported are the Lorenz-curve values at ordinates i/n = .2 (first quintile), .4 (second quintile), .6 (third quintile), and .8 (fourth quintile).

[a]This column indicates the direction of change in inequality based on shifts in the Lorenz curves from 1979 to 1987, with a "+" representing an increase, a "–" representing a decrease, and a "?" representing an inconclusive change.

curve for the 1987 distribution lies below the Lorenz curve for the 1979 distribution, implying that inequality was clearly higher in the United States in 1987 than in 1979. No conclusion can be drawn about changes in inequality over this period in Canada, since the Lorenz curve shifts in at the lower quintile points—reflecting an increase in the share of income going to those families at the bottom of the distribution—and shifts out at higher quintile points. The three inequality indices mentioned above are reported in table 7.5; focusing only on these would suggest that inequality fell in Canada, though table 7.4 tells us that it is possible this conclusion would change if other inequality indices were used. Comparing the United States to Canada, we find that family income inequality is higher in the United States than in Canada in both 1979 and 1987.

One potential explanation for the differences between Canada and the United States in the change over time in family income inequality is that the two countries' family-type distributions have shifted differently over time. We might conclude that changes in inequality are largely explained by changes in the distribution of family types if inequality did not change among families within family types.[16] But table 7.4 reveals that increased inequality within the United States is not due solely to such family-type changes, since the Lorenz curves shifted outward from 1979 to 1987 for seven of the eight family types in the United States (the exception being married couples with no children).[17] Income inequality is lower in Canada than in the United States for all eight family types.[18] Within family types in Canada, inequality clearly fell for lone females and female-headed families with children, but appears not to have changed for the other family types (except for married couples with no children, for whom inequality appears to have increased).

To construct GLCs, one can simply multiply the Lorenz-curve coordinates by average income. In order to use only factor income in calculating average incomes, we adjusted each family's income by multiplying it by the ratio of average factor income to average total income.[19] The results are reported in

16. It is also true that changes in the variation of average incomes across family types can lead to changes in overall inequality, even if the family-type distribution and the level of inequality within family types remained constant.

17. The mean logarithmic deviation (MLD) is particularly useful when decomposing inequality into contributions from subgroups of the population (see Bourguignon 1979). For both countries, we decomposed the observed change in MLD from 1979 to 1987 into portions due to (1) changes in the percentage of families within family types; (2) changes in mean incomes within family types; and (3) changes in MLD within subgroups. Roughly one-third of the increase in MLD for the United States (0.018 points) can be attributed to changes in family-type percentages; changes in family-type percentages also worked to increase MLD in Canada, but the size of its contribution in Canada (0.006 points) was only one-third the size of the U.S. contribution. In both countries, changes in group means had a negative impact on MLD, while within-group changes in MLD constituted the major source of change in the overall value for this inequality index.

18. This is true in both 1979 and 1987.

19. The same ratio (the one for the economy as a whole) was used for adjusting average total income for each of the family types. This is preferable to using the ratio of these incomes among families in the family type in question, since average well-being for a group is not necessarily

Table 7.5 **Indices of Inequality for Total Family Income**

	U.S.		Canada	
Family Type	1979	1987	1979	1987
All families				
MLD	.425	.466	.348	.295
Entropy	.263	.278	.229	.222
Gini	.398	.411	.373	.371
Lone males				
MLD	.601	.632	.426	.361
Entropy	.302	.325	.264	.257
Gini	.416	.436	.394	.394
Lone females				
MLD	.526	.596	.469	.296
Entropy	.299	.320	.276	.231
Gini	.417	.434	.407	.373
Female/1 child				
MLD	.485	.578	.312	.219
Entropy	.258	.335	.238	.203
Gini	.389	.449	.381	.353
Female/2 + children				
MLD	.464	.543	.330	.219
Entropy	.268	.354	.266	.192
Gini	.398	.457	.400	.339
Married/0 children				
MLD	.250	.252	.222	.191
Entropy	.194	.188	.172	.168
Gini	.343	.341	.327	.324
Married/1 child				
MLD	.168	.201	.150	.170
Entropy	.129	.152	.111	.119
Gini	.278	.302	.258	.271
Married/2 + children				
MLD	.186	.206	.150	.125
Entropy	.131	.144	.109	.105
Gini	.275	.295	.254	.254
Other				
MLD	.237	.272	.184	.164
Entropy	.170	.186	.137	.132
Gini	.320	.336	.290	.288

Notes: MLD is the mean logarithmic deviation. In calculating MLD and entropy, nonpositive incomes were recoded as $1. Incomes were not recoded in calculating the Gini coefficient.

related to the average factor income earned by that group. Note that the use of the same ratio in adjusting all incomes implies that the Lorenz curves for the distribution of total family income adjusted in this way will be the same as those reported in table 7.4.

It would be even more desirable to analyze a posttax, posttransfer measure of income. However, there is no information on direct taxes in the United States or on indirect taxes in either country in the data we use. Further, any assignment of the distributional burden of government borrowing or inflation would be highly speculative, given the current state of knowledge on these burdens.

table 7.6. For the most part, focusing on this set of GLCs does not change any of the substantive conclusions reached earlier for Canada: for all families, it cannot be said that welfare increased, though for families headed by females (including lone females) social welfare was clearly higher in 1987 than in 1979.

For the United States, the results suggest that for all families and within most family types increases in average income were not large enough to offset increases in inequality and unambiguously increase social welfare from 1979 to 1987.[20] Two exceptions for which welfare was clearly higher in 1987 are lone females—whose high rate of growth in average income offset their increase in inequality—and married couples with no children. The fact that average incomes fell while inequality increased for U.S. female-headed families with at least two children led to this group's being the only one in the two countries that was clearly worse off in 1987 than in 1979.

Our second method for comparing inequality and welfare in a manner that reflects needs differences across families is to standardize the income of each family for the family's size and composition. Thus, we measure the number of "equivalent adults" in families with different numbers of individuals, divide the family's income by the number of equivalent adults, and then weight each family's equivalent income by the number of individuals in the family (so that we are measuring the distribution of equivalent family income across individuals, not families; see Danziger and Taussig 1979). The equivalence scales we use are those implicit in the U.S. Bureau of Labor Statistics' poverty lines; we also use per capita family income as an alternative standardization (which, it should be noted, takes no account of any household economies of scale, unlike the first standardization described above). Lorenz curves and GLCs for these two types of distributions are reported in table 7.7.[21] These numbers suggest that income inequality fell (or at least did not increase) in Canada from 1979 to 1987, while average income increased,[22] so that both of these family income distributions in 1987 were preferable to those in Canada in 1979. For the United States, both the inequality and the mean of these distributions increased, leading to the GLCs crossing for the two years and leaving the change in welfare indeterminate.

In summary, the results of this section suggest that changes in the family income distribution from 1979 to 1987 were very different in Canada and in the United States. While average income (using factor income only) appears to have grown at a somewhat faster pace in the United States than in Canada, income inequality clearly increased in the United States but not in Canada. In

20. One implication of second-order stochastic dominance comparisons is that a necessary condition for welfare to decrease (increase) is that average income must decrease (increase). Since average income did not decrease for all but two of the family types in the United States, it follows that welfare for these family types could not have unambiguously declined.

21. We again multiply all incomes by the ratio of average factor income to average total income.

22. The fifth quintile coordinate for the GLC is by construction equal to the average income.

Table 7.6 Generalized Lorenz-Curve Coordinates at Quintiles, for Total Family Income[1]

	U.S.			Canada		
Family Type	1979	1987	Δ[a]	1979	1987	Δ[a]
All families						
First quintile	924	819		1,009	1,152	
Second quintile	3,340	3,116		3,576	3,709	
Third quintile	7,422	7,146	?	7,840	7,863	?
Fourth quintile	13,622	13,480		13,974	13,948	
Fifth quintile	23,968	24,324		23,678	23,828	
Lone male						
First quintile	553	527		622	642	
Second quintile	2,132	2,081		2,048	2,068	
Third quintile	4,816	4,773	?	4,608	4,399	?
Fourth quintile	8,855	9,022		8,349	7,993	
Fifth quintile	15,972	16,844		14,581	14,094	
Lone female						
First quintile	476	494		542	708	
Second quintile	1,502	1,623		1,555	1,969	
Third quintile	3,116	3,484	+	3,106	3,704	+
Fourth quintile	5,663	6,508		5,739	6,442	
Fifth quintile	10,499	12,328		10,460	11,375	
Female/1 child						
First quintile	456	367		505	776	
Second quintile	1,655	1,371		1,612	2,025	
Third quintile	3,728	3,203	?	3,392	3,707	+
Fourth quintile	6,786	6,255		5,971	6,470	
Fifth quintile	11,682	11,880		10,418	11,070	
Female/2+ children						
First quintile	482	384		538	898	
Second quintile	1,632	1,268		1,805	2,424	
Third quintile	3,364	2,693	−	3,584	4,335	+
Fourth quintile	6,003	5,096		6,258	7,090	
Fifth quintile	10,763	10,142		11,453	12,171	
Married/0 children						
First quintile	1,564	1,706		1,558	1,791	
Second quintile	4,676	5,096		4,514	4,758	
Third quintile	9,414	10,203	+	9,186	9,156	?
Fourth quintile	16,238	17,529		15,585	15,350	
Fifth quintile	26,794	28,186		25,187	25,194	
Married/1 child						
First quintile	2,250	2,123		2,283	2,286	
Second quintile	6,380	6,416		6,504	6,457	
Third quintile	11,964	12,454	?	11,980	12,016	?
Fourth quintile	19,095	20,496		18,803	19,091	
Fifth quintile	29,526	32,355		28,431	29,319	
Married/2+ children						
First quintile	2,358	2,191		2,456	2,610	
Second quintile	6,811	6,601		6,900	7,129	
Third quintile	12,652	12,707	?	12,509	12,915	+

Table 7.6 (continued)

	U.S.			Canada		
Family Type	1979	1987	Δ[a]	1979	1987	Δ[a]
Fourth quintile	20,064	20,712		19,466	20,174	
Fifth quintile	31,013	32,511		29,484	30,586	
Other						
First quintile	1,909	1,698		2,288	2,398	
Second quintile	6,098	5,640		6,804	6,818	
Third quintile	12,439	11,818	–	13,172	13,036	?
Fourth quintile	21,185	20,729		21,644	21,401	
Fifth quintile	33,712	33,443		33,541	33,238	

Note: The coordinates are expressed in 1987 U.S. dollars and are corrected for double-counting of transfer income.

[a]This column indicates the direction of change in social welfare based on shifts in the GLCs from 1979 to 1987, with a "+" representing an increase, a "–" representing a decrease, and a "?" representing an inconclusive change.

Table 7.7 **Welfare and Inequality Comparisons for Other Definitions of Income**

	U.S.			Canada		
Income Definition	1979	1987	Δ[a]	1979	1987	Δ[a]
Per capita income[b]						
Lorenz curve coordinates						
First quintile	.050	.042		.063	.067	
Second quintile	.162	.148	+	.183	.191	–
Third quintile	.329	.313		.353	.361	
Fourth quintile	.569	.557		.590	.597	
GLC coordinates						
First quintile	462	425		557	632	
Second quintile	1,509	1,500		1,619	1,792	
Third quintile	3,064	3,170	?	3,121	3,389	+
Fourth quintile	5,298	5,643		5,211	5,597	
Fifth quintile	9,313	10,133		8,839	9,382	
Inequality measures						
Mean log deviation	.336	.387		.253	.213	
Entropy	.249	.273		.202	.187	
Gini coefficient	.380	.401		.346	.335	
Equivalent income[c]						
Lorenz curve coordinates						
First quintile	.052	.044		.064	.069	
Second quintile	.172	.157	+	.194	.198	–
Third quintile	.350	.333		.377	.379	
Fourth quintile	.600	.588		.623	.624	
GLC coordinates						
First quintile	852	772		1,015	1,136	
Second quintile	2,816	2,725		3,062	3,276	

(continued)

Table 7.7 (continued)

	U.S.			Canada		
Income Definition	1979	1987	Δ[a]	1979	1987	Δ[a]
Third quintile	5,739	5,788	?	5,965	6,275	+
Fourth quintile	9,828	10,218		9,853	10,325	
Fifth quintile	16,388	17,380		15,827	16,551	
Inequality measures						
Mean log deviation	.305	.354		.227	.192	
Entropy	.207	.229		.164	.156	
Gini coefficient	.350	.371		.315	.310	
Total family earnings[d]						
Lorenz curve coordinates						
First quintile	.038	.035		.044	.039	
Second quintile	.149	.139	+	.166	.153	+
Third quintile	.328	.313		.352	.334	
Fourth quintile	.585	.573		.607	.592	
Inequality measures						
Mean log deviation	.366	.402		.310	.338	
Entropy	.239	.258		.208	.230	
Gini coefficient	.379	.395		.352	.371	
Average total family earnings, by number of earners						
1 earners	19,568	19,497		18,534	17,521	
2 earners	34,015	36,477		32,579	33,430	
3+ earners	45,768	47,454		43,338	44,122	
All families with earnings	28,076	29,027		26,863	28,063	

[a]This column indicates the direction of change in either inequality or social welfare (whichever is relevant).

[b]The per capita income distribution uses total family income (adjusted for transfer double-counting) per person in the family as the income measure for each individual in the family; the distribution is measured across persons.

[c]Equivalent income for each person is total family income (adjusted for transfer double-counting) divided by the number of equivalent nonelderly adults in the family; the distribution is measured across persons.

[d]The total family earnings distribution uses all earned income of individuals in the family as the income measure; the distribution is measured across all families with positive earnings.

both countries, social welfare can be said to have increased for some family-type groups but not for all groups. If corrections for differences in family needs are made using equivalence scales, however, it becomes clear that the 1987 Canadian distribution is preferable to the 1979 Canadian distribution, while no clear conclusions about changes in social welfare in the United States can be made.[23]

23. We also calculated values of the empirical cumulative distribution function for the equivalent income distribution. The results show that the first-order stochastic dominance comparisons lead to the same conclusions about social welfare changes (using the equivalent income distribution) as the second-order stochastic dominance comparisons. This is because the cumulative dis-

Increases in transfer income seem to have played a large role in keeping income inequality from increasing in Canada. Table 7.7 also presents inequality measures and distributional comparisons for total family earnings among families with positive earnings. In both countries, average total family earnings grew, but the inequality of earnings also grew. The fact that the inequality of family earnings increased in Canada, while the inequality of family income did not, suggests that the growth of transfer income—which from table 7.3 we know is strongly and increasingly negatively correlated with earnings—has had an equalizing impact on the distribution of economic well-being in Canada. The fact that inequality clearly fell in Canada only among families headed by females (including lone females) further suggests the importance of increasing transfer income, since these families are the ones most directly affected by changes in transfer policy.

7.4 Changes in the Distribution of Male Earnings

A topic of research that has begun to garner wide attention in the United States is the recent increase in the dispersion of earnings among males. As noted in section 7.3, the inequality of total family earnings increased in both Canada and the United States in the 1980s. Earnings inequality among a comparably defined sample of prime-age male earners also appears to have increased from 1979 to 1987 in both countries. In this section we examine the forces that may have worked to increase earnings inequality among males in both countries and that have potentially contributed to an increase in family income inequality in the United States.

We focus our analysis on the earnings of a sample of male workers aged 25–64, who worked full-time year-round in the previous calendar year and who were either the head of their economic family or were the husband in a married couple that headed an economic family.[24] Descriptive statistics for the samples, which are drawn from the 1980 and 1988 SCF and CPS, are presented in table 7.8. Using the variance of the natural logarithm of earnings as our measure of inequality, we see that earnings inequality among males increased in both countries during the 1980s, with the increase being slightly

tribution function for Canada in 1987 has a lower value than the 1979 function at all levels of income, while the 1987 U.S. distribution function lies above the 1979 function at lower income levels but falls below the 1979 function at higher income levels.

24. The definition of *full-time* differs slightly in the two countries—35 hours or more per week in the United States, but only 30 hours or more per week in Canada. Relatively few male workers work between 30 and 35 hours per week in the United States, however, so this difference is not likely to be of much importance to our results.

Earnings information is available in the Canadian SCF public use sample of "economic" families (defined as two or more related individuals living together, and unrelated individuals) for the household head (husband if a married-couple family) and wife only. This fact made the restriction to household heads necessary.

Table 7.8 Descriptive Statistics for the Male, Full-Time Year-Round, Prime-Age Population

	U.S.		Canada	
Income Level	1979	1987	1979	1987
Variance of the logarithm of annual earnings	.286	.320	.270	.288
Married (%)	86.3	80.7	88.4	85.5
Widowed, divorced, separated (%)	7.2	9.3	4.5	5.3
Age groups (%)				
25–34	33.2	32.4	34.1	30.8
35–44	27.3	32.2	28.2	32.9
45–54	23.0	21.9	22.9	22.9
55–64	16.5	13.5	14.8	13.4
Education groups (%)				
Less than high school	20.3	14.1	36.2	24.9
High school graduate	35.5	36.4	30.1	31.5
Some college	18.1	18.9	18.9	23.3
College graduate	26.1	30.6	14.8	20.3
Region (%)				
Northeast	20.6	24.3	—	—
North central	24.7	24.4	—	—
South	28.6	29.8	—	—
West	26.1	21.5	—	—
Atlantic	—	—	7.0	7.3
Quebec	—	—	25.5	24.5
Ontario	—	—	38.8	39.5
Prarie	—	—	17.2	17.0
British Columbia	—	—	11.5	11.7
Sample size	27,626	24,693	16,821	17,954

Notes: Prime age is defined as 25–64 years. For the United States, *full-time year-round* is defined as working an average of at least 35 hours per week for at least 50 weeks over the year; for Canada, it is defined as working 30 hours per week for at least 50 weeks. The samples are restricted to either heads of families or spouses of heads of families. Sample weights were used in the calculations for tables 7.8–7.10 for Canada, but not for the United States (where the provided weights vary relatively little).

larger in the United States than in Canada.[25] In addition, characteristics of the samples changed in a very similar fashion in both countries from 1979 to 1987, with educational attainment clearly increasing and the percentage married falling. The age composition of the population shows that the baby boom

25. Inspection of Lorenz curves reveals that earnings inequality among males increased unambiguously over the period in both countries, as did the other three inequality indices, so that our use of the variance of logs does provide an accurate indication of the direction of changes in earnings dispersion.

was of longer duration in the United States, since the age distributions look very similar in 1979, but the entering cohorts in the 1980s were relatively much smaller in Canada than in the United States.

The coefficients from OLS earnings regressions for both countries in 1979 and 1987 are reported in table 7.9. The dependent variable is the logarithm of annual earnings, and the independent variables fall into four classes: age and age squared, three educational-attainment dummies, two marital status dummies, and eight (United States) or four (Canada) region dummies. Comparing the estimates across countries for a given year, one sees that the age and marital status coefficients are reasonably similar, but the earnings differences related to education are much larger in the United States. Over the 1980s, changes occurred in the structure of earnings in both countries, but in very different ways. For instance, there was little change in the age-earnings relationship in the United States, but in Canada the rate of growth of earnings at the younger ages appears to have increased. The marital status effects decreased in the 1980s in the United States, but there was no (statistically) significant change in the marital status differentials in Canada. Most important, there was an increase in the education-related earnings differences in the United States, but from our estimates there appears to have been no such change in Canada.

Figures 7.1 and 7.2 provide more detail concerning the change in the education-earnings relationship by plotting estimates of the education-

Table 7.9 OLS Estimates of Annual Earnings Equations

	U.S.		Canada	
Independent Variable	1979	1987	1979	1987
Age	.055	.056	.051	.056
	(.002)	(.003)	(.003)	(.003)
Age^2/100	−.057	−.057	−.057	−.061
	(.003)	(.003)	(.003)	(.004)
High school graduate	.274	.270	.175	.152
	(.008)	(.010)	(.010)	(.010)
Some college	.372	.402	.226	.222
	(.010)	(.011)	(.011)	(.011)
College graduate	.570	.652	.475	.465
	(.009)	(.010)	(.012)	(.011)
Married	.230	.176	.220	.197
	(.012)	(.011)	(.015)	(.013)
Widowed, divorced, separated	.125	.080	.107	.145
	(.016)	(.015)	(.023)	(.021)
R^2	.18	.21	.13	.13

Notes: The regressions also include eight region dummies for the United States and four region dummies for Canada, as independent variables. The dependent variable is the natural logarithm of annual earnings.

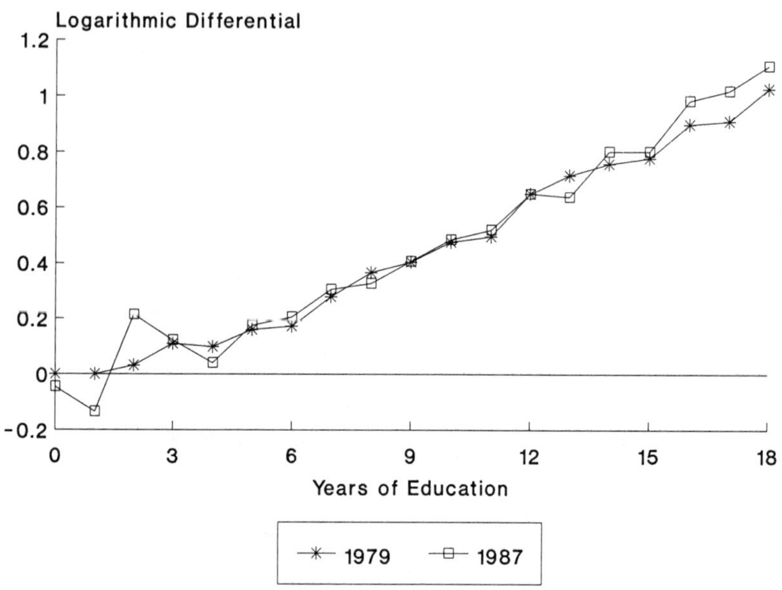

Fig. 7.1 Education-related earnings differentials in the United States
Note: The differentials in 1987 were scaled so that the 1979 and 1987 high school differentials are equal.

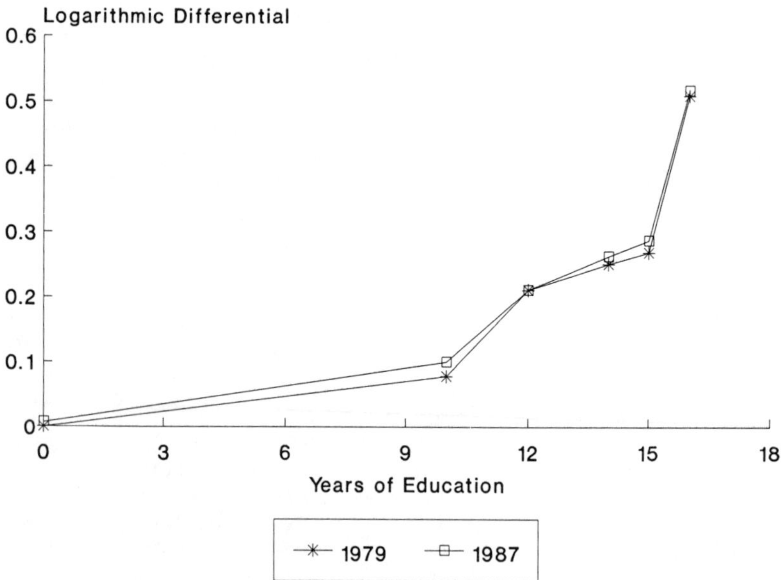

Fig. 7.2 Education-related earnings differentials in Canada
Note: The differentials in 1987 were scaled so that the 1979 and 1987 high school differentials are equal.

earnings profile using the complete years of schooling information available in the data (i.e., eighteen education dummies in the United States, one for each year of education, and five education dummies in Canada). The regressions from which the statistics in these figures are drawn also include as independent variables thirty-nine age dummies (one for each age) and the marital status and region dummies. In the figures, the 1987 regression coefficients were rescaled so that the value for the high school–dummy coefficient was equal to the same country's 1979 value for that dummy's coefficient; any changes in the plotted relationship can thus be interpreted as changes in how workers with a given number of years of schooling are doing relative to high school–only workers.[26] Inspection of the graphs shows that the only major change for either country is among U.S. workers with sixteen or more years of schooling, a group whose relative earnings clearly increased from 1979 to 1987.[27]

Using these estimated earnings equations, the variance of logs can be decomposed into variation contributed by the variances and covariances of the independent variables; this allows us to measure the contribution of each independent variable to the increase in the variance of logs (see Blackburn 1990). In particular, if earnings (w) can be represented as

$$w = \exp\left(\sum_{j=1}^{J} \beta_j' x_j + \varepsilon\right), \tag{2}$$

where x_j is a vector of associated independent variables, β_j is the corresponding coefficient vector, J is the number of subsets of regressors (e.g., $J = 4$ in this analysis because we consider vectors of age, education, marital status, and region dummies), and ε is an independently distributed error term, then the variance of logs can be represented as

$$\sigma^2_{\ln w} = \sum_{j=1}^{J} \beta_j' \Omega_{jj} \beta_j + \sum_{j=1}^{J} \sum_{k=j+1}^{J} 2\beta_j' \Omega_{jk} \beta_k + \sigma^2_{\varepsilon}, \tag{3}$$

where Ω_{jk} is the covariance matrix for x_j and x_k. The coefficient vectors and coefficient matrices were estimated for both countries in both years, and the different components of the decomposition are referred to as "primary variance effects" in table 7.10.

The results for the United States suggest that the biggest contributor to the increase in earnings variation from 1979 to 1987 was education (i.e., the composite effect of changes in the covariance matrix for the education dummies

26. The rescaling involved subtracting the difference between the 1987 and 1979 high school–dummy coefficients from all of the other 1987 education-dummy coefficients (including the zero value for the coefficient for zero years of schooling).

27. For several recent analyses of the reasons behind the increase in the return to education among males in the United States, see Murphy and Welch 1988; Bound and Johnson 1992; Katz and Revenga 1989; and Blackburn, Bloom, and Freeman 1990.

Table 7.10 **Decomposition of the Variance of Logarithms**

	U.S.			Canada		
Effect	1979	1987	Δ	1979	1987	Δ
Primary variance effects						
Age	.009	.010	.001	.005	.007	.002
Education	.043	.052	.009	.025	.026	.001
Marital status (MST)	.004	.003	−.001	.003	.003	.000
Region	.004	.005	.001	.003	.003	.000
Cov(age, education)	−.004	.000	.004	−.002	−.002	.000
Cov(age, MST)	.002	.003	.001	.001	.002	.001
Cov(education, MST)	−.002	−.001	.001	−.002	−.002	.000
Residual variance effects[a]						
Age	—	—	−.002	—	—	.001
Education	—	—	−.001	—	—	−.002
Marital status	—	—	.003	—	—	.002
Region	—	—	−.004	—	—	−.001
Variance of logarithms	.286	.320	.034	.270	.288	.018
Δ accounted for	—	—	.012	—	—	.004
Δ unaccounted for	—	—	.022	—	—	.014

Notes: The log earnings regressions included two marital status dummies, thirty-nine age dummies, seventeen education dummies (five education dummies for Canada), and eight region dummies (four region dummies in Canada) as independent variables. The residual variance regressions used the same independent variables. The covariance effects between the region variables and the other three sets of variables were small and inconsequential and are not reported.

[a]The effects were calculated by multiplying the change in the means of the independent variables over the two years (for any one country) by the residual variance equation coefficient estimates in 1979 for that country.

and changes in the education-dummy coefficients). The other important contributor to the increase in the variance of logs in the United States is the covariance between age and education. Educational attainment actually declined slightly among the youngest cohorts in the 1980s, thereby increasing the covariance between age and education, which added to the increase in the variance of logs, since both age and education are positively related to earnings.[28] In contrast to these results for the United States, the education effect and the age-education covariance effect are not important to the increase in the variance of logs in Canada; in fact, the difference in the magnitude of these two effects explains 75 percent of the difference between the two countries in the increase in the variance of logs from 1979 to 1987.

28. The change in the variance of logarithms can be more finely decomposed into portions due to changes in the coefficients and changes in the covariance matrices. This decomposition shows that the increase in the education effect in the United States is due entirely to changes in the education-dummy coefficients, and that the increase in the age-education covariance effect is due entirely to an increase in the covariance between age and education.

For both countries, more than half of the increase in the variance of logs is attributable to the increase in the residual variance (i.e., σ_ε^2 in equation [3]). Following Blackburn (1990), we also consider the possibility that the magnitude (and therefore the change in the magnitude) of the residual variance is related to the composition (and the change in the composition) of the population. For example, the residual variance may be expected to increase as the age of the working population increases (e.g., as is predicted by the job-matching theory of Harris and Holmstrom 1982). Therefore, we estimated equations with the squared error term (ε^2) as the dependent variable, and with the same independent variables as in equation (2); of course, ε^2 is not observed, so we used the squared residual from the earnings equations as the dependent variable, that is, we estimated

$$\hat{\varepsilon}^2 = \exp(\sum_{j=1}^{J} \gamma_j' x_j + \nu),$$

where $\hat{\varepsilon}$ is the predicted error term from equation (2), γ_j is a vector of coefficients, and ν is an error term. Using the estimates of γ_j for 1979, we estimated how the change in the independent variables would be expected to change σ_ε^2 by multiplying the change in the average of each independent variable by the associated coefficient from the residual variance equation. The resulting predictions are reported in the "residual variance effects" section of table 7.10.

In both countries, marital status changes have tended to increase the residual variance (and therefore the variance of logs), since unmarried (and especially never-married) males tend to have larger unexplained earnings variation. In the United States, the movement toward the Northeast (where the residual variance is lower) has tended to decrease the variance of logs. The increase in educational attainment has also tended to lower the residual variance. Overall, changes in the residual variance associated with changes in the independent variables sum to zero in Canada and are slightly negative for the United States.

Consistent with Juhn, Murphy, and Pierce (1989) and Blackburn (1990), the increase in the variation of earnings that is explained in this section is much less than the total increase in the variation of earnings. This is especially true for Canada, where only 22 percent of the increase in the variance of logs is accounted for by our analysis (35 percent is accounted for in the United States). Nevertheless, it is clear that earnings inequality increased more in the United States in the 1980s than in Canada (for males). Our analysis suggests this to be predominantly an education-related difference. Insofar as changes in the distribution of individual earnings contribute to changes in the distribution of total family income, the fact that total family income inequality increased in the United States but not in Canada in the 1980s also appears to be at least partly related to education.

7.5 Summary

Ex ante, one might have expected that changes over time in the Canadian and U.S. income distributions would be similar. This expectation would be reasonable if it were true that the labor markets in the two countries have been similar (and to some extent interrelated), and if the nature and role of the family in the two societies have been similar. Our findings do not verify this expectation but instead suggest that changes in the family income distribution were quite different in the two countries. Average family income from factor-of-production sources (i.e., total income less transfer income) grew slowly, by postwar standards, in both countries, but the rate of growth in average income from 1979 to 1987 was higher in the United States than in Canada. However, income inequality among families clearly increased in the United States over the same period, while in Canada there was no clear change in inequality (or perhaps a decline in inequality if equivalent income is used). In neither country can it be conclusively said that families were better off in a social welfare sense (assuming welfare is directly related to income), although evidence that social welfare increased in Canada does emerge when we analyze distributions of equivalent and per capita income.

What was different about the countries that led to differences in how the income distributions were changing? One factor that played a role was differences in how the structure of families changed in the 1980s. In the United States, there was an increase in the relative prevalence of female-headed families with children, but not in Canada; there was also a more pronounced shift toward unrelated individuals in the United States than in Canada. Both of these groups tend to have relatively high levels of inequality, so these differential shifts likely played a role in increasing inequality in the United States relative to Canada. Yet inequality increases occurred within all family types (except one) in the United States but did not clearly increase within family types (except one) in Canada, so family-type changes are not the entire story. One especially interesting difference between the countries pertains to how the economic status of female-headed families with children changed in the 1980s, since the economic welfare of these families increased dramatically in Canada but either remained constant or declined in the United States. These results suggest that income transfers play an important role in explaining the different changes in inequality in the two countries, since female-headed families are one of the primary recipients of transfer income, and transfer income increased much more over the period in Canada than in the United States.

While family income inequality increased in the United States but not in Canada, earnings inequality among prime-age males increased in both countries in the 1980s. In addition, the increases in earnings inequality in both countries are largely not explained by changes in observable characteristics of the populations (i.e., age, education, marital status, region), though slightly more variation is explained in the United States. Interestingly, the size of the unexplained portion of the increase in earnings inequality is very similar in the two countries. The primary reason why the explained portion is higher in the United States is that the return to education for males increased in the 1980s in the United States but does not appear to have increased in Canada.[29]

29. While we do not explore this possibility in any detail here, this difference in the change in the returns to education could be due to the more rapid growth in Canada in the supply of more-educated workers (see table 7.8).

Appendix A

Table 7A.1 Studies of Changes in Canadian Income and Earnings Inequality

Study	Data	Period	Distributional Aspect	Results	Important Factors
			Studies at the family level		
Henderson and Rowley (1977)	Survey of Consumer Finances	1965–73	Inequality of family income (Gini coefficient)	Trend toward greater inequality over period	Family size and the number of families with male earners declined.
Wolfson (1986)	Survey of Consumer Finances	1965–83	Inequality of "census" families, with equivalent adjustment	Increase from 1965 to 1971, decline to 1979, increase to 1983	Family-type changes and changes in labor force participation, especially among females, are most important; increase in investment and transfer income was equalizing.
Dooley (1988)	Survey of Consumer Finances	1973–86	Low-income status, and mean income, for families	Increase in economic status in the 1970s, decrease in the 1980s (except for elderly)	Decline in family size was important to the increase in economic status, as was the increase in government transfer payments and the increase in wives' earnings.
Dooley (1989)	Survey of Consumer Finances	1973–86	Low-income status among children	Decline in low-income percentages over period, slight increase in the 1980s	Declining family size and increasing educational attainment explain all of declining poverty for children in married couples but only about one-half for female-headed families.

McWatters and Beach (1990)	Published data using the Survey of Consumer Finances	1965–87	Inequality and mean incomes for families	Large increases in mean and some decline in inequality up to 1980, little change in mean and some increase in inequality after 1980	Increase in women's labor force participation has increasing impact on inequality, as has the fall in male labor force participation.
			Studies at the Individual Level		
Buse (1982)	Individual tax returns	1947–78	Inequality of individual income	Upward trend in inequality (from regressions that control for income definition changes)	Changes in the labor force participation rate are the factor most important to changes in inequality, with higher participation leading to lower inequality.
Dooley (1986)	Survey of Consumer Finances	Various years from 1971 to 1981	Return to education, and age, for males aged 20–64	Decline in the return to education, mostly in 1971–75; no change in age-related differentials	The entrance of the baby boom seems to explain some, but not all, of the change in the return to education.
Dooley (1987)	Survey of Consumer Finances	Various years from 1971 to 1982	Inequality of weekly and annual earnings	No clear trend for all workers, increases for some young workers and decreases for some old workers	Changes in the unemployment rate are important to changes over time in inequality.
Myles, Picot, and Wannell (1988)	Survey of Work History (1981); Labor Market Activity Survey (1986)	1981 and 1986	Inequality and mean of hourly earnings	Increase in percentage of jobs at very low wages, but no clear change in inequality	Only a small part of the observed change is attributable to industry and occupation shifts.

References

Atkinson, Anthony B. 1987. On the Measurement of Poverty. *Econometrica* 55(4): 749–64.

Beach, Charles M. 1989. Dollars and Dreams: A Reduced Middle Class? Alternative Explanations. *Journal of Human Resources*. 24(1): 162–93.

Blackburn, McKinley L. 1990. What Can Explain the Increase in Earnings Inequality among Males? *Industrial Relations* 29(3): 441–456.

Blackburn, McKinley L., and David E. Bloom. 1987. Earnings and Income Inequality in the United States. *Population and Development Review* 13(4): 575–609.

Blackburn, McKinley L., David E. Bloom, and Richard B. Freeman. 1990. The Declining Economic Position of Less Skilled American Men. In *A Future of Lousy Jobs? The Changing Structure of U.S. Wages*, ed. Gary Burtless. Washington, D.C.: Brookings Institution.

Bound, John, and George Johnson. 1992. Changes in the Structure of Wages During the 1980s: An Evaluation of Alternative Hypotheses. *American Economic Review* 82(3): 371–92.

Bourguignon, Francois. 1979. Decomposable Income Inequality Measures. *Econometrica* 47(4): 901–20.

Burtless, Gary. 1990. Earnings Inequality over the Business and Demographic Cycles. In *A Future of Lousy Jobs? The Changing Structure of U.S. Wages*, ed. Gary Burtless. Washington, D.C.: Brookings Institution.

Buse, Adolf. 1982. The Cyclical Behaviour of the Size Distribution of Income in Canada: 1947–1978. *Canadian Journal of Economics* 15(2): 189–204.

Danziger, Sheldon, and Michael Taussig. 1979. The Income Unit and the Anatomy of Income Distribution. *Review of Income and Wealth* 25: 365–75.

Dasgupta, Partha, Amartya Sen, and David Starrett. 1973. Notes on the Measurement of Inequality. *Journal of Economic Theory* 6: 180–87.

Dooley, Martin D. 1986. The Overeducated Canadian? Changes in the Relationship among Earnings, Education, and Age for Canadian Men: 1971–1981. *Canadian Journal of Economics* 19(1): 142–59.

———. 1987. Within-Cohort Earnings Inequality among Canadian Men: 1971–1982. *Relations Industrielles* 42(3): 594–609.

———. 1988. An Analysis of Changes in Family Income and Family Structure in Canada between 1973 and 1986 with an Emphasis on Poverty among Children. Program for Quantitative Studies in Economics and Population Research Report no. 238. McMaster University.

———. 1989. The Demography of Child Poverty in Canada: 1973–1986. Program for Quantitative Studies in Economics and Population Research Report no. 251. McMaster University.

———. 1990. Changes in the Economic Welfare of Lone Mother Families in Canada since 1970. Unpublished paper, McMaster University.

Freeman, Richard B. 1976. *The Overeducated American*. Orlando, Fla.: Academic Press.

Hadar, Josef, and William Russell. 1974. Stochastic Dominance in Choice under Uncertainty. In *Essays on Economic Behavior under Uncertainty*, ed. M. Blach, D. McFadden, and S. Wu. Amsterdam: North-Holland.

Harris, Milton, and Bengt Holmstrom. 1982. A Theory of Wage Dynamics. *Review of Economic Studies* 44(3): 315–33.

Henderson, D. W., and J. C. R. Rowley. 1977. The Distribution and Evolution of Canadian Family Incomes, 1965–1973. Economic Council of Canada Discussion Paper no. 91.

Jain, S. 1975. *Size Distribution of Income: A Compilation of Data*. Washington, D.C.: World Bank.

Juhn, Chinhui, Kevin Murphy, and Brooks Pierce. 1989. Wage Inequality and the Rise in Returns to Skill. Unpublished paper, University of Chicago.

Kakwani, Nanak. 1984. Welfare Ranking of Income Distributions. In *Advances in Econometrics,* vol. 3. Greenwich, Conn.: JAI Press.

Karoly, Lynn A. 1988. A Study of the Distribution of Individual Earnings in the United States from 1967 to 1986. Ph.D. thesis, Yale University.

Katz, Lawrence F., and Ana L. Revenga. 1989. Changes in the Structure of Wages: The United States vs Japan. *Journal of the Japanese and International Economies* 3: 522–53.

Levy, Frank. 1988. *Dollars and Dreams: The Changing American Income Distribution.* New York: Norton.

Lillard, Lee, James P. Smith, and Finis Welch. 1986. What Do We Really Know about Wages? The Importance of Nonreporting and Census Imputation. *Journal of Political Economy* 94(3): 489–506.

Lydall, Harold F. 1978. Some Problems in Making International Comparisons of Inequality. In *Income Inequality,* ed. John Maroney. Lexington, Mass.: Lexington Books.

McWatters, Catherine J., and Charles M. Beach. 1990. Factors behind the Changes in Canada's Family Income Distribution and the Share of the Middle Class. *Relations Industrielles* 45(1): 118–33.

Murphy, Kevin, and Finis Welch. 1988. Wage Differentials in the 1980s: The Role of International Trade. Unpublished paper, University of Chicago.

Myles, J., G. Picot, and T. Wannell. 1988. The Changing Wage Distribution of Jobs, 1981–1986. *Canadian Economic Observer* 11(4): 1–33.

Shorrocks, Anthony F. 1983. Ranking Income Distributions. *Economica* 50(1): 3–17.

Summers, Robert, and Alan Heston. 1988. A New Set of International Comparisons of Real Product and Price Levels: Estimates for 130 Countries, 1950–1985. *Review of Income and Wealth* 34(1): 1–25.

van Ginneken, Wouter, and Jong-goo Park. 1984. *Generating Internationally Comparable Income Distribution Estimates.* Geneva: International Labour Office.

Wolfson, Michael. 1986. Stasis amid Change: Income Inequality in Canada 1965–1983. *Review of Income and Wealth* 32(4): 337–68.

Contributors

McKinley L. Blackburn
Department of Economics
University of South Carolina
Columbia, SC 29208

Rebecca M. Blank
Department of Economics
2003 Sheridan Road
Northwestern University
Evanston, IL 60208

David E. Bloom
Department of Economics
International Affairs Building
Room 1014
Columbia University
420 West 118 Street
New York, NY 10027

George J. Borjas
Department of Economics, 0508
University of California, San Diego
9500 Gilman Drive
La Jolla, CA 92093

David Card
Industrial Relations Section
Firestone Library
Princeton University
Princeton, NJ 08544

Richard B. Freeman
National Bureau of Economic Research
1050 Massachusetts Avenue
Cambridge, MA 02138

Maria J. Hanratty
New York State School of Industrial and Labor Relations
255 Ives Hall
Cornell University
Ithaca, NY 14850

Thomas Lemieux
Department of Economics
University of Montreal
P.O. Box 6128, Station A
Montreal, Quebec
Canada H3C-3J7

Karen Needels
Economics Department
Princeton University
Princeton, NJ 08544

W. Craig Riddell
Department of Economics
University of British Columbia
997-1873 East Mall
Vancouver, B.C.
Canada V6T 1Z1

Author Index

Subject Index